MW00562161

ENTREPRENEURIAL AND BUSINESS ELITES OF CHINA: THE CHINESE RETURNEES WHO HAVE SHAPED MODERN CHINA

海归推动中国:中国当代海归创业及商界精英

Entrepreneurial and Business Elites of China: The Chinese Returnees Who Have Shaped Modern China *provides up-to-date and comprehensive coverage of top overseas returnees who have made noteworthy contributions to the Chinese economy since the reform era began. These elites are the men and women who mattered, both in the early years when returnee migration was rare and in recent years when it has become much more prominent. Understanding the stories of the entrepreneurial and business elites is an important step for understanding the international migration force overall.*

—Dr. William Kerr, Harvard Business School

Animal spirits are the basis of entrepreneurial economies such as China's and knowing more about the lives of successful businessmen is therefore crucial to understand that country's economy. By focusing more in particular on the role of talent circulation in the global economy, this book adds a very welcome perspective to the study of Chinese business elites. It is recommended reading to anybody interested in the Chinese economy and globalization.

—Dr. Andrea Goldstein, Senior Economist,
OECD (Organization for Economic Cooperation and Development);
Consultant, the Inter-American Development Bank

Observing the rising tide of the Chinese economy, it is easy to forget that it is driven by critical human element – the Chinese returnee, who serves as a conduit for the transfer of technology, know-how, and business practices. It is difficult to fathom the rise of China without attending to this growing human stream, which will continue to play a major role in the country's transformation.

—Dr. Oded Shenkar, Ford Motor Company Chair,
Fisher College of Business, Ohio State University

This is a fascinating book for the general public and particularly for those who have a keen interest in business China. The information is current and the entries are at appropriate length, which are short enough to general readers but long enough to be comprehensive, providing adequate information on the individual entrepreneur and the field associated with him/her. Highly recommended for the public, but particularly for business students as well as professionals.

—Mr. Haipeng Li, Executive Director, Chinese American Librarians Association;
Chair, American Library Association IRC East Asia & Pacific Committee;
Associate Director, John Cotton Dana Library, Rutgers University

A complement to A Guide to the Top Companies in China *and to* The Biographical Dictionary of New Chinese Entrepreneurs and Business Leaders, *this timely volume completes the trilogy that makes a valuable asset for every academic and investor.*

—Dr. Leo-Paul Dana, University of Canterbury, New Zealand;
Senior Advisor, World Association for Small and Medium Enterprises;
Founding Editor, Journal of International Entrepreneurship and
Journal of Enterprising Communities

Entrepreneurial and Business Elites of China: The Chinese Returnees Who Have Shaped Modern China *is an important contribution to the analysis of the human capital factor, which explains the great success of Chinese companies both on the domestic and international markets. The authors provide interesting insights on how companies have attracted competencies and overcome cultural factors which generally arise among joint ventures and foreign invested companies in this country. An essential reading.*

—Dr. Xavier Richet, Professor of International Business,
Sorbonne University, Paris and French Center of
Contemporary China, Hong Kong

ENTREPRENEURIAL AND BUSINESS ELITES OF CHINA: THE CHINESE RETURNEES WHO HAVE SHAPED MODERN CHINA

海归推动中国:中国当代海归创业及商界精英

EDITED BY

WENXIAN ZHANG

Arthur Vining Davis Fellow and Research Associate, Rollins China Center, Winter Park, FL, USA

HUIYAO WANG

Vice Chairman, China Western Returned Scholars Association, Director General, Center for China and Globalization, Beijing, People's Republic of China

and

ILAN ALON

George D. and Harriet W. Cornell Chair of International Business, Executive Director of Rollins China Center, Winter Park, FL, USA Visiting Scholar and Asia Fellow of the Harvard Kennedy School of Government, Cambridge, MA, USA

United Kingdom • North America • Japan
India • Malaysia • China

Emerald Group Publishing Limited
Howard House, Wagon Lane, Bingley BD16 1WA, UK

First edition 2011

Reprints and permission service
Contact: booksandseries@emeraldinsight.com

British Library Cataloguing in Publication Data
A catalogue record for this book is available from the British Library

ISBN: 978-0-85724-089-7

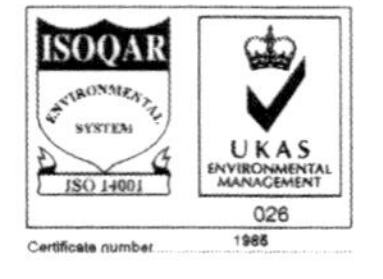

From Wenxian Zhang:
To the Teachers in My Life

From Huiyao Wang:
To Angela Wang and Anthony Wang

From Ilan Alon:
To Anna

From all of us:
To All Contemporary Chinese Returnees

Contents

Contributors to the Volume and their Entries

M. Elena Aramendia-Muneta, Universidad Pública de Navarra, Pamplona, Spain
Cheng Yuan, Hao Quan, Xie Lina, Yang Lijun

Jing Bai, Rollins College, Winter Park, FL, USA
Xiang Bing, Zhang Hongjiang, Zhao Yang

Eadie Hua Chen, Harvard University, Cambridge, MA, USA
Jing Ulrich

Hao Chen, University of Texas, Dallas, Richardson, TX, USA
Cao Guowei, Ding Jian, Fu Chengyu

Miao Chi, Rollins College, Winter Park, FL, USA
Wang Boqing, Wang Weijia, Wu Shangzhi

Jennifer Crossman, Rollins College Winter Park, FL, USA
Gao Xiqing, Wang Chaoyong, Zhang Ligang

Qun Du, University of Central Florida, Orlando, FL, USA
Liu Changle, Qin Xiao, Wang Boming

Yuping Du, Guangdong University of Foreign Studies, Guangzhou, China
Feng Ziping, Han Xiaohong, Jiang Ruxiang

Terence R. Egan, Central University of Finance and Economics, Beijing, China
Ji Weidong, Sun Wei, Zhen Ronghui

Elisabeth K. Gilbert, Production & Operations Management Society, USA
Liu Xiaocheng, Wang Lifen, Yan Wangjia

James P. Gilbert, Rollins College, Winter Park, FL, USA
Liu Xiaocheng, Wang Lifen, Yan Wangjia

Kawal Gill, Sri Guru Gobind Singh College of Commerce, New Delhi, India
Hu Shengfa, Wang Shen

Ying Huang, Jiangsu University of Science & Technology, Zhenjiang, Jiangsu, China
Tang Min, Tian Suning, Zhang Yaqin

Loi Teck Hui, Loi & Mokhtar Consulting, Malaysia
Ge Ming, Yuan Yue, Zhang Xin

Jonatan Jelen, Parsons the New School for Design, School of Design Strategies, New York City, NY, USA
Wu Ping, Xu Xiaoping, Zou Shenglong

Shuqin Jiao, Saint Louis University, St. Louis, MO, USA
Han Gengchen

Robin E. Kelly, Cuyahoga Community College, Cleveland, OH, USA
Chen Ge, Liu Jiangnan, Wang Yafei

George L. Kuan, International School of Management, Shanghai, China
Jing Muhan, Ning Gaoning

Zicheng Li, Riello Group, Shanghai, China
Li Xiaojia, Wang Zhongwei

Hao Liang, Tilburg University, Tilburg, the Netherlands
He Xin, Kuang Ziping

Eric Liguori, Louisiana State University, Baton Rouge, LA, USA
Chen Naike, Mao Daqing, Xu Changdong

Tai Wei Lim, Chinese University of Hong Kong, Hong Kong, China
Li Yi

Xueyuan Liu, Wuhan University, Wuhan, China
Cheng Changqing, Liu Erfei, Shu Qi

Margaret Minnis, Pepperdine University, Malibu, CA, USA
Gu Yongqiang, Hu Zuliu, Zhu Min

Everlyne Misati, Rollins College, Winter Park, FL, USA
Chen Hong, Gao Qunyao, Gao Zhikai, Xu Tiantian, Xu Xin

Michael A. Moodian, Chapman University, Orange, CA, USA
Gu Yongqiang, Hu Zuliu, Zhu Min

Mark Munoz, Millikin University, Decatur, IL, USA
Chang Zhaohua, Zhu Yunlai

Zhaochang Peng, Rollins College, Winter Park, FL, USA
Chen Xingdong, Wang Chunyan, Xiao Zhiyue

Wei Qian, New Tigers Consulting Ltd., Ontario, Canada
Deng Feng, Shen Nanpeng, Zhang Yichen

Liesl Riddle, George Washington University, Washington DC, USA
Xu Tiantian

Amir Shoham, College of Management Academic Studies, Rishon LeZion, Israel
Li Yanhong

Ashley Snyder, Rollins College, Winter Park, FL, USA
Xie Guozhong, Xue Lan, Yang Zhuang

Barbara L. Strother, Azusa Pacific University, Azusa, CA, USA
Liang Jianzhang, Yang Ning, Zhang Fan

Sunny Li Sun, University of Missouri, Columbia, MO, USA
He Xin, Kuang Ziping, Xu Xin

Xiaowei Sun, Siemens Energy Inc., USA
Yao Naxin, Zhou Ge, Zou Qifang

Kirsty S. F. Tan, KST Consulting, Los Angeles, CA, USA
Yan Yan, Zhang Fan, Zhu Demiao

Mian Wang, Jiangsu University of Science & Technology, Zhenjiang, Jiangsu, China
Tang Min, Tian Suning, Zhang Yaqin

Tonia Warnecke, Rollins College, Winter Park, FL, USA
Li Yifei, Tina Ju, Zhang Lan

Chunjuan Nancy Wei, University of Bridgeport, Bridgeport, CT, USA
Qian Yingyi, Zhang Weiying, Zuo Xiaolei

William X. Wei, Grant MacEwan University, Edmonton, Alberta, Canada
Lee Kai-Fu, Mo Tianquan, Zhou Yunfan

Yinglu Wu, Louisiana State University, Baton Rouge, LA, USA
Chen Naike, Mao Daqing, Xu Changdong

Xiaoqi Yu, Kent State University, Kent, OH, USA
Huang Jin, Mao Daolin, Tang Yue

Wenchao Zeng, Wuhan University, Wuhan, China
Shu Qi

Syntia Zeni, Rollins College, WinterPark, FL, USA
Lin Yongqing, Liu Yun, Zhang Xingsheng, Zhang Yan

Shanshan Zhang, Wuhan University, Wuhan, China
Cheng Changqing

Weidong Zhang, Winona State University, Winona, MN, USA
Shi Zhengrong, Yang Lan, Zhang Chaoyang

Wenxian Zhang, Rollins College, Winter Park, FL, USA
Li Yanhong, Wang Zhongjun, Wu Ping, Zhang Ligang

Xiaotian Zhang, University of Tartu, Tartu Parish, Estonia
Deng Zhonghan, Hong Huang, Wu Ying

Yan Zhang, Wuhan University, Wuhan, China
Liu Erfei

Yifang Zhang, Pepperdine University, Malibu, CA, USA
Gu Yongqiang, Hu Zuliu, Zhu Min

Peiling Zhao, Millikin University, Decatur, IL, USA
Chang Zhaohua, Zhu Yunlai

List of Abbreviations

AAMA	Asian American MultiTech Association
ABAC	APEC Business Advisory Council
ABC	Asia Business Council
ACM	Association for Computing Machinery
ACPAA	All-China Patent Agents Association
ADB	Asian Development Bank
ADF	Asian Development Investment Fund
ADLAB	Active Defense Laboratory
ADS	American Depository Shares
AIESEC	Association Internationale des Étudiants en Sciences Économiques et Commerciales
AIF	Asia Infrastructure Fund
AIG	American Insurance Company
AIPPI	Association Internationale pour la Protection de la Propriete Intellectuelle
AIST	National Institute of Advanced Industrial Science and Technology (Japan)
AMR	Academy of Macroeconomic Research (China)
AP	Application Processor
APEC	Asia-Pacific Economic Cooperation
ATC	Advanced Technology Center
ATM	Automated Teller Machine
ATSE	Academy of Technological Sciences and Engineering (Australia)
BA	Bachelor of Art
BBC	British Broadcasting Corporation
BICI	Beijing Investment Consultants Inc.
BMW	Bayerische Motoren Werke
BOC	Bank of China
BiMBA	Beijing International MBA, Peking University
BP	British Petroleum
BPEA	Beijing Private Equity Association
BRIC	Brazil, Russia, India and China
BS	Bachelor of Science

CAD	Computer-aided Design
CAE	Chinese Academy of Engineering
CALT	Chinese Academy of Launch Vehicle Technology
CAS	Chinese Academy of Sciences
CAST	Chinese Association of Science and Technology
CBA	Chinese Basketball Association
CBC	China Broadband Capital Partners
CBD	Central Business District
CBN	Chinese Business News
CCID	China Center for Information Industry Development
CCTV	China Central Television
CDN	Content Delivery Network
CDPD	Cellular Digital Packet Data
CDRF	China Development Research Foundation
CEIBS	China Europe International Business School
CEO	Chief Executive Officer
CETV	China Education Television
CFO	Chief Financial Officer
CHEFS	Chinese Higher Education Follow-up System
CIA	Chinese Institute of Accountants
CIC	China Investment Corporation
CICC	China International Capital Corporation
CIMG	China Interactive Media Group
CIMMYT	International Maize and Wheat Improvement Center
CISP	Certified International Security Professional
CITIC	China International Trust and Investment Company
CIW	Center for Information Work
CKGSB	Cheung Kong Graduate School of Business
CLSA	Credit Lyonnais Securities Asia
CMG	China Merchants Group
CMHI	China Merchants Holdings International
CMOS	Complementary Metal Oxide Semiconductor
CNBC	Consumer News and Business Channel
CNC	China Netcom Corporation
CNN	Cable News Network
CNOOC	China National Offshore Oil Company
CNPC	China National Petroleum Corporation
COFCO	Cereals, Oils and Foodstuffs Corporation
COO	Chief Operating Officer
CPA	Certified Public Accountant
CPPCC	Chinese People's Political Consultative Conference
CPU	Central Processing Unit
CRBT	Color Ring-Back Tone
CRIC	China Real Estate Information Corporation
CSAR	Computer Structure Analysis Research Corporation

CSFB	Credit Suisse-First Boston
CSR	Corporate Social Responsibility
CSRC	China Securities Regulatory Commission
CTO	Chief Technology Officer
CUNY	City University of New York
CUSPEA	China–US Physics Examination and Application
DFJ	Draper Fisher Jurvetson ePlanet Ventures
DITC	Darcy International Trading Company
DSP	Digital Signal Processor
DUSL	Duke University School of Law
DVD	Digital Versatile Disc
EDN	Electronics Design News
EMBA	Executive Master of Business Administration
ESOMAR	European Society for Opinion and Marketing Research
ESP	Embedded Server Page
ESPN	Entertainment Sports Programming Network
ESS	Electronic Switching System
ETS	Educational Testing Service
FICPI	Federation Internationale des Conseils en Propriete Industrielle
FMC	Food Machinery Corporation
FPI	Focused Photonics (Hangzhou) Inc.
GDP	Gross Domestic Product
GE	General Electric
GEM	Growth Enterprise Market
GFA	Gross Floor Area
GIC	(Singapore) Government Investment Corporation
GIEC	Guangzhou Institute of Energy Conversion
GIS	Geographic Information System
GM	General Manager
GMAC	Graduate Management Admission Council
GMAT	Graduate Management Admission Test
GPRS	General Packet Radio Service
GRE	Graduate Record Examination
GRIC	Global Roaming Internet Consortium
GSK	GlaxoSmithKline
GSM	Global System for Mobile communication
GSR	Gold Sand River
GTE	General Telephone and Electronics
HEC	Hautes Études Commerciales (Paris)
HIT	Harbin Institute of Technology
HK	Hong Kong
HKEx	Hong Kong Exchanges and Clearing Limited
HKFE	Hong Kong Futures Exchange Limited
HKSFC	Hong Kong Securities and Futures Commission
HMO	Health Maintenance Organization

HP	Hewlett Packard
HR	Human Resources
HSBC	Hong Kong and Shanghai Banking Corporation
HYSTA	Hua Yuan Science and Technology Association
IBM	International Business Machines
IAC	International Advisory Council
IC	Integrated Circuits
ICBC	Industrial and Commercial Bank of China
ICP	Internet Content Provider
IDG	International Data Group
IDMS	Intrusion Detection and Management System
IDRC	International Development Research Centre
IEC	International Electro-technical Commission
IEEE	Institute of Electrical and Electronics Engineering
IFC	International Finance Corporation
IMF	International Monetary Fund
ING	International Netherlands Group
INSEAD	Institut EuropÅen d'Administration des Affaires
INTA	International Trademark Association
IP	Intellectual Property
IPO	Initial Public Offering
IPR	Intellectual Property Rights
IPS	Investment Promotion Section
IPTV	Internet Protocol Television
IQ	Intelligence Quotient
ISI	Internet Securities Inc.
ISP	Internet Service Provider
IT	Information Technology
ITC	Internet Technologies China
IVR	Interactive Voice Response
JD	Juris Doctor
JSPS	Japan Society for the Promotion of Science
JV	Joint Venture
KLM	Koninklijke Luchtvaart Maatschappij (Royal Dutch Airlines)
KMG	Klynveld Main Goerdeler
KPCB	Kleiner, Perkins, Caufield and Byers
KPMG	Klynveld Peat Marwick Goerdeler
LCD	Liquid Crystal Display
LCTS	Lord Chancellor's Training Scheme for Young Chinese Lawyers
LES	Licensing Executives Society
LG	Life's Good
LLB	Bachelor of Laws
LLP	Limited Liability Partnership
LOMA	Life Office Management Association
LP	Limited Partners

M&A	Mergers & Acquisitions
MA	Master of Art
MBA	Master of Business Administration
MBO	Management Buyout
MD	Managing Director
MEMS	Micro Electro Mechanical System
MIT	Massachusetts Institute of Technology
MMS	Multimedia Messaging Service
MOE	Ministry of Education
MOU	Memorandum of Understanding
MPA	Master of Public Administration
MS	Master of Science
MSC/PDA	MacNeal–Schwendler Corporation Project on Defense Alternatives
MSR	Microsoft Research
MSRA	Microsoft Research Asia Lab
MTV	Music Television
MVAS	Mobile Value-Added Service
MyCOS	My China Occupational Skills
NACSA	North America Chinese Semiconductor Association
NASDAQ	National Association of Securities Dealers Automated Quotation
NASA	National Aeronautics and Space Administration
NASTRAN	NASA Structural Analysis
NATO	North Atlantic Treaty Organization
NBA	National Basketball Association
NBC	National Broadcasting Company
NCER	National Center for Economic Research
NEA	New Enterprise Associates
NGO	Non-Governmental Organization
NJU	Nanjing University
NTT	Nippon Telegraph & Telephone
NYSE	New York Stock Exchange
NYU	New York University
OB/GYN	Obstetrics-Gynecology
OCR	Optical Character Recognition
OECD	Organization for Economic Co-operation and Development
O*NET	Occupational Information Network
OS	Operating System
P&G	Procter & Gamble
PAS	Personal Access System
PC	Personal Computer
PCCW	Pacific Century CyberWorks
PCS	Personal Communications Services
PDA	Personal Digital Assistant
PE	Private Equity
PhD	Doctor of Philosophy

PICC	People's Insurance Company of China
PLA	People's Liberation Army
PMI	Peat Marwick International
PMP	Portable Media Player
PRC	People's Republic of China
PSI	Policy Studies Institute
PTCA	Percutanueous Transluminal Coronary Angioplasty
P2SP	Peer to Server and to Peer
PV	Page View
PV	Photovoltaic
R&D	Research and Development
RMB	Renminbi (Chinese currency)
RRA	Russell Reynolds Associates
SAIF	Softbank Asia Infrastructure Fund
SARFT	State Administration of Radio, Films and Television (China)
SARS	Severe Acute Respiratory Syndrome
S&T	Science and Technology
SCOBA	Silicon Valley Chinese Overseas Business Association
SCUT	South China University of Technology
SEACE	Software Engineer Advanced Career Education
SEC	Securities and Exchange Commission
SEEC	Stock Exchange Executive Council
SEHK	Stock Exchange of Hong Kong
SFDA	State Food and Drug Administration
SK	South Korea
SMIC	Semiconductor Manufacturing International Corporation
SMIH	Sun Media Investment Holdings Limited
SMS	Short Messaging Service
SOE	State-Owned Enterprise
SOHO	Small Office, Home Office
SPDB	Shanghai Pudong Development Bank
SPIEF	Saint Petersburg International Economic Forum
STAQ	Security Traders Automated Quotation
SWUFE	Southwestern University of Finance and Economics
TCL	The Creative Life
TDF	Templeton Dragon Fund
TD-SCDMA	Time Division Synchronous Code Division Multiple Access
TEDA	Tianjin Economic Development Area
TFMIM	The Double Faces Individual Move Information Machine
3G	Third Generation
TICH	TEDA International Cardiovascular Hospital
TNT	Turner Network Television
TOEFL	Test of English as a Foreign Language
TPG	Texas Pacific Group
TRW	Thompson Ramo Wooldridge Inc.

TMT	Technology, Media, and Telecommunication
TV	Television
UBS AG	Union Bank of Switzerland Aktiengesellschaft
UESTC	University of Electronic Science and Technology of China
UIBE	University of International Business and Economics
UK	United Kingdom
UN	United Nations
UNESCO	United Nations Educational, Scientific and Cultural Organization
UNICEF	United Nations Children's Fund
UNIDO	United Nations Industrial Development Organization
UNSW	University of New South Wales (Australia)
US	United States
USTC	University of Science and Technology of China
UV	Unique Visitors
VC	Venture Capital
VLSI	Very Large Scale Integration
VP	Vice President
VRML	Virtual Reality Modeling Language
VV	Video View
WAP	Wireless Application Protocol
WEF	World Economic Forum
WIIG	Walden International Investment Group
WRBF	Western Returnees Beijing Forum
WRSA	Western Returned Scholars Association
WRSACC	Western Returned Scholars Association Chamber of Commerce
WTO	World Trade Organization
XJTU	Xi'an Jiaotong University
ZII	Zhejiang Innovation Institute
ZTE	Zhongxing Telecommunication Equipment Company

Acknowledgements

The publication of *The Entrepreneurial and Business Elites of China: The Chinese Returnees Who Have Shaped Modern China* is the result of the collaborative efforts across the globe. Over 40 scholars from the United States, mainland China, Hong Kong, Canada, the Netherlands, Estonia, Israel, India, and Malaysia contributed to this collective endeavor, to whom we are most grateful for their scholarly contributions. We are also indebted to Ms. Kim Foster, Commissioning Editor and Ms. Rebecca Forster, Assistant Commissioning Editor of Emerald Group Publishing, for their assistance in the review of our initial proposal and the publication of the manuscript. Ms. Mary Miskin, Development Editor, Emerald Group Publishing and the Production staff of MPS Ltd., who have provided professional guidance and helped us move toward the final publication, have our sincere gratitude.

We would like to express our thanks to the China Western Returned Scholars Association and Dr. Han Qide, Association Chairman and the Vice Chairman of the National People's Congress of China for the support of returnee research in China. We would also want to give our special appreciations to the Center for China and Globalization for their strong supports to this project overall, and would like to acknowledge the research assistance provided by Ms. Bai Yan and Ms. Miao Lu of the Center for China and Globalization based in Beijing, China.

It is a daunting task to compile a biographical profile of key entrepreneurial returnees while the country is still undergoing rapid and unprecedented economic development, and every research project like this requires enormous support and encouragement. We deeply appreciate the patience and good humor of our families, friends, and colleagues. In addition, we are grateful to Miss Lei Guo, Student Assistant at Rollins China Center, for her work on the project website. Finally, we would like to express our genuine appreciation to President Lewis Duncan, Interim Provost Laurie Joyner, and Director Jonathan Miller of Rollins College for their understanding of the essential relationship between teaching and scholarship, and their strong support to our academic undertaking.

Foreword

The world changes quickly these days. Although the drivers of change are numerous, China commands particular attention. China's economic, political, and social development has been a defining force for its citizens and for the world over the past 30 years. Many of these drivers – for example, China's general economic growth – have been fairly consistent over time. Moreover, these drivers are understood conceptually and descriptively, even if the translation into business practice or policy design, domestically and abroad, is often less certain.

This book deals with a very important aspect of China's development – the international migration of some of its most talented people. The powerful nature of this driver is not disputed, but it is also substantially less understood than most other forces. Moreover, as discussed later, the nature of China's international migration has dramatically changed over time. We know much more about the way it was, rather than the way it is or the way it will be. *Entrepreneurial and Business Elites of China: The Chinese Returnees Who Have Shaped Modern China* addresses this deficit, which is essential for proper policy design, business choices, and similar actions.

The Way It Is

The international migration of talented Chinese to the United States and other advanced economies began in earnest in the 1980s. Data regarding science and engineering are the most available and reliable. It is hard to believe, but just three (3!) US PhD graduates in science and engineering were of mainland Chinese nationality in 1980. Decades of exponential growth increased that number to 4774 by 2006, or 11% of all US PhD graduates. This is well over twice as many as the next country.

Through much of this rapid growth in student enrollments, talented Chinese chose to remain in the United States or other host countries if allowed to do so. In its annual survey, the National Science Foundation asks graduating PhDs about their future career intentions. Throughout the 1990s, over 90% of graduating Chinese doctorates were intending to stay in the United States for employment after school.

These tremendous dynamics brought China front and center in the debate on the impact of high skilled migration for sending countries. The oldest theories – which may still have the most adherents – frequently took a *brain drain* perspective. These theories argued that the migration of the best and brightest talent from developing and emerging economies to advanced economies substantially hurt the economic and social development of the sending countries. These losses could come in many forms, from a weakened local business sector to fewer role models.

Observing the contemporaneous explosive growth in Chinese economies, however, led many scholars, business leaders, and policy makers to suggest an alternative theory of *brain gain*. This model emphasizes more the positive effects that developing and emerging economies can derive from having the migration of talented people to frontier nations. Example of the beneficial transfers include technology and knowledge flows, remittances, business contacts and investment, and similar. Some observers further proposed that developing and emerging nations could leap frog traditional economic growth stages due to the power of these trans-national ethnic networks.[1]

The Way It Was

For the most part, these basic theories of brain drain and brain gain had a static view of international migration. That is, talented individuals migrated to advanced economies and remained, causing either a net loss or gain to their homelands depending on the relative strengths of their subsequent interactions. And, for the world of even a decade ago, this simplification might not have been so bad.

The 1990s paradigm, however, melted away sometime after 2002 or thereabout, as many Western-trained Chinese students and workers are returning home for private-sector jobs, university positions, and entrepreneurial opportunities. Among my own MBA students at Harvard Business School, it is hard to find a Chinese student not returning to China after graduation for work (or taking a job that will bridge advanced economies and China). Often times these students are also taking some of the best of the United States with them – for example, the US venture capital investment into their companies.

Matching these changing facts, with China again as one of the poster cases, the newest theories emphasize a *brain circulation* phenomenon. These new theories suggest that the best way that developing and emerging economies can obtain beneficial transfers from advanced economies is through people moving regularly back and forth between the countries. This includes both permanent return migration and continuous moving between locations.[2]

1. For survey evidence regarding China, see AnnaLee Saxenian, Yasuyuki Motoyama, and Xiaohong Quan (2002), *Local and Global Networks of Immigrant Professionals in Silicon Valley*, San Francisco, CA: Public Policy Institute of California. For empirical evidence pulling across multiple countries and industries, see William Kerr (2008), Ethnic scientific communities and international technology diffusion, *Review of Economics and Statistics* **90**, 518–537. A recent, unpublished survey by FrÅdÅric Docquier and Hillel Rapoport provides a comprehensive academic overview of the themes discussed in this introduction.
2. For a broad introduction, see AnnaLee Saxenian (2006), *The New Argonauts*, Cambridge, MA: Harvard University Press.

Although these theories continue to grow in prominence, we unfortunately have very little collected information about the returnees themselves. We need to move from singular case studies to developing more comprehensive data collections to ultimately large-scale empirical analyses. Bringing more data to this question will allow us to refine our theories and formulate more sophisticated accounts of international migration.

This book is a step in this direction. *Entrepreneurial and Business Elites of China: The Chinese Returnees Who Have Shaped Modern China* provides up-to-date and comprehensive coverage of top overseas returnees who have made noteworthy contributions to the Chinese economy since the reform era began. These elites are the men and women who mattered, both in the early years when returnee migration was rare, and in recent years where it has become much more prominent. Understanding the stories of the entrepreneurial and business elites is an important step for understanding the international migration force overall.

This book is the product of great work by many contributors. The editors – Wenxian Zhang, Huiyao Wang, and Ilan Alon – are each very steeped in the returnee phenomena and the dynamics of international migration. Many contributors moreover developed the biographies that are central to this book. Each biography acknowledges the author, and their careful work shows. The final product will be an important reference volume in years to come.

WILLIAM KERR
Harvard Business School, 2010

Introduction: Chinese Returnees, a Globalization Force in Reshaping Modern China

Ever since the imperial army of Qing was defeated by the British royal navy in the first Opium War, China, in hopes of revitalizing its ancient civilization, began sending students overseas. Thousands of Chinese attended schools and universities in Europe, North America, and Japan. Upon returning, they assumed key roles in the country's modernization drive. Among the returnees was Jeme Tien Yow (Zhan Tianyou 1861–1919), a Yale graduate who became the chief engineer of the Imperial Peking-Kalgan Railway, the first railroad constructed in China without foreign assistance.

Even the core leadership of the Chinese Communist Party studied abroad, Both Zhou Enlai (1898–1976) and Deng Xiaoping (1904–1997) spent some formative time studying in France in the early twentieth century. In 1978, upon returning to power after the disastrous Cultural Revolution, Deng Xiaoping initiated the "open door policy" and launched the reform era. That same year, he also decided to send a large number of students and scholars overseas. This visionary strategy had a profound impact on the transformation of the People's Republic of China (PRC) over the past 30 years. Chinese students, often graduates of top universities at home, have gone abroad in the tens of thousands each year to acquire advanced degrees along with new knowledge and skills. Those who returned to China have generally made solid contributions in all areas of the country's development, ranging from science, technology, agriculture and medicine to business, education, law, and politics.

Among all overseas returnees, one group that stands out consists of Chinese entrepreneurs who have launched their own businesses after studying in the West. Armed with experience working at multinational corporations (MNCs), they seized the unique growth opportunities in a reformed China to start their own enterprises. For example, Li Yanhong (1968–), a graduate of Peking University and the State University of New York, worked at Dow Jones and Infoseek before founding Baidu, a company that beat Google in Chinese Internet searches within a few years; Fu Chengyu (1951–), after studied at the Northeast Petroleum Institute in China and the University of Southern California, led the China National Offshore Oil Co. into an era of growth and prosperity; Shi Zhengrong (1963–), a graduate of the University of New South Wales in Australia, returned to China to launch Suntech Power, a leading solar energy company listed on the New York Stock Exchange and the largest solar module manufacturer in the world. In sum, they represent the bright future of China, and that future is beginning to take shape. These business leaders have reshaped the country's economic landscape and begun to play a more active role on the social and political stages. As agents of change, they will have a significant impact on China and the rest of the world in years to come.

Haigui, a pun on *haiwai guilai*, meaning "returning from overseas" (Liu and Hewitt, 2008), is a very popular term in China today. Its pronunciation also suggests the Chinese phrase for sea turtles returning to shore after leaving to grow up in the sea. To most people in the Western world, the notion of "returnees" is a foreign concept. In the United States, Canada, Europe, and Australia, a person who studies abroad almost always returns to the home country. However, for students from large developing countries such as China and India, this is not always the case. Out of more than one and one half million Chinese who went abroad during the past three decades, between two-thirds to three-quarters decided to settle in the countries where they studied, a simple fact that makes the subject of this book much more striking. However, in recent years, both the number and the rate of returnees have steadily increased. As one of the fastest growing economies in the world, China provides unprecedented opportunities to overseas returnees, who are increasingly recognized as a driving force in the country's economic development.

In this book, a returnee is defined as a person born in China who left to study overseas as a student, visiting scholar or guest researcher for over one year, and who has returned to China to work on a permanent or long-term basis. In the sections below, we first review the historical background of the Chinese returnees, and then outline their key roles and contributions as a major globalization force in reshaping modern China.

Background of the Returnee Trend in China

The history of Chinese who went abroad for study and returned with new knowledge and cultural outlooks can be traced back to at least the seventh century. During the Tang Dynasty (618–907 CE), Xuan Zhuang (602–664 CE), a Chinese monk and scholar, traveled to India to study Buddhism, and his translation of Buddhist writings from Sanskrit into Chinese helped spread Buddhism in China. He may have been the first returnee.

Learning and cultural exchanges from returnees were always two-way communications. People from Japan, Korea, Vietnam, Persia, and West Asia came to China to study Confucianism, mathematics, and military strategies as well as advanced technologies of the time. As Albert Feuererker, a Harvard economic historian put it, between 1000 and 1500, "no comparison of agricultural productivity, industrial skill, commercial complexity, urban wealth, or standard of living (not to mention bureaucratic sophistication and cultural achievement) would place Europe on a par with the Chinese empire" (Fairbank and Goldman, 2006).

Historically, China was one of the largest economies in the world until the industrial revolution, when it began a continuing, substantial decline in economic output for more than a century. In 1800, during the Qing Dynasty, China's relative share of world manufacturing output was 33.3% whereas Europe's was 28.1%. However, by 1900, China was only at 6.2% whereas Europe's jumped to 62%. By that time, China had fallen well behind Europe and the US economically and technologically. With its humiliating defeats in the two Opium Wars in the mid-nineteenth century, some Chinese leaders realized that, to reverse the declining trend, China had to learn about the more advanced developments in science and technology from Western countries. With this mindset, the country began to send waves of young students to Western countries. Based on our research, the historical movement of the Chinese overseas students and returnees can be divided into five generations, described in the later section.

First Generation (1872–1900): *Learning from the West*

Arriving in the United States in 1847 and graduating from Yale University in 1854, Yung Wing (Rong Hong 1828–1912) became the first student in modern Chinese history known to study in the Western world. Led by Yung and pushed by other open-minded Chinese, the imperial Qing government developed a 15-year plan to send out "Chinese boy students" for overseas education. Starting in 1872, four groups of students were dispatched to the United States, with an average age of 12. After initial training, many of them were accepted to top US universities such as Harvard, Yale, Columbia, and MIT. However, in the tenth year of its implementation, the overseas educational plan was terminated by the Chinese government. By then, a total of 120 students had studied in the United States. Around the same time, another group of students was sent to Europe to study naval warfare. One of these students, Yan Fu (1854–1921), later introduced many Western books to China, including Darwin's works.

Although the total number of this generation of students was small (about 200), many graduates later played a pivotal role in the development of modern China's mining, transportation, communications, government, national defense, and higher education industries. For example, the first presidents of Peking University, Tsinghua University, and Tianjin University were returnees; the first minister of foreign affairs and the first premier of the Republic of China were all from this first group of overseas graduates. This generation of students also included the first designer of the Chinese railway, the first Chinese mining engineer, the first operator of the Chinese post office and customs and the first group of the Chinese national capitalists. Despite their small number, together they made a great impact on changing the country from an old, feudal society to a more modern and capitalist country.

Second Generation (1900–1927): *Ending the Feudal Past*

The second generation of Chinese returnees included many students who had studied in Japan, Europe, and Russia. This group launched the New Culture Movement in

China in the early twentieth century. Many giants in modern Chinese literature such as Lu Xun (Lu Hsün 1881–1936), Hu Shi (Hu Shih 1891–1962), and Guo Moruo (Kuo Mo-jo 1892–1978) belonged to this generation and brought new ideas and cultural approaches to China. Many modern Chinese political leaders came from this generation, including Dr. Sun Yet-Sen (1866–1925), the first president of the Republic of China, and Chiang Kai-shek (1887–1975), the leader of the Nationalist government. Major political reform movements during this period were often influenced or organized by returnees, including the Hundred Days' Reform and the Wuchang Uprising. The latter initiated the revolution that resulted in the toppling of over 2000 years of feudal and imperial rule in China.

Among the 12 delegates who attended the meeting that led to the founding of the Chinese Communist Party, eight were Chinese returnees. Zhou Enlai, the first Chinese premier, and many other leaders of the People's Republic of China had attended schools overseas. Among the group was Deng Xiaoping, who studied in France for five years in the earlier part of his life. Due to his overseas experience, Deng may have gained a cosmopolitan view of the world early on, which helped him become a strong reform leader who later opened up the country to the outside world and led China into a more prosperous modern era.

Third Generation (1927–1949): Founding the People's Republic

This generation of returnees studied mainly in Europe and the United States. Following the first and second generations of Chinese returnees, this group gave rise to many great Chinese scientists, educators, artists, state leaders, and politicians. During the early years of the People's Republic of China, many large-scale scientific and technological projects, including the development of nuclear bombs and satellites, were led and implemented by returnees. Many also worked in the newly established universities and colleges in China. More strikingly, among the 63 people with ranks above minister of the first PRC government, 42 were returnees. Among the 10 marshals awarded in the People's Liberation Army, six had studied or worked overseas. Further, among the seven central political bureau members, besides Mao, all were returnees, and they all played vital roles in founding the People's Republic.

Fourth Generation (1949–1965): Building the New China

After the People's Republic was founded, there was a great need for rebuilding China following the civil war, and the country was in urgent need of talent. Since China had good relations with the Soviet Union at that time, this generation of Chinese students was sent mainly to Russia and the former East Bloc countries. During this time, about 18,000 students and cadres from China were sent to study in Eastern Europe. They formed a much needed talent pool for rebuilding China. With the help of the Soviet Union and the hard work of returnees, China was able to build 156 large-scale projects throughout the country and laid a solid foundation for the development of the state economy. Among those trained in Russia were many engineers and factory managers, including former Chinese President Jiang Zeming and Premier Li Peng.

However, during the Cultural Revolution, China stopped sending students overseas. In fact, from 1965 through 1978, China sent almost no students overseas. Those who had studied or trained overseas were severely criticized and punished, and as a result China lost almost a generation of returnees.

Fifth Generation (1978–Present): Opening Up and Globalizing China

After China launched its economic reform and open door policy in 1978, an unprecedented wave of students went overseas to study and many Chinese students returned. Since Deng Xiaoping's initiative that sent thousands of students overseas, mainly to Western countries, China sends more students overseas than any other country. Chinese students today study in 108 countries and regions in the world, covering nearly all disciplines. As one pundit commented, "Wherever the sun rises, there are Chinese students." According to the Chinese Ministry of Education, in 2005, 32.1% of Chinese students chose to study in America, 27.9% selected Europe, 25.2% Asia, 14.2 percent Oceania, and 0.5% chose Africa.

By the end of 2009, over 1.62 million Chinese students and scholars had studied overseas, an average annual growth rate of 25.8% since 1978, and the total number of students went overseas increased more than 267 times compared with the number since the reform era began in 1978. On the returning side, there are already over one half million foreign-trained students and scholars. In recent years, more students and scholars are coming back to China, mainly due to government efforts and the financial crisis abroad. In 2009 alone, over 108,000 overseas students returned to China, an annual increase of 56.2% compared with 2008 (Ministry of Education, 2010).

As the newest and largest generation of returnees in Chinese history, these returnees have played a pivotal role in opening up and globalizing China. For example, they dominate China's academic and R&D sectors, accounting for 78% of Chinese university presidents, 72% of senior positions at the leading state and provincial research centers, 81% of the members of the Chinese Academy of Sciences, and 54% of the members of the Chinese Academy of Engineering (*China Daily*, 2007).

The Roles and Contributions of China's Contemporary Returnees

A sharp difference between recent and previous waves of Chinese returnees is that, from the mid-1990s on, an increasing number of returnees have pursued new business development, founding start-ups and managing business expansion for multi-nationals. This is the most striking difference in this generation of returnees from previous generations. Ever since the 1990s, Chinese returnee entrepreneurs have been a major force in the country's globalization process and economic development. We identify below various roles and contributions of Chinese returnees over recent years.

Driving Force of the New Chinese Entrepreneurs

Unlike their predecessors, contemporary returnees are entrepreneurs. Over the past two decades, the country has witnessed the formidable economic and technological power of Chinese returnees in their entrepreneurial activities. They have started numerous high tech enterprises and contributed directly to the economic development of the country. In addition, they introduced many new management concepts and new ways of financing, which benefit overall development of entrepreneurship in China. Returnees have started businesses in many sectors, including technology, the Internet, telecommunications, and media, and they have helped revitalize many traditional industries. Enterprises started by returnees are now in the mainstream of China's new high tech economy.

Fifty-seven percent of businesses started by returnees are in the scientific field, with 44% of those businesses holding patents. Most of China's high tech companies listed on European and the US exchanges are founded and brought to overseas stock markets by returnees. A core group of Chinese enterprises with a total market value of $30 billion are listed on Wall Street exchanges. Among them are Asia info, UT Starcom, Baidu, Sina, Sohu, Vimicro, Ctrip, eLong, Shanda, 51job, Kongzhong.com, Suntech Power, New Oriental School, and Home Inns. These listed companies brought advanced technology and talent to China as well as international capital and new mechanisms in business operation (Wang, 2007a). The returnees have brought China a large number of high tech enterprises, the modern management system, venture capital, and overseas listings. All these initiatives have a positive impact on the country's economic development and the lives of millions of people across the country, particularly the younger generations.

In support of returnee entrepreneurs, Chinese governments at various levels have set up more than 110 returnee entrepreneurial venture parks throughout the country. By 2008, over 8000 start-up businesses had been established in these parks with over 20,000 Chinese returnees involved. *Zhongguancun*, known as China's Silicon Valley, has more than 9800 returnees with approximately 4350 technological ventures established (Zhao and Zhu, 2009).

Key Player in China's Hi-Tech Industries

Most of the enterprises started by Chinese returnees are in high-tech sectors or in high-end services. The leadership teams of these enterprises usually consist of high-tech experts commanding the latest scientific knowledge. Some even have their own patents. With their close relationship with international companies, advanced management experience and wide contact, they function as a bridge between China's domestic companies and the international market. Since the 1990s, returnee entrepreneurs have significantly propelled the development of domestic high tech businesses and services, and improved the competitiveness of Chinese enterprises in the global market.

Returnee entrepreneurs have changed the domestic business landscape and fostered the development of the new economy. For instance, Asiainfo, founded by Tian Suning and Ding Jian, brought the Internet to China. The first generation of portal websites in mainland China established by Zhang Chaoyang and Mao Daolin changed the reading habits of the Chinese. Li Yanhong pioneered the leading Chinese search engine, which significantly improved information retrieval and access. ViMicro, founded by Deng Zhonghan, and SpreadTrum, started by Wu Ping, contributed to the development of the first "China Chip" with self-owned intellectual property.

Returnees played a key role in developing the Internet in China, although none of the returnees expected the development to be so rapid. But it made China a powerhouse in the world's Internet industry. Today, as a group of Internet enterprises that include Sina, Sohu, and Baidu established by returnees have fostered a vibrant online environment with hundreds of millions of netizens in China, they have not only enhanced transmission efficiency and improved information services across the country, but also created a flat world and fostered a new media revolution. More importantly, they have leveled the playing field and positioned China at the starting line along with the more developed countries in the field of Internet technology and development.

Leadership for the New Economy

Returnee entrepreneurs brought not only innovative technology but also new economic vitality to China. For instance, Kong Zhong Net, founded by Yang Ning, provides fast-growing wireless Internet service to the country. Baidu, founded by Li Yanhong and listed on the NASDAQ, has become a celebrated national brand with self-owned intellectual property in international fund markets. Successes like these have attracted more overseas investors to the Chinese market. Vimicro, founded by Deng Zhonghan, was also listed on the NASDAQ, another milestone in technology innovation by Chinese enterprises as they step up their efforts in the world market.

Most returnee companies listed on the NASDAQ are high-tech enterprises, catering to China's needs for economic development. The value of these high tech enterprises on the NASDAQ is not merely their market worth but their demonstrated role as pioneers in technology development. They have not only advanced the domestic economy, but also substantially improved the productivity of each industry by applying new technology such as the Internet, and they have instilled new vitality in business development. At *Zhongguancun*, China's "Silicon Valley," returnee entrepreneurs are in evidence. A group of high profile enterprises, including Sina, Sohu, Baidu, and New Oriental was born here, and the success clearly demonstrates the speed of growth of China's high tech industries. If China's future image in the new technology era is to be painted in this tiny and but swiftly growing valley of Beijing, the paintbrushes will be in the hands of a group of young returnees.

Revitalizing the Growth of Traditional Industries

Besides their prominent role in the high-tech sector, many returnee entrepreneurs are active in high-end service fields that have become leading companies. They are a dynamic force in many fields, covering finance, banking, consulting, law, broker agencies, media, public relations, advertising, tourism, exhibitions, and education, and are making a solid contribution to the growth of the service industry in China.

Returnee entrepreneurs also flourish in the more traditional industries. Soufun, Ctrip, Elong, and other companies are all using Internet technology to transform traditional industries such as real estate, tourism and hotels into highly efficient and vigorous new businesses. The New Oriental has made it possible for a traditional English training school to be listed on the NASDAQ. Ciming Medical Checkup realized that physical examinations, a peripheral service item in traditional hospitals, could be a big industry by itself. Arrail-Dental, founded by returnee entrepreneur Zou Qifang, introduced the chain operation concept to the Chinese dental industry (Wang, 2007a). Returnee entrepreneurs have played a leading role in creating a new business culture and promoting entrepreneurship in the country's swift transition from a planned economy to a market economy.

Chinese enterprises listed on the NASDAQ have recently expanded beyond the range of Internet and high technology firms, as many companies from diverse industries and fields are listed on the exchange. For example, Home Inns, an economy hotel chain in China launched by returnee entrepreneurs, went public on the NASDAQ on October 26, 2006. Its successful listing brought a new chain mechanism to China's traditional hotel industry. For its co-founder, Shen Nanpeng, who holds an MBA from Yale, this is his second IPO within three years after the success of Ctrip. Another example is Origin Agritech, the first agricultural company in China to be listed on the NASDAQ. Its chairman, Han Gengchen, is also an overseas returnee. The success of these enterprises is helping to foster renewed growth in traditional industries.

Bringing Venture Capital to China

Chinese entrepreneurial returnees brought back not only new knowledge and skills but also venture capital. This new funding mode has stimulated the growth of returnee entrepreneurship and small-to-medium enterprises (SMEs). Currently, almost all international venture capital companies in China are partly owned or managed by returnee entrepreneurs, and many of them are members of the Chinese Western Returnees Chamber of Commerce. A large amount of venture capital was imported into China by returnees or via foreign-funded companies where returnees worked. Venture capital is not only a new method of attracting foreign capital but also an effective capital input mode, as it brings new management mechanisms and teams to China. Venture capital not only stimulates domestic business development, but also promotes the growth of the venture capital industry.

As the industry becomes more mature in terms of market and talent, the rapid growth of China's economy provides huge operation space for the venture capitalists to play a more active role. Although many established VCs firms are experiencing dynamic growth, many returnee entrepreneurs have begun to set up new VC funds or incubation foundations to stimulate the development of SMEs. For example, returnee entrepreneurs such as Wu Shangzhi, chairman of CDH Venture, Yan Yan, chief partner of SAIF, Zhang Fan, Chinese partner of Sequoia Capital, Ding Jian, chairman and general manager of GSR Ventures, Xu Xin, founding partner of Capital Today, Kuang Ziping, founder, chairman and general manager of Qiming Venture, He Xin, chairman and GM of Carlyle Group, and Wang Shen, partner of Texas Pacific Group are all returnee entrepreneurs in charge of various venture capital businesses in China (Wang, 2007b).

After their initial successes in China's high-tech industries, many returnees shifted from being startup entrepreneurs to becoming venture capitalists. These returnees include Tian Suning, chairman of China Broad Band Capital, Deng Feng, founding partner of Northern Light Venture Capital, Zhu Min, chairman of Cybernaut Investment, Wang Chaoyong, chairman of China Equity, Shen Nanpeng, partner of Sequoia Capital, and Tang Yue, founding partner of Blue Ridge Capital China (Wang, 2007c).

Pioneering Enterprises Listing Overseas

Chinese returnees are also the main drivers of overseas listings of China's high-tech companies in the US financial markets. In 2009 alone, a record 33 Chinese companies were listed on the NASDAQ, with a total of 124 Chinese companies now listed on the stock market, more than any other US exchanges (NASDAQ, 2010). In November 2009, NASDAQ celebrated its 100th listing from mainland China by adding China Nuokang Bio-Pharmaceutical (NKBP), a healthcare company that provides blood and cardiovascular treatments. Most of the NASDAQ-listed Chinese companies are either funded or run by Chinese returnees.

Chinese returnee venture capitalists are active in fostering the growth of SMEs, and then listing them overseas, especially in the United States. They often reap a huge return while helping the newly listed enterprises participate in world financial markets and be evaluated by international investors. Since most of the firms are funded or managed by Chinese returnees, they advance the development of new technology and create new models of developing business in China and raising funds overseas. As noted by a NASDAQ representative, "The Chinese concepts brought about by these companies listed on the NASDAQ are also accepted by international markets. It is a good thing for Chinese enterprises. Among these Chinese companies on the NASDAQ, most of their management teams have studied overseas" (Wang, 2007a).

Among the entrepreneurial returnees this book discusses are Tian Suning, founder of Aisainfo, the first Chinese returnee enterprise listed on the NASDAQ; Li Yanhong, CEO of Baidu; Deng Zhonghan, CEO of ViMicro; Yang Ning, president of Kongzhong Corporation; Deng Feng, founding partner of Northern Light Venture Capital; Zhu Min, chairman of WebEx; Shen Nanpeng, co-founder of CTRIP and Home Inns; Liang Jianzhang, chairman of Ctrip; Xu Xiaoping, Beijing New Oriental Education Group; and Wu Ping, president of Spreadtrum.

Managing Multinationals in China

With 480 of the world's top 500 MNCs now operating in China, the demand for talented people with the management skills and transnational networks to bridge the East–West divide has mushroomed. In fact, a McKinsey report, as well as other studies, point out that China faces a serious shortage of middle- and high-level managers. As a result, Chinese overseas graduates who had already returned, or who work for MNCs or leading companies abroad, have filled many of the top management positions in MNCs, often as in-country directors. The list of MNCs that employ returnees as CEOs, executive vice presidents, and other senior posts is impressive and includes Google, Microsoft China, UBS, Alcatel, News Corps, Siemens, Hewlett Packard, Ernst and Young, BP and General Motors. Having participated in their company's strategic planning for China, these returnees are able to put the strategies into practice. They facilitate localization, improve the country's overall industrial structure, and help Chinese enterprises move up the value chain in world trade.

Although China's socialist heritage and troubled historical relationship with the West may cause some Chinese to see MNCs as threats to Chinese sovereignty, Zhang Yaqin, Microsoft VP responsible for R&D in China, believes that most returnees in senior positions feel responsible both for the growth of their company and for China's development. This dual notion is reflected in Microsoft Research Asia's motto: work in Microsoft, serve China. Further, as Wang Chunyan, VP of Siemens China, notes, returnees working in MNCs improve communication between China and the world, and therefore enhance the image of the country across the globe (Wang, 2007d).

Over the past three decades, MNCs have done their share to promote China's economic development. The Chinese Ministry of Commerce reports that, by September 2006, 570,000 foreign-invested enterprises (FIE) had contributed a total of USD$665 billion to the country's economy. Over 800 research and development centers have improved China's high-tech competitiveness, and most of them are headed by returnees (Xinhua, 2006). MNCs are also a key channel through which Chinese products are sold abroad. Since FIEs are responsible for over 55% of China's exports, returnee executives have helped MNCs sell "made in China" products to the outside world. In addition, returnees working in MNCs and investment banks drive the overseas listing of large state-owned enterprises (SOEs), since the CEOs and chairmen of the multinational investment banks are almost all returnees. People such as Liu Erfei, president of Merrill Lynch China, Sun Wei, managing director and China CEO of Morgan Stanley, and Zhu Yunlai of CSFB, receive credit for the successful IPOs of large state-owned enterprises such as Air

China, CHALCO, China Life, China Telecom, China Unicom, CNOOC, PICC, Sinopec, and Sinotrans.

The Rationale and the Goal of This Study

Chinese returnees have made great contributions to the country's modernization drive, especially after China opened up to the outside world. With their entrepreneurial spirit, they have brought talent, capital, technology, and management expertise to China's economic and social development. They play a unique role in connecting China to the outside world and in participating in the swift globalization process over the past two decades. However, despite Chinese returnees' significant influence on the development of science, technology and economy, researchers have devoted scant attention to the nature of Chinese returnee businesses. Until recently, the phenomenon of "returnees" has been examined largely from the perspectives of sociology and political economics, whereas few researchers in the areas of management or business studies have taken an interest in the development of Chinese returnee businesses, their profiles, roles, influences, and contributions. Therefore, a need exists for re-examining traditional viewpoints that often associate returnees with brain drain and brain gain theories. In today's globalized world, we need to look at returnees from the perspective of brain circulation and global talent movements.

The literature, especially academic studies, largely ignores the returnee phenomenon despite their prominent role in China's development. Most information is scattered in newspapers, websites, and magazines that are not readily accessible to college students studying international business or individuals seeking information on Chinese entrepreneurs and firms. Though a few studies in English exist as case studies for MBA students, most of the information is only available in Chinese and therefore beyond the reach of most Westerners. With China's growing importance in the global economy, there is an increasing need for a research tool that students, librarians, business professionals or anyone interested in China's economy and its key players can easily access. We believe this book fills the gap. As a reference title, this volume focuses exclusively on the elite entrepreneurs of new China. It strives to provide up-to-date and comprehensive coverage of top overseas returnees who have made noteworthy contributions to the Chinese economy since the reform era began in 1978.

We envision *The Entrepreneurial and Business Elites of China: The Chinese Returnees Who Have Shaped Modern China* as a useful tool for academic libraries of all sizes, research agencies and organizations with a focus on China and international business, and large-to-medium-size public libraries. The natural target audiences include undergraduate students, although graduate students in MBA programs may also find the work useful. Librarians searching for ready references on notable Chinese business figures and individuals who wish to understand the ins and outs of the new Chinese economy over the last 30 years will find the book valuable.

This book contains a total of 108 profiles, each 1000–1500 words in length, summarizing an individual's life and business career, with a focus on accomplishments and key roles in the new Chinese economy. The selections are based on both Chinese media sources and English publications currently available. We believe the leaders included in the book, although this list is by no means exhaustive, are among the most representative Chinese entrepreneurial returnees who helped to reshape the economic landscape of the country over the past three decades. For each biographical profile, we provide references with additional information on the subject. A list of common abbreviations and English-Chinese cross references of individual names indexed in the book are provided as well. All Chinese personal names in the book are listed according to the eastern custom, with family name first, followed by the given name (i.e., Deng Xiaoping); and all personal and place names are listed in the standard Chinese *Pinyin* system, except for people from Hong Kong, Taiwan and overseas, whose names are spelled following the traditional Wade-Giles system or their preferred Western names (e.g., Li Ka Shing).

HUIYAO WANG, WENXIAN ZHANG AND ILAN ALON

Sources

China Daily (2007), "Returnees are becoming the driving force in China's construction", 10 August.

Fairbank, J. and Goldman, M. (2006), *China: A New History*, second enlarged edition, Cambridge, MA: Harvard University Press, p. 2.

Liu, M. and Hewitt, D. (2008), "Rise of the sea turtles: China's most modern citizens aren't drawing it any closer to the West", *Newsweek*, 18–25 August.

Ministry of Education (2005), Statistics of the Study Abroad Service Center.

Ministry of Education (2010), Statistics of the Study Abroad Service Center, 15 March.

NASDAQ (2010), "33 Chinese companies listed on NASDAQ in 2009, more than any other U.S. exchange: Total of 124 Chinese companies listed on NASDAQ", available at: http://ir.nasdaq.com/releasedetail.cfm?ReleaseID = 434451 (accessed November 7, 2010).

Wang, H. (2010) *National Strategy – Talents Chang World*, Beijing: China People's Press.

Wang, H. (2009), The Chinese Overseas Educated Scholars Talents Development Report 2009, Beijing: China Huazhang Press.

Wang, H. (2007a), *Contemporary Chinese Returnees*, Beijing: China Development Press.

Wang, H. (2007b), *Wealth Creation: Top Ten Returnees in Venture Capitalism*, Beijing: China Development Press.

Wang, H. (2007c), *Movers on Wall Street: Ten Overseas Returnees Who Took Their Business Public*, Beijing: China Development Press.

Wang, H. (2007d), *Splendid Careers: Ten Overseas Returnees in Professional Management*, Beijing: China Development Press.

Wang, H. (2005), *Returning Times: An Overall Review and Analysis on Chinese Returnees*, Beijing China Central Compilation & Translation Press.

Xinhua News Agency (2006), "Foreign invested enterprises in China invested $665 billion", 5 November.

Zhao, L. and Zhu, J. (2009), "China attracting global talent: Central and local initiatives", *China: An International Journal*, 1 September.

BIOGRAPHICAL PROFILES OF CHINESE RETURNEES IN BUSINESS AND ENTREPRENEURSHIP

Cao, Guowei (曹国伟 b. 1965)

Cao Guowei is President and CEO of Sina.com, a leading online media company and mobile value-added service (MVAS) provider for China and for the global Chinese communities.

Born in Shanghai, Cao Guowei studied journalism at Fudan University, where he graduated in 1988. Like many of his fellow students, he went to the United States, first earned his MA in journalism from Oklahoma University, and then in 1991 enrolled into the MBA program at University of Texas at Austin. Cao began his professional career as a US-certified accountant in Silicon Valley, and worked his way up to a manager position in Pricewaterhouse Coopers, where he was in charge of providing audit and business consulting services to high-tech firms in Silicon Valley. In his early years at Pricewaterhouse Coopers, Cao was involved in many IPO and merger and acquisition (M&A) projects that later became the most valuable assets for his career development.

In the mid-1990s, when Internet was about to take off, Chinese entrepreneurs started to launch Internet businesses in large cities such as Shanghai and Shenzhen, and new dotcom companies began to show their potentials in the emerging market. Among portal sites that provided various information and services to Internet users, SINA was one of the most well-known companies at that time, and it was looking for talents to help its IPO on the NASDAQ. In search of a breakthrough for his own career, Cao consulted his friend Mao Daolin for advice, who was the COO of SINA at that time. Cao did not expect to join SINA, but his talents in capital management aroused interests of Mao and SINA. In September 1999, SINA invited Cao to join the company as its vice president, in charge of financial management. He was later promoted to CFO in 2001, mainly responsible for its IPO on the NASDAQ. Cao later recalled his decision of joining SINA as a natural one, not only because SINA was in media that aligned with his journalism background, but more importantly, it was a China-based company. However, Cao did not expect to stay with SINA for so many years or even become CEO, because CFO who is in charge of IPO usually leaves the position after the company goes public.

Six months after Cao had joined the company, SINA was successfully listed on the NASDAQ, the first Chinese dotcom company to do so. The IPO created a brand new way of financing for Chinese high-tech companies and became an icon for Chinese portal sites. However, an issue was soon bubbled up in the stock distribution among SINA's top management. Compared to other Chinese dotcom companies such as sohu.com and netease.com, whose CEOs held about half of the common shares, CEO of SINA held only a small portion of the common shares (6.3%). Stock dispersion weakened the consistency of strategy execution of the top management team at SINA and held back company's new market development. To offset the disadvantage, Cao waited for years to find ways to increase management stock holding. During this period, he led the buyout of Guangzhou Xunlong and Shenzhen

Wangxin, two Chinese mobile value added service (MVAS) providers in 2003 and 2004, respectively, which were the most well-known buyouts and the most cited cases in the Chinese Internet industry. These two acquisitions strengthened the leading position of SINA in wireless value-added service and stimulated its stock price on the NASDAQ.

Cao's talents in dealing with crisis helped SINA go through many challenges. In 2004, he was assigned as COO to solve the problem in SINA's advertisement sales. At that time, SINA was behind its major competitors such as SOHU. After examining the situation, Cao rebuilt a new sales team and the company's sale system, and took quick and effective actions. SINA finally exceeded SOHU and advertisement sales became the new development engine for the company afterwards. Two years later, it was Cao again who led SINA successfully prevent a takeover attempt by its competitor snda.com by suggesting a poison pill strategy. Afterwards, Cao was nicknamed Hawk CFO by industry observers, indicating him as a tough and effective executive.

In 2006, Cao was named CEO of SINA. When outsiders were predicting how long he could remain in the position, he was already pushing SINA forward by expanding market and strengthening its existing core businesses. Before him, none of the four former CEOs at SINA could continue for more than two years because of "poor performance." Cao did not take the hard way to lead and innovate. Instead, he claimed that he was a continuer not a reformer. To secure the continuous development of SINA, he focused on SINA's core business of news and related services. The 2008 Olympic Games proved him right. Other than the core focus, Cao also put emphasis on developing new businesses such as Web2.0 products and related advertisement sales, which protected the core business of SINA and promoted its development in the growing Internet market.

On September 28, 2009, Cao and SINA's top team executed a management buyout (MBO). As a result of US$180 million spent on 9.41% of SINA's common shares, Cao and his management team finally became the controlling shareholders of SINA. This ended the criticism of stock dispersion and reduced the possibility of outside controlling shareholders. A month later, Cao and SINA pushed forward the IPO of China Real Estate Information Corporation (CRIC) on the NASDAQ. Jointly owned by SINA and E-House China, a Chinese real estate services company, CRIC mainly provides real estate information, consulting, and online services in China.

From a journalist to a CEO, Cao proved that hard work and professionalism could lead to success. For his accomplishment, he has received honors from different groups and associations, including the Economic Personality of the Year award by CCTV in 2009. Looking into the future, Cao plans to lead SINA forward by building a network of Internet services across different platforms such as PC, cell phone, Internet TV, and other new media. He also hopes that he will become a CEO like Lee Scott, former CEO of Wal-Mart, who can build a stable system for the continuous development of the company but can still enjoy his own life after passing the torch to his successors.

HAO CHEN

Sources

Huang, L. (2009), "Cao Guowei", in: Zhang, W. and Alon, I. (eds), *Biographical Dictionary of New Chinese Entrepreneurs and Business Leaders*, Cheltenham, UK: Edward Elgar, p. 6.
百度百科 (2010), '曹国伟', ['Cao Guowei', *Baidu.com*], available at: http://baike.baidu.com/view/131548.htm#1 (assessed 29 June 2010).
新浪财经 (2009), '新浪CEO曹国伟简介' ['Sina CEO Cao Guowei: A brief bio', *Sina Finance*], 26 January, available at: http://finance.sina.com.cn/g/20090126/22575799107.shtml (assessed 29 June 2010).
张韬 (2010), '新浪掌门曹国伟: 现在开始创业', *上海证券报* [Zhang, T., 'SINA CEO Cao Guowei: Entrepreneurship starts from here', *Shanghai Securities News*], 26 January, available at: http://paper.cnstock.com/html/2010-01/26/content_71982637.htm (assessed 29 June 2010).

Chang, Zhaohua (Maxwell Chang 常兆华 b. 1963)

Dr Zhaohua (Maxwell) Chang is the founder, chairman, and director of MicroPort Medical Limited Corporation, and currently a professor and associate dean of the Medical Device College of the Shanghai University of Science and Technology. A Chinese returnee following a successful career in America, Chang has been committed to the research, development, and production of minimally invasive medical devices. These devices reduce pain and damage to millions of patients, save their lives at an average speed of 2 min, and embody a balanced and effective integration of Eastern and Western medical philosophies. His commitment to improve healthcare in China and around the world, in spite of the multitude and magnitude of obstacles, has earned him many awards both at home and abroad, including the title of an exemplar returnee.

Since the early stages in his life, Chang has demonstrated a keen interest in knowledge and a passion for learning. Born in 1963 at Ziboo, Shandong Province, Chang began his academic career with a focus on power engineering. Between 1979 and 1987, Chang was an intelligent and devoted student at the Shanghai University of Science and Technology (then Shanghai Mechanical Institute). Not content with a typical college education, he aimed to pursue the highest educational level possible, and subsequently earned his bachelor's, master's, and doctoral degrees from the same university. Chang's quest for learning led him to a new academic discipline that later defined his life. Armed with a doctoral degree, Chang decided to further his education and studied under Professor John G. Baust, the then president of International Low Temperature Biology, at the New York State University. Subsequently, he earned his doctoral degree in biological sciences in 1992.

In his developmental years in America, Chang built on and leveraged the most advanced research he could find. During his five years as a doctoral student, Chang accumulated cutting-edge knowledge in biomedicine and focused on ultrafast, ultralow temperature freezing technology theory. He would spend countless hours working alone in the barn at Professor Baust's farm experimenting in ultralow temperature system. While in the United States, Chang had published 40 articles in international scientific journals and received 10 US patents. He led the research team in developing the world's first ultralow temperature, deep freezing knife system, which was to be successfully applied to the minimal invasive treatment for liver, prostate, kidney, and breast cancer; brain tumors; and other diseases. Chang made theoretical and technological breakthrough that allowed such systems to be mass-produced at low cost.

Chang's academic success was replicated in the corporate environment. Between 1990 and 1997, Chang had successful experiences with a number of American medical companies. He worked as an engineering consultant, senior scientist, vice president of engineering, and director of R&D at Cryomedical Sciences Inc., a NASDAQ-listed and Maryland-based medical device company that was subsequently acquired. In 1996, Chang became the vice president of research and development of Endocare Inc., a NASDAQ-listed medical device company based in California.

Chang's entrepreneurial streak surfaced later in life. Though successful and well paid, Chang believed that to better use his talents and make more contributions to society he needed to establish his own company. Upon his return to China and with US$300,000 in hand, Chang established his business at the Zhangjiang Hi-Tech Incubation Park in Shanghai in 1998. This was the period when Shanghai decided to develop its Pudong district and encouraged foreign investment and Chinese returnees to develop the area. With support from the Shanghai government, Chang established MicroPort, which became the leading Chinese developer, manufacturer, and marketer of innovative medical products for interventional cardiology and peripheral vascular diseases.

Chang's path to success, however, was full of obstacles, failures, and competitions. Drawbacks never daunted him but challenged, motivated, and prepared him to create more innovative products. In December 1998, MicroPort produced the first-generation production equipment PTCA (percutanueous transluminal coronary angioplasty) balloon catheter, which was awarded the high-tech achievement transformation project and soon passed its first clinical validation. However at that time, most of the local Chinese hospitals could not afford the MicroPort products, in spite of their high quality and proven effectiveness. Moreover, the medical market in China at that time was monopolized by four international producers such as Johnson and Johnson, Boston, Medtronic, and Kato. Fully understanding the level of competition brought about by these well-established companies, Chang decided to challenge himself to produce equipment that would be adaptable to the Chinese market. With limited supplies, equipment, production facilities, and expert crew, Chang launched an aggressive business development initiative. He recruited experts from abroad, raised funds from various sources, directed a multitude of experiments, purchased land for a production base, and obtained the State Food and Drug Administration (SFDA) registration. In December 1999, Chang sold his first MicroPort product, an anti-invasive PTCA balloon catheter, to Shanghai Yangpu District Hospital. After its registration with SFDA in 2000, MicroPort's minimally invasive coronary stent delivery system won the first national patent in China.

Chang's business breakthroughs led to expansion into international locations and the creation of a diversity of new products. Since 2001, MicroPort, under Chang's leadership, expanded in many ways: it established branches in Beijing, received funds from multiple domestic and large international investment groups, sold to overseas markets such as Japan, Europe, and Latin America, and developed a number of innovative products such as Apollo, Mustang, Firebird, FireMagic, and Hercules. Chang's medical breakthroughs have made a significant impact on China's healthcare modernization and led to several well-deserved recognition. In recent years, Chang was honored with awards and titles such as the Second Prize of the National Scientific and Technological Progress Award, National Hundred Talents Project Candidate, the National Advanced Chinese Returnee, the Shanghai Second Science and Technology Young Talents, and Science and Technology Leader in Shanghai, among others.

Chang is sensitive about how his company is perceived and the national honor it can potentially bring. When MicroPort went public, an international company offered a high price to purchase the company, but Chang rejected the offer. He believes that MicroPort belongs not just to him but to China, and the in-roads enjoyed by the company are a symbolic success of China-based national industries. Chang's hard work and well-conceived business strategies have paid off. In 2006, *Forbes* ranked Chang 362nd among the 400 richest Chinese. The impact of Chang's work is deep and profound, especially within China, as the products his company manufactures have enhanced the lives of millions. A philanthropist, Chang has donated millions of dollars' worth of products to institutions such as the Shanghai Charity Foundation. Furthermore, he has decided to take a proactive stance in charitable work by establishing the MicroPort Charity Medical Treatment Program.

PEILING ZHAO AND MARK MUNOZ

Sources

AsiaInfo. (2002), 'Microport Medical (Shanghai) to end traditional surgical operation', 27 March, available at: http://www.encyclopedia.com/doc/1P1-51659734.html (accessed 20 May 2010).

China Daily. (2006), 'Shanghai company finds a foothold in Holland', 21-22 October, available at: http://www.holthuis.com/articles/chinadaily.pdf (accessed 20 May 2010).

Forbes. (2006), 'The 400 richest Chinese: #362 Chang Zhaohua', 2 November, available at: http://www.forbes.com/lists/2006/74/biz_06china_Chang-Zhaohua_11HK.html (accessed 20 May 2010).

Microport. (2010), 'About our people: Board of Directors', available at: http://www.microportmedical.com/eng/board_of_directors.html (accessed 20 May 2010).

PDI. (2007), "常兆华: 微创致力于造福人类健康事业" [Chang Zhaohua: MicroPort endeavors toward the health of human beings], 8 May, available at: http://www.pdi.org.cn/cn/news/show.do?id = PANW00001110 (accessed 20 May 2010).

上海青年 (2010), '常博士的企业搞大了', ['Dr. Chang's enterprise is growing larger', *Shanghai Youth*], Available at http://www.why.com.cn/abroad_3/weiguofuwu/12/2.htm (accessed 20 May 2010).

张冬冬 (2009), '常兆华: 创业要做好充分准备', *人民日报* (海外版) [Zhang, D., 'Chang Zhaohua: Entrepreneurship needs a solid preparation', *People's Daily* (overseas edition)], 15 June, available at: http://www.chinaqw.com/lxs/hggw/200906/15/167516.shtml (accessed 20 May 2010).

Chen, Ge (陈戈 b. 1967)

A mover and shaker in the fast growing Chinese entertainment industry, Chen Ge is the founder and CEO of Top100.cn, a popular website for one-stop music downloads licensed by the Chinese Ministry of Culture and the Ministry of Information Technology. He is also the former managing director of Pulay Music and Entertainment from 1998 to 2005.

After graduating from Peking University in 1988 with his bachelor's degree in business management, Chen, like many other Chinese students of the time, went to the United States for his graduate study. Two years later, he earned a master's degree in finance from Brandeis University in Waltham, Massachusetts. He subsequently spent seven years in a series of finance positions in the United States, and seemed to be well on his way for a successful career as an investment banker, whose happiest moments stem from closing the books on a quarterly financial statement, wrapping up the latest IPO capitalization, or successfully managing a currency hedge. While uniquely qualified for these activities, Chen has followed a very different path in his life. He has leveraged his love of music with his considerable business savvy to become one of the hottest entertainment entrepreneurs in China today.

Moreover, his timing could not have been more perfect. In an interview with the *New York Times*, Peter Grosslight, worldwide head of music for the William Morris Agency, noted that "China is on the tip of everybody's tongue. There's (sic) 1.3 billion people there. It is becoming a much wealthier place. How can we ignore that (Sisario, 2007)?" How, indeed? The Chinese acceptance of Western music, particularly rock music, has been a tenuous process. First emerging in the early 1980s, when Chen was still in college, adaptation was slow going until the advent of the Internet, which made fresh new sounds universally accessible.

Enter Gary Chen. In 1998, fresh from his American experience, Chen returned to China with intent to make a splash in the music industry. That was the year he founded Pulay Music and Entertainment, a music talent agency headquartered in Beijing. Chen's education in the entertainment business came largely from the School of Hard Knocks. With no background in this arena, his experience was limited to coordinating a US tour for Chinese rock singer Cui Jian. Chen reminisced, "I was totally an amateur, I didn't know about venues, the booking, I just called a lot of places … I spent all my savings and went over my credit card limit. I was the single promoter. Even though it lost a lot of money, it was greatly rewarding to do that before the age of 30 (Murphy, 2009)." Chen must have done something right in this original venture. Cui Jian, now known as the Godfather of Chinese rock music, became one of Pulay's first clients.

To understand the significance of Chen's success to the Chinese economy, it is important to understand the industry environment at the time Pulay was established. In the 1990s, the Chinese government became increasingly supportive of efforts toward greater commercialization. And the music scene in China was, as with most other emerging industries there, receiving greater notice by Western firms interested in getting in on the ground floor of China's vast market potential. Moreover, bootleg recordings and pirated materials were no longer monopolizing the music trade, and commercially produced and distributed works were increasingly available. However, music artists interested in plying their trade profitably had very few alternatives for representation at their disposal. Inspired by firms such as the William Morris Agency and Creative Artists Agency, Chen established Pulay Talent Agency to provide Chinese artists with professional promotion and negotiation support. While this may not seem a revolutionary feat, consider that the increased recognition of these Chinese artists, and the increased sales of their product, inherently served to grow the entire music industry in China. At its peak, Pulay represented 22 musicians, several top music producers, and boasted relationships with major international players such as Warner Music.

While Chen was making his mark as an agency entrepreneur, a new form of music distribution was becoming available to Chinese aficionados: the Internet. In 2004, after six exciting years in the agency business, Chen decided to redirect his energy to pursue this new distribution channel. The foremost issue in his mind was how best to support and expand the music industry sector in China, particularly in light of the availability of free, albeit pirated, downloads on the Internet. His answer was to create a means of monetization while still employing the Internet, thus the creation of Orca Digital and its website, Top100.cn.

Supported by investors Eric Zhang and US basketball superstar Yao Ming, Chen established Top100.cn in September 2005 as a "pay to download" site. Downloads cost just 1 RNB, and, while inexpensive by world standards, were still 1 RNB more than the pirated downloads available in China via a myriad of other sites. But how else was Orca to generate profit from music distribution? The dilemma was resolved by Chen's historic partnership with Google in March of 2009. The search engine giant offered an alternative method of revenue generation through paid advertising on the expanded Top100 site. For the Chinese music industry, the venture reflected the first legitimate means of offering free online music while compensating the record labels themselves.

The business world has watched the partnership with avid interest, waiting to see if the model would hold fast in light of China's unique Internet environment; and as of June 2010, the paradigm remains viable. Chinese music aficionados download or stream roughly seven million licensed songs from Top100 daily, most driven to the site through Google.cn. During its first year of operation, Top100 enjoyed advertising revenues of over 6 million RMB. While Top100.cn is currently profitable on an operating basis, Chen pursues greater financial success via the offering of smartphone apps.

Current issues related to Internet privacy and censorship in China have headlined recent business journals. In March of 2010, Google announced that it would move its search engine activities to Hong Kong, thus circumventing the government's efforts to check searchable content. Concerns regarding its continued operating status prevail. In this context, one might wonder about Top100's continued success in online music distribution. Leave it to Chen to develop a proactive strategy. The pioneer announced in July 2010 that Orca would seek the participation of social networking sites and telecom carriers to redirect traffic to Top100, and would court additional investors as well.

In spite of a turbulent economic and political environment, there is no doubt that Chen's "music republic" (Wang, 2010) will continue to be a safe haven for artists, labels, and those whose life would be incomplete without the sound of music. Chen has made this his mission. As fellow business entrepreneur Gary Rieschel of Qiming Ventures so wisely noted, "... when you get down in the weeds and talk about flexibility and tactics, Chinese entrepreneurs are hard to beat (Barboza and Stone, 2010)." Surely no one exemplifies that sentiment better than Gary Chen.

ROBIN E. KELLY

Sources

Barboza, D., and Stone, B. (2010). *China, where U.S. Internet companies often fail. New York Times*, 15 January.

Chao, L. (2010), "Google's China music partner faces unsure fate", *Wall Street Journal Online*, 19 January, available at: http://online.wsj.com/article/SB10001424052748704541004575011683006036028.html (accessed 30 May 2010).

Kennedy, J. (2006), "Unlocking the music market in China", *IFSI*, 25 May, available at: http://www.ifpi.org/content/section_views/view020.html (accessed 30 May 2010).

Latham, K. (2007). *Pop Culture China! Media, Arts, and Lifestyle*. Santa Barbara, CA: ABC-Clio.

LinkedIn. (2010), 'Gary Chen profile', available at: http://cn.linkedin.com/pub/gary-ge-chen/a/17a/a4b (accessed 26 June 2010).

Murphy, S. (2009), "Interview with Gary Chen", *Music Matters*, available at: http://www.musicmattersasia.com/2009/press_download/Press%20Release%20-%20Music%20Matters%202009%20-%20Interview%20with%20Gary%20Chen.pdf (accessed 28 June 2010).

Sisario, B. (2007), "For all the rock in China", *New York Times*, 25 November.

The Economist (2010). Free as a bard: seeking profit in the world's toughest recorded-music market. *The Economist*. Retrieved from http://www.economist.com/node/17627557

Wang, X. (2010), "Orca seeks more alliances to trim reliance on US partner", *China Daily*, 7 July, available at: http://www.chinadailyusa.com/news/NewsInfo.asp?range=1&lv2=4&id=20205 (accessed 9 July 2010).

Chen, Hong (陈宏 b. 1962)

A skillful and resourceful CEO, Dr. Chen Hong is the chairman and president of the Hina Group, a leading investment banking and private equity firm in China that he founded in 2003. At a time when people deemed China's investment banking market premature, Chen was audacious enough to pursue his dream of setting up a company that would help its clients and partners capitalize on emerging opportunities in China as well as enable Chinese companies such as Baidu.com Inc. and China Mobile realize their global aspirations by providing financial services, advice, and investment capital. His entrepreneurial efforts paid off; by 2010, The Hina Group had engaged in over 50 financing and acquisition transactions that included Framedia, Oak Pacific Interactive, China Software International, AsiaInfo, and many more, totaling US$8 billion in transaction value.

Today, The Hina Group has two principal businesses: Hina Investment Banking, which provides corporate finance, and mergers and acquisitions (M&A) advisory services for clients in the United States, China, and across the Asia-Pacific region; and Hina Private Equity, which focuses not only on technology, media, and telecommunications, but also energy, biotechnology, education, manufacturing, and other consumer service-related traditional industries. The company boasts more than 50 professionals, and offices in Beijing, Shanghai, Singapore, and Silicon Valley. Under Chen's leadership, The Hina Group has become one of the most reputable investment banking and private equity firms in China, having received numerous awards including the "Best Investment Bank in 2008," "China's 2008 Most Valuable Brand in New Economy Investment Enterprises," and "China Boutique Mergers and Acquisitions Firm of the Year." In 2010, The Hina Group was ranked among the top 25 M&A advisors in China for completed transactions by Thomson Reuters, and was in the sixth place in the ranking of top 10 local M&A advisors in China for transaction values by ChinaVenture.

A computer scientist by training, Chen at age 15 passed the national college entrance examination and entered Xi'an Jiaotong University in 1978, one of the most prestigious universities in China, and earned a BS in computer science four years later. In 1985, he went to the United States with a government-sponsored scholarship and obtained a PhD in computer science from the State University of New York at Stony Brook in 1991. Chen later also received an honorary professorship from his Alma mater Xi'an Jiaotong University.

After a short sting working as a software engineer at Litton Industry and TRW, in 1994, Chen founded AIMnet, a leading Internet service provider based in Silicon Valley and served as its chairman, president, and CEO. Realizing that it was virtually impossible for AIMnet to become one of the top three ISPs in the US market, Chen sold the company to NTT/Verio in 1996 and founded GRIC (Global Roaming Internet Consortium) Communications, leading its successful IPO on the NASDAQ on December 15, 1999. This achievement made Chen the first Chinese graduate to run a publicly traded company in the United States, earning him such accolades as *Computerworld* magazine's "Brightest Star in the Millennium" award.

Within a month of its IPO, GRIC's market value surged over 1 billion dollars, and its stock price soared from an initial US$14 to over US$60 at one point. However, the burst of the dot-com bubble dragged it down to less than US$2 a share, shrinking the company's assets to less than US$10 million, therefore forcing Chen to struggle in stabilizing the company financially. Although in 2002 Deloitte & Touché named GRIC one of the 500 fastest growing technology companies in North America, Chen had to resign as CEO in early 2003 but continues to serve as the board chairman. Chen and his wife Lynn Liu also founded another company called Aicent, run solely by Lynn. Besides the two companies he founded and the one he cofounded with his wife, Chen is also part of a group of pioneering Chinese student entrepreneurs who founded Hua Yuan Science and Technology Association (HYSTA) in the Silicon Valley in 1999 with the hope of building better connections between China and United States and helping aspiring Chinese professionals become successful entrepreneurs like themselves.

Today, HYSTA is the leading association for aspiring Chinese immigrant entrepreneurs, and has created a unique network of successful Chinese entrepreneurs and executives. At the same time, it has become the first stop for networking and exchanging business ideas between successful Chinese entrepreneurs and executives in the Silicon Valley and those in China (http://www.hysta.org, 2008). Chen served as the founding president of HYSTA from 2000 to 2003. He also served as the president and chairman of the Asian American MultiTech Association (AAMA) in 2000 and 2001, respectively. In addition, Chen is a member of Club 100, which consists of the top 100 famous and influential business and thought leaders in China.

For his resourcefulness and contribution to the business world, Chen has won various awards and recognition over the years. In 1998, China's Committee for Overseas Chinese published a book naming Chen one of the 30 most successful overseas Chinese worldwide. In 2000, *Digital Weekly/Business Week* of Taiwan named him one of the 100 most influential Chinese leaders in the new world economy. In 2001, CCTV cited Chen as one of the most successful Chinese in North America. In 2007, in celebrating China's 30th anniversary of resuming the college entrance examination after the Cultural Revolution, CETV (China Education TV) documented Chen as one of the 20 national success stories of the classes of 1977 and 1978. In 2008, Chen was elected by the "Winning in the Future: Business Leaders" Forum as one of the "Top 30 Business Leaders of the Next 30 Years," and he was also awarded "China's Top 100 Elites" in the same year. Most recently, in 2010, Chen was awarded the "Boutique M&A Investment Banker of the Year in Asia Pacific" by Global M&A Network.

Chen has spoken and keynoted numerous times at prominent universities and business forums on issues such as the global and Chinese communications markets, Chinese entrepreneurship, and new economies in Asia Pacific, and he often advises top executives of many leading Asian telecommunication carriers on their global strategies. He cites passion, persistence, and ambition coupled with a lead in technology as his recipe for success in entrepreneurship. He draws his strength from years of overseas experience as the resourceful CEO of listed companies and from his easy-going manner. Chen is a dreamer who hopes that Hina will grow to become Chinese Blackstone Group, or the next Goldman Sachs of China; and as Walt Disney said, "All our dreams can come true, if we have the courage to pursue them," Chen has certainly proved his mettle.

EVERLYNE MISATI

Sources

Businessweek.com. (2009), 'The Hina Group', available at: http://investing.businessweek.com/research/stocks/private/snapshot.asp?privcapId = 28942095 (accessed 1 March 2010).

Cbfeature.com. (2009), 'Back from Silicon Valley', available at: http://www.cbfeature.com/industry_spotlight/news/back_from_silicon_valley (accessed 1 March 2010).

Hinagroup.com. (2009), 'Dr. Hong Chen, Chairman and CEO', available at: http://www.hinagroup.com/team%20list/ceo.htm (accessed 1 March 2010).

王红茹 (2007), '陈宏: 激情打造中国的高盛', *资本推手: 10位海归投资银行家* (王辉耀主编), 中国发展出版社, 北京 [Wang, H., 'Chen Hong: Passionately creating Chinese Goldman Sachs', in Wang, H. (ed.), *Capital Movers and Shakers: Ten Overseas Returnees in Investment Banking*, China Development Press, Beijing], pp. 130-155.

Chen, Naike (陈乃克 b. 1955)

An engineer by training, Chen Naike is the president and CEO of BOYI Pneumatic Technology Institute, an R&D institution and high-tech company based in Tianjin, China, that specialized in industry control techniques and measurement equipment.

Born in Shenyang, Liaoning Province, in 1955, Chen grew up in an ordinary family, and did not have a chance to attend college when he graduated from high school in 1972. Instead, he began work in the Liaoning Hongyang mine, first as a fitter, then as a member of the project team. In 1978, after eight years in the mines and the official conclusion of the disastrous Cultural Revolution, Chen's wish to attend college came true when he received an acceptance letter from the Chinese Northeastern Institute of Technology. Despite the age barrier, he jumped on the opportunity. After four years of study, Chen graduated with his BS degree in automatic control, and started to work as an engineer in the Automatic Control Lab of the Northeastern Electric Power Research Institute, where he spent seven years and was later promoted to the chief of the research unit. This experience proved beneficial, helping set Chen on a path toward a career in the automatic controls industry. During this period, he also spent a year in Germany working at Siemens Power Generation on a joint project co-sponsored by the German Ministry of Water Resources.

A year in Europe broadened Chen's vision of the world. Although by then he had already established himself as both an effective leader and a scientific researcher, he wanted to further his education and career advancement. In 1989, Chen relocated to Yokohama, Japan, and enrolled into an intensive program in Japanese language. This endeavor was a challenge, as he had little money and securing employment would have been difficult without speaking the local language. Chen went to class from 9:00 a.m. to 3:00 p.m. daily, and soon he was able to find work as a dishwasher in a local restaurant, working in the 4:00 p.m. to 12:30 a.m. shift. In 1990, after completion of the Japanese language curriculum, he moved to Saitama, Japan, and began working on earning first a master and ultimately a doctorate of engineering from Saitama University. He focused mainly on air pressure and control, and quickly demonstrated his full potential as an academic and scientist, as his works were soon accepted for presentation and publication in 15 prestigious conferences and journals. For his contributions to innovation in new technologies, in 1994 Chen was honored with the Japan Science and Technology Exchange Award. After studying eight years in Japan, Chen graduated from Saitama with his PhD in 1996.

Chen's most noteworthy accomplishment in the business world began when he returned to China. After he personally secured US$100,000 in capital, Chen founded the BOYI Pneumatic Technology Institute in Tianjin in 1997. Now known internationally as a manufacturer of air leak testers, electropneumatic transducers, gas analyzer and testing systems, and pressure sensors, gauges, and switches, the company's product line is extremely diverse. Yet, the company's beginning was more humble. Originally, BOYI focused on R&D in the industry control sector, and its key to success was Chen's innovative approach, as he simultaneously combined automatic control techniques with advances in computing technology, something that had not been done before. Furthermore, Chen worked diligently to instill within the company both a strong customer-centered approach and focus on sales and marketing. Admittedly, sales and marketing were not natural talents of Chen's, and he described the pursuit of these capabilities as being BOYI's greatest challenge.

Chen has viewed diversity of experience, education, and collaboration as key components of success in business, and he spent the better part of the company's first decade recruiting, training, and mentoring hundreds of highly educated individuals who now make up the leadership, management, and R&D staff at BOYI. Like Chen himself, many of these individuals spent years training and working overseas prior to returning to China. Currently, 98% of BOYI employees hold bachelors degrees or their equivalent, with many holding graduate degrees and specialist certifications.

For his professional accomplishment, Chen has received many honors and awards. He is a recipient of both the TEDA (Tianjin Economic Development Area) Figure Award and TEDA Leading Talent award, recognizing his vision and commitment to one of China's leading initiatives. Additionally, he was one of the few recipients to earn China's top honor for working people – the National Model Worker Award – for his work in China's mines. As a holder of a special allowance certificate from government, Chen was recognized as a distinguished expert of the Chinese Academy of Launch Vehicle Technology (CALT), and was the first recipient of the overseas Chinese Professionals Outstanding Entrepreneurship Award. In 2009, Chen was honored to be a part of the Olympic celebrations in Beijing, serving as one only five torch runners for the city of Tianjin.

Looking back, Chen recognizes that his success came at a cost. Although he is proud of his accomplishments, he regrets greatly the amount of time he spent away from his family. From 1993 to 2003, Chen notes that he spent over one third of his time away from his family studying, working, and traveling the globe, and he feared that he had missed many key moments and events in the lives of his children. Now, as president and CEO of China-based BOYI, with a much more stable work schedule, he is unsure what choices he would make if he had to do it all over again.

ERIC LIGUORI AND YINGLU WU

Sources

BOYI Pneumatic Technology Institute. (2009), 'Company profile', available at: http://www.fukuda-tj.com.cn/english/Company.asp?id = 1 (accessed 18 July 2010).

人民网 (2007), '科技英才访谈：博益气动研究所所长陈乃克' ['Interview with technology talent: Chen Naike, Director of BoYi Pneumatic Institute', *People*], 6 January, available at: http://www.022net.com/2007/1-6/566244162232632.html (accessed 18 July 2010).

任欣 (2008), "走进奥运火炬手: 走进陈乃克", *天津人民广播电台*, [Ren, X., 'Olympics torchbearers: Chen Naike', *Tianjin People's Broadcasting Station*], 30 July, available at: http://big5.radiotj.com/zhuanti/system/2008/07/30/000110038.shtml (accessed 18 July 2010).
天津电视台 (2003), "陈乃克" ['Chen, Naike', *China Tianjin TV*], 4 July , available at: http://www.tjtv.com.cn/system/2003/07/02/000589648.shtml (accessed 18 July 2010).

Chen, Xingdong (陈兴动 b. 1960)

An economist by training, Chen Xingdong is the managing director and chief economist of BNP Paribas Asia Ltd. He entered the Chinese investment banking sector in 1993, and earned a reputation of being an insightful and influential analyst of the conditions of Chinese and global economy. Using his own words, he enjoys being a "business economist."

Chen was born and brought up in a village in Youxi County, Fujian Province in Southeast China. His family faced enormous financial difficulties when he was a child. With the selfless support of his elder sister and the encouragement of his mentor in high school, he managed to finish his schooling. This unusual childhood experience became a precious source of inspiration for Chen in his later life.

In 1979, Chen took part in the nationwide college entrance exam and was admitted to the undergraduate program in economics of the elite Peking University, where he studied hard to build a broad knowledge base spanning a wide range of disciplines from economics to other social sciences and even natural sciences. He believed that it would be more efficient to explore a new subject than continuing to spend extra time on an old subject. As an undergraduate economics major, he was already applying the famous economic "law of diminishing marginal product" to his learning process.

Upon obtaining his bachelor's degree in 1982, Chen decided to continue his academic pursuit. He rose to the challenge of a highly competitive admittance exam and became a proud member of the then newly established master's program in national economic management of Peking University. Upon graduation in 1985, he started to work in a high-profile central governmental agency – the National Commission for Economic Institutional Reforms of the State Council, which served as one of the key engines that drove China's economic reforms in the 1980s.

The opportunity of studying abroad soon came to Chen in 1986. Sponsored by the United Nations Development Program, he was among the first group of Chinese central government officials sent to the University of Oxford for advanced study. Chen was trained at the Oxford China Centre for one and a half years. Before he returned to China, he spent a half year working at the World Bank as an economic adviser. In August 1988, Chen returned to the National Commission for Economic Institutional Reforms of the State Council, where he participated in policy research and design associated with shareholding system reform of state-owned enterprises and privatization of small and medium state-owned enterprises. However, because of the political turmoil of the late 1980s, the economic reforms of China's public sector came to a halt. In June 1990, while keeping his position as an official of the National Commission for Economic Institutional Reforms, Chen started to work as an economic research fellow for the China Office of the World Bank in Beijing.

The turning point of Chen Xingdong's career came in July 1993 when he left the World Bank for a position of senior economist in Crosby Securities (later Societe Generale-Crosby Securities). There he was later promoted to chief economist. His insightful analyses of the conditions and development of the Chinese economy soon made Chen famous within the community of investment banking. Four years later, in May 1997, he joined the Peregrine Investment Group, which was acquired by BNP Paribas in February 1998 in the aftermath of the 1997 Asian financial crisis to become what eventually would be BNP Paribas Asia Limited. At BNP Paribas, Chen was initially the chief representative of the Beijing Office and chief economist for China, and later became the managing director and chief economist of BNP Paribas Asia Limited.

In his 17 years career as an economist for investment banking, Chen has won wide recognition for his excellent skills of macroeconomic analysis and prediction, exemplified well by his title of China's Best Macroeconomic Analyst that was twice awarded by *Asiamoney*. All these achievements come naturally from his solid training in economics, his deep commitment to producing best-in-class economic analyses, and his unique understanding of the profession of economist for investment banking. Chen classifies all economists into three groups: theoretical economists, policy economists, and business economists, and has set as his personal goal to become a top business economist. In his eyes, while a theoretical economist attempts to answer the two questions of "what it is" and "why it is so," policy and business economists need to answer a third question. For a policy economist, this third question is "what it ought to be," and for a business economist, the question becomes "what it could be." This distinction is important, for a business economist has to show to investors what might happen to the economy and guide the latter's money to the most profitable channels. A business economist will thus be held accountable to the investors for the decisions they make, and incur risks associated with the consequences from such decisions. Fully aware of the risks he has to take as a business economist, Chen likes this challenge and enjoys his job.

Chen's current principal task of macroeconomic analysis is to provide international institutional investors with updated reports on developments of China and other developing countries. His reports usually involve the following steps of analysis. First of all, he discusses whether or not the country under study is politically stable. Then he explores the possible changes in its economic policies. Third, he investigates in great detail the conditions and sources of economic growth. Lastly, he recommends the industries for investment.

The issue of the value and exchange rate of China's currency has been heatedly debated in recent years. Back in August 2005, with mounting pressures from the United States on Chinese central government, many investment bankers expected Chinese *renminbi* to appreciate greatly against US dollar. Chen, however, made a rather different prediction. Based on a systematic analysis of the conditions and needs of the Chinese economy and the dynamics in United States–China relations, he boldly projected that Chinese *renminbi* would not appreciate more than 3% within 2005 and would not appreciate more than 5% over 2006. The trend of Chinese *renminbi* value over the subsequent periods proved that Chen was correct. Afterwards, those investors who used to predict over-optimistically about the value of Chinese *renminbi* and debate vehemently with Chen on this issue came to admire Chen's great skills of analysis.

Chen spends about four to five months of a year in travel. As a popular business economist, he is frequently invited to speak at various occasions ranging from economic forums, professional associations, universities, and foreign embassies, to road shows. He often describes himself as hard working as shoemakers. When he attends a road show, his work intensity can go beyond imagination. Sometimes he has to give five to nine speeches in a given day, and his record was visiting five different cities giving talks at five conferences in a day. Such a busy schedule requires unusual stamina. Yet he always keeps an optimistic attitude toward life and work. He reminds himself of the great importance of being passionate and persistent about maintaining regular daily exercises. Before going to bed at night, he does 80–90 repetitions of squatting while facing the wall. "The more tiring one feels, the more one needs to exercise; the more one wants to feel comfortable, the more one will end up feeling uncomfortable," Chen noted on his life philosophy (Wang, 2007).

ZHAOCHANG PENG

Sources

廖书敏 (2010), "陈兴动: 人民币汇率或恢复挂钩一揽子货币", *和讯新闻* [Liao, S., "Chen Xingdong: *Renminbi*'s exchange rate may revert to pegging to a basket of currencies", *Hexun News*], 1 April, available at: http://news.hexun.com/2010-04-01/123189725.html (accessed 17 October 2010).

王红茹 (2007), "陈兴动: 投行中的商业经济学家", *资本推手: 10位海归投资银行家* (王辉耀主编), 中国发展出版社, 北京 [Wang, H.R., "Chen Xingdong: A business economist in investment banking," in Wang, H.Y. (ed.), *Investment Bankers: Ten Overseas Returnees in Investment Banking*, China Development Press, Beijing], pp. 156–81.

中国经济学奖 (2004), "专家介绍: 陈兴动" [China Economics Award, "Chen Xingdong"], available at: http://www.macrochina.com.cn/prize/brt/chenxingdong.shtml (accessed 17 October 2010).

Cheng, Changqing (Charles Cheng, 成长青 b. 1962)

Also known as Charles Cheng, Cheng Changqing is the chief executive officer of Standard Chartered Corporate Advisory Co., the investment-banking arm of Standard Chartered Bank in China. His main job is to provide the Chinese businesses with banking products and services that include mergers and acquisitions, cash management, trade and project financing, etc.

Cheng Changqing was born in 1962 in a working-class family and had four brothers and sisters. He studied in the No. 5 Middle School of Changsha, Hunan Province, which was ranked the fourth leading middle school in China at that time. With little interest in natural science, Cheng chose to study foreign language instead. In 1978, he was recruited into Beijing Foreign Studies University, majoring in French.

Cheng regarded the foreign language only as a tool to discover the world and learn the cultures of other countries. To be successful, he believed that one should have specialized knowledge in some professional fields. Therefore, he took some elective courses such as psychological research and determined to be a teacher later in his life. After graduation, Cheng chose to teach French in Northeast Normal University, as he had a firm goal to study educational psychology abroad, and Northeast Normal University could provide such an opportunity for him.

On July 1, 1984, Cheng went to Europe and enrolled into the management psychology program at University of Paris, an institution of higher learning with a history of more than 1200 years. While in France, he spent a year studying the effects of noise on people's behavior in Peugeot Automobile Group. As the outcome of that study, he wrote a paper entitled "Human Behavior Difference under Different Noises," which won the annual prize given by the French Noise Association. Because of his research experience in Peugeot, Cheng had a chance to serve as a translator for a Chinese delegation visiting France, and was thus fascinated by the aspects of business management. From that encounter, he formed an idea in his mind that psychology is only a part of management and management is an ever-changing and all-around discipline. Therefore, in September 1987, Cheng changed his disciplinary focus and went to the HEC business school. A year later, he furthered his study at McGill University in Canada.

After his graduation from McGill University in 1989, Cheng chose to work in Alexander Consulting Company. Headquartered in West Palm Beach, the company was mostly engaged in consulting and diagnosing the problem in business process. As consulting is a comprehensive industry, a consultant has to know a company's product development, marketing, procurement, production, inventory, transportation, services, finance, and so on. During his time in Alexander Consulting Company, Cheng had consulted for Hilton Hotel, Sears Stores, National Bank of Canada, Air Canada, and Peerless Carpet Corporation.

In May 1991, Cheng joined Toronto Dominion Bank as a senior customer manager, the first Chinese mainlander to work in that bank. Toronto Dominion Bank was one of few 3A banks in the world and the only one in Canada. During his two years in Dominion Bank, Cheng was in charge of telecommunication and mining industries, as well as helped those companies engage M&A and financing activities. That experience laid a solid foundation for his career in financial industry. In 1994, Cheng landed a position in the headquarters of First Chicago Corp., and a year later, he was assigned to the Beijing Branch as the director of the China marketing department of First Chicago Corp. So after 10 years abroad, Cheng returned to his motherland.

In 2000, Cheng left the company and decided to start his own business. Starting from scratch, he believed that happy people are those who are able to combine personal interest with professional achievement well, and for years he had dedicated himself to this goal. He founded several companies, including an interesting-but-unprofitable online model company, an uninteresting-but-profitable logistic company, an interesting-and-profitable international CEO vacation community, and so on.

In August 2002, Cheng resumed his old profession by joining the Standard Chartered Bank as a senior vice president and the general manager of Chinese corporation department. His main responsibility was to deal with all the business related to Chinese companies. In 2004 alone, he assisted several Chinese corporations in financing over US$3 billion of overseas acquisitions, which included the Sinopec's operation in Angora, one of the most famous cases in financing emerging corporations, in which he was able to seal a billion dollar deal in 36 hours that brought fame to Cheng overnight. Over the past six years in Standard Chartered Bank, Cheng has assisted a great number of leading Chinese companies going global, acquiring resources and knowledge, and expanding their businesses overseas. In recognition of his contribution to helping Chinese corporations in cross-border M&A, a group of eight leading organizations, including UNESCO, Peking University, and CCTV, named Cheng among "China Top Ten Talents (Finance) of the Year" in 2004. He was also awarded the title of "Manager with Excellent Execution" by the China Productivity Commission in 2005.

Currently, the value of M&A business accounted for only about 1% of GDP in China, while the figure is 14% in Occident. In developed countries, CEOs spend a large part of time engaging in M&A-related activities. In Cheng's opinion, M&A is a kind of borderless economy and an inevitable result of globalization. The purpose of M&A is nothing more than the market, technology, and R&D capability. Before an acquisition can take place, enterprises should have clear objectives. For instance, Lenovo took over PC business of IBM to quickly realize the internationalization of the brand, and PetroChina and Sinopec acquired foreign energy companies to increase their resource reserves. Based on his professional experience, Cheng found that the current primary target of Chinese enterprises in M&A was no more than the market, as those corporations were keen on acquiring well-known companies in developed countries and regions. After the acquisition, however, Chinese firms always found that the acquired companies had already shrunk in operation, which left much difficulty in the integration. In addition, the cross-border M&A is not a good choice for the enterprise to realize diversification, as the success rate of such acquisitions is low. It is very difficult for Chinese enterprises to become an industry leader in technology through M&A. Hence, Cheng believed that it would be a tough challenge for Chinese enterprises to buy the high-quality business of the famous companies, while it would be much easier to acquire some smaller companies or laboratories with advanced technology. When foreign enterprises spin off some noncore businesses or assets, it will be a great opportunity for the Chinese enterprise in the same industry.

During the SARS epidemic of 2003, Cheng learned how to play golf. One year later, he began to fall in love with the sport. So far, his best score is only 95 strokes. "The score is not important for me. I love golf because it is like an acquisition, full of challenges, expectations and uncertainty." He may not care about the score of his next golf game, but he does expect the next success of acquisition. According to him, "My next target is to complete an acquisition of more than 5 billion dollars, which will be a new milestone in China's cross-border M&A (Wang and Hou, 2007)." In the coming years, it looks like Cheng will continue to play an important role in the globalization of Chinese enterprises.

XUEYUAN LIU AND SHANSHAN ZHANG

Sources

王红茹, 侯兆晓 (2007), "成长青谈跨国并购内幕", *中国经济周刊* [Wang, H. and Hou, Z., "Cheng Changqing on the inside story of cross-border acquisitions", *China Economic Weekly*], 22 October, available at: http://finance.people.com.cn/GB/72020/74689/105826/6415179.html (accessed 26 August 2010).

王红茹 (2007), "成长青: 新一代跨国并购操盘人", *资本推手: 10位海归投资银行家* (王辉耀主编), 中国发展出版社, 北京 [Wang, H.R., "Cheng Changqing: A new generation of deal makers in cross-border acquisitions", in Wang, H.Y. (ed.), *Capital Movers and Shakers, Ten Overseas Returnees in Investment Banking*, China Development Press, Beijing], pp. 1–17.

Cheng, Yuan (Grace Cheng 程原 b. 1964)

Known to the West as Grace Cheng, Cheng Yuan is the managing director and country manager of Russell Reynolds Associates (RRA) in Greater China. RRA is a premier provider of senior-level executive search and assessment, having served clients globally for 40 years. The firm advises its clients on recruiting and retaining outstanding leaders, and helps them mitigate the risks associated with senior-level appointments. In recent years, RRA's clientele has expanded to the fast developing Chinese enterprises to help businesses accommodate to their globalization process in the human resources area, where Grace Cheng plays a major role. Working across Beijing, Shanghai, and Hong Kong, her work focuses on the industrial and non-profit sectors, with emphasis on general management and cross-border assignments for Chinese and Western multinational companies at the market entry and consolidated growth phases.

Cheng received her BA in English from Beijing Foreign Studies University and her MA in sociology from the University of Massachusetts, USA. She then moved to Britain and earned her PhD from the University of Oxford. Besides her impressive academic preparation, Cheng has accumulated 14 years of executive search experience. Before joining the executive search industry in 1996, she headed the human resources division for TNT's China joint venture, where she played a key role in the company's initial growth and later expansion strategies. From 1992 to 1995, Cheng lived in the United Kingdom and worked as a research fellow at the Policy Studies Institute (PSI), a London-based think tank, where she focused on employment and organizational behavior research.

Once she was back in China in 1996, Cheng first worked as a senior management consultant at Korn/Ferry International, a global human resources consulting firm. Four years later, she became the company's partner. In 2002, after China's entry into the WTO, Korn/Ferry International became the first Western consulting company authorized for business operation in China, and Cheng became the head of the company's joint venture in Beijing, leading its expansion in the Chinese market of foreign senior management personnel consulting services. In 2005, she was named the general manager of RRA and then in 2007, Cheng was promoted to the position of managing director of Greater China, responsible for operations in Beijing, Shanghai, and Hong Kong offices. Today, she also sits on the Executive Committee of RRA, helping shape the company's strategic direction at global level.

Cheng devotes herself to the education, training, recruitment, and retention programs of senior management personnel in China. Because of the fast growing economy, although there are 15,000 qualified business leaders in the Chinese market, there is a demand for 60,000 more. Given her wide international experience and academic achievements, Cheng is a regular contributor in conferences and international meetings, offering her insight into the entrepreneurial world from a Chinese vantage point. On October 28, 2007, during the fourth Western Returnees Beijing Forum (WRBF), she took part in the round table discussion on "Returnees to China: Employment and Entrepreneurship." Under the theme "New Returnees, New Missions," WRBF invited participants of social elites from different circles such as the party and state leadership, officials in charge of the economy and education, key members of international economic organizations, famous scholars from China and abroad, and chairpersons of leading enterprises in order to launch a platform for exchange of ideas and opinions. In addition, Cheng sits on the 2005 Committee of the Western Returned Scholars Association. She also heads the Beijing Committee of the China Oxford Scholarship Fund (COSF), a charity dedicated to bring in the benefits of an Oxford education to the next generation of the men and women who will lead China's state and private sectors, its arts, academia, and sciences.

In May 2008, during the "Leadership, Woman Style" session at the Women's Forum for the Economy and Society, Cheng noted that women differed in their empathy with people and their ability to encourage participation; however, she found few differences in management styles according to gender: "If you look at every level of hierarchy, leadership styles are the same for men and women," she stated. "If you're good, you're good – it doesn't matter if you're a man or a woman (Women's Forum, 2008).". In short, she believed that women in China showed the same level of team orientation as men, but women have not yet been trained to become mature managers to lead teams.

Based on her professional experiences, Cheng Yuan highlights that of the dozen Western executives, who work for Chinese companies, she has interviewed recently, many have failed in the relationship with their employers. "Most of them choose to leave within six months or even sooner, which has a negative impact not only on their own morale, but also on Chinese bosses' willingness to recruit from Western companies in the future (International Business Times, 2010)." She emphasizes that the trouble is that China is changing rapidly, both economically and socially, so getting a grip on what is "normal" is not straightforward, even for locals. Even foreigners who have worked for multinationals in China and reckon they have learned the ropes are often in for a jolt when they join a local firm. She is keenly aware that for many Western executives who have made the move to China, it is not handling bureaucracy that is the biggest headache, but cultural and language differences. "Language is perhaps the most obvious hurdle faced by Western companies," says Cheng, "but cultural differences are far harder to grasp. Language can be learned, whereas culture has to be understood (Brice, 2007)."

In recent years, with the swift development of the Chinese economy, any advantages Western firms used to hold over local private and state-owned firms have all but disappeared. Not only is the market rapidly filling with new players, but also Chinese firms are aggressively competing for the top talents emerging from colleges and universities. "In China today there is a huge imbalance between supply and demand for talent," says Cheng. "For the talents it's a sellers' market, so each good candidate can be considering two or three offers at a time (Brice, 2007)." Therefore in RRA, to ensure a successful operation, Cheng has outlined the steps that executives must take to navigate the transition from a multinational company to a Chinese company.

Besides her consulting work, Cheng is also a scholar and a writer. Her articles and viewpoints have been published in the *Harvard Business Review* (Chinese edition), *Twenty-first Century Business Herald*, *First Financial Daily*, *Wall Street Journal*, and *European Sociological Review*. She has collaborated with other academics in several books such as *Restructuring the Employment Relationship* (Oxford University Press, 1998), *Women of China: Economic and Social Transformation* (Palgrave Macmillan, 1999), and *Routledge Companion to International Business Coaching* (Routledge, 2008). As a recognized expert on human resource management in the country, she also gives interviews on Chinese TV, advising young students on career planning and professional development in the fast changing Chinese market.

M. Elena Aramendia-Muneta

Sources

Brice, A. (2007), "Culture is an obstacle to human resources in China", *ICB*, 6 August, available at: http://www.icis.com/Articles/2007/08/06/9049809/Culture-is-an-obstacle-to-human-resources-in-China.html (accessed 7 June 2010).

Cheng, G. (n.d.), "Guidelines for senior executives in transition from multinational to Chinese companies", Russell Reynolds Associates, available at: http://online.wsj.com/public/resources/documents/RussellReynolds.pdf (accessed 7 June 2010).

International Business Times (2010), "The pitfalls, perils… and rewards of expat executives working for Chinese bosses", 3 May, available at: http://www.ibtimes.com/contents/20100503/pitfalls-perils-rewards-expat-executives-working-chinese-bosses.htm (accessed 7 June 2010).

Russell Reynolds Associates (2010), "程原 (Grace Cheng)", available at: http://www.russellreynoldschina.com/consultant-area01.html (accessed 7 June 2010).

Shanghai Daily (2010), "Tough for expat CEOs to learn China ropes", 10 May, available at: http://mobile.shanghaidaily.com/article/?id=436507 (accessed 7 June 2010).

Women's Forum (2008), "Session in parallel: Leadership, woman style", 18 May, available at: http://womens-forum.com/zzRestofsite/2008_WFA/SessionSum/Day2/Session_in_parallel_Leadership_Woman_Style.html (accessed 7 June 2010).

Zhang, M. (2007), "Success and confusion: The lives of overseas returnees", 19 November, available at: http://www.china.org.cn/english/China/232355.htm (accessed 7 June 2010).

经理人 (2004), "程原女士简介", ["Brief bio of Cheng Yuan", *Executives*], 27 April, available at: http://finance.sina.com.cn/g/20040427/1854741608.shtml (accessed 7 June 2010).

Deng, Feng (邓峰 b. 1963)

A well-regarded Chinese returnee and venture capitalist, Deng Feng was awarded the Entrepreneur of the Year by Ernst & Young in 2002 and the Innovator of the Year award by CRN in 2003. A Tsinghua graduate, he is also a board member of the Tsinghua University Foundation. Deng received his MBA from the Wharton Business School, University of Pennsylvania, an MS degree in computer engineering from the University of Southern California, and an MS degree in electronic engineering from Tsinghua University. He also holds five US patents in computer system architecture and IC design. Although some say he is born to be an entrepreneur, Deng proved to the world that he can be a better venture capitalist. After selling NetScreen Technologies to Juniper Networks at a price of US$4 billion in 2004, Deng Feng founded Northern Light Venture Capital in 2005, a China-focused fund.

Deng Feng was born and raised in Beijing. In 1981, he enrolled in the elite Tsinghua University, majoring in electronic engineering. After excelling in four years of undergraduate study, Deng was directly admitted into a graduate program. While at Tsinghua, he was named one of the top 20 students among 2000 graduates in the university. Besides his academic excellence, Deng launched his business "career" early as well. In his junior year, Deng began to do some part-time jobs and then in1985, when he picked up a copy of *Fire in Valley: The Making of the Personal Computer*, his inner entrepreneurial flame was ignited.

During a science and technology contest held in Tsinghua in 1988, Deng won the championship with his first entrepreneurial project. In the following year, in a nationwide "Challenge Cup" Science and Technology Contest, he again won the first place with the same project, which was later bought by a company and implemented into actual production. Around Deng's postgraduate time, Beijing Z-park had just been established, and he began to do projects in China's Silicon Valley. He rented three rooms, one for himself and the other two as labs, and recruited some undergraduates from Tsinghua. First, he was just a contractor, and gradually he opened his own company. In the university, he was called by his fellow students as the "Richest Man of Tsinghua."

In 1990, Deng Feng went abroad and began to study computer engineering at the University of Southern California. However, half way through his learning, he dropped his study and joined Intel Group as an engineer, designing chips for Pentium laptops. The four-year tenure there was also one of the fastest growing periods for Intel. Besides technology, Deng also learned the advanced management concept from the world-class company, which set a sound foundation for his later career development.

At that time, Intel realized net security was a significant issue for future Internet applications, but could not find an effective solution for the problem. This caught Deng's attention, and he began to discuss with some friends about the idea of setting up an Internet security firm. At this point, Deng had already worked four years for Intel, and according to company regulations, employees could obtain options after five years of services. On one hand were Intel options, stock shares, and comfortable living, and on the other hand was the unpredictable hardship in entrepreneurship. Since Deng had a mortgage to pay, a child to raise, and his spouse was still in school, so at first he chose to stay with Intel. Nevertheless, another investor became interested in Deng and his friends' idea of Internet security technology, who soon established a company by himself, attracted venture investment, and later sold the firm to Nortel. This episode impelled Deng's decision to finally resign from Intel.

To do a venture was not easy. For Deng and his schoolfellow Ke Yan, who was then a senior software engineer at Cisco, the only opportunity was to develop disruptive technology, as all Internet security products of the time were based on software, and they tried to replace that with hardware. In October 1997, Deng and Ke along with another friend Xie Qing took out US$10,000 each, and established the NetScreen Technologies. Within a month a prototype was created, and with it the three cofounders obtained their first venture investment of US$1 million from angel investors who invested in start-up enterprises. After that, all three resigned from their well-paid jobs and formally set on the road of entrepreneurship.

Deng's initial idea was to sell the company once it reached a certain scale, then he could freely enjoy the rest of his life. But the tremendous growth of NetScreen surprised him. In the middle of second year, NetScreen attracted well-renowned Sequoia Capital's attention. Sequoia Capital is one of the most important venture capitals in the Silicon Valley, and it has invested in big names such as Apple, Atari, Oracle, Cisco, Yahoo, and Google over the years. Through angel investors' contact, NetScreen successfully raised US$3.7 million in the first stage of development. Then Sequoia made another US$10.8 million investment in 1999, and in subsequent capital raisings Sequoia continued to pile up its investment in NetScreen, surpassing US $20 million.

In November 1998, several months after NetScreen's first round of financing, and with Sequoia Capital's help, Robert Thomas, former CEO of Sun Microsystems, joined NetScreen Technologies as president and CEO, and Deng Feng and Ke Yan remained on the strategic executive team as founding board members, making important decisions for the company. While Ke focused on technology development, serving as vice president of software engineering, Deng turned to product development and management, and served as Chief Strategy Officer since late 2003. When NetScreen finally went public, Deng Feng and Ke Yan held 5.7% and 5.8% of stocks, respectively.

After the NASDAQ collapsed in 2000, all newly burgeoned technology companies experienced a hard time. However, opportunity for NetScreen rose after the terrorist attack of September 11, 2001. While the whole stock market was shadowed by the tragedy, the concern on security technologies by American investors provided an excellent chance for NetScreen. Although the company initially planned to issue 10 million shares with a share price between 8 and 10 dollars, the IPO road show had drawn keen interests, and the company was 30 times oversubscribed, with the purchase price rising up to US$16 per share. On December 12, 2001, NetScreen went public, and its share price soared to US$24 on the first day of trading. In the following year, the sales revenue reached US$138 million, and it surged to US$173 million in 2003. Before the NASDAQ opened on February 9, 2004, Juniper Networks, the world's second largest network equipment provider, announced the acquisition of NetScreen Technologies. Completed in May with a whopping price tag of US$4 billion, biggest deal in Juniper's history, this acquisition also put major pressure on Cisco. For Deng and his friend, two engineers from Beijing who started their business with only US$30,000, the investment had grown to more than US$500 million within seven years.

From 2004 to 2005, Feng served as vice president of corporate strategy at Juniper Networks. With his rich experience in entrepreneurship and investment, Deng returned to China in 2005 and founded a China-focused fund – the Northern Light Venture Capital with Ke Yan in Beijing Z-park. Deng's aim was very clear when setting up the Northern Light Venture, which was to "helping China to establish world class enterprises and cultivate international entrepreneurship." Northern Light Venture has offices in Shanghai and the Silicon Valley, and focuses on investing in the technology, media, and telecom (TMT) sectors. The venture's portfolio includes NASDAQ companies, such as Action Semiconductor and Spreadtrum Communications, baihe.com, the top dating site in China, and Hanting Hotels and Inns, the biggest hotel chain. With his success in China, Deng was named among the Top Ten China Venture Capitalists by Zero2IPO in 2007. Recently, Northern Light Venture has been cultivating Hillstone Networks, which is just like a Chinese version of NetScreen, as most of its management team is from NetScreen and it is also in the Internet security industry. But in Deng's mind, he is not merely investing in a similar company, but wants to surpass his NetScreen success.

From establishing a technology company in America to coming back to China and entering the venture capital industry, besides luck, Deng's entrepreneurial endeavor involves both innovations and risk taking. To him, venture capital is a new challenge, another pioneering project. He may succeed or fail, but it is the process in which he finds the most enjoyment in his life.

WEI QIAN

Sources

何莎莎 (2008), "北极光邓峰投资Hillstone解秘, 欲超NetScreen", *投资与合作* [He, S., "The secret of investment in Hillstone by Deng Feng of Northern Light Venture, to surpass NetScreen", *Investment and Cooperation*], 29 May, available at: http://www.ezcap.cn/News/20088231.html (accessed 12 July 2010).

李政 (2007), "邓锋: 上市不是终点", *叱咤华尔街: 10位海归上市公司领袖* (王辉耀主编), 中国发展出版社, 北京 [Li, Z., "Deng Feng: Going public is not the destination", in Wang, H. (ed.), *Movers on Wall Street: Ten Overseas Returnees Who Took Their Business Public*, China Development Press, Beijing], pp. 1–21.

张帆 (2004), "邓峰, 柯严完美创业记录", *财经*, [Zhang, F., "Deng Feng and Ke Yan's perfect record in entrepreneurship", *Caijing Magazine*], 5 March, available at: http://archive.caing.com/2004-03-05/100080885.html (accessed 12 July 2010).

Deng, Zhonghan (John Deng 邓中翰 b. 1968)

Dr Deng Zhonghan is the chairman, CEO, and president of Vimicro Corporation, the largest multimedia semiconductor technology company in China. On December 2, 2009, for his contribution to the development of the Chinese semiconductor industry, Deng was officially elected the newest and youngest member of the Chinese Academy of Engineering (CAE).

Deng was born in the eastern Chinese province of Jiangsu. From 1987 to 1992, he studied earth and space sciences at the University of Science and Technology of China (USTC). While under the supervision of Professor Huang Peihua of USTC, Deng had his first three papers published in the *Journal of Physics G: Nuclear and Particle Physics* and *The Chinese Science Bulletin*. After receiving his bachelor's degree, Deng went to the United States and enrolled at the University of California at Berkeley, where he earned a master's degree in economic management, a master's degree in physics, and a PhD in electronic engineering. This achievement gave Deng the distinction of being the first scholar within the 130-year history of the university, to have crossed three disciplines of science, engineering, and business.

In 1997, upon receiving his PhD from UC Berkeley, Deng joined IBM as a senior researcher with the VLSI-CMOS integrated circuit design. While in the United States, Deng published 25 academic articles, applied for several patents, and received the IBM Invention Award. After his brief tenure at IBM, Deng joined Sun Microsystems and was involved in the research and development of UltraSPARC, the world's fastest computing CPU of the time. In 1998, Deng went back to the Silicon Valley and established an integrated circuit company PIXIM Incorporated. As the first chairman of PIXIM, he led the team focusing on the development of the high-end digital imaging semiconductor sensors essential to monitoring satellites and other sophisticated space missions. The company's outstanding performance quickly lifted its market value to US$150 million.

The late 1990s was the golden period for the development of the electronic information industry in China. Because of Deng's experience in the Silicon Valley,

Zhou Guangzhao, chairman of the Chinese Association of Science and Technology (CAST), asked Deng to find a new way to help improve the semiconductor industry in China. Back in 1965, CAST had already started relevant work on integrated circuits; but until then, China still could not achieve the large-scale industrialization of these kinds of products. China needed to develop its silicon chip technology, as it was the key to the electronic information industry. The conversation Deng had with Zhou inspired his creative spirit, so he took the challenge.

On October 1, 1999, Deng was invited by the Chinese State Council to be a special guest for the 50th Year Anniversary Celebration of the People's Republic of China. During this special event, Deng felt extremely honored and proud to be Chinese. On the same afternoon, he, along with three friends who studied with him in the United States, climbed up onto the Great Wall and they pledged to use their knowledge to contribute to the Chinese high-tech industry. People might not understand why Deng gave up PIXIM and returned to China to start from scratch, but he has always explained that he did this because of his Chinese heart.

On October 14, 1999, Vimicro Corporation was established in a 100 m^2 warehouse located in the Haidian district of Beijing. Through his contact with Zhou, Deng was introduced to Qu Weizhi, the vice minister of PRC's Ministry of Information Industry of the time. According to Deng's plan, in order to develop the core technology, it was important to know how to handle the breakthrough of the market. Technology was being developed according to the development of the market. Therefore, in order to find the correct direction of technology development, the correct market position must first be found.

Taking off from this idea, Deng confirmed he should focus on the digital media field, as this area was quite new, and was not attractive to other enterprises. At that time, most of the chip designs were based on the traditional John von Neumann calculations that handled large amounts of energy during the data processing. This was not suitable for the digital media field that has high requirements of the power cost. To fill the gap, Deng bought an American model named *Fabless*, which had been developed several decades ago in the United States. Using this model meant that he only had to make chip designs without manufacturing. Deng chose the *Fabless* model because it is relatively easy to start, and there were no advanced chip producers in China. Therefore, the strategy of Vimicro was to focus on chip designs, and then hand over to a factory to be made into the final products.

On March 11, 2001, the *Starshine No. 1* was completed, which marked the first ultra-large-scale digital multimedia chip that is Chinese intellectual property. In the same year, its industrialization was finished, and in the summer of 2001, Deng visited SONY in Japan to introduce the *Starshine No. 1* chip. For a company with new products, the process of making the first sale is never easy, but it was finally accepted by Samsung, Philips, and many other international brands. Deng's chip had excellent performance with high integration, low power consumption, and fast transmission speed, and was warmly welcomed as the "Chinese Chip" in the global market. The "Chinese Chip" obstacle stopped many Chinese IT elites, but Deng broke this barrier with Vimicro. In 2003, Deng started the "Digital China" project with Wu Yin and Ding Jian. The goal of this project was to promote the digital advancement of

China and other Asian countries while encouraging the communication of digital development in developed countries. In the summer of 2005, SONY released a new notebook that was made using the *Starshine No. 5* chip.

On November 15, 2005, Vimicro reached another milestone when the company was listed on the NASDAQ. Set apart from other web service stocks, Vimicro is purely a technical concept company. It has a breakthrough "7 core" technology in the field of multimedia chip, and owns more than 500 patents. Vimicro is not only the first chip design company on the NASDAQ, but also the first one that has its own core technology and intellectual property. The signature that Deng signed at the NASDAQ Closing Ceremony became the Chinese signature in this stock market.

Since his return to China, Deng has actively involved himself in the development of the Chinese semiconductor industry. In recognition of his achievements, he has received numerous awards, most recent of which include "The National Scientific Achievement Award of 1st Class," "The National Medal for Outstanding Overseas Student Returnees," "Top CEOs of China Semiconductor Industry," and "The National Innovation Award in Information Industry." He has also served as an advisor to the Chinese Ministry of Information Industry and the Chinese Ministry of Science and Technology, as well as a visiting professor at Tsinghua University.

Dr Deng Zhonghan is not only an extraordinary entrepreneur and a scientist but also a proud Chinese with a strong desire for improving technology for China, and the rest of the world.

XIAOTIAN ZHANG

Sources

百度百科 (2010), "邓中翰" ["Deng Zhonghan", *Baidu.com*], available at: http://baike.baidu.com/view/30651.htm?fr=ala0_1_1 (accessed 24 May 2010).

陈方 (2010), "少壮院士邓中翰", *中国青年* ["Deng Zhonghan: The young fellow of CAE", *Chinese Youth*], 8 January, available at: http://elite.youth.cn/fmrw/201001/t20100108_1130561.htm (accessed 20 July 2010).

Ding, Jian (James Ding 丁健 b. 1965)

An EMBA graduate from University of California at Berkeley and a talented returnee, Ding Jian is the chairman of AsiaInfo Holdings and the cofounder of GSR Ventures. He is known as James Ding to the West, one of the most active venture capitalists (VC) in China today, who has successfully transformed himself from a well-known entrepreneur to an engaged VC.

Ding's story has inspired many youngsters who went abroad for higher education and dreamt of starting their own businesses to support the economic development in China. On one hand, he is a successful businessman who has been actively involved in the development of Internet in China. On the other hand, he is an active educator, serving on the industry advisory board of the joint research institute in science and engineering by Peking University and University of California, Los Angeles (UCLA), playing an important role in the long bonding relationships between these two world famous institutions where he spent his early years at. Story starts when Ding graduated from Peking University in 1986, as an undergraduate in chemistry. He went to the United States to pursue higher education like many of his fellow students. He was admitted by UCLA and earned his master degree in information science there in 1990.

It is the training in both Peking University and UCLA that helps Ding in shaping his business ideas. In 1993, Ding started AsiaInfo with his friend Tian Suning in the United States. In light of huge growth potentials, they moved major operations of AsiaInfo to China two years later, when Internet was still relatively unknown in China. Ding was among the first to spot the opportunity of Internet business in China. He has been actively involved in the development of Chinese Internet service and infrastructure ever since. By providing telecommunication software and IT security products and services to major Chinese telecommunication carriers at that time, AsiaInfo was one of the first companies to support Internet and telecommunication developments in China. It was the first to develop software and services for major Chinese carriers such as China Mobile Communications Corporation, China United Telecommunications Corporation, and China Telecommunications Corporation. AsiaInfo's operations are organized into two divisions: one is AsiaInfo Technologies (China) Inc., which mainly deals with traditional telecommunication business and provides software solutions to China's telecommunication carriers; and the other is Lenovo-AsiaInfo Technologies Inc., which provides IT security products and services tailored for small- to medium-sized companies and government agencies.

Under Ding's leadership, AsiaInfo went public on the NASDAQ on March 2, 2000, which helped push the company forward and ensured its continual success as a leading telecommunication software provider in China. For his accomplishment, Ding was ranked on the list of the "China's Richest" by *Forbes* in the same year, and was later named as one of the 100 New Champions by the World Economic Forum (WEF). *Forbes* named AsiaInfo on its "200 best small companies" list in 2001, and for several consecutive years *Fortune* also rated the company as one of the top 10 potential stocks. Today, AsiaInfo has grown from a three-person private firm into a billion dollar business with more than 700 employees and different branches in large Chinese cities such as Shanghai, Guangzhou, Wuhan, Chengdu, and Hangzhou. By leading AsiaInfo toward a stable path of growth, Ding himself has also become one of the leading figures in the Internet and Telecomminication Industry in China.

Being the cofounder and CEO of AsiaInfo and living through the early stage of its development, Ding had personally experienced the difficulties of operating new businesses in China – lack of funding and scientific management. It was only after his initial success with AsiaInfo that he began to ponder about possible solutions for overcoming those obstacles. With a belief that both passion from the entrepreneur and funding support from the investors are indispensible to the success of high-tech start-ups in China, Ding put much emphasis on the importance of an executive's ability and his or her team. While continuously improving himself through daily operations at AsiaInfo, he encouraged members of his top management team to improve themselves as well. Many of them have received managerial trainings in the United States or from other large multinational corporations. Although AsiaInfo has been successful, Ding was not contended, as he would like to find ways to help other early-stage Chinese high-tech firms that are facing similar difficulties. For private high-tech firms in China, funding has always been a great issue. Although many potential Chinese private firms could prosper given sufficient funding support, there are just not enough China-based VCs who really know the market. By sharing vision and talents with other Chinese entrepreneurs and VCs, Ding gradually drafted his plan. In 2003, he resigned from his CEO position and became the chairman at AsiaInfo. This move surprised the industry and the media. However, Ding was satisfied with the decision, as he finally spared himself some time to consider his plan on how to promote Internet development in China.

In 2005, James Ding joined GSR Ventures with other three partners and officially transformed from a successful entrepreneur to a VC. With US$700 million under management, GSR is a venture capital fund that invests primarily in early and growth stages of technology firms with substantial operations in China. It has a partnership with the US-based venture capital Mayfield Fund, and has offices in both Beijing and Silicon Valley. The naming of GSR Ventures is based on its Chinese name (金沙江创业投资), in which the Gold Sand River is the upstream of the Yangtze River. As its current is swift and dangerous, it is perfect for describing the potential risks GSR may encounter along the way. In addition, since GSR is the upstream wave that supports the growth of those firms in the early stage of development, it also stands for an old Chinese saying "waves in panning."

Besides his association with GSR Ventures, Ding has been serving on the executive boards of several Chinese firms such as Co-opLand, PingCo, UiTV, and Baidu. He has also actively involved in the development of Internet, wireless, and new media e-businesses in China, and is a cofounder of e-China Alliance, a nonprofit, nongovernmental organization that aims at promoting information technology development in China and the cooperation of high-tech firms in Asia. Each year e-China Alliance organizes a summit to support market research and provides a platform for academia and practitioners to communicate. After two decades of development, Chinese Internet market has grown tremendously and now has the largest population of online users in the world. This is due to the persistent efforts put forward by Chinese entrepreneurs like Ding and many others.

Ding gives credit of his success to the way of his logical thinking, his ability to integrate outside resources, and the cooperation of different partners. The experiences he gained from his early school days in both China and the United States, the operations of AsiaInfo, and the investments in different Chinese high-tech firms fully loaded this Chinese dreamer and practitioner with passion and talents. Being a sharp entrepreneur and smart VC, Ding is positive about the future development of the Chinese economy. He believes that localization is the key for Chinese firms to succeed in the information age. As for the future of himself,

AsiaInfo, and GSR, he is full of confidence. He will continue to play an active part in the Chinese Internet, wireless, and new media market.

HAO CHEN

Sources

Asiainfo.com (2010), "Overview", available at: http://www.asiainfo.com/about/ (assessed 29 June 2010).

GSRventures.cn (2010), "About us", available at: http://www.gsrventures.cn/en/index.html (assessed 29 June 2010).

陈海 (2005), "挑战心智权限: 亚信董事长丁健", *创业中国: 海归精英50人* (王辉耀主编), 中央编译出版社, 北京 [Chen H., "Challenge on people's mental competence: Chairman of AsiaInfo Ding Jian", in Wang, H.Y. (ed.), *Pioneering in China: 50 Elite Returnees*, Central Compilation & Translation Press, Beijing], pp. 1–10.

邢学军 (2007), "丁健: 始于创业, 终于VC", *财富裂变: 10位海归风险投资翘楚* (王辉耀主编), 中国发展出版社 [Xing, X.J., "Ding Jian: Start as an entrepreneur, ends as a VC", in Wang, H.Y. (ed.), *Wealth Creation: Top Ten Returnees in Venture Capitalism*, China Development Press, Beijing], pp. 1–23.

Feng, Ziping (冯自平 b. 1968)

A research associate of Guangzhou Institute of Energy Conversion (GIEC) and the Chinese Academy of Sciences (CAS), Feng Ziping is also an adjunct professor at the University of Science and Technology of China and chief scientist in the Lab of Air-Conditioning and Electric Energy Storage Technology. His work mainly includes the research and development of the technology of heat pump, ice storage, heat storage, and latent heat transferring. As a part of the "One Hundred Talented People" program of CAS, Feng was recruited back to China in April 2003 to conduct research on air-conditioning and electric energy storage technology in GIEC. Since then, he has developed the first set of dynamic ice slurry thermal storage technology with proprietary Intellectual Property Rights (IPR), the first set of heat transferring fluid technologies, and the first engine heat pump system with proprietary IPR.

Originally from Ningxia of China's inner northwestern region, Feng grew up with a strong passion for pursuing knowledge and accumulated massive academic capabilities. In 1986, he enrolled into Xi'an Jiaotong University (XJTU), majoring in energy and power engineering, which became the turning point of his life. After receiving his BS degree, he first worked as an instructor at a local technical school for two years, then went back to XJTU and earned his master's degree in 1994 and PhD in 1996. From 1997 to 1998, with a grant from the North Atlantic Treaty Organization (NATO), Feng conducted research in the Department of Mechanical Engineering and Aeronautics at the University of Patras. This turned out to be a valuable academic experience, as he was trained in the spirit of preciseness by his supervisor. For the next two years, Feng conducted his postdoctoral study on the micro-heat-exchanger program at Kyoto University that was sponsored by Japan Society for the Promotion of Science (JSPS), and was later employed by the National Institute of Advanced Industrial Science and Technology (AIST), under the Ministry of Economy, Trade and Industry of Japan, where he benefited greatly from the cultural emphasis on innovations. From 2000 to 2001, Feng worked as a senior researcher of AIST, conducting research on the development of dynamic thermal storage technology with ice slurry and latent heat flux processes, and for the next two years he worked at Daikin Air-Conditioning of Daikin Industries (Japan).

While working overseas, Feng realized that 90% of the most advanced technologies are controlled by large, multinational corporations. Upon studying the history and the cutting-edge technologies in Daikin, Feng determined to develop more advanced and compatible air-conditioners for China. Therefore, after mastering advanced research concepts and technologies, Feng returned to China and launched his own enterprise, Guangzhou Senyo Thermal Storage Technology Co., which was founded in 2003.

Overcoming various difficulties, Feng successfully conducted the stimulation of ice-rain experiment in a lab in Guangzhou. The idea was triggered by watching a TV news report of the horrible icy-snow climate in Southern China in 2003. Feng wanted to invent a hardware that could prevent ice-rain. Since China lacks the foundation for research on ice-rain prevention, Feng had to create a simulating platform based on his own related research experiences. Although Feng's original major was heat engineering, his love for challenge led him to pioneer new interdisciplinary experiments and technological breakthroughs.

Feng's another achievement was the implementation of a system that would balance energy demand between day and nighttime. This technology could store heat, usually from active solar collectors, in an insulator repository for later use at night, and a partial storage system minimizes capital investment by running the chillers 24 hours a day. At night the system produces ice for storage, and during the day it chills water for the air conditioning system. Since 2000, dynamic ice-storage system has been adopted by most developed countries, with a smaller storage tank, and a higher rate of ice-storage, and with no space limitation. What's more, comparing to the traditional one, the dynamic system could save more than 20–30% energy consumption. Since his return to China, Feng has successfully developed the country's first dynamic ice-storage system with proprietary IPR as well as the exploitation process simulation software for the first gas hydrate sediments. He has filled up the gap in this specific field in China.

Ever since 1995, Feng has recognized the importance of reducing greenhouse effect by conserving energy, and the idea was applied to his technological researches afterwards. Looking forward, he has a strong confidence in his R&D team and its technology, which is based on not only his personal vision and capabilities but also the spirit of scientific research. Once decided to invest in a project, Feng and his team would investigate thoroughly the value of the research and forecast the market demands. Moreover, Feng focuses on the technologies that can influence national economy, especially those that have been well tested in foreign nations and enterprises.

On October 29, 2009, a signing ceremony was held in the Science Park of Guangzhou Development Zone. Among 35 major investment programs with an aggregate investment of more than RMB 27 billions was the commercial production of dynamic ice and thermal storage technologies undertaken by the Guangzhou Senyo Thermal Storage Technology Co. There comes a brand new task for Feng and his team.

Yuping Du

Sources

北京科技报 (2008), "冯自平: 我们在室内制造冻雨" ["Feng Ziping: We are making ice rain indoors", *Beijing Science & Technology Weekly*], 13 July, available at: http://gb.financenews.sina.com/sinacn/304-000-106-109/2008-07-13/1930840446.html (accessed 26 June 2010).

梁正 (2010), "我司冯自平博士签约广州开发区科技领军人才创业项目", *鑫誉蓄能* [Liang, Z., "Dr. Feng Ziping has signed the agreement and will lead the entrepreneurial technology program of Guangzhou Development Zone", *Senyo Thermal Energy*], 27 April, available at: http://www.senyo-energy.com/news/html/?51.html (accessed 26 June 2010).

潘慧 (2008), "对话冯自平: 用市场理念构建技术核心竞争力", *广东科技* [Pan, H., "Dialogue with Feng Ziping: Building core technological competence with a marketing concept", *Guangdong Science & Technology*], Vol. 21, p. 28.

Fu, Chengyu (傅成玉 b. 1951)

Fu Chengyu is the chairman, president, and CEO of China National Offshore Oil Company (CNOOC), one of the largest state-owned oil companies, and the largest offshore oil and gas producer in China. As of 2010, it has 65,800 employees and a registered capital of approximately US$14 billion. The offshore oil industry was the first to open to the world after China's reform and oepning-up policy. By cooperating with overseas partners to develop offshore oil businesses, CNOOC has been serving as China's window to the outside world ever since.

Fu Chengyu is the fifth president of CNOOC since its establishment in 1982. After receiving his bachelor degree in geology from the Northeast Petroleum Institute in China, he went to the United States and studied petroleum engineering at the University of Southern California, where he gained a better understanding of Western management methods that were later applied to the operations of CNOOC. Fu joined CNOOC in 1982 and during his 28 years at the company, he has worked at various locations in China such as oilfields in Daqing, Liaohe, and Huabei, and gained valuable experiences from different projects that he has been involved in.

In his early years at CNOOC, Fu served in various capacities such as the Chinese deputy representative, chief representative, secretary to the management committees, and chairman of the management committees formed through joint ventures between CNOOC and Amoco, Chevron, Texaco, Phillips, Shell, and Agip. For his outstanding performance, Fu was promoted to the position of general manager of CNOOC Nanhai East Corporation a decade later. Since he had a background in overseas education and had been actively involved in many cross-country projects at CNOOC, Fu was chosen to be one of the leading mangers for its IPO promotion in Hong Kong. His leadership in the successful listing set the foundation for his later promotion at CNOOC. In October 2003, Fu was named the president and CEO of the company.

Fu has a vision for CNOOC. Unlike its competitors such as China National Petroleum Corporation (CNPC) and China Petroleum & Chemical Corporation (Sinopec) that aggressively invest abroad, CNOOC chooses to develop steadily by carefully choosing its foreign partners and targets. Fu emphasizes two strategies: one is to compete with foreign companies instead of domestic companies, indicating a focus on cost–benefits instead of scale economy; the other is to explore different ways for company growth and to avoid direct combats with its competitors. However, it is not easy for a state-owned company like CNOOC to remain steady while searching for breakthroughs, as overseas purchase seems to be one of the inevitable ways for its further growth. From 2002 to 2004, CNOOC successfully sealed five deals with companies from Indonesia and Australia that amounted to US$1.55 billion. The purchase of overseas oil companies formed a regional network for CNOOC, therefore strengthening its strategic position in Southeast Asia.

In 2005, while under Fu, CNOOC suffered a major setback from its failed bid for the Unocal Corporation, a US oil company based in California. Although CNOOC offered US$15 billion, the deal fell through due to political reasons. Afterwards, CNOOC experienced several rounds of failed attempts in acquiring overseas oil resources and companies, and therefore significantly reduced its buyout offers in the international market. However in 2010, CNOOC spent US$3.1 billion in purchasing 50% of the shares of Bridas Corporation, an Argentina-based oil and gas holding company. This successful deal increased CNOOC's competitiveness and put Fu and CNOOC back into the game of becoming a global player in the oil industry. Even though the total assets of CNOOC only amount to 22% of that of CNPC and 40% of that of Sinopec, CNOOC has lower risks since its investments in overseas projects are relatively more reliable. As for future investments, Fu plans to target at regions like Latin America and Africa to seek for wealth insurance.

As a state-owned company, CNOOC spends 80% of its revenue for taxation. This is a major issue for Fu to consider when making investment decisions. Although he has pushed the Western management approach at CNOOC, the firm is still viewed as a state-owned company in the international market, and foreign competitors or potential partners may consider CNOOC as a government agency instead of a corporation. The balance between state ownership and market orientation is a never-ending challenge for Fu and CNOOC.

However, different from previous presidents of CNOOC who moved to government positions after retiring from the company, Fu did not choose to become one of them. Instead, he manages CNOOC more like an entrepreneur who emphasizes the value of every investment or decision to the company and to the investors. In an interview with sina.com, he addressed that he always brought sincerity to his potential foreign partners when discussing cooperation or investment plans. People in investment banks who have worked with Fu described him as one of the genuine entrepreneurial managers in Chinese state-owned companies. As a well-received entrepreneur in China, Fu enjoys a good reputation in the media. For three consecutive years since 2005, he was named among the 25 Most Influential Entrepreneurs by the China Entrepreneur Summit.

The future of Fu at CNOOC is not clear. At age of 59, Fu Chengyu will soon face the issue of retirement from his position just like his predecessors. However, Fu stated that he would continue to push CNOOC forward in the global market as a first-rate international oil company.

Hao Chen

Sources

CNOOC (2010), "Management: Fu Chengyu", available at: http://en.cnooc.com.cn/data/html/english/channel_166.html (accessed 29 June 2010).

Miske, M. (2009), "Fu Chengyu", in: Zhang, W. and Alon, I. (eds), *Biographical Dictionary of New Chinese Entrepreneurs and Business Leaders*, Cheltenham, UK: Edward Elgar, pp. 39–40.

陈竹, 赵剑飞 (2010), "傅成玉重来", *新世纪* [Chen, Z. and Zhao, J., "Fu Chengyu all over again", *New Century*], 24 May, available at: http://finance.sina.com.cn/roll/20100524/00117987771.shtml (accessed 29 June 2010).

Gao, Qunyao (Jack Gao 高群耀 b. 1958)

Often addressed as Jack Gao beyond the Chinese borders, Gao Qunyao is currently vice president of News Corporation, the world's leading media company headquartered in New York City, the United States. As of September 30, 2010, News Corporation had total assets of approximately US$56 billion, and total annual revenues of approximately US$33 billion. It is a diversified global media company with operations in six industry segments: cable network programming, filmed entertainment, television, direct broadcast satellite television, publishing, and others. The activities of News Corporation are conducted principally in the United States, Continental Europe, the United Kingdom, Australia, Asia, and Latin America.

In November 2006, Gao was named as vice president of News Corporation and chief representative of News Corporation Beijing Office, responsible for running News Corporation's China strategy and business developments. In China, News Corporation operates broadcast channels that include Xing Kong, Channel V, Star Movies, and National Geographic Channel. News Corporation also owns 17.6% of Phoenix Satellite Television, which operates Phoenix Chinese Channel, Phoenix InfoNews, and Phoenix Movies Channel. Additionally, it broadcasts Mandarin-language sports channels ESPN and Star Sports through its 50% owned ESPN Star Sports joint venture. News Corporation's other investments in China include

MySpace.cn, Tianji Media Group, China Broadband Capital, IDG Media Fund, Dugi.com, AdChina, etc.

In addition to his responsibilities at News Corporation, Gao was also appointed chief executive officer of STAR (China) Ltd., in charge of STAR Group's overall business operations in China. STAR is Asia's leading media and entertainment company, with key operations in India and Greater China. In Greater China, STAR broadcasts six Chinese language channels and owns the world's largest contemporary Chinese film library, with more than 700 titles, featuring superstars including Jackie Chan, Chow Yun Fat, and Bruce Lee. Beyond Asia, STAR's channels reach the Chinese and South Asian diaspora in the United States, the United Kingdom, Canada, Europe, the Middle East, Australia, and New Zealand.

Gao is a director on the board of Phoenix TV, Tianji Media Group, Beijing Vanstone Industrial Co., and Digu.com, and executive chairman of MySpace China, the country's leading music communication platform. In addition, Gao serves on the advisor board of China Broadband Capital.

A Han national, Gao holds an impressive resume. He graduated from Harbin Institute of Technology and University of California, Los Angles, with a bachelor's, master's, and PhD degrees in engineering. Gao worked as a research fellow at the Computer Structure Analysis Research Corporation (CSAR Corp.), where he participated in the NASTRAN (NASA Structural Analysis) commercial code project, and led a research initiative to develop an acoustics feature for CSA/NASTRAN, a finite element analysis program that was originally developed for NASA in the late 1960s under the US federal government funding for the aerospace industry.

In 1992, Gao joined the MacNeal-Schwendler Corporation (MSC/PDA) based in Los Angeles. As the PDA/PATRAN and MSC/NASTRAN international distribution manager for Asia, he successfully implemented sales channel development and drove up sales revenue in the region. For his accomplishment, Gao was awarded MSC/PDA's "Manager of the Year" before his departure in 1994. In 1995, Gao joined Autodesk Inc., one of the largest PC software companies founded in California in 1982, and currently headquartered in San Rafael, California. The company focuses on 2D and 3D design software for use in architecture, engineering and building construction, manufacturing, and media and entertainment. As the regional director for Greater China and general manager for mainland China, he successfully established Autodesk's operations in China during his four-year tenure.

In 1999, Gao joined Microsoft as the president and general manager of Microsoft (China) Co. Ltd., responsible for its business development strategy, sales and marketing, government relations, overall business and financial administration, and human resources operations in mainland China. Within three years, while improving relations with the Chinese government, he saw a 300% increase in Microsoft's sales revenue in China. In 2002, Gao left Microsoft to join Walden International (WIIG), a leading billion-dollar venture capital firm headquartered in California, USA. He directed the company's investments in emerging innovative information technology enterprises in China until his departure a year later to return to Autodesk Inc. as its vice president for the Asia-Pacific Emerging Region. Back at Autodesk, he directed all operations in Greater China and India, and chaired the company's corporate emerging market taskforce for BRIC (Brazil, Russia, India, and China) countries. Under his leadership at Autodesk from 2003 to 2006, the company grew from 16 to 2500 employees and 400% of the regional sales revenue in China, and Autodesk was named in the Asian business media as one of the most successful multinational companies in the region.

Gao has also spoken at many conferences, including the 2004 Global Entrepreneur Conference, where he discussed whether China could continue to take the lead in the emerging markets. He also spoke at the 2007 Annual Conference of Hua Yuan Science and Technology Association (HYSTA) on China, Globalization, and the Shifting Global Power Equation. At the 2009 International Cultural Industries Forum, Gao addressed the audience on how the digital revolution is changing the traditional media.

Gao has made his mark in the information and media industry in China and abroad, and has won admirations for his vision and impressive work. He is no doubt one of the successful business executives who have combined comprehensive knowledge of the local Chinese environment with a solid Western education and expertise to carry China's economy forward.

For his accomplishment, Gao was honored as one of the Top Ten Most Influential IT Managers in China in 2000 by *China Computer News*; Multinational Outstanding Professional in 2001 by *China News*; Top 10 Manufacture Information Leaders in 2004 by *eWorks*; Top Executive of China Software Companies in 2005 by *China Software Association* and *Software World*; Most Valuable Manager in China in 2005 by Phoenix TV, Sina.com, *Talents Magazine*, and *Beijing Youth Daily*; Cover-page Influential in China IT Industry In Last 20 Years in 2005 by *China Information World*; Top 10 Most Outstanding Media Chinese Talents in the World in 2008 by *Asia-Pacific Economic Event*; and Best Professional Manager in the Decade in 2010 by *China IT Manage*. In addition, his book titled *Experience Microsoft* is quite popular in Chinese IT communities.

EVERLYNE MISATI

Sources

Chinavitae.com (2009), "Gao Qunyao: Partner for the China region of WIIG", available at: http://chinavitae.com/biography/Gao_Qunyao/bio (accessed 3 March 2010).

Hysta.org (2007), "HYSTA 2007 annual conference featured speakers", available at: http://www.hysta.org/ac2007/speakers.php?15 (accessed 3 March 2010).

Silobreaker.com (2009), "Biography for Gao Qunyao", available at: http://www.silobreaker.com/biography-for-gao-qunyao-5_2258758501444616192_4 (accessed 3 March 2010).

冯嘉雪 (2007), "高群耀: CEO的乐趣就是挑战", *巅峰职业: 10位海归职业经理人* (王辉耀主编), 中国发展出版社, 北京 [Feng, J., "Gao Qunyao: The delight of challenge for CEO", in Wang, H. (ed.), *Splendid Careers: Ten Overseas Returnees in Professional Management*, China Development Press, Beijing], pp. 156–183.

Gao, Xiqing (高西庆 b. 1953)

Gao Xiqing is currently the head of China Investment Corporation (CIC), which manages US$200 billion in state assets. Not only is he in charge of one of the largest investment funds in the world, but he is also one of the founders of the Chinese stock exchange market. His consistently optimistic attitude has allowed him to tackle multiple groundbreaking projects over his lifetime, and he does not have plans to slow down anytime soon.

In 1953, Gao was born in Xian, the capital of Shaanxi Province in Northwestern China. Although his father was a Red Army officer on the Long March with Mao, the senior was jailed for five years during the Chinese Cultural Revolution (1966–1976). His father's captivity and fear of his own imprisonment during his teen years left Gao homeless for two years. As a result, he became a manual laborer building railroads and worked in an ammunition factory for over a year. To this day, Gao claims he has loved and excelled at all of his jobs, and proudly calls himself "a *Lei Feng* type – a small cog in a huge Party machine, and wherever they put me I'm happily there" (DUSL, n.d.).

In the face of his struggles, Gao's optimistic perseverance helped him pursue a Bachelor of Arts, and he graduated from the University of International Business and Economics (UIBE) in Beijing in 1978. During his time at UIBE, he became interested in reforming China's primitive capital market. He continued his education at UIBE and earned a Master's Degree in Law in 1981. His achievements enabled him to attend the Duke University Law School, where he earned his Doctor Juris as a Richard Nixon Scholar in 1986. Gao became the first Chinese citizen to pass the New York Bar Exam.

For the following two years, Gao was an associate of Mudge Rose Guthrie Alexander & Ferdon, a prestigious Wall Street law firm, where he learned the operations of the New York Stock Exchange and the Securities and Exchange Commission (SEC). In conversations with his friend Wang Boming and other fellow Chinese expatriates, Gao became convinced that establishing such a stock exchange in China was what the country would need to transform from a planned economy. "Even [Karl] Marx praised stock exchanges and banking systems. He regarded them as tools, rather than goals, and tools can be used by anyone – they can be used to serve the purposes of the poor people and the working class. So in [his] mind, in order for China to change for the better and compete, we needed a better financing system. Stock exchanges were an inevitable part of that" (*ibid.*).

Gao believed "Building the economy is the best way to change China … the most effective way to create a more democratic nation" (*Esquire*, 2008). He was determined to follow through with his plans, and on his return to China in 1988, Gao toured European stock exchanges, specifically the newly established one in Hungary. He came back at right moment, when the new national laws and regulations were to be created, and Shanghai and Shenzhen were just allowed to create their own financial markets within certain guidelines. The following year, Gao spent "sleepless weeks" developing corporate laws and securities regulations for the first Chinese stock exchanges he helped create for Shanghai and Shenzhen, which were fully established by 1990. Gao was also faced with a language barrier, because it was difficult to convey the new concepts and laws and regulations in the Chinese language for the first time. He used the US stock exchange as his model and incorporated ideas from the German, Taiwanese, British, and Japanese systems; however, the enforcement was different. The Chinese government required a more transparent and controlled capital market. "As long as you disclose what you are selling, you can sell almost anything – the government won't stop you from selling bad things, as long as you disclose that they are 'bad things'" (DUSL, n.d.). The government insisted on approving all listed stocks; however, Gao believed these approvals would give the false impression that the stock is a good stock to invest in. According to him,

> Since 1990, the number of listed companies has grown to 1,400 from the eight originally listed. Probably only 100 are worth investing in. To me, that shows the failure of our approval system. No matter how good the intention, the state can't possibly do the job. Business is a complicated thing. And the government can't make up all these numbers and decide which is good and which is bad. Nobody is able to do that (*ibid.*).

As a founding member of China's first stock exchange and Stock Exchange Executive Council, Gao became the general counsel and director of Public Offerings Supervision Department of China Securities Regulatory Commission (CSRC), a position he held until 1995. He then joined the banking industry and became vice-chairman and CEO of the Bank of China International (BOC), which was the investment banking arm of the Bank of China in Hong Kong. Afterward, Gao rejoined the CSRC as vice-chairman and remained in this position from 1999 to 2003. During this time, he also served as an adjunct professor of law and finance at Peking University, Tsinghua University, and UIBE.

Gao enjoyed working with investors in China, but he felt he was not doing enough for the people of China; especially he wanted to help those who could not help themselves. The retired population in China was growing to numbers greater than 750 million. China's Social Securities Fund was established in 1997. However, this $20 billion fund was available only to retired urban residents, and investments were extremely limited. As the vice-chairman of the National Council for Social Security Fund, Gao wanted to expand the fund and invest the money in the international markets. Since then, the state has decided to allow international investment, but in a restricted fashion. Gao served as vice-chairman of this operation until 2007.

In September of that year, Gao became president and chief investment officer of CIC, one of the largest sovereign investment funds. CIC has foreign reserves up to $1.5 trillion, and Gao has $200 billion in state assets for investment purpose. Initially he planned to invest in the United States; however with the recession of 2008, companies were hesitant to accept large investments, and American companies feared that China was trying to take over the United States and even the rest of the world. Gao went his way to put everyone at ease and made special efforts to disprove this myth. He assured the media he only wanted to invest in the United States financially, noting that it was not part of the Chinese culture to want so much attention: "the Chinese culture is being self-effacing, try to hide yourself, don't stick your head out for people to knock on" (*CBS News*, 2008). According to him, China's goal was simply to make money, not to have active control in other countries.

Among Gao's most recent accomplishments is the founding of a charity fund for children in Tibet and Mongolia, which offers money to families for allowing their children to go to school rather than have to work to earn income to support the family. A recent visit to the recipients of these scholarships was a humbling experience for his family as well. "It was a good experience for my son. He gave a report to his teacher, and I talked to his class about how lucky they are, and how sympathetic they should be to poor families."

Gao has served on numerous boards and panels, such as the Board of Trustees at Duke University. He has significantly reshaped China through his contribution to the establishment of a modern capital market and expansion of the country's Social Security Fund. "Party politics are still closed, but everything else in China – economic reform, finance, sports, daily life, sex – are more freely discussed than in most countries in the world" (DUSL). His optimistic attitude is a breath of fresh air, and this is only the beginning for the future of China: "I'm not done yet – there are many worthwhile things still to do" (*ibid.*).

JENNIFER CROSSMAN

Sources

CBS News (2008), "China Investment an open book? 60 Minutes: Sovereign-Wealth Fund's president promises transparency", 6 April, available at: http://www.cbsnews.com/stories/2008/04/04/60minutes/main3993933.shtml?tag=contentMain;contentBody (accessed 12 April 2010).

China Vitae (2009), "Gao Xiqing", available at: http://www.chinavitae.com/biography/Gao_Xiqing/summary (accessed 12 April 2010).

Duke University School of Law (DUSL) (n.d.), "Duke Law in China: Gao Xiqing '86", available at: http://www.law.duke.edu/magazine/2005fall/profiles/prcgaoxiqing.html (accessed 12 April 2010).

Esquire (2008), "Gao Xiqing: Investor of China's money, 55 Beijing", 17 September, available at: http://www.esquire.com/features/75-most-influential/gao-xiqing-1008 (accessed 12 April 2010).

Fallows, J. (2008), "Be nice to the countries that lend you money", *Atlantic Magazine*, December, available at: http://www.theatlantic.com/magazine/archive/2008/12/-8220-be-nice-to-the-countries-that-lend-you-money-8221/7148/ (accessed 12 April 2010).

Gao, Zhikai (高志凯 b. 1962)

A lawyer by training, and known as Victor Gao, Esq., beyond China, Gao Zhikai is a licensed attorney-at-law in the State of New York. Gao has extensive work experience as a lawyer, an investment banker, and a senior corporate officer spanning multiple industries over a period of about 27 years. He is currently in private equity business in China as an executive director of Beijing Private Equity Association (BPEA), chairman of its International Committee, and a director of the China National Association of International Studies.

Gao holds an enviable resume, entering the elite Soochow University at age 16 with the highest English score in Suzhou in 1978. Before earning his BA degree in English literature in 1981, he again passed the graduate admission exam and enrolled into an MA program in English literature at Beijing University of Foreign Studies, where he graduated two years later. He then worked for the Chinese Ministry of Foreign Affairs from 1983 to 1989, during which period he was an English interpreter for the late Deng Xiaoping, the paramount leader of the People's Republic of China from 1978 to the early 1990s and widely regarded as one of the greatest men of the twentieth century. In November 1986, while serving as interpreter, Gao had a deep impression of Deng's meeting with John Phelan, chairman of the New York Stock Exchange (NYSE), who was visiting Beijing. The Chinese leader, who had great admiration for the positive elements of American capitalism, implored Phelan to teach China about finance and capital markets, so that the country would also have its own stock exchange in the future. Things have changed a great deal since then.

That meeting had a profound impact on Gao's future career plans. A fervent desire to learn prompted Gao to pursue further studies at Yale University, where he earned an MA degree in political science from Yale Graduate School in 1990, and later a JD degree from Yale Law School in 1993. Soon after law school, Gao practised securities law with Milbank Tweed Hadley & McCloy in New York for a while before joining the Hong Kong Securities and Futures Commission, and later served as vice president of Morgan Stanley Asia in the mergers and acquisitions practice from 1994 to 1999. Soon after, Gao was recruited by China International Capital Corporation, where he served as general manager of the Investment Banking Department, head of Mergers and Acquisitions, and head of Hong Kong Investment Banking Division.

From 1999 to 2000, Gao worked with the Hong Kong Securities and Futures Commission as a China policy advisor. He then left this position to work with two major Hong Kong conglomerates: Pacific Century CyberWorks (PCCW) and Henderson Land. Gao was the executive director for China as well as director of Venture Capital and Mergers and Acquisitions Departments at PCCW; at Henderson, Gao was also an executive director and was actively involved in major business transactions in China in property, infrastructure, and Initial Public Offering investment.

In November 2008, Gao joined the Chinese National Offshore Oil Company (CNOOC) Limited, a major oil company listed on Hong Kong Stock Exchange and NYSE, as senior vice president, general counsel, company secretary, as well as member of the CNOOC Investment Committee and director of CNOOC International. Gao was also recently elected the first Secretary-General of the China Private Equity Association, which will be the principal self-discipline body for the private equity industry in China (to be formally incorporated pending the People's Republic of China government approval).

Gao's other credits include serving as a current affairs commentator for China Central Television International (CCTV) and a regular speaker at international conferences, which included the 2009 Milken Institute Global Conference, where he spoke on "the U.S.-China Relationship: The Uneasy Ties That Bind", and the 2009 Jamestown Foundation—China in Africa Conference—where he delivered a keynote speech. A highly experienced speaker who presents in both English and Mandarin Chinese, Gao is in great demand around the world. At those gatherings, Gao drew upon his rich government and corporate experience to offer fascinating and in-depth insights into today's world, deliberated on global issues, and helped his audiences understand not only the changes occurring within the PRC, but also the country's rising status on the international stage. His topics of interest include energy, sustainable development, China's international relations, anticorruption, China and Africa, the issues of Taiwan and Tibet, the Beijing Olympics security issue, the North Korea nuclear issue, among others.

A family man who is married and has two daughters, Gao is regularly interviewed by the Chinese media, and has published in a wide variety of domestic and international publications, including the *People's Daily, Caijing Magazine, New York Times, Wall Street Journal, Guardian*, Bloomberg, CNN, CNBC, BBC, Al Jazeera, and many more. Notable among his many articles was an essay titled "China's Heart of Gold," published in the *New York Times* on May 13, 2009, in which he discussed the transition in Chinese impressions of the American dollar as the gold standard. In another article titled "Toward a New Security Order in Northeast Asia" that was published on cnn.com on July 4, 2009, Gao discussed the North Korea nuclear issue.

Gao is a leading observer of China and its impact on international business and globalization. In January 2009, he plainly told CNN's Christiane Amanpour that the relationship between China and the United States is the most important bilateral relationship in the world, and that the two countries need to give each other due respect and incentivize each other so that they can work together toward peace and a better world. As one of China's elite entrepreneurs, Gao is no doubt a voice that cannot be ignored.

EVERLYNE MISATI

Sources

Chinaglobalspeakers (2009), "International affairs speakers: Victor Zhikai Gao, Esq.", available at: http://chinaglobalspeakers.com/?p=2723 (accessed 25 February 2010).

English.cri.cn (2009), "Victor Z. Gao, Esq.", available at: http://english.cri.cn/6909/2009/01/12/301s442844.htm (accessed 25 February 2010).

Globalcast (2009), "GlobalCast Networks – Board of Advisors", available at: http://www.globalcastnetworks.com/board.htm (accessed 25 February 2010).

Milkeninstitute (2009), "Milken Institute Global Conference 2009 – Speaker's biography", available at: http://www.milkeninstitute.org/events/gcprogram.taf?function=bio&EventID=GC09&SPID=3836 (accessed 25 February 2010).

Ge, Ming (葛明 b. 1952)

The professional accountant, Ge Ming is the current chairman and director of Ernst & Young Hua Ming in China. Born in 1952 and brought up in a humble family in Beijing, Ge, like any other Chinese youth, was fueled with Chairman Mao Zedong's communist ideologies prevalent at that time. When the so-called Great Proletarian Cultural Revolution was launched in 1966, Ge's early high school education was halted. In 1968, at the age of 16, he joined the Red Guards, a mass movement of mostly students and other young people during the Cultural Revolution, and relocated to rural area in attempting to raise the education standard of the poor farmers. Based on his personal zealousness, Ge decided to "stay in the area where he was mobilized for life." Along with him in Shanxi Province at that time was Deng Zhifang, the son of Deng Xiaoping, the chief architect of the Chinese economic reform since 1978. Ge and the younger Deng became close friends, and later conducted a general survey with several others on the Chinese society. The result of that study had a profound impact on Ge, which enlightened him not to learn aimlessly but rationally by having clear objectives in mind.

In 1972, when US President Nixon visited China, Ge experienced a major turning point in his life. As the social life slowly returned to normal after the chaos of the Cultural Revolution, people began to return to school for education. Initially, Ge's family background shattered his dream of pursuing a Chinese language study at Peking University; however, he was later admitted to the Beijing Teacher's Institute, a multidisciplinary institution of higher learning founded in 1954. With a major in English language, a subject area unpopular at that time, Ge's college education also paved the way for the second turning point in his life. Upon graduation in 1975, Ge started working for the Beijing Yuying High School as an English teacher, and made a remarkable leap in his English proficiency. With the death of Chairman Mao and the conclusion of the Cultural Revolution in 1976, Deng Xiaoping emerged a year later to oversee the education and technological development in China. When the nationwide college entrance examination was reintroduced, Ge passed it in 1979 and was enrolled into a graduate study program at the Research Institute for Fiscal Science under the Ministry of Finance of PRC. Following the liberalization of Chinese economy in 1978, as joint venture initiatives between Chinese enterprises and foreign investors increased steadily, the need for skilled accounting professionals familiar with the Western accounting systems became critical. Ge's English proficiency proved to be his valuable asset for a later inclusion along with seven others for a year of practical training at Ernst & Young and Coopers & Lybrand, USA.

On May 15, 1981, at the age of 29, Ge departed from China to the United States, which marked the beginning of his career of over 20 years with Ernst & Young Hua Ming. While in Cleveland, Ge experienced the vast differences in terms of the level of economic development and quality of life between America and China. Shortly after their arrival, Ge and others captured the attention of local media and often became subjects of ridicule and laughter. The cultural shock broadened Ge's horizon about the Western social and economic systems, which greatly motivated him to acquire advanced knowledge and skills so that he could soon bridge the economic gaps between China and the developed nations.

In 1981, Xu Yi, Ge's mentor at the Research Institute for Fiscal Science, together with some others, established the Chinese Institute of Accountants (CIA中华会计师事务所), a state-owned organization. A year later, Ge return to China to complete his master's degree in accounting, and was admitted as a registered accountant of China the following year. At the CIA, Ge was mainly responsible for overseeing the audit in the area of jointed Chinese and foreign investments. When Ernst & Young and CIA formed an alliance by establishing a joint financial consultation service in Hong Kong in 1985, Ge, as the deputy general manager of the CIA, became the executive director of the corporation. The consulting firm served as the gateway for advising Hong Kong businesses and overseas investors interested in investing in Mainland China, and for providing services to Chinese businesses from Mainland China planning to go for public listing on the Hong Kong Stock Exchange. From 1985 to 1992, the firm trained close to 1000 accounting personnel from mainland China, thereby effectively narrowing the gaps between the Chinese accounting systems and the Western practices.

Since the 1990s, Ge has held senior posts in five different accounting-related entities including CIA and Ernst & Young Hua Ming. With approval from the Chinese Ministry of Finance, which regulates CIA's operation, Ernst & Young formed an alliance with Hua Ming to establish an accounting office in Beijing under the name of Ernst & Young Hua Ming. As a result, Ge returned to Beijing and joined that company as the general manager, where he made efforts to reform the accounting practice and align China's growing market orientation with international standards. After China's entry into WTO and the disconnection of Ernst & Young Hua Ming from the Ministry of Finance, Ge became a partner with Ernst & Young Hua Ming. Before those strategic moves, accounting scandals were quite rampant in China. The clear distinction made between what constitutes a business enterprise and a political entity and the separation of their interconnection therefore encouraged transparent financial reporting and good corporate governance. The changes also provided Ernst & Young Hua Ming and other major international accounting firms the golden opportunities to gain share of the large and fast growing Chinese market. In 2002, in an effort to reinforce its localization plan, Ernst & Young Hua Ming merged with Shanghai Dahua, the largest local Chinese accounting firm. One of Ge's recent missions is to train new generations of accounting personnel to become registered accountants, thus meeting the needs of growing Chinese economy and the development of local accounting professions.

Ge described himself as being luckier than most of his peers in the journey to success. On the face of it, this could be understood as his good connections with Deng Xiaoping's son and his own academic mentor Xu Yi, both of them the early movers and shakers of the Chinese economy. Ge's other assets include being progressive, hardworking, eager to learn, humble, and optimistic about life, and having a sense of responsibility toward others, which all contributed to the success of his life. In his leisure time, Ge enjoys classical music, and involves himself in charitable work to assist the less fortunates.

LOI TECK HUI

Sources

方圆 (2010), "安永华明会计师事务所董事长: 葛明", *中国企业新闻网* [Fang Y, "Ge Ming: Chairman of Ernst & Young Hua Ming", *CENN*], 6 January, available at: http://www.hyzc.net/qiyemingjia/2010-1/6/20100106286681 2.html (accessed 3 March 2010).

葛明: 享受艺术与生活是放松身心最好的方式 [Ge Ming: Enjoying art and life is the best way to relax], available at: http://e.mymb.com.cn/english/sedan/focus/content/353 (accessed 8 April 2010).

冯嘉雪, 郭玉梅, 郭俐君 (2007), "葛明: 安永华明掌门人的人生之字路", *巅峰职业: 10位海归职业经理人* (王辉耀 主编), 中国发展出版社, 北京 [Feng, J., Guo, Y., and Guo, L., "Ge Ming: The Life journey of Ernst & Young Hua Ming's Chief", in Wang, H. (ed.), *Splendid Careers: Ten Overseas Returnees in Professional Management*, China Development Press], pp. 215–233.

Gu, Yongqiang (Victor Koo 古永锵 b. 1966)

A successful entrepreneur and former COO of Sohu.com, Gu Yongqiang is the founder and CEO of Youku.com, a leading video website and one of the top Internet destinations in China. Founded in 2006, the online premier video brand offers a mix of professionally produced and user-generated video for Chinese people around the world to watch and share. As of December 2009, Youku attracted more than 30 million unique viewers a day and 200 million a month according to Nielsen and iResearch. The total user time spent exceeded 40 billion minutes per month.

Born in 1966, Gu grew up in Hong Kong. His father was a civil engineer, who sent Gu to study in Australia at age 14. Being the first and only Chinese student in the local school district, Gu demonstrated a remarkable sense of maturity. He soon overcame the initial hardship and excelled academically. Upon graduation from high school, he was admitted into an undergraduate chemistry program at the University of New South Wales. When his family moved to the United States in 1985, Gu planned to transfer to UC Berkeley and earn his undergraduate degree in economics instead. However, his application was rejected twice. His friends and family suggested that he should look into other less prestigious schools, but UC Berkley is where he wanted to enroll. Gu described himself as being persistent in pursuit of what he was passionate about. After his third attempt, he became a junior at UC Berkley and graduated two years later. In 1992, Gu also studied at the elite Stanford University, where he earned his MBA.

From 1989 to 2005, Gu successively worked for various companies: for Bain, a management consulting company (1989–1992); P&G Hong Kong (1993); Richina, a venture investment firm (1994–1999); and Sohu, one of the leading Internet information providers in China (1999–2005). Among them, the experiences at Richina particularly deepened his understanding about the rising Chinese market and helped him build the social network in the capital investment field, which later proved to be useful when he helped Sohu finance its business venture. In 1999, Gu joined Sohu, and successively served as the CFO, COO, and president before leaving the company in 2005 to found Youku.

One of the most memorable accomplishments of Gu while working at Sohu was the purchase of 17173.com. In the early 2000s, there was fierce competition in the Chinese Internet industry, as companies such as Sina, 163.com, and Tom were all demonstrating strong competitive advantages. In particular, Sina was holding the top position in portal ranking, while 163.com was showing a strong capability in online games. Hence, how Sohu could regain its leading position in the Chinese Internet industry had become very crucial to the company's long-term success. After thorough research, Gu suggested that Sohu purchase 17173.com, the largest online game information and community website. The rationales behind the purchase were that, first, he believed the online game service would be a fast growing business, as the market data indicated that the Chinese online game players almost doubled from 2002 to 2003, which implied the huge revenues generated by this industry; second, because of its sufficient cash flow, acquisition would help the company take a leading position in the Internet industry. With US$20.5 million spent on 17173.com, a venture that had less than $800,000 annual revenue and mere $200,000 profit, many industry experts believed the purchase was not a good deal for Sohu. Nevertheless, Gu steadfastly insisted that the acquisition would greatly enhance Sohu's position as a leading Internet enterprise in China and strengthen the company's ability to market its consumer services. Later on, the market proved the purchase was strategically right; by 2007, Sohu's financial report showed that online game revenues of the company reached US$42.1 million, up 394% from the previous year.

In 2005, after achieving all the goals he had set when he joined the company several years earlier, Gu resigned from Sohu. His new ambition was to pursue entrepreneurial opportunities. After several months' consideration, Gu decided to enter into the Internet video industry because he believed that the world was marching into a new era, where online video as one of the major Internet applications will generate new business opportunities. Moreover, all of his experiences in Sohu, from the knowledge of the Internet industry's ups and downs, to financing, to the relationship with the government, would greatly help him in starting up his own company.

Officially launched in 2006, Youku allows users to upload video so that people around the world could watch and share them. Unlike its Western counterpart YouTube, which focuses on the short-form, user-generated video content with an average 2 to 3 minutes on a page view, Youku's hybrid model consists of 70% professionally produced content and 30% user-generated content, creating a much longer page view time of 10 minutes. It works so well that it attracts more users, which in turn brings more advertisers. Another critical feature to the company's success, according to Gu, is that unlike other major Chinese competitors, Youku relies on its self-developed technology as well as self-operated video content delivery network (CDN), which produces the fastest speed in terms of searching, viewing, delivering, and uploading contents, and is very attractive to visitors and advertisers.

In 2007, Gu put forward the concept of video view (VV), in contrast to the concept of page view (PV) used by other web portals. While web portals use page view to attract advertisement, Gu believed that the video view approach would bring more advertisements, because web surfers spend more time watching videos than viewing the pages. Today, Youku uses several metrics to measure its performance, including user time spent, video views, page views, monthly unique visitors (UV), etc. By all of these metrics, Youku has led its Chinese counterparts with a comfortable margin. Because of these competitive advantages, Youku has been growing into a leading Internet video website in China in a short period. Its revenues were increased by over 500% from 2008 to 2009, reaching 200 million RMB.

One of the major challenges faced by Gu and Youku is that the competition for the Chinese online video sharing market is getting more and more intensifying. On the one hand, the company needs to compete with other privately owned online video sharing companies such as Tudou. On the other hand, the emergence of the state-owned video websites such as the soon-to-be-launched Hualu will definitely bring tremendous pressure on Youku, because the state-owned counterpart owns a large number of copyrights and media industry resources that privately owned firms have to spend enormous money to purchase. To further complicate the matter, in 2009, Youku was involved in a major copyright dispute of the online video and Internet industry. The China Internet Video Anti-Piracy Alliance, comprised of Sohu, some Internet video companies, and copyrights owners, sued Youku and several other Internet video websites for broadcasting unauthorized videos of Chinese movies and TV dramas. To clamp down on piracy, Youku launched its "copyright identification management platform" in early 2010 to track and disable pirated materials. Moreover, Youku joined the China Network Copyright Committee and the Chinese Online Video Anti-Piracy Alliance to fight against piracy in online music, movie, and television streaming.

Despite the challenges, Gu believes Youku's future is promising. As the only video site on the list, the company was named by *China Entrepreneur Magazine* as the top winner of the 2010 Future Stars. In terms of the company's future strategy, Gu believes that the year 2010 was the beginning of the 3G application in China, and Youku as the largest online video website in the country is ready to spread videos to mobile phones based on 3G networks. As mobile Internet video is becoming increasingly popular in China, Youku under Gu's able leadership will seek to become the major 3G platform to further improve the viewing experiences of millions of Chinese people around the world.

MICHAEL A. MOODIAN, YIFANG ZHANG AND MARGARET MINNIS

Sources

ChinaTechNews (2010), "Chinese state-owned company enters Internet video industry sector", 18 June, available at: http://www.chinatechnews.com/2010/06/18/12225-chinese-state-owned-company-enters-internet-video-industry-sector (accessed 20 June 2010).

CNETAsia (2010), "Chinese video-sharing sites launch huge attack on piracy", available at: http://asia.cnet.com/blogs/sinobytes/post.htm?id=63016419 (accessed 4 July 2010).

PRNewswire (2010), "Youku tops 2010 China Entrepreneur Future Stars List", 23 January, available at: http://www.prnewswire.com/news-releases/youku-tops-2010-china-entrepreneur-future-stars-list-97373854.html (accessed 5 July 2010).

Sohu.com (2004), "SOHU.com announces President and COO Victor Koo's resignation", 18 November, available at: http://corp.sohu.com/20041118/n240555214.shtml (accessed 15 June 2010).

Wang, X. (2009), "Web video piracy war heats up", *China Daily*, 28 September, available at http://www.chinadaily.com.cn/bw/2009-09/28/content_8744294.htm (accessed 2 July 2010).

百度百科 (n.d.), "古永锵" ["Victor Koo", *Baidu Encyclopedia*], available at: http://baike.baidu.com/view/251879.htm (25 June 2010).

廖庆升 (2009), "古永锵的3G视频梦", *通信信息报* [Liao, Q.S., "Victor Koo's 3G video dream", *Communication Information News*], 30 December, available at: http://tech.163.com/09/1230/14/5RPNJP0O000915BF.html (5 July 2010).

Han, Gengchen (韩庚辰 b. 1955)

Dr. Han Gengchen is the founder, chairman, and CEO of Origin Agritech Limited (Origin). Han is also the executive chairman of Beijing Origin and its affiliated companies, a position that he has held since founding the business in 1997. Origin is a technology-focused crop seed company serving Mainland China and specializes in research and development, production, and sales. The company markets crop seeds including corn, cotton, rice, and canola throughout China. With its focus on the production of higher-quality seed products, Origin's nationwide distribution network consisted of approximately 3,800 first-level distributors and approximately 65,000 second-level distributors and retailers at the end of 2009.

Han has more than 20 years of experience in maize breeding and seed industry. He has worked and lived in the United States, Mexico, the Philippines, and Thailand for 12 years before returning to China to found his company. Han calls himself "a farmer," having grown up in the countryside. After graduating high school, he returned to the countryside and later worked on a backbreaking irrigation construction project in the rural Henan Province during the Chinese Cultural Revolution. His fortune was changed in the 1970s, when Han was ranked first among more than 500 people competing for college entrance, and was recommended to attend the Henan Agricultural University, where he majored in crop genetics and breeding. In 1978, Han continued his study in a master's degree program and became a lecturer after graduating from the same institution. In 1984, Han went to the United States to pursue an advanced degree, and received his PhD in plant breeding and cytogenetics from the Iowa State University in 1987. Thereafter, he worked for two years for his postdoctoral study at the International Maize and Wheat Improvement Center (CIMMYT) in Mexico. In1990, Han joined Pioneer Hi-bred International as a technical coordinator for Asia/Pacific and regional supervisor for China Business.

Having learned the advanced technologies of the seed industry of the world, Han began to seek opportunities to return to his homeland. In 1997, when the Chinese Overseas Student Pioneer Park was established by the Beijing municipal government in the Haidian District, the entrepreneurial bud in Han's heart began to sprout. "I will let the Chinese farmers use the best seeds" is Han's goal for his agriculture-oriented company. After launching the Origin Agritech Limited, Han recruited his friend Dr. Yang Yasheng, who has since served as president, treasurer, and chief operating officer of Origin.

At the beginning of its operation, Origin aimed at "high quality, high value, with emphasis on services and innovation." Owing to his overseas working and management experiences and his expertise in biotechnology and seed industry, Han introduced both advanced biotechnology and a new business model to the Chinese seed production arena. He took the lead in improving the quality of seed processing and packaging and in promoting services and technical support for farmers. In addition to adding values to his products through branding, marketing, and after-sales services, Han also developed and incorporated research, production, sales, and services into his operating mechanism, which has made Origin stand out compared to the existing government-run seed companies.

Under Han's leadership, the company has rapidly grown and thrived. With more than 30% steady growth of profit over the recent years, Origin has quickly established its leading position in China's seed industry, and has become a marvel among the flourishing IT companies in Beijing's Zhongguancun High Tech District. In 2000, Origin was named among "China's top 100 strong enterprises" by the Ministry of Agriculture, and one year later, the company ranked third among 100 fast-growing small and medium-size enterprises in China. Han received an "Entrepreneurship Award" sponsored by the Beijing municipal government, which honors Chinese overseas returnee scholars and scientists. In addition, Han was one of the distinguished entrepreneurs recognized at the fifth "Shining Light of the Sciences and Technologies" award. In 2003, Origin was ranked among the "Top 50 Strongest Seed Companies" in China, and was recognized as the "Future Star" in *Digital Fortune*. More recently, Origin has received the Bio-safety Certificate from the Chinese Ministry of Agriculture for the commercial distribution of the world's first genetically modified phytase corn.

With the fast growth and huge success in the domestic arena, Origin began to aim at the international market. In 2005, Origin became China's first agricultural biotechnology enterprise that joined the American Seed Trade Association and landed on the NASDAQ. By the end of 2008, Origin had expanded to 13 marketing centers, 8 production centers, 8 breeding stations, in addition to 1 winter nursery base and 1 research and development center. Origin also subsidized three of China's top 50 seed companies. By the end of April 2010, Origin's market value reached over US$204 million on the NASDAQ, yet its initial registered capital was just 3 million RMB in 1997. All these impressive accomplishments serve as a convincing testimony to the vision and entrepreneurial spirits of its capable leader, who has never forgotten his deep roots in the yellow earth, and given the importance of agriculture in the global economies, it seems that Dr. Han and his agricultural endeavor will continue to flourish and make solid contributions to the general well-being of the Chinese society in the years to come.

Shuqin Jiao

Sources

Origin Agritech (2010), "About Origin", available at: http://www.originseed.com.cn/en/about/ (accessed 1 May 2010).

北京农业 (2007), "让中国人用上最好的种子" ["Let Chinese people use the best seeds", *Beijing Agriculture*], 26.

农博种业 (2006), "自称是'农民'的海归育种专家: 韩庚辰", ["Oversea returnee breeder who called himself 'a farmer': Han Gengchen", *Nongbo Seeds*], 14 March, available at: http://seed.aweb.com.cn/news/2006/3/14/17500112.shtml (accessed 1May 2010).

Han, Xiaohong (韩小红 b. 1967)

A doctor in oncology and a member of the Board of Chinese Returnee Entrepreneurs, Han Xiaohong is a trailblazer in the Chinese physical checkup field, as she has magnified a link from the clinical process—body checkup—into an industry. Her name, along with the Beijing Ciming Health Checkup and Management Co. that she founded, and the health care concept "to be discovered early, to be diagnosed early, to take treatment early," has spread out all over China.

Born into a medical family in 1967, with her grandfather and both parents being doctors, Han naturally had a dream of becoming a medical professional since childhood. After high school, she entered Dalian Medical University, and later received her graduate degree from Beijing Medical University in 1997. Then she went to the best military hospital in China—the 301 Hospital of the People's Liberation Army (PLA)—and became an oncologist. However, in the Oncology Department there, Han found herself suffering a great deal psychologically from her work, since 90% of the patients who came to her care were in the late-stage cancers. She could do nothing but watch the terminal patients leave desperately, which made her feel extremely helpless.

In 1999, Han went to Germany on an academic exchange, where she observed the advanced medical technologies and all kinds of people-oriented services in the hospitals. That experience shed new light on Han and inspired her to launch the service processes in Ciming a few years later. More importantly, she received the Western concept of health care that it would be too late to take treatment after people got very sick, even if they would spare no penny from the property. The earlier the discovery of the disease, the higher the possibility of cure and the less the expense incurred. This inspired her to notice the potential demand of health checkup in China.

While in Germany, Han applied for the PhD program in medicine from Heidelberg University and was admitted. In 2001, she returned to the Oncology Department of 301 Hospital in Beijing. However, even with her newly minted doctoral degree, Han still could not make any difference for those patients suffering from late-stage cancer. After some struggles, she decided to forgo what many considered the best job, and turned to help her husband in his clinic. In 2002, Han launched her Ciji Health Checkup, which was later changed to Ciming Health Checkup and Management Co. At the beginning, many people had serious doubts; however, with her strong faith and hard work, the institute began to generate profit after the first three months. Thus, Han became a trailblazer in the professional health checkup field, while she gradually demonstrated her great potential in entrepreneurship and management.

Along Ciming's path of growth, Han had to overcome all kinds of obstacles and challenges. In 2003, when the second branch of Ciming Checkup was just opened up, Severe Acute Respiratory Syndrome (SARS) broke out in China and all the checkup appointments were canceled overnight. Han had to take immediate measures. By supplying what was badly needed in the market such as masks and sterilizing drugs, she barely earned the rent and the salary for her staff. Then in 2004, Ciming's third branch center was damaged by fire only one day after its opening, and Han had to rebuild the confidence of her team one staff member at a time. As she remarked, "I am just like the sea that can absorb everything. Every setback was only an experience gained on my way to success." Nevertheless, setbacks did not end. When the fourth branch of Ciming opened for business, her father came to take the physical exam for the first time, and was diagnosed with late-stage cancer. Even worse, around the same time Han herself was diagnosed with an early stage of stomach cancer. Coincidently, Han shared the same ward with her father in the 301 Hospital for three months of treatment. Although Han recovered, she had to again witness a late-stage patient losing his life, this time her father.

The loss of her father reinforced her belief and further motivated her to push the Ciming health care model forward. She vowed: "I do hope that none of my customers will suffer from what I have been through. Thereby, I shall dedicate all myself to this health checkup business." With determination, Han boldly put forward the management output model in order to expand the scale of her business and benefit more people. According to her plan, Ciming would build stores, offering manpower and materials and training the staff while collecting a certain amount of fees. Thus, the receiving party can promote their brand and Ciming can benefit more people in the second-tier and third-tier cities.

With Han's brave strategies and managerial approach, Ciming grew rapidly. In April 2008, Ping An Insurance Co., one of China's largest insurance companies, became the largest shareholder of Ciming by investing 100 million RMB ($14.60 million) in Ciming Health Checkup and Management Co. Ltd. Later that year, the company purchased Beijing Baizhong Checkup and Guangdong Very Good Health Care Center, and 12 health checkup centers run by Wojia Checkup. Now the Ciming Group Chain is the largest professional chain industry in health checkup. Ciming Group has more than 40 health checkup centers in major Chinese cities such as Tianjin, Shanghai, Chengdu, Wuhan, Guangzhou, and Shenzhen, among others.

Besides over 10 centers in Beijing, there are more than 30 centers in the other cities. Under Han's leadership, Ciming continues to develop alongside the improvement of people's outlook toward health. Han believes that she is making a difference for the helpless oncologist she used to be: "It's different now. Diseases can be discovered and treated earlier and with better treating results, the cancer patients will no longer be desperate. So are the oncologists." With her tireless promotion of the importance of regular checkup, Han and her Ciming will continue to contribute for a better health care system in China.

YUPING DU

Sources

陈楠 (2009), "我是一个智商很高, 情商中等的人", *商务周刊* [Chen, N., "Han Xiaohong: I am a person of high IQ with medium EQ", *Business Week*], 29 April, pp. 26–30.

季长亮 (2009), "坚毅拓荒的铿锵玫瑰: 慈铭健康体检管理集团总裁韩小红", *首都医药* [Ji, C., "A perseverant lady pioneer: The general director of Ciming Health Checkup Group Han Xiaohong", *Capital Medicine*], Vol. 16, No. 17, pp. 26–30.

慕容 (2008), "韩小红: 中国体检第一人", *新西部* [Mu, R., "Han Xiaohong: The first person in Chinese health checkup", *New West*], No. 9, pp. 48–50.

谢娜, 杨生文 (2005), "你的健康需要'管理': 访北京慈济健康体检连锁机构总经理韩小红", *职业* [Xie, N. and Yang, S., "Your health needs 'management': An interview with Beijing Ciji CEO Han Xiaohong", *Occupation*], No. 6, pp. 4–7.

Hao, Quan (Sherry Hao 郝荃 b. undisclosed)

An accountant by training, Hao Quan is the first Chinese partner of KPMG, a firm created in 1987 with the merger of Peat Marwick International (PMI) and Klynveld Main Goerdeler (KMG). KPMG is a global network of professional firms providing audit, tax, and advisory services. Hao has spent most of her professional career at the firm. The company operates in 146 countries and employs 140,000 people working in member firms around the world. In China alone, KPMG employs over 9000 people and operates in 12 major cities across the country.

Hao started her education at the 7th Primary School of Beijing Railway, where she studied from 1965 to 1972. She then attended the 8th High School in Beijing until 1977. Afterward, she was among the last group of Chinese youths dispatched to the countryside following a national policy initiated during the Cultural Revolution. At that time, there was turmoil in the Chinese political life, and she was uncertain about her choice of future career; fortunately, she decided to pursue a college education, encouraged by some of her teachers. In November 1977, excelling at mathematics, she wanted to participate in the newly resumed college entrance examination, but fell ill and was unable to take the test. She tried again in the following year, and was admitted to the undergraduate financial accounting program at the Renmin University of China in 1978, although originally she was hoping to study either journalism or literature.

Hao had never considered going into the accounting profession, because at that time, people in charge of accounting left a lot to be desired as regards their professional competence. Nevertheless, she accepted the reality and excelled in her academic work. After graduation in 1982, Hao became a member of the accounting faculty at Renmin. Nowadays, Professor Wang Jinxing of the Finance Department at Renmin still has vivid memories of Hao Quan: "Our people here are particularly fond of Sherry, she was always smiling and she was very thoughtful, logical and showed very powerful communication skills" (Xie, 2007). It was also at her alma mater that Hao met her future husband, Jesse Wang, whom she married right after graduation. Himself a leading accountant in China, Wang once worked as an assistant to the chairman of the China Securities Regulatory Commission. Although there were some periods in which they could not be together, fluent and open communication with each other was the key to the success of their marriage.

Encouraged by her professor, Hao underwent advance training in the United States, and such valuable work experience abroad laid a solid foundation for the future success of her professional career. Hao entered the world of accounting by first obtaining her US Certified Public Accountant (CPA) status, and from 1985 to 1987, she worked as an intern auditor at the New York office of KPMG. At the end of her internship, although the company offered her a permanent position, she turned it down and returned to China to resume her teaching career. Staying in the United States would not have made her stand out in her area of work, but if she returned home, she could pass on what she had learned overseas, as she was among the first group of Chinese professionals from Mainland China who had first-hand experience of working in a foreign country.

A few years later, she decided to further her education in the United States. In 1992, Hao received her master's degree in business administration from the Business School at Temple University in Philadelphia. Afterward she was able to rejoin KPMG in Los Angeles. Initially she intended to spend only two years in the United States, but she ended up staying overseas for over a decade. Hao was aware that if she decided to continue working at the same company, she would need between four and six years to be promoted to a position of responsibility and as long as 10–14 years to become a manager. She still vividly remembers her time in America, where she had to work hard and overcome both language barriers and cultural shock to gain confidence in her capabilities. As she had to start from scratch again, Hao worked extra-long hours, often until midnight or early in the morning, but still she would be back at her desk by 9 o'clock. Unwearied, she was determined to improve herself and move up the corporate ladder. For her, job and life are connected, and she was grateful to KMPG, because the company has always encouraged her to try hard and get to the top, even though she was a foreigner and an outsider.

In 1997, Hao was transferred to the firm's London office, and finally in 1999 she was relocated to the Beijing office of KPMG. Once back in China and spurred by the fact that the Internet business was in full swing, she decided to switch companies and started working as CFO for TOM.COM, a newly created dot.com funded by Hong

Kong billionaire Li Ka-shing. However, after a brief spell in this new venture, she was recruited back by KPMG and promoted to a partner in 2001, the first person from Mainland China to have ever risen to such status in the history of the company. Besides her leadership role in accounting services, throughout the years Hao has been instrumental in getting KPMG China to become actively involved in numerous activities to support local communities. She represented KPMG at the New Great Wall, a China foundation for helping students, where she encouraged her staff members to participate. According to her, "These events, not only do they improve staff loyalty and work-life balance, but they also raise awareness among the employees of our corporate social responsibility" (Xie, 2007).

Given her background in teaching, Hao eagerly shares her insights as a successful Chinese returnee with many young and aspiring students. In 2004, she was invited to take part in the Students Career Forum at the Renmin University of China. Based on her professional experience, she not only talked directly to students about the general career outlook and what expectations a firm could have from job applicants, but also made useful suggestions about writing a résumé, and highlighted the need for applicants to include quality training such as team building and group spirit in their applications. Hao has also stressed that when employers evaluate a prospective candidate in the employment process, they look at a person's overall qualities and development potential, not just academic achievements.

In addition to her professional services at the global accounting firm, Hao has joined the China Western Returned Scholars Association, Chamber of Commerce (WRSACC). In April 2004, she was a guest speaker at the Seventh Annual Conference at Harvard Conference Center under the theme of "China's Quest for Balanced Development." She also took part at the annual China-U.S. Symposium on Building the Financial System of the 21st Century held at Harvard Law School in 2009 and in Nanjing, China, in 2010. For her professional accomplishments, Hao was recently named among the top 100 corporate talents in China by *Talents* magazine. She is also a member of the American Institute of Certified Public Accountants and California State Society of CPAs. Despite her achievements, Hao is gentle mannered, soft spoken, and shy, depicting traditional Chinese characters, unlike a Western white-collar professional who typically projects a strong and powerful image. These attributes make her unique in her field of work, and being herself has always contributed to the success in her professional career.

M. Elena Aramendia-Muneta

Sources

KPMG (2010), "Who we are", available at: http://www.kpmg.com/CN/en/WhoWeAre/Pages/default.aspx (accessed 6 June 2010).

WRSACC (2005), "Sherry Hao, Partner of KPMG", available at: http://www.2005committee.org/english.php/member/ls/914 (accessed 6 June 2010).

解红, 孟繁颖 (2007), "毕马威中国合伙人郝荃: 在工作中体会成长乐趣", 人大新闻网 [Xie, H. and Meng, F.Y., "KPMG China Partner Hao Quan: Enjoying the pleasure of growth from work", RUC News Network], 31 October, available at: http://news.sina.com.cn/c/2007-10-31/172614205660.shtml (accessed 6 June 2010).

天下金融 (2010), "毕马威郝荃：在大学生就业过程中的一些建议", ["Hao Quan of KPMG shared her thoughts on college students employment process", 21jrr], 20 March, available at http://www.21jrr.com/html/jrzy/kjs/2010/0320/11257.html (accessed 6 June 2010).

中国扶贫基金会 (2010), "新长城项目高校2010年工作会议暨爱心包裹项目总结会圆满结", 中国财富 [China Foundation for Poverty Alleviation, "New Great Wall Project Conference successfully concluded", Zgcaifu], 14 January, available at: http://www.zgcaifu.com/web/gongyixiangmu/xinchangcheng/20100513/706.html (accessed 6 June 2010).

He, Xin (何欣 b. 1964)

He Xin is one of the first VC investors in China. Born in Hangzhou, He grew up with his father in the Zhoushan Islands. As a teenager, he dreamed of being a scientist. Even during the Cultural Revolution, He read broadly and was distinguished student at a young age, especially in science subjects such as mathematics, physics, and chemistry. In 1981, He entered Zhejiang University, majoring in civil engineering. Upon graduation, He worked as an engineer for the Beijing Design Institute of Nonferrous Metal, and a few years later he obtained a scholarship from Transport Canada for studying at Carleton University in Ottawa.

In 1988, He left China with only $25 in pocket, and began his study at Carleton University. In Canada, he lived through some tough time in his life taking part-time jobs such as dishwashing at the school's café and some other work to support himself. After obtaining his master's degree in 1991, He began to work for the Waterloo office of CH2M HILL Engineering Consulting Corp. Headquartered in the United States with more than 18,000 employees, CH2M is one of the world's largest companies in environmental and engineering consulting services. Working as an engineering consultant in Canada in a small college town, with very good salary and high social status, is enviable in most people's minds, but He gradually got bored with his job. After serious considerations, he decided to enroll into the MBA program at the Schulich School of Business, York University. From 1992 to 1994, He studied very hard at Schulich, learning not only his academic subjects but also the spirits of diligence, teamwork, and integrity.

After receiving his MBA in 1994, He joined a consulting firm in Canada. Due to the economic recession of that time, the job market in North America was sluggish. However, the financial market in Hong Kong began to boom, with extremely strong-performing H shares and Red Chips from Chinese business. Analysts proficient in the Chinese language were highly demanded, as most financial analysts in Hong Kong are foreigners without knowledge of Chinese, which created a huge opportunity for overseas returnees such as He Xin, who soon joined DBS (Development Bank of

Singapore) in Hong Kong as a security analyst, and established his own investment philosophies at work. In 1996, He was headhunted to Nikko Global Asset Management and worked on fund management.

Once He had a conversation with a Zhejiang University alumna about the VC industry and career path, which made him become very interested in this unfamiliar field that always made headlines on the *Wall Street Journal*, especially during the Internet boom and the NASDAQ mania period. Since then He began to pay attention to relevant information about VC. In 1998, He joined Intel Capital and began to work under Eric Levin, who interviewed him and was impressed by his qualifications. Later when Levin moved to Carlyle and formed the Carlyle Asia Venture Capital Fund, He began to help him by meeting with many potential entrepreneurs who were also overseas returnees with various plans seeking for huge funding, a scenario very much like the NASDAQ and Internet boom of the time. In 2001, He joined the Carlyle Group as the vice president of Carlyle Asia Investment, supervising direct investments in mainland China, Taiwan, Japan, and Korea. In a 10-year period, from engineer to MBA, to financial analyst, to fund manager, until direct investment manager, He Xin has taken a typical path for professional managers in multinational corporations.

In 2002, Carlyle Asia Venture Capital Fund II was founded with total capital of US$164 million. It was at the end of the Dotcom Bubble, and new investment opportunities began to emerge. Carlyle recognized the increasing value of investing in traditional enterprises. Under the referral of Morgan Stanley Asia, Carlyle approached Target Media, which focused on the business of LCD TV advertising in buildings, and He was leading the VC team for this investment. Although the market for LCD TV advertising was growing, Target Media was competing with Focus Media in the Chinese market, both in business and in attracting venture capital investments. Upon careful review, He believed Target Media held several unique advantages: first, early entrance position and sufficient experiences to enlarge the market space; second, a top-notch entrepreneurial team with very good expertise and professional experiences; third, clear strategy and highly reliable team members. Having recognized these, Carlyle entered a long-term strategic partnership with Target Media. By 2004, the growth of Target Media had exceeded Carlyle's expectation, and in July 2005, Carlyle invested an additional US$5 million in Target Media for its market expansion plan. In order to reduce friction and better compete internationally, under the facilitation of Carlyle, Target Media later merged with Focus Media to become a giant in advertisement business.

Within a few years, Carlyle Group had an impressive investment record in Asia. By 2009, Carlyle closed its Asia Growth Capital Partners Fund IV, which mainly focused on China, India, South Korea, and other key Asian markets, with US$1.04 billion in capital, about 50% bigger than its previous Asia Growth Fund, which raised $680 million in June 2006. Until June 2010, the fund had made eight investments, including $60 million in three Chinese companies: Nantong Rainbow Heavy Industry Co., a supplier of ship components and port and marine-related large steel structures; China Agritech Inc., which provides agricultural products; and iTour, an online travel services company. All these had He's involvement and leadership. As a veteran in China's VC industry living through the first Internet investment boom as well as various successes and failures, He is still busy looking for companies that have emerged from the global financial crisis relatively unscathed and that have potential for rapid growth.

Hao Liang and Sunny Li Sun

Sources

Sheng, E. (2010), "Carlyle Invests in Asian Firms", *Wall Street Journal*, 6 June, available at: http://online.wsj.com/article/SB10001424052748704025904575291793589301162.html (accessed 11 June 2010).

Zero2ipo (2010), "Sean He: The Carlyle Group, Managing Director", available at: http://character.zero2ipo.Com.cn/en/character/2009330185157.shtml (accessed 11 June 2010).

王佑 (2007), "凯雷投资集团何欣: 如何将创意变为真实项目很重要", *第一财经日报* [Wang, Y., "He Xin: It is important to transfer ideas into real projects" *First Finance Daily*], 10 December, available at: http://fund2.jrj.Com.cn/news/2007-12-10/000003031561.html (accessed June 11, 2010).

邢学军 (2007), "何欣: 10年VC激荡岁月", *财富裂变: 10位海归风险投资翘楚* (王辉耀主编), 中国发展出版社, 北京 [Xing, X., "He Xin: A decade of excitement in venture capitalism", in Wang, H. (ed.), *Wealth Creation: Ten Overseas Returnees in Venture Capital Investment*, China Development Press, Beijing], pp. 101–127.

Hong, Huang (洪晃 b. 1961)

A celebrity with many roles, Hong Huang is the CEO of the China Interactive Media Group (CIMG), and editor and publisher of the magazines *Time Out*, *Seventeen*, and *i LOOK*. In the public's eyes, she is a publisher, a popular blogger, the ex-wife of famous film director Chen Kaige, and a woman from a diplomatic family.

Hong's grandfather, Zhang Shizhao, was a well-known scholar and democrat in China. Her mother, Zhang Hanzhi, was the English teacher of Mao Zedong, and the wife of Qiao Guanhua, a famous Chinese diplomat and former minister of PRC's Foreign Affairs. Originally, Hong's mother wanted her daughter to have a diplomatic career as well. In 1974, when China joined the United Nations, the bilateral relations between the United States and China also improved. The result was that the Chinese government sent a group of young students to study in the United States, among them 12-year-old Hong Huang. Her excellent English language skills are due to living her teenage years in America. Then four years of higher education at Vassar College, a highly selective, residential, coeducational liberal arts college in Hudson Valley, NY, helped to create her unique character with a truly artistic temperament. After graduating, she felt that now was the time for her to return to her homeland.

By the time she was 25 years old, Hong had already become the representative of a foreign company in Nanjing, China, with a large annual income that meant she could buy property. However, Hong felt that she would appreciate the money more if she would become rich later. For a young woman, having fun at a friend's party was much more attractive than having a large salary. At that time, Hong Huang thought the life she had as a business executive was boring, as the credit letters, appointments, and all kinds of agreements ruled her life. She enjoyed having money to do what she pleased, but she preferred to tell her family how she had accomplished something meaningful with her life.

Therefore, in 1996, she resigned from her job, and this young woman who had no experience in managing a magazine, decided to become a publisher. With some of her friends who shared common interests, they established a publishing company. All the investors of this company had overseas study experiences, and all of them had a strong desire to contribute to the growing and blossoming Chinese culture. Remembering her early years spent in New York City, Hong located her office and home in a loft building in 798, a district that has become very fashionable for many avant-garde artists to live. Initially, whenever she invited friends to her new home, they would not come as it was too far away from the downtown area. She then persuaded them as well to relocate to 798, thus encouraging development, and making this a very new and popular residential district.

In March 2000, Hong as CEO, along with several other young entrepreneurs, established the CIMG, which has the world's leading and the biggest Internet interactive media platform in China. It gathers together both domestic and foreign media professionals and excellent resources, and focuses on offering the high-level service to the Chinese media market, including print, online, and other media. The company pays special attention to cooperation with international media companies, and promotes the best international media and successful business models to China. CIMG provides content for media production from a new perspective, in which the magazine, Internet, and TV are not separated, but makes them become the unity of diverse media forms of communication to the massive Chinese market.

CIMG's content mainly focuses on three important marketing areas: women, commercial, and entertainment. The goal of CIMG is to combine all forms of media and divide them according to the topics during the editing, instead of dividing them according to the type of media. With the processes of the diversification of media modes and the development of existing print media, CIMG creates a wide interactive platform that offers the possibility for the communication between the advertiser and emerging Chinese consumer groups. As a prominent Chinese media and public relations company, with offices located in Beijing and Shanghai, CIMG has been authorized to edit and publish some of the well-known magazines in the world, such as *Time Out Fun-Beijing*, *Time Out Fun-Shanghai*, *Time Out Fun-English*, and *i LOOK*. CIMG is also involved in radio broadcasting, TV, and other media projects.

Recently, blogging has become very popular in China, and one of the most popular web blogs belongs to Hong Huang, although she originally did not want to start a blog. Ranked among the top five on Sina.com, her blog had a record of over 100 million hits. In contrast with other celebrities, Hong Huang is a woman who speaks from her heart, and her straightforwardness creates a deep impression on the public. While her friends attribute Hong Huang's character to how her life has been influenced by her education, her friends and family, the literature that she reads, and her successful business and financial independence, she attributes inheriting her father's optimistic character to what keeps her happy, and this lets her continue to look for more unique ways of having fun in her extraordinary life.

XIAOTIAN ZHANG

Sources

China Culture (2006), "Publisher Hong Huang", 14 June, available at: http://www.china.org.cn/english/NM-e/171331.htm (accessed 14 June 2010).

He, J.P. (2006), "Hong Huang: CEO of China Interactive Media Group", *CCTV*, 24 April, available at: http://www.cctv.com/program/upclose/20060424/101135.shtml (accessed 14 June 2010).

百度百科 (2010), "洪晃" ["Hong Huang", *Baidu.com*], available at: http://baike.baidu.com/view/346812.htm (accessed 24 February 2010).

Hu, Shengfa (Norman Hu 胡胜发 b. 1962)

As the cofounder, president, and CEO of Anyka Microelectronics Technology Co. Ltd, Hu Shengfa is a pioneer in mobile multimedia application processor in Mainland China. His mobile solution module has gradually been adopted by high-end smart phones like Apple iPhone and Google gphone, and some of his application processors (AP) have also been used extensively in portable electronics field such as educational electronics, netbooks, and portable media players (PMP), thus marking a milestone in the development of China's semiconductor industry.

Born in 1962, Hu attended Tsinghua University in 1980, where he obtained his bachelor's, master's, and doctoral degrees in succession. Besides his academic achievement, Hu had an active student life and demonstrated a remarkable talent in leadership during his 13 years on campus. He was elected as vice president of All-China Students Federation (1988–1989) and president of Tsinghua Graduate School Student Union and the university's Student Science & Technology Association, and was the cofounder of Sanlian Science and Technology Development Center. After obtaining his doctoral degree in electronics engineering from Tsinghua in 1993, Hu decided to pursue further study in sociology at the University of Colorado in Boulder. During his study in the United States, Hu participated in an academic conference and met with Dr. Lewis Branscomb, a well-known American physicist and chief scientist of IBM, who advised Hu to return to the engineering field. Therefore, he began to work in some top IC design corporations in Silicon Valley. Prior to the founding of Anyka, Hu had worked in Sigma Designs, ESS Technology, and Sykes Enterprises, cumulating rich experience in corporate management, DSP, firmware development, and VLSI design. His time in Silicon Valley also firmed his resolution in devoting himself to the industry.

After obtaining his PhD from the University of Colorado, in 2000, Hu registered Anyka in Silicon Valley. Since its inception, he has served as president and CEO of Anyka Microelectronics Technology Co. Ltd. In 2001, in light of the enormous market and great opportunities, Hu decided to move the headquarters of Anyka to Mainland China, a familiar place and his motherland, and strategically set up offices in Guangzhou, Shenzhen, Beijing, Shanghai, and Hong Kong, with a vision that one day China would play a leading role in the global semiconductor industry.

During the early stage of Anyka, Hu faced two major challenges: lack of money and talents. Since the concept was so new, it was very difficult for Hu to receive the initial funding from investors just based on the idea of AP. After rounds of presentations to Angel Funds, Hu finally obtained his first support from Monet Capital, which decided to finance Anyka based on not only Hu's novel concept but also his rich experience and strong determination to succeed. After this initial success, it was much easier to convince other investors, and a total of US$30 million was raised.

The second bottleneck issue for Hu and Anyka was the lack of a professional team. Since IC design industry had not started up in China until 2000, there was almost no company like Anyka that set its R&D center in Mainland China then. As there were few qualified professionals in microelectronics, Hu made a brave decision to train some fresh graduates with the help of his team from Stanford and Silicon Valley. He recruited graduates from top domestic institutions such as Tsinghua and Peking Universities and taught them from the very basic to advanced concepts. Because of his attractive career plan accompanied by good salary package, Hu was able to build a talented team in a relatively short time.

Hu and his team focused on innovation that they considered as the core competitiveness of the enterprise. To meet the diversified customers' need and growing demand, differentiated integrated circuits and solutions have been created, and those innovative products led Anyka as well as the national semiconductor industry to new stages. Besides multimedia application processor, Hu also helped promote the national 3G developments. In 2004, Anyka and Chongqing Chongyou Information Technology Co. signed a contract for a joint venture focusing on the development of TD-SCDMA, a national 3G standard, and an important step for a self-innovated TD-SCDMA chip in China. Presently, the company holds a leading position in research and implementation of mobile multimedia coding/decoding algorithms and protocols in China and, together with cellular phone makers, network equipment providers, mobile operators, and content providers, is pushing out the next-generation solutions of mobile multimedia products for both Chinese and global markets.

With years of devoted work and a large amount of investment, Hu has led Anyka to become one of the major chip vendors in mainland China. Under his leadership, Anyka has eventually attracted a group of world-class R&D engineers, and grown to become a key leader in mobile multimedia AP, offering open platforms and total solutions for handheld communications and consumer electronics products. Most of its partners and customers are leaders in the mobile communication industry as well. By focusing on integrated circuits and building software platforms of independent intellectual property right, Hu and his team are pushing the age of "Made-in-China" forward into a new era. As Anyka chipsets are widely applied in educational electronics (including learning machine, electronic dictionary, and synchronous reading machine), PMP, mobile TV, smart phone, and other portable products, Hu and his company are able to regain a large share of the market from the giant foreign competitors. For his contribution to the national semiconductor industry, Hu was recognized as one of the top 10 returned scholars in Guangzhou in 2008, and served as a returned scholar consultant for the Guangzhou Municipal Government.

KAWAL GILL

Sources

Entrepreneur (2006), "Anyka selects arm architecture advanced multimedia processor", 1 September, available at: http://www.entrepreneur.com/tradejournals/article/print/149501943.html, (accessed 24 June 2010).

Merritt, R. (2008), "Inside Shenzhen: A tale of two chip entrepreneurs in China's manufacturing hub", *EE Times*, 4 August, available at: http://www.eetimes.com/news/latest/showArticle.jhtml?articleID=207100411 (accessed 24 June 2010).

Tsinghua Entrepreneur and Executive Club (2009), "Norman S.F. Hu", 6 September, available at: http://teec.eefocus.com/article/09-09/346971252198671.html (accessed 24 June 2010).

Hu, Zuliu (Fred Hu 胡祖六 b. 1963)

Former executive director of economic research and managing director of Goldman Sachs Asia, Hu Zuliu is known as a leader in global investment banking, securities, and investment management. Based in Hong Kong, he had been working with the Wall Street investment firm since 1997 before stepping down in 2010, which made him one of the longest serving Chinese executives.

Born and brought up in Miluo County, Hunan Province, Hu at age 17 attended the Henan University of Science and Technology in Luoyang, where he later received his BS in engineering. Subsequently, Hu earned his MA in engineering science from Tsinghua University, and both MA and PhD in economics from Harvard University. From 1991 to 1996, he was employed by the International Monetary Fund (IMF) in Washington, DC, where he engaged in macroeconomic research and policy consulting with member countries such as the People's Republic of China. Based on his professional belief and experience, Hu has been a strong advocate for companies involved in Chinese enterprise to immerse themselves in the international market; such experience, Hu proclaimed, would improve quality, the effectiveness of management, and general business competitiveness for all parties involved. After traveling abroad extensively and having made a name for himself, Hu became an active figure on the international capital market and a major dealmaker in China.

Hu originally joined Goldman Sachs in 1996 as a chief economist for Greater China, before assuming the role of general manager, and eventually, co-head of investment banking and chairman of Greater China, a position that he was named to in 2008. As managing director of Goldman Sachs Asia, Hu oversaw a division with its headquarters in Hong Kong and Tokyo, and additional offices in Beijing, Mumbai, Singapore, Taipei, Seoul, and Shanghai. Hu established himself as an executive who was well connected among business and policy leaders; for example, he was recognized as the primary point person for former US Treasury Secretary Henry Paulson when Paulson was chief executive of Goldman Sachs. Additionally, he was known to have very close relations with Chinese Premier Zhu Rongji. During his tenure with the company, Hu led some of the firm's landmark transactions. He helped manage some of the world's biggest foreign exchange reserves, and established China's largest public equity fund. He has come to be known as one of the top investment executives in China, with his main accomplishment being a $3.78 billion investment in the Industrial and Commercial Bank of China. The bank is now the world's largest lender by market value. Earlier in the decade, Hu was instrumental in helping Bank of Communications, one of China's top banks by assets, sell a 20% stake to HSBC Holdings based in London. He had a reputation for helping spearhead multibillion-dollar landmark deals in China, all of these feats accomplished before reaching the age of 50.

To add to his business success, Hu has been an active scholar and author. In 2003, he co-wrote *The Five Great Myths about China and the World* with Jonathan Anderson. Originally published as a series of intensive research reports for clients of Goldman Sachs, the book explored various myths that pertain to China and the Chinese market. One such myth is the notion of China as an economic juggernaut. The book also provided a detailed analysis of China's external industrial and trade relations, monetary policy, structural price pressures, real exchange rate trends, wage and product trends, and a thorough analysis of China's major impact on the rest of Asia. Besides this title, Hu has published extensively on China and the various aspects of financial market. In addition, he has served as a member on the editorial boards of numerous academic journals, including the *International Economic Review*, and as a columnist for *Caijing*, one of the most influential financial and business magazines in China.

Since 1996, Hu has been affiliated with the National Center for Economic Research (NCER) at Tsinghua University, where he teaches a graduate course in international finance and macroeconomics. Beyond this, he has served on the advisory boards of Shanghai Pudong Development bank, China Huarong Asset Management Company, and the *South China Morning Post*, while advising the Chinese government on financial and pension reforms and various aspects of macroeconomic policies. Furthermore, he has worked closely with Chinese companies such as Bank of China, Bank of Communications, China Development Bank, Industrial and Commercial Bank of China, Ping An, and ZTE, consulting them on strategy, raising capital, and mergers and acquisitions. Because of his close connection with Hong Kong, Hu has been a member of the strategic development committee for the Hong Kong Special Administrative Region and the advisory committee for the Hong Kong Securities and Futures Commission.

Over his professional career in international finance, Hu has established himself as a global leader in investment banking and management. When describing his experience at Goldman Sachs, Hu noted, "I regard Goldman Sachs as a global company. If Goldman Sachs enters in China and sets up Goldman Sachs (China), then I see Goldman Sachs as a Chinese company, because it is supervised by the Chinese government, it pays taxation to Chinese government, and possibly employs excellent laborers from China. So it is a local enterprise. Foreign investments or multinational enterprises are attracted to China, and they would be used by China, then become Chinese enterprises." Hu is one of the most successful returnees in Chinese commerce of recent years, and many attribute his ability to transcend across cultures as a secret to his success, ultimately benefitting Chinese commerce in general.

In 2010, the *Wall Street Journal* reported that Hu had planned to write a book in Chinese that would detail his experiences as head of Goldman Sachs Asia. During the same year, there was also a deliberate effort by the Chinese government to bring together some of the top Chinese professionals in Western firms to work for state-owned organizations. After entertaining a position with the foreign-exchange division of the People's Bank of China as vice-governor or another position with one of China's state-run lenders, Hu instead established a private equity fund of $10 billion that was focused on China. Named Chunhua, reportedly several investors, including Ping An Group, the nation's second largest insurer, have expressed an interest in investing heavily in the fund. Other investors have included China Construction Bank, Temasek Holdings, and Hu's former employer Goldman Sachs. The fund would also seek to attract foreign investors. As a successful returnee, Hu will likely continue to play an active role in the development of Chinese economy in the years to come.

MICHAEL A. MOODIAN, YIFANG ZHANG AND MARGARET MINNIS

Sources

Chen, G. and Shen, S. (2010), "Top Goldman partner Hu to launch China fund", Reuters, 10 March, available at: http://www.reuters.com/article/idUSTOE62A03120100311 (accessed 1 May 2010).

China Daily (2010), "Fred Hu", 16 April, available at: http://www.chinadaily.com.cn/business/2010-04/16/content_9741085.htm (accessed 15 June 2010).

Harvard China (2005), "Speaker profile, Dr. Fred Hu", available at: http://www.harvardchina.org/conference/conf2005/speakers/HuFred.html (accessed 25 May 2010).

McMahon, D. (2010), "Next phase for Fred Hu", *Wall Street Journal*, 31 May, available at: http://blogs.wsj.com/chinarealtime/2010/05/31/next-phase-for-fred-hu/ (accessed 3 June 2010).

McMahon, D., and Gopalan, N. (2010), "Goldman Greater China Chairman to retire", *Wall Street Journal*, 10 March, http://online.wsj.com/article/NA_WSJ_PUB:SB10001424052748704655004575113270527934684.html (accessed 8 June 2010).

Wang, B., and Mao, L. (2010), "Fred Hu takes the private path, to float $10b PE fund", *China Daily*, 21 May, available at: http://chinadaily.cn/cndy/2010-05/21/content_9875236.htm (accessed 17 June 2010).

Huang, Jin (黄劲 b. 1966)

An information technology expert and outstanding overseas returnee, Dr. Huang Jin was well recognized by the Chinese government even before she launched Ambow Education Co., Ltd. in 2000. With the vision to leverage China's cost-effective software talents and great potential in educational market with the advanced American Internet technology, Huang has made Ambow the indisputable leader in providing e-learning technologies and educational services in China. In 2007 and 2008, Ambow Education Group received funding of $54 million and $103 million, respectively, a record for private equity investment in China's education industry despite the challenging economic conditions. In 2009, Ambow Education Group was named in the China Entrepreneur Investment Value List as one of the "Top 50 Enterprises with the Most Investment Potentials."

Huang was born in Lanzhou, Gansu Province in northwestern China, and grew up in a teacher's family. In 1981, while most 15-year-old girls worked on their high school assignments, Huang had already become an exceptional college student majoring in computer science. After earning her BS (1985) and MS (1988) from the elite University of Electronic Science and Technology of China (UESTC) in Chengdu, Huang enrolled into a joint PhD program sponsored by UESTC and University of California in 1988, went to study at Berkley in 1990, and received her doctoral degree a few years later. While in the United States, Huang was determined to leave her mark in Silicon Valley. She was one of the founding engineers at Avant!, an early leader in the development of integrated circuit computer-aided design (CAD) automation software solutions, where Huang was responsible for product design and engineering management. Gradually her titles were expanded to engineer director, senior technological supervisor, and project engineer and manager of the corporation. During her eight-year tenure at AVANT!, she worked on everything from technology development to product creation, marketing, and management, and thus accumulated valuable experience and first-hand knowledge of how to operate a high-technology enterprise. In 1998, Huang resigned from AVANT! and launched Ambow Corporation in Silicon Valley, which focused on Internet-related software design and e-commerce management. Besides running her company, Huang has an easy-going character and personal charisma that made her an activist and a leader in many influential associations in Silicon Valley, which include *Silicon Valley Chinese Overseas Business Association (SCOBA), Chinese Internet Technology Association, and North America Chinese Semiconductor Association (NACSA).*

Being an outstanding Chinese overseas talent and entrepreneur, Huang's success captured the attention of the Consulate General of PR China in Los Angeles. In 1998, she was named the group leader of Silicon Valley Chinese Overseas Entrepreneur Delegation organized by the Chinese consulate, and visited Beijing, Shanghai, Jiangsu, and Liaoning to explore potentials for business development and collaboration. Being recognized as an extraordinary representative of 100,000 Chinese overseas students, Huang was invited in 1999 to attend the official ceremony of the 50th National Day celebration in Beijing, an honor beyond the reach for many. Frequent visits to China provided Huang with opportunities to reassess her business focus, and she believed the country was ready for huge growth in educational market based on new technologies. Therefore, Huang decided to return to China and help reshape the country's fast-growing educational market.

In less than a year, with support from various government agencies, Huang registered her Ambow Software Engineering Co. in Beijing and Suzhou, which specialized in developing long-distance education software. Her company in Beijing was based in Zhongguancun, also known as the Silicon Valley of China. With a vision and commitment to the principle of personalized education, Huang brought back to China not only the know-hows of Silicon Valley but also its creative spirit. Along the way, Ambow has created many "firsts" in the history of Chinese education, and quickly grew to become the leading provider of personalized education and training services in China. In 2000, Ambow pioneered the establishment of China's own e-learning education platform. In the same year, the company became the first founding corporate member of China's National Information Technology Standardization Committee and a founding member of the National e-Learning Standards Committee. In 2003, Ambow was the first in China to be recognized by the Ministry of Education (MOE) for developing and operating a citywide education network linking schools together. Two years later, Ambow became the first in China to establish the training program for IBM's Software Engineer Advanced Career Education (SEACE). In 2006, Ambow launched IT Practical Training System Promotion Project, and started its research institute with Beijing Normal University. During the same year, Ambow's e-learning system was endorsed by MOE as a priority project in China's 11th Five-Year Plan. In 2007, Ambow broke the record of single round of private placement in China's education sector by raising $54 million from Avenue, CID, Cisco, and Macquarie Group, which was only surpassed by yet another record-breaking fundraising of $103 million in 2008, led by new investor Actis and existing investors Avenue and Macquarie Group.

With its highly effective "learning engine" technology and responsive business model, Ambow has consistently set the standards of excellence to which others aspire in the personalized education services in China. A pioneer in the sector, Ambow strives to become a leading technological innovator and trendsetter in the delivery of effective teaching and learning practices. Its learning engine personalizes the way in which a student absorbs information, and a learning tracking system records the student's progress and achievements. The company also provides software and technology solutions, which include i^3-builder application architecture for the deployment of Internet-based cross-platform applications, e-learning platform that provides online education and training solutions, and Learning Management System, a school administration management system for education providers to support online teaching and learning environment for distance learning. In addition, it offers School Online Platform for schools to create online schools for interactive instruction, electronic whiteboard, file sharing, and teacher–student interaction, and an online training platform for companies to conduct online training activities. Furthermore, the company also offers IT job-readiness programs that focus on skills enhancement, training, and internships for students, and distributes vocational and e-learning contents.

Since a good education is much emphasized and appreciated in Chinese culture, the success of Ambow made Huang a frequent consultant to governmental officials during the recent educational policy-making process. She also served as a visiting professor at Beijing Normal University and her alma mater University of Electronic Science and Technology of China. More recently, during the 2009 NetEase Education Summit and Award Ceremony at Peking University, Huang was named among the "Top Ten Leaders in the Education Industry," and the Ambow Education Group was honored as one of the "Top Ten Most Influential Education Companies," "Top Ten Companies in Improving Employment Competitiveness," and "Top Ten Educational Companies with the Most Investment Value." Clearly, these awards are a valid recognition of Huang's vision and Ambow's contribution in ensuring the continual growth and innovation of Chinese education industry.

XIAOQI YU

Sources

Ambow.com (2009), "Ambow named one of 2009 China Entrepreneur Investment Value List's Enterprises with the Most Investment Potential", 9 December, available at: http://www.ambow.com.cn/en/20091209/10001786.shtml (accessed 7 February 2010).

Ambow.com (2009), "Ambow receives four awards from NetEase Education", 26 November, available at: http://www.ambow.com.cn/en/20091126/10001744.shtml (accessed 8 February 2010).

Sohu.com (2009), "中国教育60年60人荣誉获得者: 黄劲", *搜狐教育* ["Huang Jin honored among the Sixty People in Sixty Years of Chinese Education"], 12 December, available at: http://learning.sohu.com/20091212/n268895450.shtml (accessed 8 February 2010).

白瑜，马彦军 (2006), "中关村群英谱: 黄劲—成功背后有大智慧", *华声报* [Bai, Y. and Ma, Y., "Heroes of Zhongguancun: Huang Jin—Wisdom behind the success", Chinaqw.com], 5 April, available at: http://hs.cns.com.cn/news/2006/0405/68/23099.shtml (accessed 8 February 2010).

张艳 (2008), "安博教育CEO黄劲博士：传递成功的女船长", *腾讯教育* [Zhang, Y., "Ambow Education CEO Dr. Huang Jin: A female captain who delivers success", Rednet.cn], 11 November, available at: http://news.rednet.cn/c//2008/11/11/1633494.htm (accessed 7 February 2010).

Ji, Weidong (Richard Ji 季卫东 b. 1968)

Ji Weidong is a managing director of Morgan Stanley and heads China Internet and media investment research for his company. His life is a classic tale of unbridled talent meeting relentless passion, resulting in a meteoric rise within one of the world's most competitive industries.

Ji Weidong was born in Shanghai. His mother was a well-known scriptwriter and his father a manager for a leading shipping company. They were affectionate and supportive parents who held high aspirations for young Ji, instilling in him a loving heart and a passion to achieve greatness. Growing up, he was an intelligent, caring, and self-driven boy who read extensively and enjoyed sharing stories with his friends, who called him "Dr. Ji," a status that would be conferred upon him formally by Harvard University. With his strong convictions about always giving 100%, Ji excelled academically and earned the highly sought-after high school scholarship endowed by one of China's elite educational institutions, Jiaotong University. In his leisure time, Ji shined at his "twin loves." He was the star of his local street basketball competition thanks largely to the athletics culture of his elementary school that, several years later, also raised basketball superstar Yao Ming. Ji's eclectic interests also included the arts, where he became the youngest member of the poetry club of a popular national magazine. Through these nonacademic pursuits, Ji learned valuable lessons about creativity and teamwork that he would continue to apply to his personal life and his career.

In 1986, with a top academic record, Ji was accepted into Shanghai's Fudan University, another of China's prestigious academic institutions. He studied biology, one of the most popular and competitive majors at that time, and found himself teaming up with highly talented classmates who were among the top scorers in the national college entrance exams. "I saw some of the best academic stars in our country during those days," Ji said. "They helped me to broaden my learning scope by miles and to sharpen my way of thinking."

Upon graduating as one of the highest achievers in his class, Ji earned a full scholarship for doctoral studies at Harvard University, a rare accomplishment for a Chinese student at that time and the first in the history of his department. At Harvard, Ji was like a boy at a candy bar, seizing every opportunity to learn from peers, alumni, and mentors. With his characteristic enthusiasm and refusal to rest on his laurels, Ji was soon elected vice president of the Harvard Chinese Students and Scholars Association. In that capacity he and his colleagues organized a forum entitled "The Path to Success" and succeeded in attracting elite Chinese leaders as keynote speakers. The forum provided valuable insights into wide-ranging business topics and, as Ji himself later noted, "opened my eyes to the importance of growing a powerful business network."

In the meantime, Ji maintained his record of outstanding academic performance under the guidance of his supervisor Dr. Judah Folkman, a renowned scholar and a member of the US National Academy of Sciences, who recognized Ji's creativity and ambition. While the field of medical sciences tended toward a culture of secrecy, Folkman was open, generous, and encouraging. He impressed upon Ji the importance of matching one's passion with one's strengths when choosing a career.

In 1996, upon graduating from Harvard with his Doctor of Science degree, Ji joined a leading pharmaceuticals company as a research scientist. While it was a decent job with a good salary, it quickly became apparent to him that it would never provide the passion that he was seeking. It was at this time that Ji co-founded the North American Chinese Association of Science and Technology, then one of the largest Chinese professional organizations in the United States. He organized a successful program called "Future China" and invited Chinese leaders in many fields to discuss the outlook and opportunities in China. As a result, he was also elected a member of the All-China Youth Federation, an elite organization that hosts some of the most talented young Chinese in China and from overseas. These valuable networking activities, with influential people across many walks of life, placed Ji on a steep learning curve and convinced him of the unprecedented potential of the China market.

Meanwhile, Ji began to take a serious interest in personal investment and became fascinated by the dynamics of the stock market. It was the late 1990s and the Internet was booming. In 1999 alone, the NASDAQ index almost doubled. In his first year as a stock market investor, he achieved a sizeable return outperforming most mutual funds in the United States. Ji often recounted the experience saying that he felt like an "investment genius" during that period. But then, the Internet bubble burst and his previously inflated "paper" wealth dissipated. This humbling experience reminded him that he still had much to learn about financial markets. However, he knew that he had found his passion. In 2001, he quit his research job in the pharmaceuticals company and enrolled in the elite MBA program at Wharton Business School.

Ji noted that most of the world's renowned investors had a first-class education. Taking people like Warren Buffett, George Soros, Peter Lynch, and John Templeton as his role models, he determined to become a lifetime student of investment. Possessing a photographic memory, he was a voracious reader in two languages; however, his appetite exceeded even his huge capacity for absorbing knowledge. His apartment was totally dominated by his books, leading to his friends' teasing remarks that he was living in a library. Ji read hundreds of books on the strategies of acknowledged investment gurus and the building of the world's great corporations. Accordingly, Warren Buffett became his biggest hero and "virtual mentor." As Ji explained it, "Every great investor has his unique style. Buffett's approach suits me the best."

For his outstanding academic achievements, Ji was added to Wharton's Director's List and was awarded the Meyer Scholarship. To gain valuable experience during summer breaks, he pursued internships in two investment banks: JP Morgan in Hong Kong and UBS in New York. This gave him the opportunity to evaluate and compare the risks and rewards of working in China and the United States, and helped him to consolidate his decision to return to China once he completed his studies. "I love the people, the culture and the 'home court' advantages that I have in China. By tapping into the world's most robust emerging economy, I knew the odds would always be in my favor."

Upon graduation in 2003, Ji embarked upon his investment-banking career, joining Goldman Sachs Hong Kong as a security analyst covering the Internet and media sectors. It was a time of great turmoil within the market. Alarm surrounding the SARS epidemic was at its peak and Hong Kong was at the epicenter. Furthermore, the effect on Internet stocks was compounded by lingering negative sentiment attached to the sector's crash just two years earlier. At that time, only three Chinese Internet companies were listed and they all traded in the single-digit range. However, Ji remained unflustered. Like many of the great investors whom he had studied so intensely, he had a keenly honed contrarian mindset. While others panicked, he foresaw enormous opportunity. Given his outlook that the Chinese Internet market promised a robust future for investors, the stocks were at bargain basement prices and represented extraordinary value. Soon after, Ji's success was widely recognized and he became known on Wall Street as a strong advocate for the Chinese Internet industry.

Ji believed that he had two distinct advantages in the investment industry: his nontraditional background, which gave him an additional and often unique perspective on the dynamics of the market, and his wide and influential network of investors and entrepreneurs that he had begun developing from as early as his college years. In less than two years with Goldman Sachs, Ji produced innovative investment analyses of many leading media and Internet companies including Sina, Sohu, NetEase, and Phoenix TV. He also played a significant role in high-profile IPOs such as Shanda and Tencent, which were dominant in online communities and gaming industry in China and subsequently achieved multifold price increases.

Ji's success in persuading investors of the underlying value of these companies amid market skepticism distinguished him as one of Goldman Sachs' most highly regarded young analysts. With his reputation growing rapidly, it was no surprise that he received a call from the "Queen of the Net" herself. Mary Meeker, Morgan Stanley's managing director and the world's most renowned and respected Internet analyst, offered Ji a world-class platform for his burgeoning career. In April 2005, he joined Morgan Stanley as its vice president overseeing Chinese media and Internet investment research. As he later acknowledged, "I've been incredibly fortunate to have had two superstar mentors in my career. Both Ms. Meeker and Dr. Folkman inspired me with their vision and their passion."

Under Ji's leadership, Morgan Stanley became a thought leader in China's Internet and media sectors. Within a short period, he had produced comprehensive and groundbreaking reports on sectors such as entertainment, sports, advertising, and the Internet. Since 2005, as part of his comprehensive investigations, Ji has visited more than 1000 Internet, media, and consumer companies. He has also led many high-profile IPOs including Alibaba, China's leading online business-to-business platform; Perfect World, a leading online game developer; MakeMyTrip, the dominant online travel service player in India; and DangDang, the No. 1 online bookstore in China. In 2008, Ji's efforts were recognized with his promotion to managing director of Morgan Stanley. In just five years, he had advanced from the position of an entry-level analyst to a regional sector leader, a rare merit in one of the world's most competitive industries.

Ji's investment philosophy was based on a belief that he had to be the "virtual CEO" of the companies he tracked, paying due regard to issues such as competitive strategies, product pipelines, branding initiatives, and cost minimization. "By taking this 'insider' perspective, I manage to focus more on the company value instead of the market 'noise.'" Recognizing that modern financial theory was based on the Western conditions and Western values, Ji had localized his strategy to fit China's robust and volatile market. He believes in betting on the "All-star" companies, which have first-class business models plus first-class management teams, hopefully in first-class industries. "By owning these 'All-star' companies, you will have the Michael Jordan, Yao Ming and Tiger Woods of the business world working for you."

Ji Weidong is regarded internationally as a leading investment expert in China's media and entertainment industries and has been listed among the top investment analysts by *Institutional Investor* and *Greenwich Survey*. He was named "the best investment bank analyst in the new economy" by *iResearch*, while the *Financial Times* lauded him as the "No. 1 stock picker in software and IT services in Pan-Asia." His views are well known through hundreds of articles published in the world's leading financial press and media interviews.

Ji Weidong's enthusiasm and dedication to his work are legendary. Clearly, the words of his Harvard mentor continue to light his path: "only through work about which you are passionate can you develop a rewarding career and a happy life."

TERENCE R. EGAN

Sources

Ji, W.D. (2010), "Interview with Terence Egan", 21 June.

王红茹 (2007), "季卫东: 笑傲数字江湖, *资本推手: 10位海归投资银行家* (王辉耀主编), 中国发展出版社, 北京 [Wang, H.Y., "Ji Weidong: Proudly smiling at the digital world", in Wang, H.Y. (ed.), *Capital Movers and Shakers: Ten Overseas Returnees in Investment Banking*, China Development Press, Beijing], pp. 182–206.

Jiang, Ruxiang (姜汝祥 b. 1965)

Known as the pioneer of business execution study in China, Jiang Ruxiang is the CEO of Zion Management Consulting Ltd. He has been praised as a brilliant, practice-oriented expert in strategic consulting circle by many top business leaders including Liu Chuanzhi of Lenovo Group, Li Dongsheng of TCL, and Wang Shi of China Vanke. Committed to the formalization, internationalization, and sustainability of Chinese business development, Jiang's company has long been recognized as the first brand in executive management for Chinese companies and has been nicknamed the BMW of China's consulting business, and his lectures have inspired and enlightened more than 2000 managers nationwide. Jiang is a best-selling author and his books are warmly received; Galanz even adopts the policy of one copy for each of its managers in China.

Jiang was born in 1965 in a small town in Guizhou Province, southwestern China. By doing part-time job to finance his schooling, he obtained his BS in mechanical engineering from Luoyang Institute of Technology, and was later admitted to the Capital University of Economics and Businesses in Beijing. After receiving his master's degree in economics there, Jiang went to study economic sociology at

Peking University. Graduating in 1993 with his PhD, he worked for the Academy of Macroeconomic Research (AMR), a subsidiary of State Planning Commission until 1997. Afterward he was a strategic manager at Motorola for the next three years.

In early 2000, Jiang gave up his well-paid job and cozy life and went to the Business School of Columbia University to conduct research on multinationals' competitive advantages. In a small room in New York where Jiang lived, with little chance to enjoy sunshine, he experienced some profound awakening and established his personal mission there: on the basis of respecting diversities, to be a broad-minded man with a win-win mentality, and at the same time, encouraging everyone to fight for his or her own dreams. After returning to China in May 2000, Jiang first worked at the Executive Education Center of Guanghua School of Management, Peking University. A year later, he established Zion Management Consulting Ltd. Since then, Jiang and his Zion have concentrated on providing consultations and solutions on strategic planning and management for all kinds of businesses. With his consistent effort, Zion has gradually become one of the leading consulting companies in China.

The year 2004 was a period of great leap forward for Zion. The company beat some well-known international competitors such as McKinsey and Roland Berger Strategy Consultants by winning the contract of the Medium and Long-term Development Planning with China Vanke. Over the past nine years, Zion has successfully provided various consulting services to many first-class companies in China, which include TCL, Bosideng, and Softto, and about 2000 Chinese growing companies have witnessed Zion's remarkable achievements.

With years of studies and researches, Jiang has formed his own system of management principles. The strategic thinking that he actively promotes is that at the top level of execution, operational strategy should be in accordance with a wolf principle, which focuses on powerful leadership; at the medium level, it should be implemented by using monkey management principle; and at the bottom level, a mirror thinking, which means that service consciousness should be enhanced. Moreover, Jiang is also a modern intellectual with great social responsibilities, studying and commenting on various social issues from his distinct professional perspectives. He is the columnist for both Chinese and American mainstream media such as *Fortune*, *Fast Company*, *Economic Observer*, *China Business,* and *Global Entrepreneur*. In 2004, when the worship of Jack Welch in China caused a sensation, Jiang contended that the legend was always inspiring and encouraging. However, overstating the power of hero would likely cover up the actual motives that push the progress behind the scenes. In his view, Welch has been overrated to a point that few can observe GE's profound institutional organization and culture that supported Welch's success. As a result, Jiang advocated that more emphases should be placed on the establishment of long-term and stable mechanism. Only in this way can misreading be avoided.

Jiang is an accomplished author with numerous influential books; among them is *The Gap*. Through a contrast and comparison of top Chinese businesses and the world-class companies, including Haier versus GE, Lenovo versus Dell, Huawei versus Cisco, Glanz versus Wal-Mart, Jiang emphasized the importance of sustainable development for Chinese businesses, and designed a 4C model for strategic planning:

C1 stands for Convergence, which means establishing visions and core values for businesses; C2 stands for Coordination, which solves the issues of arranging businesses at different levels; C3 stands for Core business, the determinants of relative competition advantages; and C4 stands for Core competence, the determinants of sustainable competition advantages.

At the beginning of 2010, in his New Year's greetings to all Zion employees, Jiang declared, "we are not merely acting for ourselves, but also representing the most intellectuals in our society. We should shoulder the missions and responsibilities not only for ourselves, but also for this era." At the end of his letter, to express the attitude they should adopt toward the coming decades, he quoted the famous words from *I Ching*: "As heaven maintains vigor through movements, a gentleman should constantly strive for self-perfection; as earth's condition is receptive devotion, a gentleman should hold the outer world with broad mind." Evidently, Jiang and his Zion team are writing their own *Analects* of modern business management.

YUPING DU

Sources

姜汝祥 (2003), *差距*, 机械工业出版社, 北京 [Jiang R., *The Gap*, China Machine Press, Beijing], pp. 12.

商业周刊 (2007), "建立品牌而不是知名度: 专访姜汝祥教授", ["Establishing brand, not popularity: Exclusive interview with Professor Jiang Ruxiang", *Business Weekly*], December, pp. 61.

尹生 (2004), "姜汝祥访谈: 韦尔奇不是神", *公司* [Yin, S., "Welch is not omniscience: Interview with Jiang Ruxiang", *Company*], August, pp. 38–39.

张永乐 (2007), "走近华为: 专访姜汝祥教授", *中国信息界* [Zhang, Y., "A study of Huawei: Exclusive interview with Professor Jiang Ruxiang", *Chinese Information Times*], February, pp. 60–63.

招商周刊 (2004), "姜汝祥: 为什么只有偏执狂才能生存" ["Jiang Ruxiang: Why only paranoid can survive?", *Merchants Weekly*], No.18–19, pp. 12.

中国新时代 (2004), "跨国公司本地化逆潮: 专访北京锡恩顾问总经理姜汝祥" ["The Localization of multinationals in China: Exclusive interview with Zion CEO Jiang Ruxiang", *China New Time*] July, pp. 44–45.

Jing, Muhan (景慕寒 b. 1973)

Jing Muhan is the current CEO of Mapbar.com, the largest online map provider in China with millions of Internet and cell phone users and over 70% market share. Founded in 2004, Mapbar is an online map application that combines telecommunication, GIS (geographic information system), and web technology covering over 2 million kilometers of roadways throughout China.

Graduating from Xian Jiaotong University in 1995, Jing then studied abroad at the University of San Francisco, where he received his Master of Business Administration and Master of Science in Computer Science. After graduation, he worked on research and application of electronic map and information systems in the Silicon Valley, California. While living in the United States, Jing and his friend Dai Donghai became accustomed to having detailed maps as part of everyday normal life routine, and Dai later became Jing's business partner in founding the Mapbar a few years later. In an interview Jing recalled, "In the U.S., whenever we take a trip, even if you know the place, you always print out a map that tells you which streets to take, and then you would drive according to that route instruction" (Oushe, 2009). In other words, accurate maps were taken for granted. Upon returning to China in 2002, Jing and his friend Dai were shocked to find out how little and unreliable the local maps were. Equally unreliable at the time was the use of the Internet for searching information or business locations in China. Initially frustrated, Jing sensed the opportunity in combining powerful search engine technologies with online map services, which would provide the growing China Internet users with fast, convenient, and reliable services. The result was the formation of Mapbar in 2003.

Mapbar is competing in one of the hottest and untapped markets in the online search sector–map search, which Jing believes has become the new focal point in the global search market. By 2004, website giants such as Yahoo, Microsoft, and Google had launched their new map search services, while the Chinese portal companies had also tapped into the emerging Chinese map search market. For example, China portal giant Sohu merged with Go2Map, a domestic professional map service company, to enter the market. The market was further complicated by the fact that many popular local sites such as Netease, QQ, and Elong had also been providing their own mapping solutions to their users; at the same time, these sites were themselves customers of Mapbar. While both global and local players were busy exploring the new markets, Mapbar started to emerge and differentiate from the others. Jing's vision for Mapbar was to set it apart by combining map data, search engine, and GIS technology to launch the most practical map search solution. For instance, if a user wants to search for all Sichuan restaurants in the Zhongguancun area of Beijing, he or she could simply click on Zhongguancun Sichuan dish in Mapbar to locate all necessary information. Mapbar also allows map search by key information such as a street number or telephone number, and provides detailed location of destination indicating public transportation system and driving routes. To further expand its market share, Jing has also set his eyes on the growing mobile market by extending Mapbar services to mobile telephones. As a result, Mapbar has daily online visits of more than 50 million hits, propelling the company to become the leading map search company in China within a few years.

Under Jing's leadership, Mapbar focuses on providing services to three core groups of users: first, Internet users who are often referred to as "netizens," those who will use the map search service for general daily needs such as locating a specific destination or route planning. For them, Mapbar has taken an open source and organic approach in building up of and keeping current its database information through its users—such as metro bus daily routes information. For the second group of enterprise customers, Mapbar provides map flag products, wireless satellite navigation for cars, and public transportation information to mobile phone users. Industrial clients will likely use GIS mapping technology to explore potentials in natural resources such as oil, coal, and so on. While this group of clients does not use this technology in as large a volume as do the consumer users for Mapbar, it does represent a lucrative business segment.

Jing believes Mapbar's business strategy and development should be based on a direct and distribution system. At present, Mapbar has around 500 sales agents and distributors in China. Mapbar's sales team is responsible for not only selling its products but also building up the distribution system. Therefore, the marketing team has to recruit and train new qualified local distributors. So far, this strategy of expanding the business via multiple distribution layers has proven to be a successful approach in China for a couple of reasons. First, China represents a vast geographic mass complicated by different cultures and languages. In order to expand the business to beyond the first-tiered cities, Mapbar chooses to leverage a network system of distributors. Second, Mapbar instituted a 50/50 profit sharing plan with its distributors, which has established a solid business relationship and connections with agents and distributors. This partnership has also helped Mapbar receive accurate information to populate its mapping data at a lower cost, hence setting Mapbar apart from its competitors, most notably Google. Mapbar currently provides its information and data to nearly 1000 partner sites and from there to the end users; in addition, it is integrated with about 3500 local business portal sites and industrial customers to form the largest online mapping platform in China. The success of Mapbar is evident by the US$10 million investment from IDG in 2005.

In this new and highly competitive industry, companies that can provide the fastest and most accurate information with value-added services will prevail as the market leader. Map search has undoubtedly become an indispensable tool for China's netizens who want to find information or need to conduct business in an unfamiliar area. Under Jing's vision and leadership, Mapbar has gained a 74% market share in China. By making customized map solution to serve the local special needs such as Chinese Spring Festival holiday travel map, 2008 Beijing Olympics transportation map, and detailed subway map, Mapbar has touched the lives of many ordinary Chinese people, and will likely continue to play an important role in the information age of the twenty-first century.

GEORGE L. KUAN

Sources

Oushe.com (2009), "景慕寒生平简介", *偶社* [Brief biography of Jiang Muhan], 11 January, available at: http://www.oushe.cn/intro/33718 (accessed 14 May 2010).

Sina.com (2007), "Mapbar图吧CEO景慕寒 ：培养用户是当务之急" [Mapbar CEO: It is imperative to have a user base], 2 February, available at: http://tech.sina.com.cn/i/2007-02-02/17501367808.shtml (accessed 10 May 2010).
高永钰 (2007), "Mapbar图吧的移动 '指南针' " [Gao, Y., "The mobile 'compass' of Mapbar"], 11 April, available at: http://eeo.com.cn/industry/it_telecomm/2007/04/11/54717.html (accessed 11 May 2010).

Ju, Tina (Ru Linqi, 汝林琪 b. 1969)

Tina Ju is one of the leading venture capital investors in China. A founding and managing partner at Kleiner, Perkins, Caufield and Byers (KPCB) China, as well as managing director and founder of TDF (Templeton Dragon Fund) Capital, Ju has played a central role in coordinating more than 20 investments since 2000, backing some of China's most successful entrepreneurs and enterprises—Alibaba, Baidu, Cgen, China Netcom, Focus Media, and Hurray being a few examples. Known for her determination, vision, and extraordinary work ethic, Ju has been recognized as one of the Top Ten Active Venture Capitalists by Zero2IPO (2005), one of China's Top 50 Best Venture Capitalists by *Forbes* China (from 2006 to 2009), Best Private Equity Investor by *China Business News* (2007), and Best Venture Capital Investor by *China Business News* (2008).

At the age of 12, Ju immigrated to the United States from Taiwan with her parents, who were originally from Qingdao, Shandong Province of mainland China. Always interested in learning, she pursued her undergraduate degree from the University of California at Berkeley, where she earned a BS in industrial engineering and operations research, gaining expertise in mechanical and electrical engineering. Afterward, she worked for one year as an industrial engineer for IBM. Ju originally chose engineering because many prominent Chinese at the time had backgrounds in this field. During her tenure at IBM, however, she found herself thinking more and more about a career in business and finance. Her first introduction to investment banking was through a job at Goldman Sachs from 1987 to 1990; she began in the real estate investment banking division, and then transitioned to the investment financing of businesses of many different sectors—consumer goods, technology, and transportation, among others. Ju then completed an MBA at Harvard Business School, and after graduating in 1992, immediately moved to New York to work for JP Morgan in the investment banking division.

Soon after, she accepted a job with more responsibility at Merrill Lynch. Ju worked on Wall Street from 1993 to 1995 and then moved to Hong Kong as the co-head of Merrill Lynch Hong Kong's corporate finance execution group. In 1997, Ju initiated Merrill Lynch's Asia investment banking efforts, serving as the head of Asia Technology. She successfully led more than 15 transaction teams at Merrill Lynch, altogether raising more than US$3 billion in capital from the private equity market. In 1998, Ju transitioned to a job at Deutsche Bank, where she served as a director and head of the Technology, Media and Telecommunications (TMT) and Transport sector. In this position, she raised capital for Asian technology and transport companies.

Ju's experiences in investment banking at Deutsche Bank, Merrill Lynch, and Goldman Sachs were very demanding; she regularly worked up to 90 hours per week. Yet these efforts prepared her for what lay ahead: a successful career as a venture capitalist. In the fall of 1999, while briefly serving as the CFO/COO at Privylink, a portfolio company of TDF, Ju noticed an opportunity emerging at Venture TDF. She joined TDF in Shanghai as managing director and co-founder of Venture TDF China Fund, bringing extensive experience with capital markets, financial restructuring, and strategic advisory services across a broad range of industries. In October of 2000, TDF China Fund was established to actively manage US$33 million of capital. Ju had a vision: to find worthy investments in Chinese consumer, media, and technology entrepreneurs in the early to expansion stage of their companies. While this may seem similar to any venture capital fund, TDF China Fund is unique because it is locally based and independent, connecting local talent to global resources.

For Ju, venture capital is a service business and so relationship networks are very important, especially within the Chinese market. Known for being unhurried, methodical, and convincing, she has cultivated an impressive network of contacts within the Chinese business community, which has helped her gain a reputation of being well tuned into the pulse of China's business environment. In selecting investment projects, Ju has supported IPOs as well as mergers and acquisitions; in either case, she commits to working with entrepreneurs every step of the way. She does think, however, that "true venture capitalists pride themselves on finding the company early, having significant ownership and being a partner from zero all the way to IPO" (*China Economic Review*, 2008). Her highly successful investments in Alibaba (Chinese web auctioneer), Focus (Digital Media Group), and Baidu (Internet search firm) won widespread acclaim—both for TDF and for Ju herself. In Baidu's first day of trading, its stock nearly quadrupled!

These successes in the early 2000s enabled Ju to found TDF Capital China in 2005, with an even larger stock of capital—supported by global blue chip investors and leading university endowments. Her continued success brought an amazing opportunity. In the mid-2000s, Silicon Valley–based KPCB—considered by many to be the world's top venture capital firm—decided to do something it had never done before: open an office outside the United States. KPCB selected China for this expansion, in order to capitalize on the opportunities presented by emerging markets. While KPCB had plenty of expertise on venture capital operations, it did not have insider knowledge of China's business world. This was one of TDF's strengths, so in 2007 an alliance between TDF Capital and KPCB was formed, and KPCB China opened offices in Beijing and Shanghai. Still based in Shanghai, Ju became one of five partners establishing a US$360 million China Fund for KPCB to invest in high-growth industries.

While KPCB China still invests in Internet, media, wireless, health, and green technologies, "greentech" or "cleantech" has been a major focus of late. According to Ju, KPCB China likes "to bet on early-stage companies with big innovation, either with technology risk or business model risk" (*China Economic Review*, 2008); given the current global challenges of urbanization and climate change, greentech could be the largest economic opportunity of the 21st century. In 2007, KPCB forged an alliance with Al Gore, former US vice president and current chairperson of Generation Investment Management, in order to expand the global reach of KPCB in these areas—and help Chinese entrepreneurs change the world.

Apart from her considerable duties at KPCB China and TDF Capital Fund, Ju serves on the Board of Directors for five portfolio companies in the TDF China Fund—including Alibaba and Hurray. She also has many leadership roles within China; currently, she is the chairperson for Women in Leadership (the premier organization for female entrepreneurs and venture capitalists in China), vice president of the Shanghai Venture Capital Association, and governor of the China Venture Capital Association. This demonstrates her interest in cultivating relationship networks of people with similar interests. Yet her passion for venture capital does not stop there; Ju likes to communicate the importance and relevance of venture capital to business audiences at all levels. Hence, she is a frequent speaker at conferences around the world.

There is no doubt that Ju's dedication and skill have led to the flourishing of many new Chinese companies over the last decade. The business world is certainly noticing; in 2008, *Business Watch Magazine* named Ju one of China's 25 most powerful women in business. With her prolific achievements, does she plan to slow down? Well, Ju says it best: "I hope to have more normal working hours, but not now. Because there are so many investment opportunities in China" (*CEO*, 2007).

TONIA WARNECKE

Sources

Business Watch Magazine (2008), "The 25 most powerful women in business", 20 March.

CEO (2007), "凯鹏华盈汝林琪: 中国主流VC界最早女掌门" [Tina Ju of KPCB China: The lady boss of Chinese mainstream venture capital market], 24 July, available at: http://capital.cyzone.cn/article/46120/ (accessed 12 June 2010).

China Economic Review (2008), "Kleiner comes to China", 1 May, available at: http://www.chinaeconomicreview.com/industry-focus/in-the-magazine/article/2008-05-01/Kleiner_comes_to_China.html (accessed 12 June 2010).

Ju, T. (2004), "The opportunities and challenges of a foreign VC investing in China", available at: http://www.slideshare.net/p2045i/vcs-in-china (accessed 10 June 2010).

Marshall, M. (2007), "Kleiner Perkins repents – goes to China with $360M fund", *Venture Beat*, 23 April, available at: http://venturebeat.com/2007/04/23/kleiner-perkins-repents-goes-to-china-with-360m-fund/ (accessed 12 June 2010).

TDF Capital (2005), "Introduction", available at: http://www.tdfcapital.com/about.php (accessed 8 June 2010).

US-China Green Energy Council (2010), "Ju, Tina", available at: http://ucgef.org/en/bio/tina-ju (accessed 8 June 2010).

Kuang, Ziping (Duane Kuang 邝子平 b. 1963)

As the previous chief strategic investment officer of Intel and the current managing director of Qiming Venture Capital, Kuang Ziping is a brilliant star in China's emerging venture capital industry; and as an overseas returnee, Kuang has a touching and amazing story about pursuing his ambitious dream over the past several decades.

In his childhood, Kuang dropped from school and was boarded in his relatives' family due to the impact of the Chinese Cultural Revolution. Shortly after resuming his high school in 1979, an overseas friend of Kuang's family persuaded Kuang's father to send Kuang to the United States to study. In 1980, Kuang moved to California and began his overseas life at age 17, without knowing any English words. Right after he settled down in San Francisco, Kuang went to local school studying English while working part-time, insisting on not relying on others. He rented a 20-m^2 apartment in San Francisco's Chinatown with a Chinese roommate Xin Guan, who later became Kuang's close friend in Shanghai's VC industry. Kuang studied English from scratch in a community college and worked as a waiter and bus boy to support his study at the same time. In his spare time, Kuang read martial arts novels but had no time to watch movies or enjoy other forms of entertainment.

After his enrollment into the University of San Francisco, Kuang still worked part-time to support himself. It was the time when the high-tech industry was booming, which was led by semiconductor, computer, and software sectors, and the computer science major was the hottest career choice among college students, as its graduates were in high demand on the job market with top compensations. Naturally, Kuang took computer science as his major, but he had to change three universities to finish his undergraduate degree. In 1986, with an outstanding academic record and strong recommendation from his professors, Kuang entered the elite Stanford University to pursue his graduate degree. His teaching assistantship also provided him with tuition waivers and monthly stipends, which released him from the high pressures of making a living while pursuing graduate study. The positive environment, the stimulating atmosphere, and the support of faculty and fellow students quickly helped Kuang build up his self-confidence. At Stanford, Kuang made his first circle of friends, many of them later returned to China and established their own businesses; they became Kuang's friends both in work and in life when Kuang started his business in China.

Upon graduating from Stanford in 1988, Kuang first joined 3Com Corporation as a computer engineer in charge of software development. After three years at 3Com, Kuang was promoted to the position of senior software engineer and became the key leader in his department. In 1990, when a senior vice president at 3Com was recruited to become CEO of Kalpana Co. in Silicon Valley, he took several team members including Kuang to Kalpana, where Kuang was among the first batch of professional managers and engineers outside the entrepreneurial team and the only software engineer in the new company. With the rapid development of the new venture, Kuang was soon promoted to the software manager position, leading 30 people. Two years later, Kalpana encountered some technical problems with its new products, and after some restructuring and streamlining, the company was acquired by Cisco in

1994. Despite the setback, this experience gave Kuang a valuable lesson on almost every aspect of a new venture: how to manage, how to deal with corporate crisis, and the importance of leadership and taking responsibilities.

Kuang established his second friend circle in life during the three years at Kalpana, such as Charlie Giancarlo, the chief development officer at Cisco. From 1991 to 1994, while working for Kalpana, Kuang attended a part-time MBA program at UC Berkeley, and completed his thesis titled "Privatization of State-Owned Enterprises in China." While writing his thesis, he paid much attention to China's development and visited the country regularly. After years of experience from software to hardware, from R&D to marketing, from technology development to overall management, Kuang had become versatile in business operation. Having lived in the United States for more than 15 years, Kuang began to think about developing his career path back in China, as the emergence of IT industry in China had created many unparalleled opportunities that could not be obtained in United States. Just then a friend who was leading Cisco's Hong Kong office introduced Kuang to the company.

After Cisco acquired Kalpana, Kuang became the system engineer in the sales department at Cisco Hong Kong. The acquisition by Cisco was a great opportunity for Kuang, as he was very familiar with Ethernet Switches that was Cisco's main target product. Therefore, Kuang took the responsibility of developing Asian markets, and was soon promoted to market manager of the Asia-Pacific region, in charge of the Ethernet Switches business of the whole Asia-Pacific market. However, Kuang was still eager to work in the mainland. In June 1995, Kuang got a chance to move to Guangzhou to lead Cisco's South China office there. Two years later, Kuang was assigned to the Beijing office, which gave him a bigger platform for his career development. During the five years working at Cisco, Kuang had made many Chinese friends who were all IT elites and helped Kuang a great deal.

At the end of 1999, Kuang joined the Intel Capital Division, and was in charge of investments in Asia's telecommunications industry, and later the whole Greater China region. Intel Capital was then one of the few VCs investing in early-stage ventures in China. Under Kuang's leadership, Intel Capital had made successful investments in AsiaInfo, UT Starcom, Sohu, TechFaith, ChinaCast, Legend, Hoi Fai, etc., and had established close cooperative relationship with those companies. Even in the trough of the IT industry during 2000–2002, Kuang implemented the smooth investment strategy by investing in six to eight projects, which won him the "Best Investor of the Year" award in 2001 and 2002. From 1999 to 2005, Kuang had led his team to invest in more than 40 Chinese companies, with more than 10 listed, merged or acquired.

Kuang believes that seizing market opportunities is very important for VC investors. Since Intel Capital is the earliest and biggest institute in China's VC industry, it is often called the "Whampoa Military Academy of China's venture capital industry." Although the company has cultivated many outstanding talents for China's venture capitals, Kuang felt that there were many defects in Intel Capital's later-stage development. Moreover, Kuang was not satisfactory with only being observers of his invested ventures. He was more inclined to make major decisions at those ventures' boards, which he believed could professionalize the new venture and serve them better. Meeting with his old friend Gary Rieschel, former managing director and founder of Softbank America's VC fund Mobius, had convinced Kuang that running his own business was the best choice. Hence, Kuang left Intel Capital and decided to set up his own VC fund along with his friend so that he could implement his own investment strategies at discretion. Qiming Venture Capital was therefore established, and its first funding of 200 million was raised within three months, which included some prestigious institutional investors such as Princeton Fund and Sloan Fund. The name Qiming was thought out by Kuang at the Boston Airport, which means "starting and bright."

The investment style of Qiming was basically long-term investing, instead of short-term following suit. Qiming also built alliance with the famous US VC fund Ignition: while Ignition focused on the US market, Qiming focused solely on the Chinese market. This division allowed them to share mutual demands and partners. At Qiming, Kuang set three levels of promotion channel: managing director, partner, and analyst, and everyone had equal opportunity. In the first year of Qiming's operation, Kuang paid great attention to team building, and conducted in-depth research in several industries and made cautious investments. By the end of 2006, Qiming had established a team of more than 10 members, and finished investments in seven projects, four of which were in the technology, media, and telecommunications (TMT) field, and another three were in the medical industries. Entering 2007, Kuang began to sense the increasing market competition, and had enlarged the amount of investment. The major investment fields were still concentrated in TMT and medical industries in the early stage, but Qiming also selectively invested in a few mature projects and in other industries. By October 2007, Qiming had invested in 13 ventures within 20 months, ranging from the smallest investment of less than US$1 million as an eagle investor to the largest single investment of over US$10 million, with the average investment on each venture about US$5 million. Kuang himself was sitting on the board of directors for four companies including Fangtek Technology, 2duche. Com, Shanghai Gamma Star, and Lensun.

Kuang summarized that the most important element of being a successful VC investor in China was diligence. "When you work abroad, many things could be finished just in office because people around you are all professional experts in the field. However, in China, you have to go out to contact with people directly to secure your projects," Kuang said, "therefore you have to like what you are doing, and like those who you are contacting with." Kuang feels very happy and satisfactory about his current work-life style, and his impact is clearly felt in China's fast growing venture capital industry.

HAO LIANG AND SUNNY LI SUN

Sources

Business Wire (2006), "Top Chinese investors and Ignition announce Qiming Venture Partners: Fresh approach and on-the-ground commitment to investing in China", available at: http://www.thefreelibrary.Com/Top+Chinese+Investors+and+Ignition+Announce+Qiming+Venture+Partners%3B...-a0142078828 (accessed June 11, 2010).

Chinaventurenews.Com (2006), "Qiming Fund signifies new day for partners", available at: http://www.chinaventurenews.Com/50226711/qiming_fund_signifies_new_day_for_partners.php (accessed 11 June 2010).

Nmgmzbwg.Com.cn (2010), "Qiming venture capitalists Kuang Ziping: Not because of undertaking board change investment strategy", available at: http://www.nmgmzbwg.Com.cn/archives/2428 (accessed 11 June 2010).

邢学军 (2007), "邝子平: 投资人生三级跳", *财富裂变: 10位海归风险投资翘楚* (王辉耀主编), 中国发展出版社, 北京 [Xing, X, "Kuang Ziping: A life of Triple jump in investment", in Wang, H. (ed.), *Wealth Creation: Ten Overseas Returnees in Venture Capital Investment*, China Development Press, Beijing], pp. 62–80.

Lee, Kai-Fu (Li, Kaifu 李开复 b. 1961)

When asking any Chinese youth, who are the most admirable people in the IT field, Kaifu Lee's name is definitely on the list. Former head of the Microsoft Research Division, Lee later became the corporate vice president of Google and the president of Google Greater China. As an expert in speech recognition, an influential leader in computer science, and an idol for millions of young students, Lee has played a key role in the development of information technology industry in China over the recent years. From an immigrant student to an accomplished computer scientist, from an academic to a successful entrepreneur, his legendary experiences have inspired many young students. Lee knows that making a difference is the meaning of one's life, and he tries his best to make the huge difference in his life, while changing the world along the way.

Lee was born in Taiwan in 1961. At age 12, he immigrated to the United States along with his family and attended high school in Oak Ridge, Tennessee; there he started his first business – making napkin rings with his friends. Because all customers were their parents, so they made some money easily. A year later, Lee wanted to do it again, with real customers. This time he seized the opportunity when the school lunch time was reduced from 70 to 50 minutes, an unpopular measure objected by all students in his school. Lee and his friends made T-shirts with a few words such as "we want long lunch" printed on and sold them to fellow students, which turned out to be a great success. This first business experience made Lee believe that one should choose a cause he would be passionate about as lifetime career. A person needs to spend the time and find out what is his or her true avocation and then figure out where one's gift lies.

In 1983, Lee graduated summa cum laude from Columbia University, receiving his BS degree in computer science. He then went on to earn a PhD in computer science from Carnegie Mellon University in 1988.While studying at Carnegie Mellon, Lee focused on machine learning and pattern recognition. In 1986, he and Sanjoy Mahajan developed *Bill*, a Bayesian learning-based system for playing the board game *Othello* that won the US national tournament of computer players three years later. In 1988, Lee completed his doctoral dissertation on Sphinx, the first large-vocabulary, speaker-independent, continuous speech recognition system, which was published as a Kluwer monograph, *Automatic Speech Recognition: The Development of the Sphinx Recognition System*. Lee has since written two books on speech recognition and more than 60 papers in computer science.

After graduation, Lee started his professional career at Carnegie Mellon, working as an assistant professor, later joining Apple Computers in 1990 as a research and development executive. After six years, he moved to Silicon Graphics in 1996 and spent a year as president of its VRML (Virtual Reality Modeling Language) division, Cosmo Software. In 1998, Lee moved on to Microsoft in Beijing, China, where he played a key role in establishing the Microsoft Research (MSR) division. MSR China later became MSR Asia. Lee returned to the United States in 2000 and became vice president of interactive services at Microsoft for the next five years.

In July 2005, Lee left Microsoft to take a position at Google. Due to a one-year, noncompeting agreement that he signed in 2000, this job-hopping made the world's two biggest IT companies Google and Microsoft confront in court, and Lee himself became the focus of the sensational legal dispute. When the dust finally settled, Google was able to march into the Chinese market under Lee's leadership. At Google China, Lee helped establish the company in the fast-growing market and oversaw its development in the country. He was responsible for launching the Google.cn regional website, and strengthened the company's team of engineers and scientists in the country.

Since Lee was once a professor at Carnegie Mellon University, sharing learning experiences with students was among the most favorite things he enjoyed to do in life. Believing that the youth is the future of China, since 1990, Lee has been in touch with young students on tours of visiting Chinese universities. In 2000, when Lee became the vice president of Microsoft, he wrote two open letters to Chinese students sharing his view on talents and career options, which were soon spread on the Internet and followed by another six letters, shedding new light on important life choices for the young people. This time, Lee wanted to realize another dream of his life. Deeply moved by those eager learners, Lee saw the new mission of his life was to help young Chinese students. So he created a website called kaifulee.com and was later renamed to 5xue.com (开复学生网), which provides students an open platform for study, growth, and practice. As an elite Chinese returnee, Lee is known to a large number of young people in China. His experiences have inspired many students, as his personal blog is widely followed in China. Among other important life lessons, he has been promoting the value of being "the best of yourself" to the young people and made them know that the world can be changed out of their sheer determination and hard work.

In September 2009, Lee left Google to establish Innovation Works, which is a platform focusing on Internet, mobile Internet, and cloud computing. As a first step in his new business plan, Innovation Works incubates new Chinese high-tech companies and mentors the next generation of Chinese entrepreneurs. On the stake of US$800 million and his reputation, Lee seeks to create the new business model that will combine angle investment and venture capital with software development, headhunting, and incubator together.

William X. Wei

Sources

Innovation Works (2009), "Founder", available at: http://en.innovation-works.com/founder.asp (accessed 4 September 2010).

Wikipedia (2010), "Kai-Fu Lee", available at: http://en.wikipedia.org/wiki/Kai-Fu_Lee (accessed 4 September 2010).

李开复 (2010), "世界因你而不同", *李开复的博客* [Lee, K., "The world will be different because of you"], 16 March 2010, available at: http://blog.sina.com.cn/s/blog_475b3d560100hcur.html (accessed 28 September 2010).

李开复 (2009), "成长中的十个启发", *都市快报* [Lee, K., "Ten inspirations in my life", *Hangzhou Urban News*], 17 October 2009, available at: http://edu.sina.com.cn/j/2009-10-22/0936179822.shtml (accessed 28 September 2010).

张凯峰 (2009), "李开复: 创业乌托邦", *创业家* [Zhang, K.F., "Kai-fu Lee: Utopia of future entrepreneurs", *Founder Magazine*], 13 October 2009, available at: http://tech.163.com/09/1013/09/5LGDL34M000915BF.html (accessed 4 September 2010).

Li, Xiaojia (Charles Li 李小加 b. 1961)

Li Xiaojia, widely known as Charles Li in the financial world, is the chief executive officer of Hong Kong Exchanges and Clearing Limited (HKEx), the first person from mainland China to hold the position. HKEx is the holding company of the Stock Exchange of Hong Kong, Hong Kong Futures Exchange Limited, and Hong Kong Securities Clearing Company Limited. As of the end of November 2010, HKEx is the largest listed exchange in the world in terms of the market capitalization of its own shares.

Li was born in Beijing in 1961 but grew up in Gansu Province after his parents were offered employment in the region. Following his graduation from middle school, Li went on to a petroleum technical school, and at the age of 16, began working in the offshore oil fields in Bohai Sea. At that time, the Cultural Revolution was in full swing, and Li spent three years enduring poor working conditions on the platform. However, as the Cultural Revolution wound down, oil platform workers became more highly regarded and received decent salaries with free meals and other perks.

Although his job on the platform provided him with a relatively better life than in remote Gansu, Li began to deeply reflect on his own purpose and future. At that time, the government had just restarted the national college entrance examinations, and Li decided that his future was dependent on a university education. Wasting no time, he taught himself the high school curriculum and listened to English-language programs on the radio after work. In 1980, Li passed the examinations and was admitted to Xiamen University, majoring in English literature.

After graduating from university four years later, Li put his English skills to good use as a journalist for the *China Daily*, the only national English-language newspaper in China at that time. He immediately grew fond of journalism. In 1986, he received two scholarships to further his study in the field from the University of Alabama. He and his wife made the journey to the southern United States, working part-time in the evenings to help offset living expenses as he pursued his education. During his five years in the United States, he did not visit his parents once because of the prohibitive cost of flying home. Although he earned his master's degree in journalism and loved the trade, he soon realized it was too difficult for a foreigner to survive in the journalism field in the United States. This was the second time he reflected on his own life's path and had to make a decision.

Li decided to make a change once again. He entered the top-ranked Law School at Columbia University where he earned his Juris Doctor. He began his legal career in 1991 as an associate in Davis Polk & Wardwell in New York, where he stayed until 1993. He then joined Brown & Wood of New York.

In 1994, Li joined Merrill Lynch when the firm started to play a key role in helping the Chinese Ministry of Finance issue bonds in the US market. Merrill Lynch provided Li with a platform to demonstrate his talent, and by 1999, he was promoted to managing director and CEO of Merrill Lynch China responsible for business development in the country. Amid the growing number of listings of Chinese state-owned enterprises and the rapid development of the mainland economy, Li was involved in several major IPOs including Jiangxi Copper, China Mobile, and China Telecom, and was responsible for global sales of US$1 billion in Chinese national bonds. Also in 1999, Li was involved in both the New York and Hong Kong listings of China National Offshore Oil Company (CNOOC), the same company he had worked for 20 years prior.

Seeking another new challenge, Li was appointed the chairman of J.P. Morgan China in 2003. On June 23, 2005, CNOOC offered US$18.5 billion to purchase US-based Unocal Oil, with Goldman Sachs and J.P. Morgan serving as project consultants. Although the high-profile bid fell through, the event had far-reaching global implications. Under Li's leadership, J.P. Morgan China became a leading underwriter; in 2006 alone, it completed 9 acquisitions and 14 fundraising projects.

Li has also served as a director of the China Entrepreneurs Forum, and was a nonexecutive director of a number of large Chinese enterprises such as Shanghai Pudong Development Bank and China Vanke. In December 2009, Li joined HKEx as its CEO. He believed it was time for him to help facilitate the general economic development of the country. While Li used to be a link to connect finance and law between Western countries and China, now he serves as another bridge that connects Hong Kong and the international financial market with mainland China. With his global vision and rich experience in law and finance, Li is well positioned to lead HKEx to new heights.

ZICHENG LI

Sources

HKEx (2010), "Li Xiaojia: Executive director, chief executive", 16 January, available at: http://www.hkex.com.hk/eng/exchange/org/boardirect/charles_li.htm (accessed 30 June 2010).

百度百科 (2010), ["李小加", *Baidu.com*], available at: http://baike.baidu.com/view/1581797.htm?fr = ala0_1_1 (accessed 30 June 2010).
郦晓 (2009), "聚焦李小加：一个石油工人的后传", *腾讯财经* [Li, X., "Focusing on Li Xiaojia: Biography of a former oil worker", *Tencent Finance*], 27 May, available at: http://finance.qq.com/a/20090527/004333.htm (accessed 30 June 2010).

Li, Yanhong (Robin Li 李彦宏 b. 1968)

Known to the West as Robin Li, Li Yanhong may one day be known for something beyond the success of Baidu, the search engine company he founded and that has become the number 1 website in China and outpaces Google in Chinese Internet search. On August 5, 2005, the day he took Baidu public, the share price started at US$27 and when the NASDAQ closed later that day, share prices had risen to US$122, up over 350%.

In one fell swoop, Li Yanhong became a billionaire; in one glorious moment, the mindset of China's IT business community broke free from their fetters and rose to greater heights. It is not that he became a billionaire, although that is really phenomenal; it is the fact that he had developed many inventions in web search technology that are still in use, at a time when China was seen elsewhere in the IT world as having also-ran technology. The Baidu moment was the result of a life's work. However, it also meant that China's IT expertise was on par with the best available in the world. For that achievement, Li Yanhong will be well remembered. He has been recognized among the Top Ten People in the IT World in 2002, and CCTV Economic Personality of the Year in 2005.

He started modestly enough. When Li was born in 1968, the only boy and fourth in a family of five children, his hometown of Yangquan, Shanxi Province in Northwestern China, was still quite impoverished. He spent an active childhood collecting stamps and dreaming to become a performer in traditional opera. His interests in computers progressed when he was still in high school. Li participated in the national youth programming competition and did not rank nationwide. By then he realized that he needed to look outside of the city he grew up and compete with all the better programmers. Li had a quick mind, and this enabled him to gain entrance into China's most prestigious academic institution, Peking University, in 1987, following the step of his elder sister. He enrolled in a library and information science major but continued pecking away on his enduring interest, computer science. In the fall 1991, after receiving his bachelor degree in information management, he was admitted with scholarship to a computer science program at the State University of New York at Buffalo, where he worked hard on his schoolwork and excelled academically. In the ensuing summer, Li had a successful internship at Matsushita, where he calculated a better way to improve the recognition rate of the newly developed optical character recognition (OCR) technology. After publishing his research findings, Li made a name for himself among the IT circle, and was quickly recruited to work for the online edition of the *Wall Street Journal*. Bowing out the pursuit of his PhD, he received a master's degree in 1994 and started his corporate career in New York.

Li soon developed a real-time information system for Dow Jones, which has since been used in the websites of several Wall Street businesses. He then focused on trying to find a solution to one of the most perplexing problems in the early stages of the Internet industry: how to sort information. Two years later, he had his eureka moment. He invented Embedded Server Page (ESP) technology, a search program that he called link analysis, for its ability to study the links that a website had to others and come up with a ranking of the website's popularity. It was a moment of great excitement. He told his boss about it, but he was not interested. However, this technology caught attention of William Chang, chief technology officer of Infoseek, where the ESP technology was later implemented. In 1998, Li wrote a book titled *Silicon Valley Business War*, in which he tried to draw attention to the commercial possibilities of Internet search and described his own insights on the industry as it was in the 1990s.

In 1999, after Infoseek began shifting toward content, Li decided instead to establish his own Internet search company with Eric Xu, another Peking University graduate and a friend with a doctorate in biochemistry and a network of contacts in Silicon Valley. Because of the concept of emerging China and Li's proven technical capabilities, the team easily raised US$. 1.2 million from Peninsula Capital and Integrity Partners and flew to China to establish Baidu. When the Internet bubble was pricked in the United States, Baidu was beginning its ascent in China. The company began its life as a business offering search services to large Chinese portals such as Sina and Sohu. Li soon changed course, despite some opposition from the board, as he was sure that the success of Overture, the company that made paid search engine advertising a real business, signaled a change in the industry. In 2001, Li was able to obtain another US$10 million from venture capital funds DFG and IDG. After its Chinese search engine was launched in September 2001, Baidu began to provide pay-per-click advertising, ahead of Google. The offering became popular among businesses and by 2004, Baidu became profitable, and as the largest search engine in Chinese language, Baidu had built links to more than 300 million pages and daily traffic reached over 60 million. By that time, the company was ripe for an initial public offering, which it finally did in August 2005. While Li still held 25% of Baidu, five others became billionaires and more than 400 people also became millionaires. By 2009, Baidu's stock price had reached over US$400 per share on the NASDAQ.

Baidu still faces a strong challenge from its rival Google. The Internet giant has spent hundreds of millions of dollars in its China offensive. However, Li believes the Chinese market has different characteristics than Western markets, and Baidu has the better ability to serve that market. The company may be right so far: it continues to gain market share in pay-per-click advertising with at least 50%, while Google and Yahoo both lost market shares. By 2007, Baidu had 5500 employees and 75% of Chinese market. On the legal front, there are also challenges involving copyright infringements. Lawsuits have been filed claiming that Baidu is breaking copyright laws on music files; however, Baidu insists it only provides links. Investors are also concerned about its earnings, which are low relative to its share price, and Baidu needs to find ways to increase income.

Despite the mounting technological challenge from Google, Li is confident that Baidu will prevail. "Know ourselves, build our strength, cut our weakness, improve, improve and improve!" The Baidu internal magazine carries this quotation from Li Yanhong on the top page. As one of the best-known brand names in China, a front-runner and outstanding leader in the domestic high-tech industry, Baidu already touches the lives of hundreds of millions of Chinese netizens. Li Yanhong is leading his team to the day when every Chinese will know to "Baidu" it whenever there is a problem.

AMIR SHOHAM AND WENXIAN ZHANG

Sources

Baidu.com (2009), "The Baidu story", available at: http://ir.baidu.com/phoenix.zhtml?c=188488&p=irol-homeprofile (accessed 29 November 2009).

Barboza, D. (2006), *The rise of Baidu (that's Chinese for Google*, 17 September, *New York Times*, available at: www.nytimes.com/2006/09/17/business/yourmoney/17baidu.html?ex=1185336000&en=fedbeba9cb4214a8&ei=5070 (accessed 29 November 2009).

BizChina (2006), "Li Yanhong", *China Daily*, 13 March, available at: www,chinadaily.com.cn/bizchina/2006-03/13/content_533967.htm (accessed 29 November 2009).

李政 (2007), "李彦宏: 众里寻她千百度", *叱咤华尔街: 10位海归上市公司领袖* (王辉耀主编), 中国发展出版社, 北京 [Li Z., "Li Yanhong: In searching of her hundreds of times", in Wang, H. (ed.), *Movers on Wall Street: Ten Overseas Returnees Who Took Their Business Public*, China Development Press, Beijing], pp. 91–110.

Li, Yi (David Y. Li 李一 b. 1962)

Known to the West as David Li, Li took charge of UBS overall China strategy building and implementation since June 1, 2005. As the chairman and country head, Li is credited by some quarters for contributing to the establishment of the UBS Securities JV platform in China.

Li is highly regarded for his skills in running China-based multinational corporations, the recognition of which was symbolized by being awarded the "Financial Figure of the Year" in the 2008 Financial Values Standings organized by the leading China media group, *China Business News*. The Award emphasizes the valuable efforts made by companies towards Chinese socioeconomic development since the start of the economic reform period in 1978. The event is made even more significant for Li because UBS is the sole finance-related recipient of the Award, a fact that was covered in the Chinese state media.

Other China-based awards received by Li include the "Pioneer Leader" in the Multinational Leadership Ranking organized by *Global People*, a related publication of the *People's Daily* on the toopic of finance, and the Special Award of Top Ten Chinese Business Talents cosponsored by Sohu, China Education TV, etc. These are all public recognition of Li's achievements by Chinese institutions and establishments. He had received other prestigious awards before. In 2004, Mr Li won the

"Asian Best Business Leaders for 2004" award cohosted by CNBC and Dow Jones. He was also named one of the "Ten Most Influential Chinese from the Financial Industry" during the Asia Pacific Investment and Finance Annual Meeting in 2007.

Li's academic record is as distinguished as his illustrious career in the corporate sector. He obtained a Bachelor of Education at the Beijing University of Physical Education in 1984; an LLB from the China University of Political Science & Law in 1988; and an MBA from the Wharton School of Business at University of Pennsylvania in 1992. In terms of extracurricular activities, between 1983 and 1985 (some sources indicated 1982–1984), Li was vice chairman of the National Student Federation in China (also known as All-China Students Federation), and from 1984 to 1988, he was the deputy secretary-general of Beijing Students Federation. Besides having been a student leader, he was also an accomplished sportsman as a professional player at the Shaanxi Professional Soccer Club between 1976 and 1980.

Li started his career in the finance sector, spending more than seven years in securities trading, direct investment, and investment banking on Wall Street. Between 1992 and 1997, Li worked for Citicorp in New York in a number of positions, which was his first job after graduating from Wharton. From 1997 until 1999, he was senior vice president (VP) at First Capridge Corporation, while in 1995–1996 he was appointed chairman of the China Finance Society in New York.

As opportunities for China returnees beckoned, Li moved to China in 1999. Before joining UBS China operations, Li's skills came in handy for China-based companies keen to venture into finance activities when he was later appointed executive vice president of China Merchants Securities with the portfolio of building and developing the group's investment banking services. Li started off with China Merchants Holdings (International) (CMHI) from November 2001 until May 2005 as the managing director (MD) in charge of general operations with the strategic task of overseeing the refocusing strategy on the port industry and restructuring business lines through asset swaps, M&A, and divestments as part of that company's new strategy.

During Li's term, the company became a constituent (component stock) of the Hong Kong Hang Seng Index. Under Li's watch, CMHI's net profit increased 2.5 times and its share price almost quadrupled; the company was added to the Hang Seng Index and was the third best performing constituent of the index in 2004 (UBS Hong Kong, 2005). Li's term coincided with a gold rush in Chinese stock market. Chinese companies sold as much as US$55 billion of stock in 2007, up from US$50 billion in 2006. By 2007, the Zurich-based UBS only ranked behind Goldman after tripling its share of the market since 2000 by targeting issuers in China.

The transition of China Merchants Holdings (International) from a multicategory investment company into an industry leader emphasizing port operation has been attributed to Li's management skills and may be one of the factors that attracted UBS' attention. This may have been validated by Rory Tapner, chairman and chief executive officer of UBS in Asia Pacific to whom Li reports: "David's demonstrated excellence in both strategy development and implementation will complement our already strong China team. As our businesses in China continue to expand, exploiting opportunities across the breadth of our group will become ever more critical" (UBS Hong Kong, 2005).

Rob Rankin, who had 16 years experience in UBS previously managing the Asia-Pacific telecommunications, media, and technology group, led UBS' efforts in China from 2004 to 2007 after the bank deployed him to run a business operation that was bringing in lower than US$100 million yearly revenue. Under Rankin's watch, investment-banking fees from China more than doubled in 2006 to US$200 million in 2007, and thereafter, UBS strategized the need for an even stronger team to sustain and expand such encouraging results. Li was part of this stronger team strategy. Along with David Li, UBS also hired seven bankers from BNP Paribas Peregrine led by Henry Cai in 2006 to solicit business opportunities from the private sector in China and to beef up the China team.

Other appointments that Li has held include chairman of the Board for UBS Securities, China; member of the Chinese People's Association for Friendship with Foreign Countries; and member of the Asia Executive Board, Wharton School of the University of Pennsylvania.

TAI WEI LIM

Sources

Chan, C. (2007), "Goldman beware: UBS, via China, may be new stock king (Update2)", *Bloomberg News*, 22 January, available at http://www.bloomberg.com/apps/news?pid=20601109&sid=aeqkZs7fGAo8&refer=home (accessed 8 February 2010).

Euroweek (2005), "David Li leaves China Merchants to run UBS show in China", Issue 905 - 27 May, available at: http://www.euroweek.com/Article.aspx?ArticleID=1147479 (accessed 7 February 2010).

UBS (2009), "UBS China head receives two distinguished awards", 5 January, available at http://www.ibb.ubs.com/News/jan09.shtml (accessed 9 February 2010).

UBS Hong Kong (2005), "Chairman and country head of UBS AG, China", 24 May, available at: http://www.ubs.com/1/e/media_overview/media_asiapacific/search1/search10?newsId=78788 (accessed 8 February 2010).

Wharton (2007), "Yi David Li, WG'92 managing director, chairman and country head UBS China", available at: http://www.wharton.upenn.edu/alumni/wharton125/events/finale/panels.cfm?panel=panels%5Cday1%5Csession3%5Cpanel1.xml#4 (accessed 7 February 2010).

W. Beijing (2009), "David (Yi) Li, WG'92", available at http://www.whartonbeijing09.com/bio-li.html (accessed 8 February 2010).

Li, Yifei (李亦非 b. 1964)

As the chairperson of VivaKi in China, Li Yifei oversees US$50 billion in global advertisement spending and influence, and is known for her powerful combination of business acumen and marketplace knowledge. In fact, she has been a star in the media and digital world for quite some time. In 2001, Li was on the cover of *Fortune* magazine, as one of the 25 rising stars of the next generation's global leaders. In 2005 and 2006, *Wall Street Journal* named her one of the Top 10 Remarkable Women in

Asia. Today, Li is perceived to be one of the most well-connected and powerful women in China.

Li's interest in the media world should not surprise anyone familiar with her childhood. A Beijing native, Li was a national tai-chi champion at the young age of 13, and was literally in the spotlight as a stunt double for the leading actress in China's first martial arts film after the Cultural Revolution. She could have continued in that line of work, but her parents were both professionals (her father an astrophysicist and her mother a teacher) and they wanted Li to be well educated. They told Li to aim high, so Li attended the city's most prestigious foreign-language university – China Foreign Affairs University – and earned a BA in international law.

Li was curious about the West and searched for a university in the United States that would offer her a scholarship to undertake graduate studies there. Baylor University, in Texas, did, so Li began her studies there in 1985. This was a life-changing decision for Li; she wanted to experience new things, but had never left China before. She did not know if she would be able to return to China, saying, "I was the first student ever to leave my college for overseas" (Cremer, 2009). But leave she did, and at Baylor she earned an MA in international affairs. Upon graduation, her language skills and educational background made Li a shoo-in for a prestigious short-term internship at the United Nations. Moving to the "Big Apple," Li worked for the UN public information department before producing and hosting a television program called UN Calls for Asia. Through this position, Li honed skills that proved crucial for her future career: reading an audience, and creating and delivering a clear, effective message.

In 1990, Li began to work for a New York law office, where she was in charge of business in China. During her residence in New York, Li also met her future husband, and after he was offered a job transfer, they decided to return to China. This was not an easy decision for Li, who had been away from China for several years and did not know what moving back would feel like. She was pleasantly surprised to discover that the combination of Chinese heritage, American education, and business experience she possessed set her apart from most other job candidates at the time. The circumstances of the global economy were fortuitous for Li as well. China had undergone considerable economic reform (becoming more market-oriented) and as a result, was experiencing a rapid growth spurt. More and more multinational firms perceived an opportunity for expansion in China, and were seeking out employees with "East meets West" experience.

After returning to China, Li's first job was at Burson-Marsteller, a leading global public relations and communications agency. Li started at Burson-Marsteller in 1995 and worked her way up to the position of managing director in two short years. At that time, the focus of Burson-Marsteller was to help foreign multinationals navigate through Chinese government regulations. Li provided strategic counseling to clients such as BP, Intel, Philip Morris, and Motorola, helping them define and develop their entry strategies. She also worked on accounts for News Corporation, a global media company; she did so well consulting for them, having such "character, competence, and conviction" (Xinhua News Agency, 2003) that Viacom (News Corporation's main rival) decided to steal Li away. She was hired in 1999 to run

MTV China. For the next nine years, Li's work for Viacom fundamentally changed the face of media business and youth culture in China.

Many argue that Li is singlehandedly responsible for the widespread growth of MTV in China since 1999; she sold programs to more than 300 cities in China, oversaw programming, found new artists, staged unplugged concert series, and dramatically increased advertising revenue. Li established the first 24-hour MTV channel in China. She coordinated a deal between MTV and China Mobile, offering MTV branded content to 200 million cell phone subscribers in China. She also negotiated a joint venture between Nickelodeon and Kids Channel of Shanghai Media Group, offering Nickelodeon Orient to 3.5 million Chinese households. In 2005, Li was promoted to senior vice president of MTV Asia.

The effort it took to expand the reach of MTV in China should not be understated; Li had to gain acquiescence of often-conservative Chinese government officials, who were not altogether accepting of international innuendo-laden music. Li believes her awareness of and respect for different cultural traditions and different regulatory traditions (including censorship) aided her quest. She is strategic, ever-aware of moments when she needs to be aggressive and when she needs to be more restrained; she notes that "as a woman in China, you have to be a little bit softer and humble" (Grayson, 2006). In many interviews, Li has referred to Confucius, who said that in order to succeed, you have to walk the middle line. For Li, there are many middle lines – between the older and the younger generation in China, and between the East and the West. Many think that walking the middle line signifies weakness, but according to Li "it is a strategy" that facilitates successful negotiation (Li, 2004).

Li briefly left the media world in 2008, when she became managing director of GLG China, a global asset management company. Though this represented an entirely different industry, Li believed the skills needed for the position – decision-making, negotiating, and networking skills; the ability to find commercial opportunities and bring different parties together to create win-win situations; brand management; team management and motivation skills; and financial management skills – were not very different from her previous positions. Still, Li missed the media sector and in the autumn of 2009, she left GLG China to become the Greater-China chairman of VivaKi.

VivaKi is the media and digital division of Publicis Groupe, one of the world's largest advertising and media companies. Li oversees China Media Exchange, two leading digital marketing agencies (Digitas and Razorfish), and two global media agencies (Starcom Mediavest and ZenithOptimedia) in China; the agencies' CEOs and the CEO of the China Media Exchange all report to Li. Her main task is to figure out how to connect brands to people in meaningful ways, considering how consumers communicate and connect in an increasingly digital world, including blogs, wikis, and increased reliance on social media and networking.

At VivaKi, Li develops cross-brand initiatives and delivers operational and financial goals for the company. Since VivaKi is one of the largest media buyers in China, Li is well positioned to capitalize on the comparatively high growth of China's economy as compared with most economies around the world. To Li, China's economic growth means more room for advertising growth. She believes the country is close to an exponential increase in advertising outlay, because clients are now ready to pursue online digital options (Cremer, 2009). One thing is crystal clear: with Li at the helm, China's media sector will continue to reach new heights in this increasingly internationalized world.

Tonia Warnecke

Sources

All-China Women's Federation (2007), "Li Yifei: New Media will change us", *Women of China*, 22 January, available at: http://www.womenofchina.cn/Profiles/Businesswomen/13414.jsp (accessed 11 June 2010).

All-China Women's Federation (2010), "First Chinese woman to make the *Fortune* list", *Women of China*, 19 May, available at: http://www.womenofchina.cn/news/Spotlight/217558.jsp (accessed 16 June 2010).

China Economic Review (2004), "Viacom pushes ahead with China JV", 29 November, available at: http://www.chinaeconomicreview.com/dailybriefing/2004_11_29/Viacom_pushes_ahead_with_China_JV.html (accessed 14 June 2010).

Cremer, J. (2004), "Kung Fu double finds her niche", *Classified Post*, 12 December, available at: http://www.classifiedpost.com/career-centre/leadership-lessons/working-women/kung-fu-double-finds-her-niche (accessed 13 June 2010).

Grayson, I. (2006), "Li: Narrowing the cultural divide", Cable News Network (CNN), 26 June, available at: http://edition.cnn.com/2006/BUSINESS/06/25/forward.li/index.html (accessed 14 June 2010).

Li, B. (2009), "Yifei Li hired as head of Publicis Groupe's Vivaki in China", 25 August, available at: http://www.campaignasia.com/Article/210837,yifei-li-hired-as-head-of-publicis-groupes-vivaki-in-china.aspx (accessed online 15 June 2010).

Li, Y. (2004). "*New Leaders in a new China*", *Baylor Business Review* Texas: Spring, Baylor University. (available at: http://www.baylor.edu/bbr/index.php?id = 16331 (accessed 14 June 2010)).

Xinhua News Agency (2003), "Yifei Li: a Chinese businesswoman and MTV in China", 5 December, available at: http://www.baylor.edu/pr/index.php?id=13595 (accessed 15 June 2010).

Xu, W. (2009), "Li Yifei, one of the most successful women in China", 24 June, interview available at: http://english.cri.cn/4406/2009/06/24/1941s496210.htm (accessed 17 June 2010).

ZenithOptimedia Review (2009), "VivaKi of Publicis Groupe names Yifei Li as Greater-China chairman", No. 43, September, available at: www.zenithoptimedia.com.cn/publication/vol43/en/zom_message.html (accessed 16 June 2010).

Liang, Jianzhang (James Liang 梁建章 b. 1969)

With the founding of Ctrip, a travel booking website and service, Liang Jianzhang revolutionized the Chinese travel industry, turning US$250,000 seed money into a US$1.3 billion travel powerhouse in less than a decade. He broke new ground in the Chinese hospitality industry by introducing the idea of budget hotels with the creation of the popular Home Inn chain. Liang's pioneering entrepreneurial efforts have been perfectly timed with the rise in tourism to one of the most prominent industries in the nation due to newly burgeoning wealth from China's economic transformation. His efforts to bring profitable change to the travel industry have profited him well; he has made it to *Forbes* List of China's Richest with an estimated personal worth above US$200 million.

Liang gives the impression of being wise beyond his years. Smart, curious, rational, and forward thinking, he dresses casually and prefers spending time with his family rather than working long hours at the office. He would much rather think than talk. Introverted but confident, he does not talk much, even to his closest associates, but certainly a lack of words in no way hints at a lack of strategic thought. With a cunning laugh, he will be quick to remind you not to judge what you see on the surface.

Born in Shanghai in 1969, Liang was a computer prodigy as a young child in an era when most Chinese hardly even knew what a computer was. Liang's prodigal bent continued into his teens when he entered Fudan University directly after middle school at just 15 years old, and transferred to Georgia Institute of Technology less than a year later. He finished his bachelor's and master's degrees in computer science at Georgia Tech by the age of 20.

After graduation, Liang moved on to Silicon Valley, working in R&D at Oracle for three years. Around this time, he took a trip back to China to visit relatives, and was surprised by the dramatic changes he saw: China had become a place charged with business opportunity. He applied for a transfer to Oracle's ERP implementation in order to learn the customer service and management side of the software development industry, which laid a foundation for managing his own tech business in the future. This move opened the door to spend three years in China as a consulting director of Oracle China, allowing him to learn the Chinese market in final preparation to become a successful tech entrepreneur in China.

Liang first proposed the idea for Ctrip when having lunch with a friend, Neil Shen, an old middle school pal. Chatting about the potential of the Internet, together they brainstormed business ideas just for fun, and Liang proposed what would one day become Ctrip, China's leading travel consolidator of hotel and airline reservations. The conversation between the two friends clicked, realizing they had similar ways of thinking, and the rest, as they say, is history. The two recruited two more, Ji Qi and Fan Min. Liang had the technical background; Shen, the investment banking background not to mention a Yale MBA; Ji Qi, the entrepreneurial and sales management background; and Fan Min was a veteran travel agent. Classmates and friends, the group was hailed as the ideal venture combination, eventually creating two NASDAQ firms together in three years. Dubbed "the four horsemen," this dynamic team has been praised for setting an example of a cohesive team with no chief *lao ban* (boss), no emperor dominating the other members of the group, and their skill in working as a team is considered one of the key success factors for their achievements.

Liang's talented eye for long-term opportunities saw the huge potential for Internet business in China, a view not shared by many of investors in the beginning. His intention was to create a Chinese version of Expedia, at a time when the Internet bubble was bursting in the developed world and much less than 1% of the Chinese population were even online yet. Admittedly, the initial decision to form Ctrip was based more on intuition than in-depth knowledge of the tourism industry or even in-depth research. Nevertheless, the move was a smart one: barriers to entry were negligible and the only competitors, traditional tourism enterprises, were weak. Though the idea of e-commerce had not yet been accepted into Chinese society, spending money on travel certainly was. It was an easy conclusion to come to.

At the time, 95% of the travel industry in China was made up of individual travelers. These nongroup travelers were an underserved yet quickly expanding market segment, ripe for the profit picking. Ctrip offered the type of online travel services that catered to individual travelers: the flexibility of researching their many travel options and price points to make informed and cost-efficient decision, and to do so in their own time, not restricted to the office hours of their local travel agency.

Ctrip utilized business models that the four returnees brought back from their time in the West, cloning well-established foreign travel booking websites with a Chinese flair. Discovering early on that the China market was not ready for a solely Internet-based system, the business took off when they added call centers and in-person marketing promoters that went to areas where travelers gathered, such as airports and train stations. The website became secondary to the call centers as the Chinese eased their way into a newfound comfort level with e-commerce, resulting in the current click-and-brick business model. Ctrip provided a dexterous integration of the traditional Chinese travel industry with highly developed global technology.

From its beginnings in 1999 with US$250,000 in startup capital from overseas VCs, Ctrip did not take long to go public. Just four years after its creation, it became the first Chinese tourism company to successfully land on the NASDAQ, quickly climbing to double its offer price by day's close at US$33.94. Liang woke up that morning in China as a wealthy man.

Ctrip has experienced quick success well beyond the four partners' wildest imaginations, breaking even in its third year and reaching over US$1 billion business in less than seven years. It is the best-known travel brand in China today, holding 60% of the market, and it is one of the country's largest Internet companies. With 20 million members and growing, Ctrip has at times averaged 90 new customers every hour. Ctrip does as much travel business in one day as a traditional agent does in one year. In addition, with the surge in international travel among the Chinese, Ctrip's expansion into overseas hotel bookings is growing exponentially as rising demand for the international leisure travel outpaces domestic demand.

Liang served as CEO of Ctrip from 2000 to 2006, and has been a member of its board continuously since its inception, serving as chairman since 2003. He has skillfully infused Chinese travel with an American business approach, adapting the Expedia model to be "China unique," and in the process built a beloved national travel brand.

After successfully launching Ctrip, the team of four went on to add another travel-related business to their list of accomplishments: Home Inns, the first branded family hotel chain in China. Created in 2002, Home Inns went public on the NASDAQ in 2006 at nearly 60% above IPO price.

Home Inns fit a niche that was an unmet need in the Chinese hospitality industry at the time. This domestic chain focuses on standardized quality and dependably low rates, patterned after American economy hotels, which filled 88% of the US hotel industry but at the time were rare in China. Previously, the main options for travel lodging in China were either a trusted but expensive 4 or 5 star hotel chain or take a big gamble at a cheaper individual guesthouse, often less than acceptably clean or comfortable. Home Inns created the first low-price alternative that was of dependable quality and strong brand image with its yellow multistoried low-rise buildings, often sandwiched between busy malls and commercial hotspots throughout Chinese cities. In less than a decade, Home Inns has become one of the world's largest economy hotel chains.

As a natural correlation with GDP, the travel industry in China is expected to continue to see significant escalation. The recent history of double-digit annual growth is a direct result of the emergence of the Chinese middle class with its increasing disposable incomes and a strong cultural trend toward travel as a main form of consumption. For Chuppies (Chinese young urban professionals), traveling is an essential component of their newfound success. In fact, China is predicted to be largest outbound travel market by 2020; by 2015, the largest inbound travel market, surpassing France as the top world travel destination.

Liang's businesses have helped to facilitate these national travel trends, both in greatly facilitating the accessibility of independent travel with Ctrip's information and booking services as well as facilitating the affordability of domestic travel with Home Inns. The future is bright for Liang. Having helped to create these travel trends, he is now nicely situated to profit from them and to stay on the forefront of this national and international pulse, a perfect demonstration of his favorite motto: opportunities for people who are prepared for them.

BARBARA L. STROTHER

Sources

Hsu, R. (n.d.), "Make your fortune in China's second surge", Investor Place Asia, available at: http://asia.investorplace.com/free-reports/make_your_fortune_china_second_surge-part4.html (accessed 15 August 2010).

Industry Trends and Development (2006), "Travel agency grows with Chinese economy", available at: http://www.i2i-m.com/china-news/it&d1.htm (accessed 15 August 2010).

So, S., and Westland, J. C. (2009), "Ctrip: Redefine the formula of success in online travel.", *Global Times*, 6 July, available at: http://business.globaltimes.cn/industries/2009-07/443232.html (accessed 15 August 2010).

百度百科 (2010), "梁建章" ["James Liang", *Baidu Encyclopedia*], available at: http://baike.baidu.com/view/200896.htm (accessed 15 August 2010).

商务周刊 (2005), "梁建章：天才与旅游" ["Liang Jianzhang: Genius and travel", *Business Watch Magazine*], 8 December, available at: http://tech.sina.com.cn/i/2005-12-08/1618786666.shtml (accessed 15 August 2010).

Lin, Yongqing (Alex Lin 林永青 b. 1969)

In China, Lin Yongqing is seen by many as a preeminent thinker in business and an authority figure on information technology. He holds the position of founder and CEO of ChinaValue.net, the biggest communities of businesspeople and professionals, the largest business and industry knowledge base in the country, and a provider of elite business, economics, financial, investment, information technology, and industry real-time news and commentary focused on China.

Since its creation in 2004, Lin has molded the firm into becoming the first professional business news media website in China, and the first news media website to post the real names and credentials of their writers. Over 500,000 members contribute contents to ChinaValue, which has a large reader base of 50–60 million people ranging from undergraduates to the managing directors of listed companies. The company is the first website to make shareholding available to all professional contributors. In a few short years, ChinaValue.net has gathered such an impressive number of prestigious contributors that it has grown to become one of the country's largest owners of intellectual property concerning business, finance, and economics. One of ChinaValue's unique advantages is its new business model built on web 2.0 technologies, which allows every member the ability to make use of all the functions and the environment, specifically designed to create relationships and invest back into the community through expertise and knowledge. Convinced that knowledge is the most powerful asset in the information age of the twenty-first century, Lin's goal was to develop ChinaValue into an engine for Chinese economy based on the power of professional knowledge and collective wisdom from its massive user community.

Besides his work with ChinaValue, Lin is also the founding partner of SuperValue International, a leading Chinese investment consulting firm. Before founding the firm, he served in China as a senior executive at Intel for seven years. Having graduated from Xiamen University in 1998, receiving this position made him the first local MBA recruited by Intel. Working for the world-class corporation, he was responsible for building and managing one of the largest IT sales channels in the country. Experience at Intel broadened Lin's horizons and helped boost his self-confidence; he learned that everything was possible if one set a higher goal and vision than normal standard and try best to achieve it.

After his tenure at Intel, Lin worked briefly as a deputy general manager and vice president of marketing for Tsinghua Tong Fang Computer Ltd., one of the top three PC makers in China. In 2005, Lin also became the first in China to earn a global executive MBA through the renowned TRIUM program, which derives its excellence by incorporating the world-class expertise of the New York University Stern School of Business, the London School of Economics and Political Science, and the HEC School of Management in Paris. Ranked as the second worldwide by *Financial Times*, it was through this program that Lin further built his confidence, and developed a strong belief that Chinese entrepreneurship could change the world. Although currently most of Chinese entrepreneurship was at a grassroots level, lacking in critical thinking and innovation, he saw them as both diligent and hardworking. Not surprisingly, his vision and expertise is sought out by many. Lin has since made appearances on China's premier media outlet, CCTV, on China's most critical business issues. In an interview with the Network Professional Association, he expressed his belief that to increase competence and knowledge, Chinese government needs to cultivate competition by further opening up the mass media market.

Besides his corporate work, Lin devoted himself to the youth education in China. He is a visiting professor of the graduate business school at Beijing Normal University, and has given lectures on Chinese entrepreneurship and served as a senior consultant to the Peter Drucker Academy in Beijing. In addition, he was also the general advisor of the Association Internationale des Étudiants en Sciences Économiques et Commerciales (AIESEC) in China, a large youth organization that engages in international student exchange and internship programs for various organizations. With his global vision and rich professional experience, Lin has become a sought-after speaker by many Chinese universities. Sharing his thoughts on how to become a successful entrepreneur, he strongly believed that Chinese youth should learn more from both the Western cultures and Chinese traditions. Under his leadership, ChinaValue has helped many foreign publishers and authors, translating their books into Chinese version, as he believed it may help students develop a better understanding of the key factors for their success.

The Ministry of Information Industry, which oversees the fast growing Chinese information technology industry, has benefited from Lin's position as a special advisor. Similarly, Lin is also advisor to organizations such as Center for Information Work (CIW) and China Center for Information Industry Development (CCID). In addition, he extends his service to some of the world's finest global organizations such as Ambrosetti and Agrion. He is also at the forefront of the vision to increase China's value in a time of globalization by augmenting online credit and trust. He is a pioneer in commencing the legislation of using Internet Real Names with The National People's Congress of PRC. In 2009, Lin was a CEO delegate and special nominee at the World Economic Forum. In an interview with the Network Professional Association, Lin outlined his belief that China would be a prominent figure in the world economy in the twenty-first century, and that ChinaValue would be a primary driver in getting China to that position. In recognition of his positive impact on China and the world as a successful entrepreneur and innovator, the London School of Economics made a profile of him in its 2009 series of Blazing Trails.

SYNTIA ZENI

Sources

ChinaValue (2010), "Alex Lin's profile", available at: http://english.chinavalue.net/Profile.aspx?UserID=1 (accessed 3 April 2010).

Ibaraki, S. (2010), "Interview with Alex Lin", 9 February, available at: http://blogs.technet.com/b/cdnitmanagers/archive/2010/02/09/alex-lin-yong-qing-shares-his-insights-into-the-world-economic-forum-nyc-global-leaders-summit-building-the-largest-intel-channel-founding-the-largest-online-professional-business-media-and-service-company.aspx (accessed 3 April 2010).

Liu, Changle (刘长乐 b. 1951)

A Chinese media tycoon and successful entrepreneur, Liu Changle is the founding chairman and chief executive officer of Phoenix Satellite Television Holdings Limited. Based in Hong Kong, Phoenix Satellite is the only private television network in China allowed to broadcast news in Chinese.

Born in 1951, Liu is a native of Shanghai, and his father was an official in the Chinese Communist Party. At a young age, Liu moved with his parents to Beijing, and then Xian. In 1964, his family settled in Lanzhou, Gansu Province. When the Cultural Revolution broke out, Liu watched his father being humiliated through public parade. In 1970, upon graduation from a local high school attached to the Northwest Normal University, Liu went to work for the Lanzhou Pharmaceutical Factory for six months. He soon joined the People's Liberation Army (PLA) and during his time in the military, Liu risked his life several times rescuing people and their property in areas of natural disasters, and was later promoted as an officer and political instructor of the 40th Army based in Jinzhou, Liaoning Province.

Entering the reform era, Liu experienced a drastic change in his life when he graduated from Beijing Broadcasting Institute (the Communication University of China) in 1980, and began to work for the Central People's Radio Station in Beijing. Because of his PLA background, Liu became a reporter of the Military Department, and was later named the editor, news commentator, and deputy director of the department. In that capacity, Liu participated in the reporting and commentary of a number of important national events such as the first rocket launches and submarine test in China, and was able to accompany Yang Shangkun, a top PLA leader and later PRC president, on an official visit to the United States in 1987. This trip not only helped his professional career but also broadened his vision and made him think about his true calling in life.

After conducting an interview with a senior executive at a state-owned oil enterprise, he asked for a job and was soon named an oil trader in its office in Houston. In 1988, Liu quit his position at China National Radio, left Beijing for the United States and began to pursue his business aspirations. With a sharp sense and bold entrepreneurial spirit, he resigned only a year into his new job to seize what he perceived a golden opportunity for building a personal wealth. At that time, Chinese economy was still in transition with a two-tier price system. Benefiting from his strong connection with government officials, Liu was able to secure permits and began to purchase crude oil at the official price under the planned economy; he then refined and exported petroleum products at the market price, and within a few years became a multimillionaire. Besides his home in California, he also established a residence in Hong Kong, and soon branched into highway construction, real estate, port facilities, hotels and hospitals, and trade, benefitting greatly from a booming economy in China.

Despite his success in business, Liu's heart is still in the Chinese media, and his long cherished dream is to establish a TV station for Chinese across the globe. In 1995, with a unique foresight, Liu won the bid for a satellite TV channel in Hong Kong. At that time, Rupert Murdoch's News Corp. controlled Asia's main TV satellite and was seeking a local partner to enter the Chinese market. Therefore, on

March 31, 1996, Liu, through Today's Asia Limited, which is 93.3% owned by him, together with Satellite Television Asian Region Limited and China Wise International, jointly founded Phoenix Satellite Television Company. His original plan was to break even within three years and going public within four years; by 2000, the company was listed on the Hong Kong Stock Exchange, and was renamed Phoenix Satellite Television Holding Limited, with Liu serving as the chairman and the chief executive officer.

Under Liu's leadership, Phoenix grew rapidly. From a single channel in 1996, it quickly became a Mandarin Chinese television broadcaster that serves the Chinese mainland, Hong Kong, Taiwan, and other markets with substantial Chinese viewers. Phoenix Television provides news, information, entertainment programs, and has five different television channels, including Phoenix Chinese Channel, Phoenix InfoNews Channel, Phoenix Movie Channel, Phoenix North America Chinese Channel, and Phoenix Chinese News and Entertainment Channel. From its early audiences of more than 20 million worldwide, of which more than 62% are Chinese-speaking people, Phoenix Television now covers over 150 countries and regions around the world with an estimated 300 million audience, half of which are viewers from the mainland China in over 42 million households. In addition, the company publishes a weekly magazine and operates its own website. By the end of 2009, Phoenix's annual revenue reached over HK$1.53 billion, with nearly HK$300 million in net income.

Phoenix Television defines itself as the window to the world for the Chinese global community. Liu sees Phoenix as a TV broadcaster that is different from channels in mainland China, Hong Kong, and Taiwan. Under Liu's vision, Phoenix is to transcend the various components of the Greater China and offer Chinese viewers a media service that is global in outlook and independent of local political attachments. Aimed to become the CNN of Chinese media, he decided to launch China's first 24-hour news station. Initially, the broadcast was blocked by the Chinese government. Without viewers and ad revenue, Phoenix suffered heavy losses, but Liu persisted. When the terrorist attacks took place on September 11, 2001, Phoenix went live immediately and its aggressive reporting won international recognition that came to be a shape contrast to the delayed broadcasting by CCTV. Gradually the blockage was lifted, and since then Phoenix has grown to become the channel of choice for much of China's new elites and the most affluent and influential citizens. Even former Premier Zhu Rongji admitted publicly that he was a regular viewer and a fan of the Phoenix programming. In January 2003, the Chinese State Administration of Radio, Films and Television (SARFT) granted landing rights to Phoenix InfoNews Channel, making it one of the few nongovernment-related television broadcasters in mainland China able to broadcast information about events not covered by the government media.

Liu has been criticized for his strong ties with Chinese government officials, and Phoenix TV has been called "better-packaged propaganda than CCTV" that helps keep the party in power. Unyielding to the criticism, Liu believes his Phoenix reaches more people in China with more news than any other media organization. Not only it has ushered the Chinese language into the world media and promoted Chinese culture, but it has also brought together Chinese viewers across the globe. Although the network routinely practices self-censorship by avoiding politically sensitive stories, it frequently challenges the Chinese government's control of information with critical reports and documentaries that revealed the dark moments in contemporary Chinese history, and probed into some major social issues such as China's AIDS epidemic and rural unrest.

For his vision, entrepreneurial spirit, and achievement in the Chinese media industry, Liu has received widespread recognitions in the recent years. He was named one of the Top Ten Intellects of the Media by *China News Weekly* in 2000. In the following year, Liu ranked 17th of Asia's most influential communicators in *Asia Week*'s "Power 50" survey, and in 2004, he received the Robert Mundell Successful World CEO Award, an honor named after the Nobel Prize winning economist Robert Mundell. During the same year, Liu was also honored with the Most Creative Asia-Pacific Overseas Chinese Business Leader Award at the Asia-Pacific Overseas Chinese Commercial Leaders Forum in Singapore. His other recognitions include the Man of Year in China New Economy by *China Internet Weekly*, Man of Year for Asia Brand Innovation Award by the China Economy Information of *Economy Daily*, one of the Top 100 Most Influential Chinese Businessmen nomination sponsored by the Ministry of Commerce and Beijing Municipal Government, and the Entrepreneur in Media Industry Award by Ernst & Young.

Besides his leadership position at Phoenix TV, Liu is also a member of the International Board of the US National Academy of Television Arts and Sciences. He was appointed twice to the Board of Directors of Nanjing University since 2003, and is a visiting professor at the Communication University of China and Nankai, Fudan, Xiamen, and Sun Yat-Sen Universities. In November 2006, he was conferred an honorary doctoral degree by the City University of Hong Kong in recognition of his significant contribution to the Chinese media industry.

QUN DU

Sources

BusinessWeek (2010), "Executive profile: Changle Liu", available at: http://investing.businessweek.com/research/stocks/people/person.asp?personId=8672093&ticker=PXSTF:US (accessed 10 December 2010).

McDonald, H. (2005), "Running risks with Rupert: China's latest media magnate", *Sydney Morning Herald*, 31 October, available at: http://www.smh.com.au/news/business/running-risks-with-rupert-chinas-latest-media-magnate/2005/10/30/1130607149290.html (accessed 10 December 2010).

Pan, P. P. (2005), "Making waves, carefully, on the air in China: head of private TV network curries Party's favor while testing limits", *Washington Post*, 19 September, available at: http://www.washingtonpost.com/wp-dyn/content/article/2005/09/18/AR2005091801597.html (accessed 10 December 2010).

Yao, F. F. (2006), "Honorary Doctor of Letters: Mr. Liu Changle", City University of Hong Kong, available at: http://www.cityu.edu.hk/cityu/about/honorary/doc/Liu_en.pdf (accessed 10 December 2010).

Liu, Erfei (刘二飞 b. 1958)

The managing director of Merrill Lynch (Asia Pacific) Co. Ltd., Liu Erfei is a member of the board and the chairman of Merrill Lynch China Region. By working with senior managers of Merrill Lynch's main businesses and products in the areas of finance, insurance, telecommunications, energy, and electric power, Liu is responsible for coordinating general strategy of China among different departments of the company, as well as further consolidating and expanding the firm's leading position in the country. Prior to joining Merrill Lynch, he had worked for a number of top investment banks, and was instrumental in the launch of China operation of Morgan Stanley, Goldman Sachs, Smith Barney, and Calyon. Specialized in Chinese business, Liu has a rich experience in investment banking circle, and was once named among the world's most valuable 50 investment bankers by *Global Finance* magazine.

Liu was born in 1958 in Changchun, Jilin Province. His father worked as a civil servant in local government and his mother was a teacher. When he was 11, Liu's family was dispatched to the countryside during the Cultural Revolution, and three years later, he returned to Changchun to go to middle school. At the age of 15, he was sent to Shuangyang County, Jilin Province, where he worked for three years. During those formative years, one of his mother's friends played an important role in Liu's life, who had studied in Japan and spoke fluent English, which was rare in Northeast at that time. This had left a deep impression on Liu, and inspired him to study English during his years of hard labor in the countryside. As it is often said, hardship is the mother of success. After experiencing many difficulties at a young age, Liu was able to deal with any situation in later part of his life, whether study abroad or the high-pressure work in investment banks.

In 1977, when the nationwide college entrance examination was resumed, Liu experienced a major turning point in his life. With an excellent score in English, he was admitted into the Beijing Foreign Languages University, which turned out to be a stepping-stone for his career later. In 1981, out of a desire to explore the world outside China, Liu went to the United States and enrolled in Brandeis University in Massachusetts, a private institution named after the first Jewish American Chief Justice. As the first Chinese student there, he was given a scholarship of US$8000 annually for three consecutive years that ensured his focus on academics.

In 1984, after obtaining his bachelor's degree in economics from Brandeis, Liu was admitted into MBA program by both Columbia University and Harvard Business School. Declining the full scholarship from Columbia, he chose to go to Harvard without scholarship, and delayed his study so that he could earn enough money to cover the high tuition. Through friends' introduction, he had chance to work for British Rossier Investment Bank. A year later, with enough money, Liu joined the first batch of students from mainland China to study at Harvard Business School, where he not only learned advanced knowledge in business but also built up his self-confidence. The one-year working experience at Rossier and his time in Harvard laid the foundation for his future success in investment banking.

In 1987, upon graduation from Harvard Business School, Liu received a number of offers from internationally renowned companies. After some thoughts, he finally selected Goldman Sachs, one of the three major investment banks in the world. From 1984 when he first joined the New York branch of the British Rossier Investment Bank, Liu has had a career of over 20 years successively working in various investment banks that include Goldman Sachs, Morgan Stanley, Solomon, Calyon, and Merrill Lynch.

As one of the first people who introduced the concept of investment bank into China, Liu has left his footprints in the world's most famous investment banks. Especially since the early 1990s, with the opening of financial market, China became the most attractive land of opportunities in the world capital market. Starting from Qingling Motors in 1994, Liu had overseen the IPOs of many large state-owned enterprises, such as China Telecom, China Mobile, China Southern Airlines, and so on. In addition, he had also presided and operated the overseas IPOs of NetEase, UT Starcom, and other high-technology companies from China.

At the end of 1999, Liu joined the investment team at Merrill Lynch, and accepted the most difficult case – the second attempt of going public by China National Offshore Oil Corp. (CNOOC). Earlier in the same year, CNOOC failed to be listed in New York and Hong Kong, which made people skeptical to its re-listing effort. As the main underwriter, Merrill Lynch must make all-round readjustments to make it acceptable to the market. For security purposes, Liu united BOC International and Credit Suisse First Boston as co-underwriters during the second listing of CNOOC. He and his colleagues prepared hundreds of possible problems for the road show, especially the explanations on the operating ability that failed during the first listing. As a result, CNOOC's road show was the only one in China at the time that was completely explained in English, and thus gained the favor of investors. In February 2001, CNOOC was successfully listed on the New York Stock Exchange, which was regarded as the most successful IPO of that year, raising a total of US$1.5 billion for the company. Because of its outstanding performance on CNOOC, Merrill Lynch was brought back into China with many major projects, such as China Telecom's IPO, Lenovo's acquisition of IBM's PC division in 2005, and the Industrial and Commercial Bank of China (ICBC)'s IPO in Hong Kong in 2006. For his professional achievement, Liu was selected as the "Banker of the Year" by the *Asian Bankers* in 2006.

In order to share the benefits of the rapid growth of Chinese companies and the Chinese economy at large, Liu shifted his focus from IPO service to private equity (PE) since 2007. In his view, China is at its epic time of creating wealth, just like the United States a century ago, and many Chinese "Coca-Cola," "Time-Warner," or "Ford" are on their way of rapid growth. Therefore, it is the right time in this day and age to capitalize its investment with certain ownership, not just a commission. A recent success of Merrill Lynch's investment in Bank of China and the Chinese herbal medicine manufacturer Tongji Tang's IPO on the NASDAQ proved his judgment.

XUEYUAN LIU AND YAN ZHANG

Sources

百度百科 (2010), "刘二飞" ["Liu Erfei", Baidu.com], available at: http://baike.baidu.com/view/1299007.htm?fr=ala0_1_1 (accessed 26 August 2010).

王红茹 (2007)，"刘二飞：将投行引入中国"，*资本推手: 10位海归投资银行家* (王辉耀主编)，中国发展出版社，北京 [Wang, H.R., "Liu Erfei: Bringing the concept of investment bank into China", in Wang, H.Y. (ed.), *Capital Movers and Shakers: Ten Overseas Returnees in Investment Banking*, China Development Press, Beijing], pp. 38–51.

Liu, Jiangnan (Jean-Jacques Liu 刘江南 b. 1955)

From a soldier of the People's Liberation Army (PLA), to a medical specialist and successful entrepreneur, and finally, the CEO of Alcatel Lucent (China), Liu Jiangnan's life is both a case study for business classes and an inspiration for many young aspiring students.

Growing up, the story of Jean-Jacques Liu reads as if against the backdrop of a novel by Victor Hugo or Ernest Hemingway. Liu was raised in a family for which military service was a badge of honor. The young Liu thus found himself, at age 14, serving the Signal Corps of PLA as a communications specialist. His experience here, his first exposure to digital communications, foreshadowed his eventual success in the field of telecommunications management.

Yet, like many other returnees, Liu's life voyage was composed of many changes in direction. In 1980, in part because of his record of service, Liu was able to attend college, and was selected for advanced studies in medicine at the Second Military Medical University of PLA in Shanghai. Afterwards, he worked as a radiologist at a military hospital for several years. During this time, Liu could not help but compare the medical technologies available to him to those considered commonplace in the West. Encouraged in part by his sister, Liu made up his mind to obtain an education in France, and in 1987 secured a hospital post as a visiting scholar.

His experience there was not initially positive. Language barriers, limited contacts, and with little in the way of financial resources, Liu felt isolated and disengaged from his country and his hospital and colleagues. In addition, there was the issue of simple survival. Liu's scholarship provided for tuition, but little else. To make a living, he found himself waiting tables, performing manual labor, and even clerking at a small retail establishment. In short order his priorities shifted from furthering his education to simply making ends meet. This, he realized, was the complete antithesis of his original aspirations. Serendipitously, a friend offered Liu an alternative to his makeshift livelihood. He suggested a business partnership that would provide him a temporary means of earning sufficient funds to return to the hospital and pursue his doctoral education. Certainly, Liu did not view this option as a long-term career move. His perspective on business had been shaped by the political views of the day, which did not laud the tenets of capitalism.

Liu and several Chinese graduates also living in France at the time assembled their team and secured start-up capital of 50,000 francs. They disseminated a simple market survey to determine what markets represented the greatest opportunity for their venture. The research uncovered an untapped niche in computers and spare parts, competing with the likes of IBM largely based on price. While Liu's teammates addressed the sales and finance aspects of the venture due to their fluency in French, it was Liu's responsibility to liaise with his Taiwanese manufacturers and to assemble the startup units. He sold his first computer the day after assembling it; but sadly, his success quickly turned to chagrin. His colleagues pointed out to him that the price that he charged for this first unit was not enough to generate an acceptable profit. From this Liu learned his first valuable lesson in business.

As the venture grew, Liu and his colleagues suffered from what management guru Larry Greiner refers to as a Stage Three crisis: the crisis of control. The colleagues found themselves stretched to the limit, retaining control over most of the firm's functions to avoid the cost of additional hires. As a result, operations became increasingly chaotic. At one point, a lack of clear shipping and inventory documentation caused concern with an outside accounting firm, and Liu found himself spending an entire week reviewing documentation. Second valuable lesson? A standard operating procedure is critical to the effective operation of a business enterprise. Liu himself noted that establishing these procedures was a difficult task, particularly in the case of a partnership where colleagues were also friends.

At the end of its second year, Liu's computer firm realized a sizable profit. The business now had funds for expansion, which were then invested for growth. At this time, Liu believed that he had met his objective of financial security, and could now return to his medical education. Yet profits earned were immediately repatriated to the business. Hence his third valuable lesson: there is a significant difference between book profit and available cash.

Doing business in France was not easy for the colleagues. They found French labor law decidedly favored the employees and that the courts were not prone to side with Asian managers in labor disputes. Personally, Liu felt that, although France was one of the first nations to propone social justice and equality, it was nevertheless challenging for him to be accepted. He felt as if, in spite of his success, he was on the fringe of society. This idea crystallized after 10 years in France. He realized that his homeland called to him. He relinquished his interests in the business and returned to a new China; one very different from when he had left 10 years before.

This new China was far more prosperous and interested in foreign trade. To take advantage of this fortunate circumstance, Liu plied his knowledge as an international business consultant. In this position, Liu found that the patience and active listening skills he had learned in medical school served him well in interpreting client's concerns and clarifying their options. Liu was also able to apply both Asian and Western perspectives to developing business solutions. This ability to bridge two very different business philosophies was unique, and much sought after. Liu's reputation as an effective international business strategist grew, and he was noticed by management at Alcatel (China).

At this time, Alcatel was the world's largest telecommunications equipment company, registering sales of over US$20 million in 1992. Moreover, the potential market for telecom apparatus in China was considered the fastest growing in the world. Market analysts predicted that the country would become the biggest telecom market in the world by 2000. To exploit this opportunity, Alcatel created a veritable maze of manufacturing facilities, joint ventures and strategic partnerships designed to foment market share growth while complying with complicated government requirements for technology transfer, soft loan financing, and local content rules. The company was clearly in need of an executive with superior business acumen, sufficient knowledge of Western and Eastern business practices, and an understanding of the French business mindset. Who better for the post of vice president than Jean-Jacques Liu?

Initially, Alcatel's massive infrastructure and organization chart bewildered Liu. In comparison to his own company, the operations of Alcatel seemed unfathomable. Concerned, he went to the company's president, who suggested that Liu give the opportunity six months before making a final decision. As Liu pondered how he could best contribute to Alcatel, he realized that he could not follow the crowd. He arranged a groundbreaking meeting between the Chinese President and senior Alcatel (China) leadership, a feat that many said could not be done. This was his first imprint on the firm, and was followed by many critical successes.

With Liu's guidance, Alcatel initiated China's largest corporate merger, developed a successful aerospace business, and led the way to advanced data traffic systems and the establishment of 3G networks. Now, as CEO of Alcatel Lucent (China), Liu Jiangnan continues to pave the way for the latest in telecom technology. He also takes the time to share his knowledge with others in forums such as the US' Kellogg School of Management, Northwestern University, and the China Europe International Business School. Surely, the lessons he has learned in his own career will prove valuable to those who wish to follow in his footsteps.

ROBIN E. KELLY

Sources

Economist (1993), "The biggest prize: Alcatel in China", Vol. 326, pp. 68–69.

Greiner, L. E. (1972), "Evolution and revolution as organizations grow", *Harvard Business Review*, **50**, 37–46.

冯嘉雪, 郭玉梅, 郭俐君 (2007), "刘江南: 追随内心召唤的阿尔卡特COO", *巅峰职业: 10位海归职业经理人* (王辉耀主编), 中国发展出版社, 北京 [Feng, J.X., Guo, Y.M. and Guo, L.J., "Liu Jiangnan: Alcatel COO who follows his heart", in Wang, H.Y. (ed.), *Splendid Careers: Ten Overseas Returnees in Professional Management*], translated by Feng, L., China Development Press, Beijing, pp. 22–41.

Liu, Xiaocheng (刘晓程 b. 1949)

Liu Xiaocheng is the founder and president of the TEDA International Cardiovascular Hospital (TICH), a 600-bed, 16-operating room facility located in the Tianjin Economic Development Area in Northern China. One of the leading cardiovascular hospitals in Asia, TICH is also notable for its six tiers of service, with costs ranging from US$6.70 to about US$3200 a night.

Liu was born in 1949 in Jiamusi City, Heilongjiang Province in Northeastern China. Although little has been published about his early years, it is known that during the Cultural Revolution, his family of doctors was forced to relocate to the countryside, where they planted crops on a military farm. Liu was destined for other things than farming, though. In 1979, he entered the Institute of Cardiovascular Disease at the Academy of Medical Sciences in Beijing as a graduate student; he graduated in 1982. It was also in 1979 that he began working as a heart surgeon at Fu Wai Hospital.

In 1984, Liu had the opportunity to study at Prince Charles Hospital in Brisbane, Australia. Although he experienced a bit of culture shock for the first month – he particularly remembers knowing only the technical names of instruments, while his Australian colleagues referred to them with a variety of slang terms – he quickly settled in. Asked in one interview about his experience abroad, he said, "it not only increased my knowledge in general and broadened my horizons, but also made me realize, 'Oh, I can be a good heart surgeon' (Beijing TV Station, 2006)." He was at Prince Charles for two years before ultimately deciding to return to China, passing up the opportunity for a much higher salary in the process. It was at this point that Liu began to dream of creating a world-class cardiovascular hospital in China, but it would be more than two decades before his dream was fully realized with TICH.

Liu returned to work at Fu Wai Hospital, but found himself frustrated. While abroad, he had found that Australian hospitals were able to perform many more heart surgeries than Chinese facilities. He has said there was a perception in China that coronary artery bypass graft surgeries could be handled by only a handful of elite doctors, while in Australia younger doctors – including Liu himself – were able to perform these procedures regularly. Liu was deeply concerned with the contradiction between the supply and demand for heart surgery in China, where the backlog of cases meant many patients waited years or even died before they could be treated.

Liu decided he had to do something to combat the problem. In 1987, he resigned his job at Fu Wai and moved to the border city of Mudanjiang in his home province of Heilongjiang, which ranked first in the country in cardiovascular morbidity. He founded the Mudanjiang Cardiovascular Hospital – China's second cardiovascular hospital – in 1991. During his years there, the hospital saw 3000 cardiac surgery patients and achieved a survival rate of 98.6%. In December 1992, he and his colleagues completed China's first heart and lung transplant operation.

Two years later, in 1994, Liu was transferred to Beijing, where he took leadership roles in the Chinese Academy of Medical Sciences and the Peking Union Medical College Hospital. However, he was not satisfied with opening just one hospital. In 2000, at age 51, he once again resigned to begin a new project: the development process for the TEDA International Cardiovascular Hospital. The 720-million-yuan (about US$92 million at the time), 76,000-m^2 hospital opened its doors on September 26, 2003. It is designed to conduct 10,000 surgeries every year. That was still just a small percentage of the Chinese patients who need heart surgery – in 2003, Liu said that number was four million – but it was a start.

TICH is remarkable because it aims to bridge the gap between the two extremes of Chinese health care: low-priced public hospitals where patients may have to wait years for surgery and inefficiency can be high, and privately owned facilities (only about 5% of China's hospitals) that are affordable to only a small percentage of wealthy Chinese. Most patients also do not have health insurance and must pay out of pocket. Liu has likened TICH's levels of service to a commercial airline flight that offers first-, business-, and economy-class seats: every passenger reaches the same destination, but they choose individually how to fly. Like a good airline, Liu says he aims to keep the average length of his "passengers'" stays as short possible, to keep their costs low.

The more expensive service levels help subsidize the hundreds of low-cost surgeries TICH has provided to orphans and children from impoverished families (for whom it also receives about US$2500 apiece from the Chinese government, not enough to cover the full cost of care). In addition to the Chinese citizens it treats, the hospital is also part of the medical network of China Connection Global Healthcare Inc., a Christian healthcare organization that markets China's relatively low-cost treatment to foreigners.

One reporter noted the medical equipment and white-coated staff members are the only reminders that visitors to the TEDA International Cardiovascular Hospital are not in a five-star hotel. The facility is equipped with imported beds, LCD televisions, telephones, full air conditioning, and a pure-water plant. The VIP suite goes even further, with amenities such as an indoor garden, a private gym, and a massage chair. More important than its creature comforts, however, are TICH's technological innovations, which include electronic patient medical record cards that cut down on waiting in lines, visual visiting systems that allow patients and their families to talk remotely, and a mobile Clinical Pathway Information Terminal System that matches with nurses' code cards and is designed to cut down on unnecessary patient treatment. Services such as cleaning, security, and food are subcontracted to an outside company. As for the hospital's full-time employees, they work on one- to two-year contracts – and Liu makes it clear that any doctor who accepts kickbacks in the form of "red envelopes" will not have a job for long. Instead, TICH's employees receive bonuses linked to the quantity and quality of their work. "We run the hospital like a corporation (Zamiska, 2007)," Liu has said.

As for himself, Liu says, "I am a paving stone; I was paving the way for the construction and management of this hospital (*China Hospital CEO*, 2005)." That may be the case, but as a heart surgeon, hospital administrator, and innovator, Liu's role in Chinese health care is far from over.

JAMES P. GILBERT AND ELISABETH K. GILBERT

Sources

Binhai New Area Network (2010), "Binhai New Area public hospital reform stands out in the nation", 28 July, available at: http://www.bh.gov.cn/eng/system/2010/07/28/010057544.shtml (accessed 31 August 2010).

China Connection Global Healthcare (2010), "TEDA International Cardiovascular Hospital", available at: http://chinaconnection.cc/tich.html (accessed 31 August 2010).
China Daily (2003), "Cardiovascular Hospital opens in Tianjin", 28 September, available at: http://www.chinadaily.com.cn/en/doc/2003-09/28/content_268289.htm (accessed 31August 2010).
Wan, S., and Yim, A. (2003), "The evolution of cardiovascular surgery in China", *The Annals of Thoracic Surgery*, **76**(6), 2147–2155. available at: http://ats.ctsnetjournals.org/cgi/reprint/76/6/2147 (accessed 31 August 2010).
Zamiska, N. (2007), "Hospital caters to China's wealthy and poor: Innovative heart center uses market economy to subsidize treatment", *Wall Street Journal* (Eastern Edition), 4 January, available at: http://online.wsj.com/article/SB116785311279866221.html?mod=health_hs_health_providers_insurance (accessed 31 August 2010).
北京电视台 (2006), "*世纪之约*专访心血管外科专家刘晓程", ["*Century Appointment* interview with cardiovascular surgery expert Liu Xiaocheng", Beijing TV Station, 15 May, available at: http://tech.sina.com.cn/d/2006-05-15/1757938097.shtml (accessed 31 August 2010).
刘晓程 (n.d.), "个人简介" ["Biography", personal website], available at: http://liuxiaocheng.365heart.com/ (accessed 25 August 2010).
医生网 (2008), "刘晓程: 一心装着千万心" ["Liu Xiaocheng: One doctor who cares millions of others", DoctorSky.cn], 24 September, available at: http://www.doctorsky.cn/medical/20080924/40692.html (accessed 31 August 2010).
中国医院院长 (2005), 刘晓程和他的泰达试验田" ["Liu Xiaocheng and his TEDA experimental field", *China Hospital CEO*], 26 April, available at: http://business.sohu.com/20050426/n225341622.shtml (accessed 31 August 2010).

Liu, Yun (John Liu 刘允 b. 1963)

As corporate vice president of Google in charge of Greater China sales and operations, John Liu Yun remained confident even when the company itself faced uncertain future in the country while the industry was caught unexpectedly in the uproar of the global financial crisis. Convinced of the huge potential of the Internet, Liu emphatically believed the industry would endure the troublesome times and blossom into unprecedented growth opportunities in the coming years.

Originally from Gansu Province, Liu Yun attended Beijing Normal University, where he earned his bachelor's degree in mathematics in 1983. He went on to teach at the East China Normal University in Shanghai for five years before going abroad to pursue graduate studies. After receiving his master's degree in operation research (1992) and a PhD in telecommunication network management (1994) from the Technical University of Denmark, Liu held executive positions at both FreeMarkets Inc. and Singapore Telecom. In 2002, Liu became a visiting professor at the Beijing University of Posts and Telecommunications, and joined SK Telecom China, serving as CEO and president for six years. One of the major mobile operators in South Korea, SK Telecom purchased a 6.6% stake in China Unicom, a cell phone operator, and became the second largest holder of its shares. Another achievement for SK

Telecom was being among the first foreign businesses to be a part of the development of China's first 3G technology, TD-SCDMA. Liu was credited for his smooth handling of the relationship with the Chinese government, which was critical for SK Telecom to close the deal.

It was Liu's strong telecom background and expertise concerning the new 3G technology that first drew Google's attention toward him. With most of Beijing's population constantly detained in terrible traffic, half of the 338 million Internet users were using their phones to surf the Web. Those 155 million potential customers were of great interest to Google, and they began an intense focus on their 3G mobile-phone technology. As part of a strategic push to gain precedence in this area, Google recruited Liu as its corporate vice president, specifically in charge of sales and business development in Greater China that includes mainland China, Hong Kong, and Taiwan. Liu began working with Kaifu Lee, also corporate vice president and president of Google China, with the goals of expanding market shares, strengthening the integration, and promoting services.

Things would not be so simple for Liu, however. In September 2009, Kaifu Lee resigned from his position. Most of the senior executive staff initially hired by Google China in 2005 had been chosen from the world's top technology firms. Lee was no exception, having come from Microsoft himself. Although those executives had impressive backgrounds and titles, many believed they were not the best choices for running a Chinese Internet business. Lee's departure placed a heavy burden upon Liu, who was elevated to vice president of sales and operations, taking up a majority of Lee's operational responsibilities. Even though Liu was not as well known as the other executives, it was expected that he would be a better candidate. As Liu was born in China, studied in China, and taught in China, he would have a more in-depth knowledge of Chinese culture and the needs of its people.

However, once again complications arose for Liu, only this time the grievances were far more serious. In December 2009, Google discovered its corporate infrastructure was being assailed in a very sophisticated and focused manner that resulted in stolen intellectual property. As Google looked further into the issue, they realized it reached much farther than Google alone. At minimum, 24 other companies were also being attacked, which came from a wide variety of industries such as the Internet, finance, technology, media, as well as chemical sectors. Even more disturbing, Google found evidence that implied the main goal of these assailments were the Gmail accounts of activists for Chinese human rights, not only those in China but also those based in the United States and Europe.

Google has openly shared all of this information with the public, not only out of the security and human rights implications, but also underlying the much larger issue over freedom of speech. The company agreed to allow some censoring in China because Google believed it was a worthy compromise in order to make more information available to the people of China. These discomforting attacks as well as China's push to further restrict free speech on the Internet in the past year have brought Google to the decision that it would not be continuing censorship in China. On March 22, 2010, the decision was implemented, and all Google search services became censor free. It required a switch from Google.cn to Google.com.hk, which is now in simplified Chinese and delivered via Hong Kong servers to those in Hong Kong and mainland China.

The future is uncertain for Google in China, a country where working without the government's blessing is highly unadvised. However, with Liu as corporate vice president, Google has a strong ally and leader on its side. The China Computer and Information Industry Development Center honored Liu as one of the "Ten Outstanding Information Technology Business Leaders of China" in 2006. The following year he was awarded for his achievements in China with the Robert Mundell World Executive Award, which is the highest honor possible within the economic, management, and commercial circles of China. At the end of 2009, in the midst of the attacks at Google, he still found time to be one of the main speakers at the First International Conference on Cloud Computing. Liu Yun has overcome many obstacles in his life, and it will be interesting to see how he excels through this one.

SYNTIA ZENI

Sources

Google (2010), "Corporate information: Google management", available at: http://www.google.com/corporate/execs.html#johnliu (accessed 15 April 2010).

Hof, R. (2009), "Google China Head Kai-Fu Lee leaves to start new venture", *Businessweek*, 4 September, available at: http://www.businessweek.com/the_thread/techbeat/archives/2009/09/google_china_he.html (accessed 15 April 2010).

Sol, S. (2009), "Google, Baidu do battle in China's 3G frontier", *Asia Times*, 3 September. available at: http://www.atimes.com/atimes/China_Business/KI03Cb01.html (accessed 15 April 2010).

So, S. (2009), "New broom may sweep Google China ahead", *Asia Times*, 20 October, available at: http://www.atimes.com/atimes/China_Business/KJ20Cb01.html (accessed 15 April 2010).

Mao, Daolin (茅道临 b. 1963)

Also known as Daniel Mao in the West, Mao Daolin is most remembered as the former CEO of Sina, the largest Chinese portal in the world. With an estimated wealth between $35 million and $60 million, Mao was ranked the 351st on the 2005 Hurun Report of The Richest People In China and the 35th on 2004 Audi Euromoney China IT Rich List. However, in recent years much of the spotlight has been shed on him for reasons that are not so relevant to Internet business. In 2003, Mao married Chinese president Hu Jingtao's daughter Hu Haiqing, and was since nicknamed "fuma" (emperor's son-in-law) by Chinese online media. No official explanations were given as why he left Sina at its best, and people speculated that his resignation from Sina's CEO position in May 2003 had direct correlation with this marriage. Despite the mystery, one fact remains unchallenged—Mao rescued Sina and reestablished its standing as the largest Chinese website in the world.

This Internet tycoon was not born with a silver spoon in his mouth. On the contrary, Mao grew in an ordinary family in Shanghai. While studying computer science at the elite Shanghai Jiaotong University, he was also actively involved in the young Chinese IT industry. With support from his department chair, Mao opened a firm designing software for accounting management. In 1987, two years after graduating from Jiaotong, Mao went to Stanford University and earned his master's degree in economic management shortly after. In 1993, he started his business career at Walden International Investment Group (WIIG) in Los Angles. This experience coincidently interweaved his destiny with Sina. During the six years of working at WIIG, Mao rose to become its vice president in charge of investment business in the IT industry sector of the United States, mainland China, and Hong Kong. Mao's decision to invest in Beijing Stone Richsight Information Technology Co. played a vital role in the growth of Stone. He also strongly advocated for the merger between Stone and Sinanet, which resulted in the birth of Sina, currently the largest Chinese portal in the world.

Established in 1993 by two top Chinese computer programming engineers, Stone Richsight specialized in Chinese software development, sales, and services. In June 1996, Stone successfully developed RICHWIN 4.3 Beta 1, the standard Chinese-language operation platform for the Internet. A year later, Stone became the first company in Chinese IT industry history to receive international venture capital $8.5 million, which included investment from WIIG, Bank of America, and Ivanhoe Group. Consequently, Stone was able to attract overseas talents, reconstruct its operation, and expand business beyond software design and services to Internet. Meanwhile, Sinanet was the largest Silicon Valley–based Chinese portal established by three Taiwanese students from Stanford University, and its CEO, Jiang Fennian, was seeking business opportunity in mainland China. In August 1998, Mao set up a meeting for Jiang and Wang Zhidong, CEO of Stone. In 1999, after the merger was finalized, Mao was named the chief operating officer (COO) of Sina as well as its board member. A year later, Sina was listed on the NASDAQ.

Mao's experience in finance and investment situated him as an ideal successor to Wang in June 2001, who was ousted as CEO, president, and director of the company he founded, due to his failure in tacking Sina's financial crisis. During Mao's term in Sina, he not only turned losses into profit, but also took Sina's quarterly income from $5 million to historical peak of $10.3 million in September 2002. Key to Mao's success was the reconstruction of Sina management model and the implementation of the TMT (technology, media, and telecommunication) strategy and the "Central Kitchen" concept, under which Mao distinguished three categories of Sina's core business: Sina.net, Sina.com, and Sina online. According to Mao, Sina.net mainly facilitated Internet service and the need from government and enterprises. While Sina.com was all about content websites, and Sina online focused on combining ISP (Internet service provider) and ICP (Internet content provider) services, the "Central Kitchen" itself possesses the centralized authority in management, developing Sina brand, and contents editing, etc. Under Mao's visionary leadership, Sina's capital focus was clarified and its sector efficiency was greatly enhanced. Furthermore, Mao also led Sina in seeking horizontal corporations with various enterprises. Utilizing Sina's Internet platform, information was categorized and reorganized, and Sina Sports, Sina Real State, and Sina Finance all became strong brands in the industry. In 2002, Sina established an online shopping model and built the first online sports community with Nike. In the following year, Sina acquired Xunlong, a wireless provider in Guangzhou, which allowed the company to reclaim its position as the leading online media and service provider in Chinese portal by surpassing Sohu and NetEase, its two competitors in mainland China.

To the surprise of many people, Mao stepped down as CEO in May 2003, but kept his seat on the board. According to media report, Mao claimed that he had accomplished his mission and it was his personal wish to continue facilitating Sina's development as a board member rather than a CEO. Some market analysts regarded Sina's comparatively weaker performance on global capital market the cause of Mao's departure; however, such a hypothesis was never confirmed by Sina.

XIAOQI YU

Sources

Shanghai Daily (2006), "Sina.com to announce CEO's departure", 10 May, available at: http://news.xinhuanet.com/english/2006-05/10/content_4528646.htm (accessed 10 February 2010).

首席执行官 (2007), "夫妻档案: 新浪前CEO茅道临与胡锦涛女儿" ["Couple profile: Former Sina CEO Mao Daolin and daughter of Hu Jintao", ceo.icxo.com], 26 January, available at: http://ceo.icxo.com/htmlnews/2007/01/26/994474_0.htm (accessed 10 February 2010).

张军 (2009), "茅道临'功成身退', 汪延接任CEO", *羊城晚报* [Zhang, J. "Mao Daolin stepped down, Wang Yan named Sina CEO", *Yangcheng Evening News*], 6 August, available at: http://www.netcoc.com/news/content_v4494.html (accessed 11 February 2010).

张念庆 (2003), "汪延接替茅道临担任新浪首席执行官, 茅道临留任董事", *北京青年报* [Zhang, N. "Wang Yan replaced Mao Daolin as Sina's CEO, Mao remains a board member", *Beijing Youth Daily*], 13 May, available at: http://tech.163.com/tm/030513/030513_93032.html (accessed 10 February 2010).

中国名人录 (2003), "茅道临" ["Mao Daolin", Chinavitae.com], available at: http://www.chinavitae.com/biography/Mao_Daolin/bio (accessed 10 February 2010).

Mao, Daqing (毛大庆 b. 1969)

Mao Daqing is the vice president of China Vanke and general manager of Beijing Vanke, the largest residential developer in the People's Republic of China and a leading player in the fast-growing real estate market of China.

Born in 1969, Mao came from a traditional family of intellectuals; his grandfather was a well-respected architect and one of the principal architects responsible for designing both the Great Hall of the People and the Beijing Exhibition Center. His father was an expert in nuclear physics, who studied in the Soviet Union in the 1950s, and his mother was among the first group of people to go abroad after China's reform and opening-up policy, studying aerospace technology in the UK. As both of his parents had experience studying abroad, it was natural for Mao to follow his parents' steps. However, he decided to stay in China, and went to Southeast University for his college education in architecture. Later, Mao earned both master's and doctorate degrees in management from Tongji University, completed some postdoctoral coursework in regional economics at Beijing University, received a certification in real estate finance from Columbia University, and finally earned an EMBA from UC Berkeley.

After his graduation from Southeast University in 1991, Mao found a job in an architectural design firm in Hong Kong. One year later, Mao went to Thailand and joined Saha Patana Interholdings Co., where he was responsible for developing industrial parks in China. In 1994, Mao moved to Singapore and joined Nikken Sekkei International. At that time, he was 25 and the only Chinese designer in the firm. Mao demonstrated great talent as an architect. His designs have won various awards in international design competitions, including the Fourth International Competition for Architecture and Environmental Design in Japan in 1990 and the International Competition for Interior Design in UK in 1992. In 1995, Mao won the project of Somerset Apartment Shanghai (originally named Regent Court) with his unique design that integrated traditional oriental elements and modern style. As a designer, Mao frequently flew to Shanghai to guide the construction. It was at that time that he realized the city's rapid growth and tremendous potential for future development. Mao decided to return to China after five years of living abroad.

With the idea of returning to China market, Mao left Nikken Sekkei and joined Singapore Liang Court Holdings (later changed to Ascott Group), a subgroup of Singapore real estate company CapitaLand Ltd. Working as a senior designer and project manager, he was responsible for the design and construction of Somerset Serviced Apartment in Shanghai and Guangzhou Supreme Golf Club and Villa. Somerset Shanghai is located in Xuhui district, a vibrant area filled with business, dining, shopping, and entertaining centers. Positioned as a luxury corporate housing and marketed to executives and professionals, Somerset Shanghai has 167 fully furnished residences and provides comprehensive personalized services and facilities. During the construction phase, Mao efficiently managed the project development and reduced the cost by nearly 50 million RMB. When Somerset was named outstanding architecture in Shanghai, Mao was also honored with a White Magnolia Award for his outstanding contributions to the city's economic construction and social development. The great success of Somerset Shanghai opened a new chapter for Mao's career as a real estate developer, who has since become one of the key forces that facilitated CapitaLand's development in the China market.

In 1999, Mao was named the chief representative of Ascott Beijing. In the same year, Ascott Group, along with the Government of Singapore Investment Corporation (GIC), acquired the office building that was located to the south of the China Merchants Tower and transformed it into Ascott Beijing, a serviced apartment that consists of 272 residences and provides luxurious service accommodation. The project set the record for foreign capital acquisition of Beijing real estate. Mao participated in the last stage of acquisition and led a development team converting the building into serviced apartment. The transformation was completed within a year and became a classic case of real estate conversion in the history of China real estate development. With its outstanding quality, Ascott Beijing was awarded high-quality project prize and became the flagship project of Beijing luxury serviced apartments.

Later, Mao developed and managed other serviced apartment projects in Beijing including Somerset Grand Fortune Garden, Luxury Serviced Residence, and Ascott Raffles City. In 2002, Mao was promoted to the China general manager of CapitaLand Bohai Rim Region, responsible for the management of nine serviced apartments at the same time. During his 14 years with CapitaLand China, Mao developed various types of real estate that include residence, serviced apartment, office building, and shopping center, and he helped the company become the largest serviced apartment owner and operator in China, which possesses 36,000 residential units, 50 shopping centers, and 5,000 serviced apartments in over 40 cities and more than RMB 45 billion worth of real estate assets.

In August 2009, Mao left CapitaLand and joined China Vanke, the largest real estate company in China, as its vice president and general manager of Vanke Beijing. Mao has cumulated extensive knowledge in design, project planning, financing, operation, management, and other aspects related to real estate development. Through this career change, he found an opportunity to assist Chinese enterprise with his international perspective and management experience, and to contribute to the development of China real estate market. Mao believes that the real value of a commercial real estate is reflected in its operating stage, and the key to improving Chinese commercial real estate development lies in the management and operation. As one of the founders of China Commercial Real Estate Association and China Real Estate Professional Association, and vice president of the Chamber of Commerce of the Western Returned Scholars Association (WRSA), Mao is dedicated to bringing advanced management expertise to the Chinese real estate industry, facilitating skill and information exchanges between China and the outside world, and promoting the development of real estate professionals.

From architect, to project executive, real estate developer, and professional manager, Mao has achieved tremendous success in each chapter of his career. Proficient with every aspect of real estate, Mao cannot be defined by any specific title. To him, real estate development is a process of creating social living. Each project, whether it is serviced apartment, office building, or shopping center, is the creation of a lifestyle. In the coming years, he will continually be driven by the goal of improving the quality of Chinese urban living and the development of China's real estate industry.

YINGLU WU AND ERIC LIGUORI

Sources

陈建波 (2009), "毛大庆: 塑造做梦的'壳'", *经理日报* [Chen, J., "Mao Daqing: Building the 'shell' for dreams"], *The Manager's Daily*, 1 November, available at: http://bbw.cenn.cn/info/nid_16495.html (accessed 18 July 2010).

商务周刊 (2005), "毛大庆: 见证从来没有经历过的大时代" ["Mao Daqing: Witness the great unprecedented era", *Business Watch Magazine*], 9 December, available at: http://finance.sina.com.cn/manage/cfrw/20051209/19292187315.shtml (accessed 18 July 2010).
新浪财经 (2002), "新加坡凯德置地中国控股集团北京副总毛大庆博士" ["Dr. Mao Daqing, vice president of CapitaLand China in Beijing", *Sina Finance*], 26 November, available at: http://finance.sina.com.cn/roll/20021126/1703282941.shtml (accessed 18 July 2010).

Mo, Tianquan (Vincent Mo 莫天全 b. 1964)

Mo Tianquan is the founding chairman and CEO of SouFun Holdings Limited, one of the largest online real estate information and service platforms in the world, with 5000 employees and 630,000 registered real estate service personnel, covering over 100 cities and regions in China.

Mo holds a bachelor's degree in engineering from the South China University of Technology (SCUT), a Master of Science degree from Tsinghua University, and a master's in economics from Indiana University. Despite his impressive academic accomplishment, he had a very humble beginning. Born in a rural county in Guangxi in 1964, Mo spent his childhood in the isolated but peaceful and beautiful region of southwestern China. At age 17, Mo completed his high school in Shaoyang, Hunan Province, and participated in the national college entrance examination together with 2.58 million high school students. The competition was very fierce, with only 10% of admission rate. In such an intense environment, Mo learned the value of endeavoring. Consequently, he had the highest score in his hometown, and was accepted into the SCUT in Guangzhou, a key institution of higher education in the country. Majoring in mechanical engineering, he was influenced by his uncle, who taught him that math, physics, and chemistry were the key to a successful career among the world's elites.

At SCUT, Mo was a very intelligent and diligent student; every semester he held the top spot academically in his class. In addition to his study, Mo also liked to practice martial arts and free-style combat during his spare time, through which he believed that he could cultivate his perseverance. Till today, Mo's interest in martial arts has not changed, and he continues to practice *Taiji* in his leisure time.

During his sophomore year, Mo sent a petition to the school dean requesting to skip his junior courses and directly study the senior curriculum. As this appeal was unprecedented, the dean brought the application to the university president, who was very supportive of the idea, on the condition that Mo would pass all sophomore and junior exams with minimum score of 80%. Though it seemed like a mission impossible, Mo surpassed the challenge. Therefore, he became the first student to successfully complete his undergraduate studies in three years at SCUT. Whenever recalling his college era, Mo is always smiling, as he regards those simple and pure times the best part of his life.

After graduation, Mo was assigned to Tianjin, where he engaged in research work in the area of environmental protection. Two years later, aspiring to be a leader, he shifted his attention to the science of management, and left his job to pursue postgraduate studies at Tsinghua University. During this period, Mo published several papers in top-tier academic journals such as *Management World* and *Journal of Economics*, which left a deep impression among the editorial team members, since those authoritative publications were normally reserved for the more established academics in the field.

In 1989, Mo gave up a very attractive job opportunity at the Development Research Center of the Chinese State Council, left for the United States, and enrolled into a PhD program at Indiana University. During the following few years, besides his academic work, he also partnered with two friends to establish a wine company in Guangxi. Unfortunately, the factory closed three months later; however, in early 1994, Mo was offered the chance to join Teleres, a joint venture of Dow Jones and Aegon USA. There he became familiar with the real estate market, and within three years, was made the general manager of Teleres China. Years later, Mo reflected on his overseas experience: "Life is constantly changing, when I first entered Indiana University, I was always thinking that I would become some kind of professor of economics. But this job changed my career; I started to learn how to make money from then on" (Xin, 2006). Nevertheless, his full-time engagement in business activities made him too busy to finish his dissertation, a decision he regrets till today.

In 1994, Mo became the Asian and Chinese director and general manager in the Dow Jones Teleres, and later the executive vice president of the Asian Development and Finance Corporation (ADF). By the end of the last century, the Internet was booming and the Chinese market economy was accelerating. In 1999, Mo bought a number of servers and computers, and hired several technicians to run his website Chinaproperties.com, which later became SouFun.com. Chinaproperties mainly engaged in providing information about real estate and IT services. In order to support his website operation, Mo pursued venture capital fund, which he was able to raise along with his friend and Tsinghua alumnus Li Shan, who later became the founder of the Three Mountain Foundation. The process of negotiation was also quite dramatic; with no detailed project plan but only "one-page idea" and a meal with the investor, Mo secured his first venture capital investment of US$1 million. It was his professionalism in IT information that won the trust of IDG. After that, SouFun was able to secure bridge loans without any guarantee from the IDG. Mo later recalled in an interview: "I do not know how they treated other investees; but to me, their support is like a blind faith, they believe in me and my decisions no matter what I do" (Zhou, 2010).

From 2000 to 2005, SouFun rapidly expanded its operations to more than 70 cities across the country, becoming the largest and most popular website on real estate development in China. SouFun holdings have several divisions: new housing, second-hand housing, home furnishing and improvement, and research group (Chinese Index Academy). Its services cover the new and second-hand housing, apartment, villas, office buildings, shops, industrial plants, and home renovation and decoration. In 2006, with the successful investment made by VC, Telstra, the largest IT Company in Australia, acquired 51% of SouFun's shares for $254 million, which was one of the largest private equity investments in Chinese Internet history of the time. A year later,

SouFun's earnings reached 500 million RMB, with 90% of the revenue originating from advertisement.

Since the ownership change, SouFun has grown aggressively with the support of its major shareholder Telstra. However, for the benefit of the company's future, it looks better for the management to gain back the control of the company. Therefore, Mo sought to introduce other financial investors or public shareholders through IPO to regain the actual leadership position for the company's development. In August 2010, it was announced that two PE companies, General Atlantic and Apax, joined the partnership, and on September 2, 2010, SouFun filed its request to the US Securities and Exchange Commission for listing on the New York Stock Exchange, with the Code SFUN, price range between US$40.5 and 42.5 per ADS, and a proposed fund-raising of US$140 million. Its stock price jumped 73% in its first day trading on New York Stock Exchange.

When reflecting on the past, Mo concludes that his experience gained early in life was critical and that no matter if one succeeds or fails, the experience is what counts. When a company is economically stable, one should be attentive to market opportunities and take some risks with caution in order to be the leader in their field.

WILLIAM X. WEI

Sources

百度百科 (2010), "莫天全" ["Mo Tianquan", *Baidu Encyclopedia*], available at: http://baike.baidu.com/view/730815.htm (Accessed 4 September 2010).

百度百科 (2010), "搜房网" ["SouFun", *Baidu Encyclopedia*], available at: http://baike.baidu.com/view/1104016.html?wtp=tt (accessed 11 September 2010).

辛苑薇 (2006), "莫天全: 从商如习武贵在坚持不懈", *京华时报* [Xin, Y., "Mo Tianquan: Doing business is like practicing martial arts, the key is perseverance", *Beijing Times*], 20 November 2006, available at: http://net.chinabyte.com/131/2676631.shtml (accessed 12 September 2010).

周惟菁 (2010), "莫天全借道IPO'赎回'大股东", *21世纪经济报道* [Zhou, W., "Mo Tianquan 'redeem' controlling shareholder position via IPO", *21st Century Business Herald*], 3 September 2010, available at: http://www.21cbh.com/HTML/2010-9-6/5OMDAwM-DE5NTg5OQ.html (accessed 12 September 2010).

周云成 (2008), "莫天全和搜房的成功密码", *商界评论* [Zhou, Y., "Mo Tianquan and the secret of SouFan.com", *Biz Review*], 12 May, available at: http://it.hexun.com/2008-05-12/105898348_5.html (Accessed 4 September 2010).

Ning, Gaoning (宁高宁 b. 1958)

Also known as Frank Ning, Ning Gaoning is the chairman of the state-owned China Cereals, Oils and Foodstuffs Corporation (COFCO), the largest oils and food importer and exporter and a leading food manufacturer in China.

Ning was born in Shandong Province, China, and graduated from Shandong University in 1983. Four years later, Ning received his Master of Business Administration from the Katz School of Business Administration at the University of Pittsburg. Upon graduation, Ning joined Huarun Groups (China Resources) in 1987 and became a director in 1990 at one of Huarun's subsidiaries. Ning distinguished himself and rose the corporate ladder steadily through a series of mergers and acquisitions that would later contribute to the development of the capital market in China. He was also able to identify Huarun's internal inefficiency that resulted in a restructure of Huarun's operations into four business units: distribution, real estate, technology, and investment. Equally significant to Huarun and the industry was that Ning moved Huarun from Hong Kong to mainland China, which provided a symbolic and strategic advantage for the company. By 1999, Ning was appointed the vice chairman and general manager of China Resources (holding) Co., and in 2004, he was named the chairman of COFCO.

As the largest food manufacturer and leading cereals, oils, and foodstuffs group in China, COFCO has been on the list of *Fortune* 500 and has ranked first in China's Top 100 Food Enterprises for many years. In addition to foods, COFCO has also real estate, hotels, and financial services, and currently employs more than 100,000 employees. Over his short tenure, Ning has led COFCO through several phases of the company's growth; equally important as the company's growth is the market-oriented culture he has instilled that serves as the foundation of COFCO, which has helped not only boost the company's customer satisfaction ratings but also enhance the employee's performance standard.

After thorough research and data analysis, Ning thought that the food business would grow optimally by controlling and monitoring both quality and quantity in the entire value chain–from manufacturing to retail food market. In an interview with *China Entrepreneur,* Ning stated that he saw a young lady selling honey in a supermarket, standing next to some broken paper boxes and holding a spoon with honey. The saleslady was uttering, "COFCO product, exported quality, RMB 59 a bottle." Ning believed that a company as big as COFCO should not be selling its products in a traditional method. This was a wakeup call for him, and in order to make COFCO a truly giant food enterprise, he had to do what the Japanese had done by linking industry, manufacturing, finance, trade, and investment. Thus, in 2009 Ning proposed a "whole production chain" at the board meeting of COFCO. Although different points of views and concerns were expressed and no one knew exactly when this idea would become successful, most of the participants were motivated by the new proposal titled "Dream and Perseverance Can Change the World." In order to compete effectively on the global stage, Ning is convinced that linking up seamlessly the entire value chain should be an ultimate goal for COFCO. To design a unique value chain is to emphasize its effectiveness of business daily operation, to decrease the expenditure, to reduce the risk of failure, to allocate fund reasonably, and to make the best use of current and future resources. This vision will also change the previous cooperative relationship between COFCO and its suppliers to a strategic relationship toward a higher level of mutual growth, and the underlying foundation for success of this new model is a process and system powered by teamwork.

In order to build up a strong and healthy infrastructure for COFCO, Ning adopted a systematic management approach to stimulate innovative idea and utilize open door policy toward instructive suggestions as well as constructive criticisms. According to him, a good manager should keep his company steadily growing year after year and assure its products are more competitive in the marketplace. In light of recent food safety issue in China, Ning believes it is COFCO's social responsibility to ensure its product's quality and consumer's safety. COFCO is the largest enterprise of food service in China, with a history of more than 50 years, so while an employee can be accustomed to work with outdated operation system and become complacent, the recent financial crisis should serve as a reminder for each COFCO employee to reexamine and make certain that COFCO will continue to produce and sell high-quality products, be able to change, and compete effectively on the global market.

For his accomplishment, Ning was named Asia Business Leader of the Year by CNBC Asia Pacific in 2009. He has also been recognized five times as one of the 25 most influential business leaders by *Chinese Entrepreneur* magazine. In addition, Ning has served as a mentor at the New Champions, a gathering of 1500 leaders from 80 counties that is sponsored by the World Economic Forum. Commenting on his achievement, University of Pittsburg Chancellor Mark A. Nordenberg noted: Frank Gaoning Ning's extraordinary record of high achievement and impact, so visibly recognized by his selection for this prestigious award, should be an inspiration to everyone who believes in hard work and the power of higher education. To know that he travelled to our University from the other side of the world as a young man, earned his MBA here at Pitt, returned to China to begin building his career, and now has been named the outstanding business leader in all of Asia is remarkable. Every institution of higher learning makes many of its most important contributions through the work of its alumni. Just a year ago, we publicly declared our own pride in the many accomplishments of Frank Ning when we honored him as a Legacy Laureate. For obvious reasons, our sense of pride in this distinguished Pitt graduate deepens with each passing year (*PittChronicle*, 2009).

George L. Kuan

Sources

PittChronicle (2009), "Pitt alumnus Frank Gaoning Ning named Asia Business Leader of the Year", 7 December, available at: http://www.chronicle.pitt.edu/?p=4378 (accessed 1 June 2010).

Sun, J., and Shi, H. (2009), "Ning, Gaoning", in: Zhang, W. and Alon, I. (eds), *Biographical Dictionary of New Chinese Entrepreneurs and Business Leaders*, Cheltenham, UK: Edward Elgar, pp. 130–132.

中国知识网 (2009), "宁高宁简历" [Brief biography of Ning Gaoning], 23 July, available at: http://www.zhishi5.com/shrw/2009/0723/article_923.html (accessed 1 June 2010).

Qian, Yingyi (钱颖一 b. 1961)

Former professor of economics at University of California (UC), Berkeley, and current dean of the Economics and Management School at Tsinghua University, Dr. Qian Yingyi is a prolific economist who has made significant contributions to transitional and institutional economics. Qian has especially focused on explaining China's stunning economic success. Unlike many of his Western colleagues, Qian does not believe that gradualism is the right word for Chinese reform. In fact, he describes Chinese economic restructuring as a combination of calculated moves with intermittent drastic measures. As an academic, his impact is also keenly felt. Qian's writing style is accessible to general readers, with his articles widely used to educate students on China's transitional economy.

Born in Beijing in 1961, Qian was admitted into Tsinghua University's mathematics program immediately upon China's resumption of its college entrance examination in 1977. After his graduation in 1981 with a BA, Qian pursued further studies in the United States. He subsequently earned two master's degrees in management and statistics from Yale and Columbia Universities, respectively. In 1984, Qian began to study under the guidance of future Nobel laureate Eric S. Maskin (awarded for his mechanism design theory in 2007) at Harvard University. Employing Western economic theories to analyze Chinese economic problems, Qian received a PhD in economics in 1990. He then served academia as a professor of economics at Stanford University (1990–1999), University of Maryland (1999–2001), and the UC Berkeley (2001–2006), where he received tenure. In 2006, Qian returned to his Chinese alma mater, Tsinghua University, to serve as the fourth dean of the Economics and Management School, which was founded in 1984, with former Premier Zhu Rongji as its founding dean. Since 2002, Qian has also served as guest speaker and research fellow for a number of US and Chinese higher education and research institutions.

As a prolific writer, Qian has published extensively on broad Asian topics in numerous papers, articles, book chapters, and single volumes, in both Chinese and English. His explorations include China's and Russia's entrepreneurs, their organizational forms, reform approaches and strategies, relationships of the market and the associated rule of law, China's corporate governance and finance, Chinese-style budgetary federalism, the Japanese banking system, and American economics. Qian has introduced Chinese reform rationales to the English-speaking world, and in recent years, has similarly introduced the American economy to a Chinese audience. Among various studies, Qian boldly concludes of China's reform that the dual-track approach to transition was a reform that did not produce losers.

In an article titled "Why Is China Different from Eastern Europe? Perspectives from Organization Theory," Qian and his colleagues Gérard Roland and Chenggang Xu (1999) brought to attention how different central organizational structures may produce different reform preferences. They pointed out that, prior to economic reforms, former Soviet Union and East European countries were organized in a specialized or functional way, with major government departments each controlling enormous resources and large factories. The benefit of this "branch organization" is that it significantly reduces setup costs. China's style of central planning, on the other hand, drew on regional characteristics. While it had the advantage of local information, the Chinese M-form organization suffers from duplication of setup costs. The Soviet U-form approach enjoyed the advantage of higher specialization of tasks and economies of scale, but China's M-form structure promoted localized experiments in reform period without destroying the whole system. China's relatively flexible organizations thus allowed Deng Xiaoping's gradual and piecemeal reform strategy to succeed. China's trial-and-error approach, if applied in the Soviet and East European U-form structures, would have caused significant confusion and additional costs without achieving desirable results.

Conventional wisdom assumed that "best-practice institutions" such as information transparency, rule of law, and secure property rights are prerequisites for economic growth. Qian and colleagues challenged that thought by demonstrating how counterintuitive second-best practices can promote economic development and enhance social stability in developing nations. In his article "How Reform Worked in China" (2003), Qian pointed out that these "transitional institutions" must simultaneously meet two criteria: being both "efficiency-improving and interest-compatible" (p. 305). He further identified some of China's institutions and practices that improved allocation efficiency and created win–win results for both the Communist party and common citizens. Such institutions included the dual-track approach and anonymous household banking accounts. Though opaque, these approaches provided incentives for competition and produced much better results than Russia's "shock therapy" approach.

Among his Chinese publications, Qian writes of good governance and rule of law, as well as incentives and constraints in China's unique party-state system. His book *Modern Economics and Chinese Economic Reform* (2003) is a popular text among Chinese economics students. In his book he analyzes many unique behaviors in China's transitional economy and provides policy options on how to correct them. Most Western economists view government ownership either as a necessary evil (the standard conclusion extended from "Market Failure" perspective) or as a needless design that tends to produce "crony capitalism"; Qian instead perceives China's government ownership of enterprises as a transitional institution that is compatible with important social interests and enhances allocation efficiency. This perspective can be found in his 2002 article published in the Beijing-headquartered Chinese journal *Economic Herald*.

As an economics professor at UC Berkeley, Qian taught Comparative Economics I and II, with a macro and micro foci, respectively. Both courses dealt with the theoretical and empirical aspects of economics, describing how firms, markets, and the state work together to promote or hinder economic growth. His macro course focused students' attention on the economic effects of different institutions, while the micro course centered on the interactions of various forms of contracts, organizations, and the mechanisms of institutions. At Tsinghua University, Qian mentors students on the introductory Principles of Economics as well as Transitional

Economy and Development. He focuses on spreading knowledge of modern economic theory to a Chinese audience as well as helping students to understand China's economic reform.

Qian has published numerous articles singly or with colleagues in top economic journals such as the *Journal of Public Economics, Journal of Political Economy, American Economic Review, European Economic Review, Quarterly Journal of Economics, Economics of Transition*, etc. Among colleagues he has published with are economists Barry R. Weingast, Wu Jinglian, and the Nobel prize winning Joseph Stiglitz.

Beyond academia, Qian is also co-editor of *Economics of Transition* and on the editorial boards of *China Economic Review* and *China Journal of Economics*. Other board positions in several Chinese and US business and organizations include the Board of Directors of Industrial and Commercial Bank of China (ICBC), the Board of Dean's Advisors of Harvard Business School (HBS), and the Council of the Association of Asia Pacific Business Schools (AAPBS).

CHUNJUAN NANCY WEI

Sources

Qian, Y. (2003), "How reform worked in China?" in: Rodrik, D. (ed.), *Search of Prosperity: Analytic Narratives on Economic Growth*, Princeton, NJ: Princeton University Press, pp. 297–333.

Qian, Y., Roland, G., and Xu, C. (1999), "Why is China different from Eastern Europe? Perspectives from organization theory", *European Economic Review*, **43**(4–6), 1085–1094.

Qian, Y., Roland, G., and Xu, C. (2006), "Coordination and experimentation in M-form and U-form organizations", *Journal of Political Economy*, **114**(2), 366–402.

Qian, Y., and Wu, J. (2003), "China's transition to a market economy: How far across the river?" in: Hope, N. C. Yang, D. T. and Li, M. Y. (eds), *How Far across the River: Chinese Policy Reform at the Millennium*, Stanford University Press, pp. 31–63 available at: http://elsa.berkeley.edu/˜yqian/how%20far%20across%20the%20river.pdf (Accessed 17 August 2010).

Qian, Y. (n.d.), "Yingyi Qian articles in English", UC Berkeley, available at: http://elsa.berkeley.edu/˜yqian/research.html (Accessed 17 August 2010).

Qian, Y. (n.d.), "Yingyi Qian recent writings in Chinese", UC Berkeley, available at: http://elsa.berkeley.edu/˜yqian/research.chinese.html (Accessed 17 August 2010).

钱颖一 (2002), "第三种视角看企业政府所有制: 一种过渡性制度安排", *经济导刊* [Qian, Y., "A third perspective: Government ownership as a transitional institution", *Economic Herald*], 5, 1–7.

钱颖一 (2003), *现代经济学与中国经济改革*, 中国人民大学出版社, 北京 [Qian, Y., *Modern Economics and China's Reform*, Renmin University of China Press, Beijing].

钱颖一 (2009), "回国是时代的召唤", *光明日报* [Qian, Y., "Returning to China is the calling of the time", *Guangming Daily*], 5 January, available at: http://news.xinhuanet.com/politics/2009-01/05/content_10605963.htm (Accessed 17 August 2010).

Qin, Xiao (秦晓 b. 1947)

A Cambridge PhD and an influential leader of China's large state-owned enterprises, Qin Xiao has served as chairman of China Merchants Group (CMG) and China Merchants Bank for the last 10 years. Prior to his CMG tenure, he also worked as president of China International Trust and Investment Corporation (CITIC) from April 1995 to July 2000, vice chairman of CITIC from July 2000 to December 2001, and chairman of CITIC Industrial Bank from 1998 to 2000.

Born to a military family during the Chinese Civil War, Qin Xiao moved to Beijing along with his parents after the founding of the People's Republic, and went through the elite education reserved for the children of revolutionary cadres in the state capital. However, before graduating from Number 4 High School in Beijing, the Cultural Revolution occurred. Like many youths of the time, Qin eagerly joined the massive political movement and became a district leader of the local Red Guards. Nevertheless, unlike other zealous revolutionaries, he demonstrated not only leadership potential but also independent thinking at a young age by issuing a series of orders prohibiting the physical abuses of high-ranking officials and the violent raids of their family possessions. Because of his unusual, empathetic actions, Qin himself became a subject of investigation, and his fraction was soon outlawed by the Party's Central Steering Group of the Cultural Revolution. In 1968, to escape further political prosecution, he left for Inner Mongolia along with his classmates and became a herdsman for the next several years. While there, besides hard labor, Qin was able to read some banned books and gained a first-hand understanding of the struggles of ordinary Chinese.

In 1972, when some colleges resumed limited admissions after the initial turmoil of the Cultural Revolution, Qin went to Shanxi Mining Institute and studied mechanical engineering for three years. Upon graduation, he began to work for the International Department of the Ministry of Coal Industry. Soon after, the launch of the economic reform in China provided him a new growth opportunity. In 1980, at age 33, he enrolled in the graduate program in enterprise management at China Mining University. Three years later, Qin was appointed assistant to Song Renqiong, a Politburo member and secretary of the Secretariat of the Chinese Communist Party. This key post enabled Qin gain access to the core leadership of the country's economic reform movement, hence laying a solid foundation for his career advancement. Because of his outstanding English skills, he was soon appointed the deputy director of the International Department of the Ministry of Petroleum Industry.

In 1986, Qin joined CITIC, a large state-owned investment firm based in Hong Kong, and steadily moved up the corporate ladder; by 1995, he was named the president of CITIC. With increased responsibilities, Qin did not regard himself as a mere storekeeper of a large SOE, but corporate leader of a modern enterprise, and the strategic decisions he made were based on the market conditions in the fast-growing economy with little regard to the issues of ownership and role of the government. During his spare time, he began to write a series of articles on a wide range of subjects such as the Chinese economic reform, strategies for large enterprises, optimal asset allocation, corporate restructuring, mergers and acquisitions, banking and finance, and the globalization and human capitals. In 1997, at age 50, Qin began to study for his PhD in economics, and in 2003 he graduated from University of Cambridge after completing his dissertation titled *From Production Function to Substitution Function: A Study of on the Functions of the Headquarters of Modern Large Corporations*. Reflecting on his academic work, Qin believed that through his hard labor he has gained a systematic approach to comprehensive issues and was ready for new challenges in his life.

At the turn of the new century, Qin was named by the Chinese State Council as the chairman of the China Merchant Group (CMG), another large SOE of the PRC. CMG traced its history to a transportation company founded on December 16, 1872, by then Prime Minister Li Hongzhang during the Self-Strengthening Movement in the late Qing Dynasty, which was the first transportation firm in China using modern technology not based on foreign ownership, as most of the startup capitals were provided by native Chinese. When Qin stepped in, CMG was struggling for its survival in the aftermath of the Asian Financial Crisis. Initially, he maintained a low profile eating box lunches like others, but quickly won wide respect for his vision, dedication, and professionalism. Qin then built a consensus among all employees of the need for further reform, and established a team and system for modern enterprise management. Within a few years, through restructuring and a series of acquisitions, he was able to turn around the company, and led CMG into an era of extraordinary growth and prosperity. For his accomplishment, in 2003, Qin was named among the most influential enterprise leaders in China.

Besides his leadership with CMG, Qin has been a member of the 11th session of the Chinese People's Political Consultative Conference since 2008, a member of Lafarge's International Advisory Board since 2007, and chairman of the Asia Business Council since 2009. He is also the honorary chairman of Hong Kong Chinese Enterprises Association, a deputy to the Ninth National People's Congress, an advisor on the Foreign Currency Policy of the State Administration of Foreign Exchange, and a guest professor at the School of Economics and Management of Tsinghua University and the Graduate School of the People's Bank of China. In addition, Qin has served as an independent nonexecutive director and a member of the audit committee of HKR International since 2009 and of China Telecom Corporation since 2008, and is responsible for, among other things, reviewing the financial statements of these public companies and overseeing their financial systems and internal control procedures. He also served as chairman of the APEC Business Advisory Council (ABAC) in 2001, and was a member of Toyota's International Advisory Board from 1997 to 2005.

As a well-respected leader of large SOEs in China, Qin is the author of several papers and books in economics, management, and social transformation. In August 2010, he announced his retirement from CMG, and began to devote his energies on the development of the Boyuan Foundation. With a focus on economic and social research, the Boyuan Foundation seeks long-term solutions for the problems that emerge during China's rapid transformation from an agricultural to a postindustrial society. Reflecting on his life, Qin does not regard himself elite, but a "reformer working from inside the establishment" (Xiao, 2010). Influenced by his experience in both China and the West, this intellectual and businessman feels a deep sense of responsibility for the future direction of Chinese social and economic reforms.

QUN DU

Sources

Xiao, J. (2010), "Interview with former chairman of China Merchants Group Qin Xiao", *Economic Observer*, 25 October, available at: http://www.eeo.com.cn/ens/finance_investment/2010/11/04/184874.shtml (accessed 23 November 2010).

乐楚 (2010), "士大夫秦晓", *南都周刊* [Yue, C., "Gentleman scholar Qin Xiao", *Southern Metropolis Weekly*], 2 November, available at: http://www.nbweekly.com/Print/Article/11415_0.shtml (accessed 23 November 2010).

Shen, Nanpeng (Neil Shen 沈南鹏 b. 1967)

Known to the West as Neil Shen, Shen Nanpeng is a successful entrepreneur and investor who twice made impressive records on the NASDAQ, and is the founding partner of Sequoia Capital China.

Born in Haining, Zhejiang Province, Shen Nanpeng relocated to Shanghai with his family at a young age. His childhood dream was to become a mathematician rather than an entrepreneur or investor, as he excelled academically since elementary school especially in mathematics, and was called a whiz kid by his teachers and fellow students. In his high school entrance exam, Shen scored 594, six points shy of the perfect score. In 1982, during the first nationwide high school student computer contest, Shen Nanpeng met Liang Jianzhang and both received prizes; 17 years later, the fate of the two crossed again while founding Ctrip. For Shen, his excellence in academic did not happen by chance but through hard work, as he participated in a math tutor program every week and whole-heartedly devoted his time to the subject, and this devotion and concentration are the natural reasons for his achievements.

In 1985, upon school recommendation, Shen Nanpeng was directly admitted into the elite Shanghai Jiao Tong University, majoring in mathematics. During his freshman year, he joined a survey group and subsequently broadened his horizon. He realized that he had spent too much time merely on the books and neglected many important things in life. After he was admitted to the mathematics program at Columbia University, Shen became more and more aware of the fact that mathematics was not the ultimate goal for him. Through all those years of math study, he strengthened his logic thinking, but that was still far from the ideal of becoming a math expert. During that time, a Chinese student's experience enlightened Shen. That student failed one exam and did not even finish his PhD study, but he was recruited by a top firm on Wall Street. After some thoughts, Shen decided to give up math and enrolled into the School of Management at Yale University. In retrospect, Shen thinks that was a wise decision.

After graduation from Yale in 1992, Shen worked for more than eight years in the investment banking industry in New York and Hong Kong. First he applied for a job in the Citibank. After five rounds of intense interviews, he joined the Wall Street branch of Citibank. In 1994, he worked at Lehman Brothers in an investment banking position. After another two years, he became director and head of debt capital markets for China at Deutsche Bank Hong Kong, where he worked from 1996 to 1999.

Eight years of investment banking experience became Shen's most important capital for career success. At the end of 1998, he made an individual investment in an antihacker software company. At that time, Internet just began to take off. Influenced by his contact in investment banking and his schoolfellows in California, Shen was convinced of the bright future of the new Internet industry. He understood that his skills were in macrostrategies and capital operation, but lacked knowledge of Internet technology and travelling industry, so Shen invited Liang Jianzhang, who was the technical director of Oracle at that time, and Fan Min, who had more than 10 years of experience in the travelling industry to cooperate with him. Over a lunch in Shanghai in 1999, the three had a chat and Ctrip.com came into being. In May of that year, Shen, Liang, and Fan co-founded Ctrip.com International Limited with a capital of 2 million RMB. Serving as president and CFO, Shen bid farewell to the investment banking industry, and began to focus on financing for Ctrip. Though he had eight-year investment banking experience, the task was not easy because of the small business size of Ctrip. After being turned down by many investors, Ctrip finally attracted IDG's attention, which made an initial US$430,000 investment in Ctrip after a two-month discussion with the Ctrip team in return of 12.5% equity of the company. After that, Ctrip successively secured $4.5 million investment from Softbank and another $11 million investment from Carlyle Group.

As Ctrip continually grew its market share, many companies wanted to copy its model, but through competition and elimination, only one or two companies are still in the game, with Ctrip being the firm leader. During the IPO road show for Ctrip in 2003, the most frequently asked questions were where Ctrip's competitiveness was and how it managed to maintain a 30%–40% net profit, together with an annual growth rate of 70%–80%, for which Shen confidentially attributed to Ctrip's service system and executive team. On December 9, 2003, Ctrip went public on NASDAQ with an issue price of $18 per share; by the end of the day, the share price reached $33.94.

Shen once drove through Dallas during a trip in the United States. In his 30-minute drive from outskirts to the city, he observed that there were more than 30 economy hotels along the way. The capacity of market surprised him, and this became the sparkle for his later development of Home Inns. After setting Ctrip on the right track with a leading position in the market, the co-founders were no longer satisfied with the current situation and wanted to explore and develop a new line of business. Seeing many high-rating hotels with foreign investment entering China while the market for the low-end hotel chains remained almost empty, Shen and his partners set their sights on this market sector. The Home Inns Group arose at this moment. From its incorporation in 2001 to 2006, the properties run by Home Inns had exceeded 110, and the general income reached 249 million RMB by 2006. Due to its rapid expansion, Home Inns surpassed Jinjiang Inns and ranked first place in the Chinese market. On October 26, 2006, Home Inns went public on NASDAQ with an opening price of $22 per share, an increase by 59.4% compared to the issue price of $13.8. In its successful IPO, a total of 7.9 million American depositary receipts were issued, and Home Inns raised a capital of $109 million.

A year before Home Inns went public, Shen stepped down from his president and CFO position, and began to cooperate with Sequoia Capital on investing in the Chinese market. The famous venture capital Sequoia was founded in 1972 with a total capital exceeding $4 billion. Over the years, it has invested in more than 500 companies, among which more than 200 went public and more than 100 were acquired, including Apple, Cisco, Oracle, Yahoo, Google, and PayPal. Together with Zhang Fan, former director on the board of DFJ, Shen co-founded Sequoia Capital China with $200 million of registered capital. Within the first half of 2006, Sequoia Capital China has announced its plan to invest in nine companies, covering the technology, telecom, agriculture, media, and comic industries. Since its inception in 2005, led by Shen and Zhang, Sequoia Capital China successively invested in over 50 companies, including Land V. Group, Waps.cn, China Concord Insurance, Qihoo.com, Greatdreams Cartoon Media, and so on. Not content with his accomplishments, Shen Nanpeng is still busy exploring the best method of investing in China, and the "special gene" of Sequoia Capital China.

WEI QIAN

Sources

李政 (2007), "沈南鹏: 功夫在NASDAQ之外", *叱咤华尔街: 10位海归上市公司领袖* (王辉耀主编), 中国发展出版社, 北京 [Li Z., "Shen Nanpeng: Laboring beyond the NASDAQ", in Wang, H. (ed.), *Movers on Wall Street: Ten Overseas Returnees Who Took Their Business Public*, China Development Press, Beijing], pp. 132–158.

中国证券报 (2009), "纳斯达克常客沈南鹏: 从数学天才到耶鲁MBA" ["NASDAQ regular Shen Nanpeng: From math genius to Yale MBA", *China Securities Journal*], available at: http://news.cnfol.com/090831/101,1596,6443028,00.shtml (accessed 12 July 2010).

中投顾问 (2008), *沈南鹏: 个人投资明星与红杉资本* [*Shen Nanpeng: A Star in Individual Investment and Sequoia Capital*, China Investment Consulting], available at: http://wenku.baidu.com/view/a0e9f9ec4afe04a1b071dea0.html (accessed 12 July 2010).

Shi, Zhengrong (施正荣 b. 1963)

Once an unknown physicist, Shi Zhengrong is the founder, chairman, and chief executive officer of Suntech Power Holdings, an NYSE-listed leading solar energy company and the world's largest crystalline silicon photovoltaic (PV) module manufacturer based in Wuxi, China. Shi is ranked by *Forbes* among the world's richest people and one of the wealthiest living in China. People hail him as "China's sunshine boy" and "hero of the environment."

Shi came from a farming community on Yangzhong Island in Jiangsu Province. Born in 1963 during the years after great famine, Shi's parents gave him, the younger twin, up for adoption. Young Shi excelled at school and his adoptive parents honored his teachers with a great banquet before their 16-year-old son left for university in Northeast Jilin Province. He received a bachelor's degree in optical science from Changchun University of Science and Technology in China in 1983, a master's degree in laser physics from the Shanghai Institute of Optics and Fine Mechanics, the Chinese Academy of Sciences in 1986.

In 1988, Shi arrived in Australia as a foreign-exchange scholar. Four years later, he earned his PhD in electrical engineering from the University of New South Wales (UNSW), under the supervision of Martin A. Green, a well-known world leader in PV. In 1991, Shi obtained his PhD in multicrystalline silicon thin film solar cells. He was soon chosen an international expert by the research journal *Progress in Photovoltaics* for its special issue on crystalline silicon solar cells, and was subsequently recognized as a world authority in the area. From 1992 to 1995, Shi was a senior research scientist and the leader of the Thin Film Solar Cells Research Group at the Centre of Excellence for Photovoltaic Engineering at UNSW, the only government-sponsored PV industry research center in Australia. For the next six years, he worked as a research director and executive director of Pacific Solar, an Australian PV company engaged in the commercialization of next-generation thin film technology. During this period, he was involved in the development of the thin film technology now being commercialized by CSG Solar in Germany, and was one of the inventors on the key patents for this breakthrough.

In 2001, Shi returned to China as an Australian citizen, and headed a solar-cell startup company with 20 workers in Wuxi, Jiangsu Province. With the support of $6 million arranged by Wuxi municipal government, the assistance of ex-colleagues at UNSW, and his own unrelenting drive, Shi soon had his first factory up and running. Sales boomed as the market for solar technology rapidly expanded. In August 2005, Suntech Power Holding CO. was incorporated.

On December 15, 2005, Suntech successfully completed its initial public offering (IPO) on the New York Stock Exchange. Through the IPO, Suntech Power issued 26.38 million American Depository Shares (ADS) priced at US$15 per share. The company raised a total of US$400 million, at that time becoming the Chinese private enterprise to raise the largest amount of funds in the New York Stock Exchange. It is China's first high-tech private corporation that started to attract investment from the mainstream international capital market and earned the highest market value in the world PV industry.

Shi is China's new generation of entrepreneurs. He is the inventor for 11 patents in PV technologies and has published or presented a number of articles and papers in PV-related scientific magazines and at conferences. In October 2005, he was awarded "PV-SEC Prize" at the International Photovoltaic Science and Engineering Conference, the only award winner who was from business, in recognition of the great contribution to China and the world's PV industry and PV technology applications. On May 25, 2006, Shi was awarded the "Best Entrepreneur Prize" by the Southern California Asian Society. On August 8, 2006, he was appointed as a member of the advisory board of NYSE. Shi is the first entrepreneur in China to be honored with the employment of MOU (*Memorandum of Understanding*), whose members are presidents and general managers of top-class enterprises around the world. In January 2010, he was also honored as a finalist for the Zayed Future Energy Prize.

Suntech's production capacity has increased from 10 megawatts a year in 2002 to well over 1000 megawatts in 2010. Under Shi's leadership, the company continues to grow at a phenomenal rate, with a current market capital of nearly US$2 billion. Suntech Power has diversified its portfolio in the solar market by offering solar energy for off-grid systems, government, homes, and large solar plants across the world. The company has offices in over 13 countries and its solar modules have been installed in over 80 countries. One of the unique products that Suntech offers is the Ab & Ad+, which offers residential users 175–190 watts of electricity. These solar panels are made from monocrystalline silicon, come with a 25-year warranty, have lower power bills, and are ideally set up on the roof of a house. As a badge of honor and a validation of its technology, Suntech's PV system was installed on the Bird's Nest Olympic Stadium in Beijing.

As a prime mover in the development of photovoltaic technology, Shi has played an important role in making China a powerhouse in the global photovoltaic technology market. In January 2009, Suntech achieved a record of 1 gigawatt solar cell and module production capacity. Looking forward, Shi is full of energy, and envisions his company growing to the size of oil conglomerates as the world increasingly shifts from fossil fuels to renewable energy. His next ambition is to make solar power as cheap as conventional electricity. His trailblazing efforts have also inspired six other former UNSW students to play a leading role in successful Chinese solar ventures of their own. As a result, China is poised to overtake Japan as the global leader in solar-cell manufacturing.

For his accomplishment, Shi was named one of the "Heroes of the Environment" by *TIME* magazine in 2007. During the same year, he was also honored as one of China's Green Persons of the Year for his outstanding contribution to environmental protection initiatives and environmental awareness within China. In January 2009, *Fortune* magazine named Shi Asia Businessman of the Year. Later that year he was also elected to the fellowship of the Australian Academy of Technological Sciences and Engineering (ATSE) for his outstanding achievement in research and management in the large-scale commercialization of photovoltaic technology. Although a citizen of Australia since 1995, he was one of first 19 people who were granted a permanent resident green card in Wuxi in 2010.

WEIDONG ZHANG

Sources

Bullis, K. (2010), "Solar's Great Leap Forward", *Technology Review*, July/August, available at: http://www.technologyreview.com/energy/25565/ (accessed 25 July 2010).

China Public Companies (2010), "Solar Power breaks new boundaries in China", available at: http://chinesepubliccompanies.com/solar-power-breaking-new-boundaries-in-china-638/ (accessed 30 July 2010).
Green, M. (2007), "Heroes of the environment: Shi Zhengrong", *Time*, 17 October, http://205.188.238.181/time/specials/2007/article/0,28804,1663317_1663322_1669932,00.html (accessed 2 June 2010).
Suntech (2010), "About Suntech", available at: http://ap.suntech-power.com/en/about.html (accessed 2 June 2010).
Zhang, W.D. (2009), "Shi Zhengrong", in: Zhang, W.X. and Alon, I. (eds), *Biographical Dictionary of New Chinese Entrepreneurs and Business Leaders*, Cheltenham, UK: Edward Elgar, pp. 154, 155.

Shu, Qi (Jack Shu 舒奇 b. undisclosed)

Known as a star of public relations, Shu Qi is the vice president of China Hewlett-Packard Co., Ltd., who has helped expand HP's business development by working closely with other senior managers in shaping public decisions and strengthening HP's sustained operation and positive exposure and visibility in China over the recent years.

Born in Beijing, Shu Qi has three elder sisters. His parents were Chinese returnees as well—while his mother was a graduate from NYU with a master's degree, his father Shu Hongyuan once studied at Columbia University, and was one of the most successful businessmen of the 20th century in China. During World War II, the Chinese Communist Party founded a commercial company to import medicines for the war effort, and Shu Hongyuan was appointed as the deputy director. After the founding of the People's Republic of China, Shu Hongyuan returned to China and founded China Resources in Hong Kong, which has now become one of the world top 500 companies.

Because of his notable family background, Shu Qi received a solid education during his childhood. A serious student himself, Shu studied very hard, especially English and math. His outstanding performance caught the attention of a famed scientist from the East China Electric Power Institute, who became his after-school tutor later on. In 1977, when the national college entrance examination was resumed, Shu was admitted into the University of Science and Technology of China (USTC), one of the most prestigious universities in China. However, his mentor convinced him to study in the Physics Department of Nanjing University (NJU) instead, from which he graduated originally. So in the spring of 1978, Shu came to the campus of NJU, and after some efforts, he again excelled in his academic work. Shortly after, Shu fell in love with a girl from the computer science department at NJU, who was also the captain of track and field team of the university and the record holder of female hurdles in Jiangsu Province. Upon graduation, they both went to Beijing and got married soon. While she worked for the Beijing Software and Computer Service Company (which later became China National Software and Service Co.), Shu Qi became an assistant engineer at the Chinese Center for Medicine and Disease Prevention under the Ministry of Health of China.

In the autumn of 1984, Shu went to study at the Manhattan Institute of Engineering in New York. Although he changed his major from physics to computer science, he found that it was not difficult, and always challenged his professors. If a teacher made any mistake, he would point out right away. Once when a faculty member who was the authority in computer science came and gave an exam, Shu quickly objected to one of his questions. Deeply impressed by his response, his professor decided to offer Shu a scholarship for PhD study together with some other benefits. However, around the same time, he was also offered a position in the world renowned Bell Laboratory. After some thoughts, Shu chose to work for Bell, joining its Unix OS department.

At Bell Lab, Shu started as a basic software engineer, and soon was promoted to the director of a team, the manager of planning technology, and later the market development. In the eight years of working for Bell, Shu learned a great deal about modern business operation of the technological undertaking, and was very much content with his job until he met a Chinese employee of senior age. That old gentleman had been working in Bell for many years and had made great contribution to the laboratory; however, he received no promotion. Shu soon realized that further career advancement opportunity was rather limited for being an ethnic minority member, so he decided to return to China, although he and his family already had a comfortable life in the United States.

In 1992, Shu Qi returned to China, and a year later, he founded an investment and consulting firm with his friends, and travelled extensively across China to meet the raising demands due to the accelerated economic reform activities in the country. However, at that time, the investment environment in China was not well developed, and Shu soon found that he was not good at this kind of business operations. Therefore, he changed his career again and joined Schmidt Electronics Group, a German company that worked as the general agency in China for many of the famous electronics brands around the world. Schmidt Electronics Group started selling ESI Group's products in the early 1990s but was not successful. Therefore, Schmidt Electronics invited Shu to join the company and appointed him as the manager of the Shanghai Branch. Under his leadership, the market share of ESI was soon raised from 50% up to 90%.

On August 3, 2000, Shu joined Hewlett-Packard as the general manager of Government Affairs Department and Strategy Development Department. Months later, he was appointed as the vice president of Hewlett-Packard (China) Co., Ltd. In April 2003, when SARS broke out in Beijing, Shu made a quick decision to donate equipment to the public, and his judgment was soon approved by the HP headquarters. He quickly checked the demand with the Chinese Center for Disease Control and Prevention, and gathered all urgently needed equipment and sent them to the major hospitals swiftly. Due to its active involvement in the public welfare, HP China had been awarded the title of "the Most Respected Company in China" for six years since 2002.

To be the best in business is not only one of the connotations of HP, but also the life goal of Shu Qi. Besides his professional work at HP, he is also a senior member of the Chinese Institute of Electronics, HP's corporate member in American Chamber of Commerce in China, vice chairman of Entrepreneur Advisory Committee of Zhongguancun Science Park, and adviser for the mayor of Wuhan.

XUEYUAN LIU AND WENCHAO ZENG

Sources

US-China Green Energy Council (2008), "Jack Shu, HP Vice President", available at: http://ucgef.org/en/bio/jack-shu (Accessed 26 August 2010).

冯嘉雪 (2007), "舒奇: 永远用微笑面对挑战", *巅峰职业: 10位海归职业经理人* (王辉耀主编), 中国发展出版社, 北京 [Feng, J.X., "Shu Qi: Always facing challenges with a smile ", in Wang, H. Y. (ed.), *Top Careers: Ten Overseas Returnees in Professional Management*, China Development Press, Beijing], pp. 234-261.

中国国际广播电台 (2008), "海归推动中国: 对话舒奇" ["returnees who have shaped China: Conversation with Shu Qi", China Radio International], 9 April, available at: http://taobao.cri.cn/18824/2008/04/09/2185@2011589.htm (Accessed 26 August 2010).

Sun, Wei (Wei Christianson 孙玮 b. 1957)

Sun Wei is the managing director and China CEO of Morgan Stanley, one of the world's largest financial service firms. Her international finance career has been characterized by consummate relationship building, bold strategies, calculated risk-taking, and a sheer determination that has seen her succeed in one of the most competitive, high-pressure industries. If one were to propose a role model for young Chinese women, Sun Wei may very well be the perfect choice. The story of a shy but determined Beijing girl who rose to become one of the key players in the business world is not only an account of immense personal achievement, but also a tale that parallels and embodies the development and spirit of China itself.

Sun Wei was born in Beijing in 1957 to a military family. While she was fated to spend her formative years in the turbulent and impoverished environment that was China at that time, she maintained an optimistic outlook and an insatiable curiosity. Sun was an excellent all-round student who also made time to pursue extra-curricular activities. While China's Cultural Revolution (1966–1976) placed many restrictions on daily life, young Sun Wei maintained a full and happy life taking on the roles of editor of her student newspaper and on-air host of its daily broadcasts.

After graduating high school with top grades, she was assigned to work in Beijing Library, the modest forerunner to today's expansive National Library of China. Many of her colleagues were from well-connected families with political or military backgrounds as this was a sought-after position carrying a degree of status and prestige. Even at this early stage of her working life, Sun stood out as someone with acute potential and was often assigned tasks that required a high degree of diligence and talent. She excelled as a member of the editing team for foreign language books, which gave her added motivation to improve her English language skills.

To the bewilderment of her colleagues, Sun Wei had her sights set on entering university and often studied late and alone in the library offices. For her, study was a means by which to expand one's range of opportunities, and she was determined to lift herself beyond the life path to which she had been designated. Finally, events in China were to turn in her favor. In the late 1970s, China opened up to the world and university entrance examinations were reinstated. She had no hesitation in resigning from her secure and comfortable job in order to compete for a place in university.

After recording an excellent score in the national entrance examination, Sun Wei entered Beijing Language and Cultural College in 1978, one of the foremost language schools in China. Her after-hours study at the library prepared her well for a successful college life, and due to her strong leadership skills, she secured a full four-year position as the Secretary General of the Youth League for the College.

In 1982, Sun Wei graduated with flying colors and was almost certainly in line for a prestigious job as a translator in the foreign ministry. Instead, she elected to continue her studies and set her sights on a highly ranked American university. At that time, very few students were given the opportunity to study abroad. However, with her characteristic optimism, Sun refused to be restricted by a scarcity of precedent or by the scale of the challenge that confronted her.

By chance, she met Professor Randy Edwards of the Colombia University Law School, who was visiting Beijing at that time. She was impressed with his responses to her many questions and resolved to study law. Since her education in China would not qualify her for a prestigious institution such as Columbia University, Professor Edwards suggested that she focus on gaining entrance to a high-ranking liberal arts college as a step toward receiving an offer from a prominent law school. Although this meant that she would repeat two years of undergraduate study, Sun was neither daunted nor discouraged. She was eventually accepted for enrolment to Amherst College in Massachusetts as their first Chinese student.

The cultural challenges were considerable; however, Sun Wei graduated cum laude from Amherst College in 1985. Even more importantly, her excellent academic record ensured that she was offered a scholarship to attend the Law School at Colombia University. Professor Edwards' advice had paid off.

In New York, Sun quickly became a member of the Law School's Chinese Law Institute Center that was run by Professor Edwards. Here, she met another young member, Jon Christianson, who took particular interest in her work. In 1989, she graduated from Columbia Law School and was admitted to practice in the State of New York, one of the earliest Chinese to receive a license to practice at the bar in the United States. This was also the year in which she changed her name to Wei Sun Christianson, having decided to accept Jon Christianson's proposal of marriage.

Sun's career in law began in the New York office of Orrick, Herrington & Sutcliffe; however, her path would soon take an unexpected turn. With her husband's law firm opening an office in Hong Kong, they decided that this would be the opportunity and the ideal location to launch both their careers and their family. With one child to care for – and two more soon to follow—she was already receiving excellent offers from investment banks and law firms in Hong Kong.

At this time, the Hong Kong Securities and Futures Commission (HKSFC) was investigating regulatory changes that would enable Chinese mainland companies to list on the Hong Kong Stock Exchange. Sun was invited to play a significant role in the internationalization of the Hong Kong securities market and in the first governance framework for listed Chinese companies. She was eventually engaged in the float of the first batch of Chinese IPOs. Her outstanding performance led to her appointment as associate director of corporate finance at HKSFC, where she became known for a soft appearance that belied her strength and her problem-solving skills. However, after five years—and three children—she needed a new challenge and was keen to switch to the finance industry. In 1998, with no shortage of offers on the table, she accepted a position at Morgan Stanley as its Beijing chief representative, thus beginning her illustrious career in banking.

One of Sun Wei's first projects for Morgan Stanley was an IPO for Sinopec, a large state-owned enterprise (SOE) in the oil industry. Chinese SOEs were renowned for their complicated structures and opaque accounting systems, so she spent almost 18 months entangled in a very complicated IPO execution process. A volatile market and the government's oil price policy saw the project shelved for some time; however, policy changes were eventually effected to allow the float to proceed.

As lead underwriter to some of China's most powerful SOEs, Morgan Stanley was often embroiled in conflict with clients and their stakeholders. Sun Wei frequently found herself having to make decisions that put her own job on the line; however, her record was exemplary and her growing reputation was well earned.

With the financial fallout from 9/11 causing the cancelation of most IPOs, she insisted on pressing ahead with her clients' planned floats. Learning from her Sinopec experience, and in order to avoid the additional stigma that surrounded Chinese companies at that time, she cleverly repositioned the IPOs, a strategy that achieved a level of success that ran counter to the market.

Meanwhile, Morgan Stanley's CEO, John Mack, had departed to join Credit Suisse-First Boston (CSFB) in Hong Kong and invited her to join him. She quickly developed a dynamic and successful China division within CSFB and again demonstrated her willingness to take personal risks in order to break through a regulatory or stakeholder impasse. In spite of investor concerns about regulatory risks that had already stalled several high-profile floats, Sun Wei succeeded in launching an IPO for the oil service business of CNOOC, China's largest producer of offshore crude oil and natural gas. She followed that with successful launches of China Life (US$3.5 billion) and SMIC (US$1.8 billion).

With the sudden dismissal of John Mack in 2004, Sun Wei also resigned. She spent the next 14 months as chairman of Citigroup Global Markets (Asia) Ltd., followed by a brief period with HKSFC. By early 2006, she had again joined her old boss and mentor John Mack in her second Morgan Stanley "career," this time as CEO China region. By this time, Morgan Stanley's strategic focus had shifted to Asia and particularly China. In spite of considerable turmoil within the finance industry, Sun brought together a team that developed a portfolio of business with a solid core of profitable investment-banking revenue, overseas equity raising for Chinese clients, and key mandates to advise state companies on overseas deals. Along the way, she oversaw the establishment of Morgan Stanley's wholly owned commercial-banking operation as well as their joint ventures in asset management and trust businesses.

During her stewardship, some of Morgan Stanley's initiatives in China have been stunning in their boldness and perspicacity. In order to cope with write-downs during the subprime mortgage crisis, she was instrumental (together with her CEO John Mack) in securing a US$5.6 billion capital infusion from China Investment Corporation (CIC), the sovereign trust fund of China. Given the status of CIC, this was widely considered the most sensational transaction of 2007. In that year, she became a member of the Morgan Stanley Global Management Committee in recognition of her outstanding leadership of the important China business.

Another of Sun's recent gambits involves executing the exit from Morgan Stanley's joint venture with China International Capital Company (CICC) in order to make way for a joint venture with investment bank Huaxin Securities Co. Ltd. This will create a full range of investment banking services to rival the China operations of Goldman Sachs Group Inc., Credit Suisse Group, and UBS AG. These deals require Sun Wei and her team to manage complex relationships, conflicts between unrelated deals, and sensitive vested interests. The scale and dynamics of these initiatives can even cause occasional collisions with government policy on strategic assets.

Throughout her career, many awards and accolades have been bestowed upon her. In 2006, her achievements were recognized by Columbia Law School, where she was awarded the prestigious Columbia Law School Medal of Excellence. She has been named on the *Fortune* magazine's "Most Powerful Women" (2007–2010), the *Wall Street Journal*'s "50 Women to Watch," and *Forbes Asia*'s "Powerful Women" (2010). In addition, she topped the 2009 list of "50 Outstanding Asian Americans in Business," where she was cited as "an Asian American who has reached the highest plateau within a major corporation." During the same year, she was inducted into the Museum of Chinese in America. In 2010, she became a member of the Board of Trustees for Amherst College.

In a high-pressure industry and a hypergrowth business environment, Sun Wei still finds time to enjoy family passions such as open sea diving, snow skiing, and horse riding. The focused student with boundless energy and a determination to make time for a happy and balanced life is still clearly visible.

Sun Wei has played an important role in China's corporatization and economic liberalization and is universally admired for her integrity, her loyalty, and her unsurpassed professional skills. She is a rare talent who has achieved great success in the most difficult of industries while also choosing to enjoy a happy and enriched family life.

Terence R. Egan

Sources

Center for China and Globalization (2009), "China's diaspora and returnees: Impact on China's globalization process", 1 September, available at: http://www.ccg.org.cn/en/news.asp?id = 769 (accessed 26 January 2010).

Hung, H. (2010), "China's financial insider", *The Daily Beast*, 18 March, available at: http://www.thedailybeast.com/blogs-and-stories/2010-03-18/chinas-financial-insider/?cid = tag:all2 (accessed 6 June 2010).

Morgan Stanley (2006), "Morgan Stanley hires Wei Christianson to lead China", Press release, 31 January, available at: http://www.morganstanley.com/about/press/articles/5f0f87cb-5554-11dd-adaf-ab43576ea42b.html (accessed 6 June 2010).

王红茹 (2007), "孙玮: 不安于平淡的'金融美女'", *资本推手: 10位海归投资银行家* (王辉耀主编), 中国发展出版社, 北京 [Wang, H., "Sun Wei: A 'beauty in finance' who will not settle for an insipid life", in Wang, H. (Ed.), *Capital Movers and Shakers: Ten Overseas Returnees in Investment Banking*, China Development Press, Beijing], pp. 84-105.

Tang, Min (汤敏 b. 1953)

Tang Min is the former deputy representative and chief economist of Asian Development Bank (ADB). Tang and his wife (also an economist), Zuo Xiaolei (左小蕾), have played a key role in the development of the country's economy, especially the large-scale college expansion drive that started in the late 1990s.

Born in Beijing in 1953, Tang grew up like other typical children of that period. In 1966, during the turbulent time of the Chinese Cultural Revolution, he attended the local middle school where the main study materials consisted of *The Quotations from Chairman Mao*. Nevertheless, instead of party doctrines, Tang learned that knowledge was power. In 1971, he was sent to countryside to be "reeducated" by peasants. Two years later, he was reassigned as a high school teacher and taught mathematics.

In 1977, before reaching age 25, Tang decided to take the newly resumed national college entrance exam. According to the state regulations of the time, candidates for college education could not exceed 25 years of age. Knowing this was his last and only chance, Tang worked hard, and his intelligence and dedication paid off. In 1978, he enrolled in Wuhan University, a well-known institution of higher learning in Central China, with a major in mathematics. However, foreseeing future employment opportunities, he took many courses related to economics, which laid a solid foundation for his subsequent education and career. While in Wuhan, Tang met Zuo Xiaolei, a fellow student in the mathematics department, who later become Tang's wife.

In 1984, Tang went to the United States and enrolled in a PhD program at the University of Illinois in Urbana-Champaign. Upon receiving his doctoral degree in economics five years later, he was recruited by the ADB as an economist, overseeing East Asian economies, economic cooperation, debts, and Asian financial market research. Tang spent the next 18 years working at ADB. He chose the bank because he had a special interest in the economic advancement of developing countries. Owing to his personal experience, he saw a career in this area would be fulfilling and meaningful work.

After entering ADB, Tang relocated to the Philippines, where he lived through a military coup. That experience made Tang realize that the US model of development and the market economy was not the solution for poverty in that country; democracy alone could not solve all the nation's problems. Therefore, his interests shifted toward policy study, and he spent 11 years researching and publishing books and papers focusing mainly on the Asian economy, debt and financial markets, as well as regional economic cooperation. He was among the first generation of students going abroad after China's reform and opening up; however, the long experience living overseas did not make him more Westernized. Growing up from a developing economy gave him a unique perspective and let him put more focus on the localized issues like rural finance, thus enabling him to grow and become one of the most in-depth economists on the Asian economy. Moreover, Tang focused on China's rural development and financial markets, as he believed that financial tools and support from commercial banks would be the key for poverty alleviation in rural areas. To develop China's rural finance, Tang noted: "We now need to tackle the rural financial problem, we are short of capillaries but not large vessels, we need to establish a mechanism infiltrating as far as the farmers; more importantly, I think the next step in financial reform is to create a good capillary system" (Yuan, 2007).

During the peak of Asian financial crisis of 1997, out of professional insight, he and his wife, Zuo Xiaolei, wrote a letter to the Chinese central government expressing their views on the higher education reform. They believed that more individuals should have the rights to receive higher education, a strategy that would boost the nation's economy and pull the country out of a possible recession. This suggestion was soon implemented by the Chinese government, and in the first few years, Tang won widespread praises for his suggestion, and was nicknamed the "father of college expansion." However, the expansion drive soon went beyond his expectation, as he originally suggested to double the scale in three years, but the total college enrollment was expanded five times in just six years.

The expansion made it possible for many students to attend college who would otherwise be rejected, but its long-term impact was uncertain. When the first batch of expanded student population poured in the job market in 2002 and 2003, people began to cast double about the real benefits of the expansion drive. As a result of the decade-long expansion, China's net enrollment rate in higher education rose from 8% to 24%, and the country was fast-forwarded from an elite education system to mass public education, thus becoming the largest higher education provider in the world. Nevertheless, the meaningful curricular reform did not keep up with the school expansion, which led to a widespread problem that a large number of college graduates did not possess the knowledge and skills the society really needs, therefore compounding the challenge of a very tough employment situation for millions of students. Facing the public criticisms, Tang remained steadfast in his position on the college expansion, believing the benefits far outweighted the negative impact.

According to him, many countries have experienced the conflicts between the enrollment and short-term employment problem, and China cannot rely on only one reform to solve all the problems. Young people should go to university not only because of the need of employment, but also because it is in the best interest for the long-term, national quality improvement and social development goals of the country.

In 2000, Tang returned to China, serving as the chief economist of the ADB. In 2007, he was elected vice-president of China Development Research Foundation (CDRF) of the Development Research Center under the State Council, a nonprofit organization engaged in policy research, and promoting China's development. Leaving the job (he worked for nearly two decades for the position in CDRF), Tang felt very comfortable about his decision out of the concern about Chinese and Asian financial issues, just like when he chose the ADB over the First National Bank in Chicago 18 years ago.

Now retired form ADB, Tang lives in China as an elite returnee and frequently shares his insights into the development of the nation's economy. For his professional accomplishment, in January 2010, during the Lujiazui Summit of the Worldwide Chinese Financial Elites, Tang was named among the Chinese financial elites worldwide who have made significant contributions to the motherland.

YING HUANG AND MIAN WANG

Sources

百度百科 (2010), "汤敏" ["Tang Min", *Baidu Encyclopedia*], available at: http://baike.baidu.com/view/508684.html?wtp = tt(accessed 10 September 2010).

柳建云 (2009), "'高校扩招之父'汤敏: 不后悔谏言大学扩招", 新华网 ["Liu, J., "Tang Ming, 'The father of college expansion' in China who has no regret in his suggestion", Xinhua Net], 10 September, available at: http://news.sina.com.cn/c/sd/2009-09-10/144218622828_4.shtml (accessed 4 September 2010).

袁媛 (2007), "汤敏: 亚行18年太久, 提前退休正式'海归'", *上海证券报* [Yuan, Y., "Tang Min: Eighteen years at ADB was too long, who took early retirement to become a returnee", *Shanghai Securities News*], 27 July, available at: "http://news.xinhuanet.com/fortune/2007-07/27/content_6437609.htm (accessed 4 September 2010).

Tang, Yue (Justin Tang 唐越 b. 1971)

Known to the West as Justin Tang, Tang Yue is the former CEO of eLong and co-founder of the private equity fund Blue Ridge China. Nicknamed "Gongfu Boy" and "Deal Maker," Tang was ranked 18th on the Audi Euromoney China Rich List with an estimated wealth of $80 million in 2004. Similar to other successful overseas returnees, Tang accumulated his fortune through an Internet-related business; different from many successful Chinese CEOs, Tang came out of Wall Street rather than from Silicon

Valley. Nevertheless, his background did not hinder his understanding in managing and operating an Internet company. Tang gathered his wealth of experience mainly through working in financial service industry in the United States for seven years prior to funding eLong, a leading online travel service company in China.

Born in Nanjing, Tang went to study at the Business School of Nanjing University in 1989. Two years later, he went to the United States for his BS. He was admitted to Concordia College in Minnesota, where he majored in economics and politics. While in the United States, Tang was selected from hundreds of applicants to participate in the Disney College Program at the Walt Disney World Resort. This special, one-of-a-kind program combining education and work experience provided him with first-hand insight of business leadership and management, which later proved beneficial for Tang to get a taste of business operation from such a world-class media and entertainment corporation. After graduating from Concordia in 1993, Tang worked for two years at Merrill Lynch, where he was responsible for stock research and marketing. This experience gave him a solid foundation in understanding details of how investment banks operate. Since then Tang's résumé has been filled with various positions in the venture investment and financial services companies. In 1995, he joined investment-banking firm Brookehill Equities, and was made in charge of investment in the sector of emerging bioscience technology companies. Two years later, Tang was involved in the establishment of a new branch of New York–based investment banking firm Oscar Gruss & Son Inc., which focused on investing in high-tech companies in the United States and bioscience companies in Israel. With years of experience of investment in high-tech companies, Tang decided to start his own Internet company, convinced that the field represented a new exciting frontier in China. In May 1999, together with several Chinese overseas students and $1 million, Tang funded eLong in the United States. Five months later, eLong.com was officially launched in Beijing, targeting at providing information regarding life style, fashion, and entertainment.

Similar to many Web companies of the time, eLong was deeply involved in rapid expanding by acquiring other smaller websites. Within one year, eLong had acquired four other companies and established about 10 branches in China and overseas. However, by early 2000, the capital market began to dry out and Tang decided to sell eLong. At that time eLong was neither famous nor well known for its contents, and everyone thought it would be a difficult task for Tang to find a buyer. Nevertheless, the "Deal Maker" proved that anything was possible. He soon initiated a merger with Mail.com for $68 million, which was regarded as the most successful deal of the year in Chinese Internet business. Shortly after the merger, the dot.com boom went bust. The share price of Mail.com on the NASDAQ collapsed, and eLong was about to be sold by its parent company. In May 2001, Tang led the buyout of eLong from Mail.com with an investment of $3 million from two of his friends in the investment business. Those two cases led by Tang were regarded by market observers as the perfect demonstration of profitable deals. But for Tang, finding a suitable business model for eLong became the top priority.

From 2001 to 2006, Tang served as the chairman and CEO of eLong, responsible for its overall strategy and management. Under his leadership, the company established a national presence across China. Realizing that the gold mine for Chinese portals was already occupied by companies such as Sohu, Sina, and Netease, Tang redirected eLong's focus from contents to e-commerce, and its core business was providing online travel services. By the time he finished reconstructing the company, 80% of eLong's monthly income—about 64 million RMB ($9million)—was generated from its online travel service sector, and it became one of the very few websites that made a profit at the time. As a returnee, Tang had the advantage of learning from successful Western business models and incorporating advanced technologies in booking tickets and making hotel reservations. In this sense, eLong's existence fundamentally changed Chinese consumers' concept of planning a trip and shopping online, which for many people was hard to imagine mere a decade ago. In August 2003, Tiger Technology Funds invested $15 million in eLong, a strategic move that reconfirmed its leading position among Chinese online travel service providers. In the same year, eLong went public (NASDAQ: LONG), and entered into a cooperation agreement with the world's largest online travel service provider Expedia, which currently owns 52% of fully diluted stake in eLong, representing 96% of the total voting power of the company.

After setting eLong on the right track, Tang started a new chapter in his business career, motivated by his entrepreneurial spirit of always being challenged and creating something new. In January 2006, Tang resigned from eLong's CEO position and joined Blue Ridge China, a private equity fund co-founded by him along with John Griffin, former CEO of Blue Ridge Capital, a well-known hedge fund firm. Blue Ridge China was also associated with several top US hedge funds and international investors. By March 2006, Blue Ridge China successfully raised initial fund of $300 million and began to invest in growing companies in China. Within eight months, Blue Ridge China had invested approximately $150 million in companies across fields such as new energy, retail, medicine, real estate, telecommunication services, education, water, etc. Consequently, Tang was labeled a representative of the new generation of investors in China. Given his entrepreneurial insight and a proven track record, Tang will likely continue to play a key role in the rapid development of Chinese economy in the coming years.

XIAOQI YU

Sources

21世纪商业评论 (2004), "唐越: 从华尔街走来的中国小子" ["Tang Yue: The young Chinese from Wall Street", *21st Century Business Herald*], 23 November, available at: http://news.xinhuanet.com/overseas/2004-11/23/content_2250730.htm (accessed 23 February 2010).

Sina.com (2006), "蓝山中国资本唐越: 国内一些创业者口气太大" ["Tang Yue of Blue Ridge China: Some Chinese entrepreneurs are too ambitious", Sina Science & Technology], 24 August, available at: http://tech.sina.com.cn/i/2006-08-24/16471102476.shtml (accessed 24 February 2010).

王子居 (2006), "唐越: 领舞篮山" [Wang, Z. "Tang Yue: Leading Blue Ridge", Cntmu.com], 7 November, available at: http://www.cntmu.com/blog/user1/tangyue/archives/2006/2240.html (accessed 22 February 2010).
中国企业家俱乐部 (2007), "*唐越*" ["Tang Yue", China Entrepreneur Club], available at: http://www.daonong.com/huiyuan/tangyue/index.html (accessed 23 February 2010).

Tian, Suning (Edward Tian 田溯宁 b. 1963)

Also known as Edward Tian, Tian Suning is currently the founder and chairman of China Broadband Capital Partners, L.P., one of the first Chinese TMT (technology, media, and telecom) sector-focused private equity funds.

Born in 1963, Tian was a child of the Cultural Revolution, a tumultuous and brutal movement launched by Mao Zedong in 1966 to consolidate his power base. The main targets were intellectuals, including teachers, party officials, and other privileged Chinese. Before the political turmoil, Tian had a "normal life, playing under his grandmother's peach tree-free and joyful"; after 1966, however, his childhood was characterized by a single, all-pervading force: hunger. "Hunger for food, hunger for information," Tian recalled, "It's all I remember" (Sheff, 2001).

In 1968, since Tian's parents, both Russian-educated researcher and teacher, were sentenced to hard labor in reeducation camp and factory, Tian stayed with his grandparents in Shenyang. A year later, when the family's home was seized by the Red Guard, Mao's citizen militia, and turned into housing for dozens of people, Tian and his grandparents were confined to a small back room there. At one point, the family was forced to surrender its collection of world literature to a Red Guard bonfire held in the yard. Panicked and tearful, Tian tried to rip a book out of the hands of a Red Guard officer, who seized the book and knocked him down. Finally, when the Cultural Revolution concluded with Mao's death in 1976, the second stage of Tian's life began.

Revitalized, Tian delved into his studies, and in 1980 he scored high enough on the nationwide college entrance examination to gain admittance to the top local university, Liaoning. He majored in biology, and after graduation he entered the prestigious graduate school of the Chinese Academy of Sciences. While there, he married Jean Kong, whom he had met in a biology class at Liaoning. Soon after, a professor visiting from Texas Tech encouraged them to apply to school in the United States. Therefore, in 1988, Tian left China for Lubbock, and was followed by his wife the next year: she worked on her master's degree in biology, while Tian on his PhD in environmental resource management.

When he graduated in 1992, the budding Internet was just being outlined as an "information superhighway" that would transform a nation through communication, knowledge, and education, Tian knew that was exactly what China needed. He finally realized what he needed to do in life. He would return to China, and work to connect the country to the information superhighway. According to him, "We were starved for information when we grew up; but because of this technology, China will soon be part of the open world and the children will become engines of change. We are at the new dawn-the stage of the information technology entrepreneur" (Sheff, 2001). Therefore, Tian decided to follow his dream, and pave the superhighway step by step. In 1994, he established AsiaInfo Holding Inc., the first Internet technology provider in China. From 1994 to 1999, he worked as the CEO of the company, and in March 2003, AsiaInfo successfully went public, becoming the first Chinese technology company to be listed on the NASDAQ.

From 1999 to 2006, Tian was the vice chairman and CEO of China Netcom (CNC) Group, which is a leading fixed-line telecommunications company that operates an extensive network in China and a top international data communications operator in the Asia Pacific region. In November 2004, Netcom was successfully listed on the Stock Exchange of Hong Kong and the New York Stock Exchange with a total of US$1.8 billion raised, which became the largest telecom IPO in 2004. At CNC, in an effort to build a leading telecommunication company, he tried to establish an open environment for communication among everyone regardless of their levels. He knew that the only way he could depend on was talents, so he encouraged people to find their own path and accomplish the target goals for themselves and the company.

In addition to his service as vice president of China Network Communication Group Corporation, Tian has worked as vice chairman of PCCW Limited, a telecommunications holding company, from April 2005 to March 2007. He has also served as an independent director of MasterCard International, a credit card company, since April 2006; a senior advisor of Kohlberg Kravis Roberts & Co., a private equity firm, since November 2006; an independent director of Lenovo Group Limited, since August 2007; a nonexecutive director and chairman of Media China Limited (formerly Asian Union New Media Group), a media company and satellite channel operator in China, since April 2008; and an independent director of Taikang Life Insurance Company Limited, a Chinese life insurance company, since July 2008. For his professional accomplishment, Tian was named among the "Global Leaders for Tomorrow" by the World Economic Forum in 1998, and was listed as one of the "Stars of Asia" by *BusinessWeek*. He was also voted as one of the Top 10 Entrepreneurs of 2000 by *Red Herring*.

Tian attributes his success to stepping in tune with the Chinese opportunity. He has benefited from three factors of the Chinese socioeconomy. The first is globalization. China has become one of the biggest beneficiaries of globalization, which has brought Chinese economic growth to an unprecedented pace. The living standards of ordinary Chinese people have also been rapidly raised. The second factor of the Chinese socioeconomy that he has built upon is IT development. Being able to keep up with the great technical developments in global wireless communications and Internet communications since the 1990s is a key ingredient to his success. The third important factor is the high-efficiency credit and financial support of the US market. This has led to an increased consumption rate, which in turn has stimulated Chinese production capacity. Regarding this as an unprecedented opportunity in Chinese history, Tian worked diligently to seize its full potential.

Tian also attributes his success to personal motivation and the drive for innovation in his life. At an early age, his goal was to become a professor or government official. While in his thirties, he strived to become a scientist. Within a rapidly developing environment, he soon realized that, despite his constantly shifting goals, what he really needed was imagination and courage. Without these traits he would have nothing; no capital, no social networks, no influence. It is only through personal determination that he has reshaped his life, and in this process of self-realization, Tian has become a role model for many aspiring Chinese students who want to follow his steps in creating wealth and contributing to the society.

YING HUANG AND MIAN WANG

Sources

Forbes (2010), "Edward S. Tian", available at: http://people.forbes.com/profile/edward-s-tian/7762 (accessed 5 September 2010).

Media China (2009), "Mr. Edward Tian Suning", available at: http://www.mediachina-corp.com/en/tabid/230/InfoID/354/Default.aspx (accessed 4 September 2010).

Sheff, D. (2001), "Betting on bandwidth: Edward Tian has a pipe dream for China. It's called democracy", *Wired*, available at: *http://www.wired.com/wired/archive/9.02/tian_pr.html* (accessed 5 September 2010).

Zhang, Y. (2009), "Tian Suning", in Zhang, W. and Alon, I. (eds.,) *Biographical Dictionary of New Chinese Entrepreneurs and Business Leaders*, Edward Elgar, Cheltnham, UK, pp. 167–169.

Ulrich, Jing (李晶 b. 1967)

A Chinese expert to the international financial community, a foreign market expert among Chinese circles, and a renowned networker with 11,000 professional contacts in her address book, Jing Ulrich has a compelling story to tell. As the chairwoman and managing director of China Equities and Commodities of J.P. Morgan, Jing Ulrich has been twice named by *Fortune* magazine as one of the 50 most powerful women in international business in 2009 and 2010; in 2008 and 2010, *Forbes* named her among the 100 most powerful women in the world. Most recently, the same publication also included her among the world's 20 youngest power women.

Jing Ulrich's life has been a journey of experience and growth that is uncommon in the professional world. A Beijing native, daughter of a Chinese diplomat, wife of an American, Jing was fortunate to have deep exposure to both Eastern and Western cultures at a young age. In the mid-1980s, she went to the United States after being admitted to Harvard University, where she first majored in English literature before switching to international relations. Upon graduation from Harvard in 1990, she enrolled at Stanford University and earned her graduate degree two years later.

As part of the first generation of Chinese to study overseas during the reform era, Jing felt a tremendous responsibility toward her native country. "When I went to a private college there were very few Chinese students on campus, and I thought of myself as the lens through which Americans view China. I was young, but I felt an extraordinary burden on me because I was in a small way representing my country," she once told *China International Business* (Gardner, 2010). My parents were diplomats and some people now call me the 'China Ambassador'. It's a tremendous honor to share what I see, what I feel, what I hear, my analysis, my views and insights with hundreds of millions of people around the world. And in the same way I'll share with Chinese leaders [and] executives what I see in the West. I feel equally comfortable in both the Chinese culture and the Western culture, equally comfortable with the Chinese and English languages, and the background of growing up in China during very turbulent times and the experience I've had since really molded me into who I am today (*ibid.*).

After graduating from Stanford, Jing began working as a mutual fund manager for Emerging Markets Management in Washington DC. With a talent for interpreting economic, cultural, and political issues, she embarked on a path of professional growth that was in tandem with China's rise in the international arena. Before joining J.P. Morgan in 2005, Jing had gained extensive experience in the financial industry. Starting as a fund manager for Greater China in 1994, she later moved to the sell-side of the industry and spent seven years at CLSA Asia-Pacific Markets, where she led the China team. Jing later moved to Deutsche Bank in 2003 as managing director of Greater China equities.

With each change in employment, she took on more responsibility. Nonetheless, her job has consistently been to help international investors understand Chinese economic, financial, and industrial policies. "I usually integrate both macro and micro pictures together to convince our clients about our interpretation about China," she recently told Chinese media (Meng, 2010). To keep up with the latest developments in China and grasp market nuances, Jing works extremely hard. Getting up at 5:00 am, working for 12–16 hours a day, and spending countless hours on flights are basic norms of her life. "To succeed, you have to be enthusiastic and work hard. Working in the financial industry can be very stressful, but I like my work so much that I never feel pressured" (*ibid.*).

For many, an impressive educational background, unique cultural advantages, and diligence might be the necessary ingredients of a successful career. However, what really distinguishes Jing apart from others is her relentless effort at networking. In her own words, information is the most valuable commodity in her industry. She must ensure that she has access to first-hand information in a timely manner and, more importantly, that she is able to interpret complex information in an easy-to-understand way for her clients. Having spent the past 18 years helping Western investors and institutions understand how to navigate the China market, Jing is referred to by some as the "unofficial voice of China" for her knowledge of the country's culture and economy.

Everywhere she goes, she hosts lunches with dozens or even hundreds of people. The topics can be wide ranging. "It could be about US-China relations, it could be about copper, metal prices. It could be about monetary tightening, or the problems we're seeing in Greece, and other countries. There's always a China angle, but everything these days has something to link it with China," she once said, "My job is to connect people" (Gardner, 2010). This massive networking enables her to call important people and draw upon their insights anytime she needs.

Moreover, Jing is an expert at knowing how to best leverage resources. Journalists often receive her briefings and comments on red-hot policy or financial developments far ahead of other analysts, even if news breaks at midnight. These extraordinary efforts ensure that her name and comments appear in various news stories. "And I think what gives me a unique advantage is that I have among the best access to leaders in both the Chinese and foreign business communities," she remarked in a recent interview (*ibid.*). At J.P. Morgan, she established the *Hands-on China* series, which brings together a network of CEOs, leading figures in various industries, multinational executives, consultants, etc. The program works as a large think-tank for J. P. Morgan's global clients and offers invaluable insights and first-hand information.

Reflecting on her professional life, Jing recently noted, "When I first began my career, I was primarily facing to the West, but in the past five to six years I began to increasingly face towards China" (*ibid.*). As China rises steadily, Jing sees huge market potential for foreign banks to explore. Although currently China has set certain limits to foreign banks' activities, international institutions still have a vast market to engage: mergers and acquisitions, underwriting IPOs in Hong Kong and the overseas markets, advisory business, and so on. Therefore, in her view, the role for foreign banks in China in the foreseeable future is to continuously expand. Since the country has massive and almost unlimited financial resources, and because of the central government's extremely strong political will to maintain a high level of growth, the world will increasingly look toward China for future growth opportunities. This will certainly provide people like Jing an even larger stage to reshape the global financial landscape.

Eadie Hua Chen

Sources

Fortune (2010), "50 most powerful women in business", http://money.cnn.com/magazines/fortune/mostpowerfulwomen/2010/global/index.html (accessed 29 September 2010).

Gardner, B. (2010), "Jing Ulrich: JP Morgan's ambassador to China", *China International Business*, 12 April, http://www.cibmagazine.com.cn/Features/Face_to_Face.asp?id=1273&jing_ulrich.html (accessed 29 September 2010).

Wikipedia (2010), "Jing Ulrich", http://en.wikipedia.org/wiki/Jing_Ulrich (accessed 29 September 2010).

孟梅 (2010), "摩根大通董事总经理李晶: 今年A股可能前低后高", *天府早报* [Meng, M., "Morgan Chase CEO Jing Ulrich: A-shares will likely go low initially but climb up later this year", *Sichuan Moring Post*], 1 March, http://finance.newssc.org/system/2010/03/01/012603740_01.shtml (accessed 29 September 2010).

Wang, Boming (王波明 b. 1955)

A leading participant in the initial formation of China's capital markets, Wang Boming is the president of the Stock Exchange Executive Council (SEEC), CEO of SEEC Media Group, and chairman of SEEC Investment Development Co. He is also a director of the Government Bond Association and the editor-in-chief of the bestselling *Caijing Magazine* and *Capital Week* in China.

Born in Beijing, Wang grew up in an elite family. His father Wang Bingnan had served as PRC's deputy minister of foreign affairs from 1964 to 1975. However, the junior Wang did not even have a chance to complete his elementary school when the Cultural Revolution took place. After wandering for a few years, he could find a job only in a local pesticide plant. The hazardous working conditions and manual labor soon made Wang realize that to change his fate he had to improve himself first. With only a fourth grade education, he devoted all his time to study English, and eventually secured a translator position in Beijing Food Research Institute. Soon after, the nationwide college entrance examination resumed, and Wang was fortunate enough to enroll in a branch of the Second Foreign Language Institute of Beijing in 1978.

Because of his English skills and family connection, Wang was among the first group of Chinese students to study overseas. Arriving in the United States in 1980, he enrolled in the City University of New York, and then studied at Queens College. Besides his schoolwork, Wang had to work long hours as a waiter and grocer to support himself financially. Despite the hardship, he excelled academically and earned a scholarship from Columbia University for his graduate study. After receiving his master's degree in international finance, Wang went to Wall Street to work as an economist at the research department of the New York Stock Exchange, where he was responsible for macroeconomic studies and market movement analysis in the United States. Soon after, he experienced in person the turmoil of the Black Monday on October 19, 1987. Notwithstanding the chaos, he was fascinated by the magic of stock markets. A few months back, NYSE Chairman John Phelan just paid a visit to the Chinese leader Deng Xiaoping in Beijing. Although Wang already had a well-paid position in the United States, he sensed a great opportunity waiting to be explored back home. After discussing with his friend Gao Xiqing, a Chinese attorney from the Wall Street law firm Mudge Rose, Wang decided to return with his friend and take on the challenge of pushing forward an equity market in China.

Back in Beijing in 1988, Wang and Gao first launched an NGO that was backed by some reform-oriented government officials and business leaders, the Joint Office for Research and Design of Beijing Stock Exchange, which later evolved into SEEC. After Wang and his friends drafted the first proposal for a capital market in China, then Shanghai Mayor Zhu Rongji took a special interest, as he was seeking ways to develop the dilapidated Pudong area into a new international financial center. With Zhu's strong support, Shanghai Stock Exchange opened for business on December 19, 1990. Based on his experience on Wall Street, Wang also helped develop the STAQ (Security Traders Automated Quotation) system for both Shanghai and Shenzhen Stock Exchanges. Soon after, with backing from Premier Zhu Rongji, stock markets began to take off in China. Two years later, Wang also contributed to the formation of an independent regulatory authority for the Chinese financial market, the Securities Regulatory Commission. Because of his foresights, Wang was able to seize the moment and reach his seemingly ambitious goal a few years after his return.

After participation in the founding of the stock market in China, Wang devoted his attention to the growth of SEEC. Initially, he was active in the investment and finance of the burgeoning stock exchanges in China. However, early market manipulations and speculations, irrational behaviors of investors, and the lack of independent monitoring soon became major concerns for him. Since Wang had a brief yet productive experience working as a journalist for the *Overseas Chinese Daily* while a student in New York, he launched the *Securities Market Weekly*, which soon became a popular publication in China. A few years later, Wang and SEEC also launched *Caijing Magazine*, an independent, Beijing-based periodical devoted to financial information on companies and business in China. *Caijing*'s driving mission is to have an "independent standpoint, exclusive coverage and unique perspective." Led by the founding editor Hu Shuli, herself a returnee and a former reporter and editor of the Chinese newspaper *Worker's Daily*, the bi-weekly soon made a name for itself through a series of investigative reports that exposed the dark side of the financial markets in China. With its independent voice, unique perspective, and sharp writings, the magazine was named "the leading finance publication in China" by the *Wall Street Journal*, and before long, the subscription reached over 200,000 per issue.

In 1997, after some soul searching, SEEC was transferred from an NGO to an enterprise, focusing on network, media, and finance. Under the leadership of Wang, SEEC Media Group was incorporated; five years later, it was listed on the Hong Kong Stock Exchange. The investors of SEEC included China International Trust & Investment Corp., the country's biggest conglomerate, and the state-owned China Merchants Bank. Another was Hong Kong–based newspaper *South China Morning Post*, which is controlled by billionaire Robert Kuok. As an investment holding company, SEEC Media is one of the earliest Internet content providers in China, and it operates mainly in two segments: advertising income from agency services and organizing conferences and events and sale of books and magazines. Its subsidiaries include Cai Lian Advertising Co., Caixun Century Infotech Co. (investment holding), Jinzheng Ronglian Advertising Company, SEEC Book and Press Distribution Co., and Hainan Caixun Infomedia Co.

In 2009, Wang was in spotlight when he and Hu were involved in an apparent disagreement over editorial policy and financial control of *Caijing*, which eventually led to the resignation of Hu and many of her staff members. The controversy aside, Wang seemed to survive the crisis and the publication of the magazine continued. Besides his involvement with the formation of the country's stock exchanges, Wang is the vice chairman of the China Securities Industry Institute and a director of the Asia Securities Industry Institute. He has also played a pioneering role in creating the first underwriting syndicate of government bonds, which revolutionized the bond distribution system in China.

Qun Du

Sources

Businessweek (2010), "Executive profile: Wang Boming", available at: http://investing.businessweek.com/research/stocks/people/person.asp?personId=8487663&ticker=205:HK (accessed 23 November 2010).

胡冰 (2007), "王波明: 沉默的时代领跑者", *创业英雄: 10位海归创业先锋* (王辉耀主编), 中国发展出版社, 北京 [Hu, B., "Wang Boming: A frontrunner in the silent age", in Wang, H. (ed.), *Entrepreneurial Heroes: Ten Overseas Returnees in Entrepreneurship*, China Development Press, Beijing], pp. 23–48.

彭苏 (2006), "王波明: 将证券市场引入中国", *南方人物周刊* [Peng, S., "Wang Boming: Introducing stock markets to China", *Southern People Weekly*], 26 October, available at: http://news.sina.com.cn/c/2006-11-01/102911389535.shtml (accessed 25 November 2010).

Wang, Boqing (王伯庆 b. 1954)

A scholar devoted to improving the employment situation for college graduates in China, Wang Boqing is the president of MyCOS HR Digital Information Co. Ltd. MyCOS stands for My China Occupational Skills, founded by Wang in 2006 in order to create a longitudinal database of college graduates' employment outcomes, which would help universities evaluate the quality and output of their education programs, and thus address the soaring unemployment problem of recent college graduates across the country.

Born in 1954, Wang was among the first wave of Chinese to attend college after the Cultural Revolution in 1977. After graduating from Dongbei University with a degree in engineering, he worked as an assistant engineer for a year before entering the Southwestern University of Finance and Economics (SWUFE) to obtain a master's degree in industrial economics management. He joined the faculty of SWUFE immediately afterward. In 1990, Wang left China to pursue graduate studies in the United States, where he received an MS in mathematics and a PhD in economics from Washington State University in 1994. For the next decade, Wang developed his expertise in labor economics as a researcher, primarily in the public sector.

Wang's long-standing interest has been the study of employment. Despite having lived and worked in the United States for 16 years, three events in 2003 prompted Wang to reconsider his career trajectory. The first event was the World Bank's completion of a comprehensive research project on occupational skills that provided measurements for colleges to evaluate the market demand for university graduates. The second event was that American colleges began to evaluate graduates' employment outcomes and used these evaluations to improve university curriculum. The third event was the public concern over the rapidly rising unemployment rates of college graduates in China as a result of the higher education expansion plan launched in 1999. Based on his years of experience in labor economics, Wang predicted that China would soon need a system of higher education employment outcome evaluation and decided to move back to China to pioneer this new system.

Consequently, Wang rejoined SWUFE in 2006 and founded MyCOS. He led MyCOS to develop the Chinese Higher Education Follow-up System (CHEFS) by conducting nation-wide surveys and building an occupational database using the results. MyCOS efforts represented two firsts in China: the first time to measure college graduates' occupational skills and the first time to use a scientific approach to measure the supply and demand of college graduates. In the last several years, MyCOS has introduced the American O*NET (Occupational Information Network) system, conducted follow-up surveys on the employment situations of newly minted college graduates, and drafted national and provincial college graduate employment reports. Furthermore, MyCOS was the sole author of the "2009 Chinese College Graduates' Employment Report" published by the Chinese Academy of Social Sciences, which has a significant and widely-recognized impact in China.

Wang has led MyCOS to partner with research institutions such as the Chinese Academy of Social Sciences, the World Bank, and the Ford Foundation, and to conduct surveys for and write reports on college graduate employment for more than 100 universities and colleges located in 14 provinces. Wang's work has been highly valued; one university president told Wang that his approach would revolutionize the way of evaluating universities and his evidence-based outcome evaluation was about to completely change the face of college evaluation in China.

In late November 2009, Wang's MyCOS was the only noneducational institution invited to attend the Third Annual Presentation of Achievements to Pioneering Technical and Vocational Institutes, held by the Ministry of Education. The participants were highly enthusiastic toward MyCOS, commenting that it had created a historic improvement in the study of higher education in China.

Wang's leadership and knowledge has led MyCOS to become the only professional body in China with expertise in the study of higher education that has been recognized by governmental, academic, and business organizations and the public. On a survey of organizations that Chinese people trust the most, coordinated by Sina.com, MyCOS ranked among the top 10 research organizations, along with venerable organizations such as the Research Center of the State Council and the Chinese Academy of Social Sciences. At the end of 2009, Dr. Wang was honored as one of three nationally esteemed educators during the "China Echo 2009" ceremony held by QQ.com. He was also a recipient of Sohu.com's "60 Years of Education Achievement, 60 Chinese Education Achievers" award.

Wang is dedicated and passionate about his cause-assessing standards of Chinese education with data, interpreting the problem of unemployment with science, and hopes to advance the improvement of higher education in China. His ultimate goal is to use his research as an avenue to increase the number of well-trained talents in China, to raise the living standard of the general public, and to reduce the number of the poor. His work is summed up by the following statement made during the QQ.com ceremony: "Reveal substance through transparent data, address doubts with clarifying tables, tell the truth with passion-Wang provides us with these lenses to gain insight into education" (MyCOS, 2010).

As a responsible overseas returnee, Wang believes that the various avenues through which returnees contribute to China are of crucial importance to the nation.

He also encourages overseas scholars to work for several years abroad before returning to China so that they can bring back advanced concepts and mode of operation. In the future, Wang aims at leading his team to provide continuous assistance to China's education industry.

MIAO CHI

Source

MyCOS Corporation (2010), "About MyCOS", available at: http://www.mycos.com.cn/ (accessed 10 October 2010).

董尧尧 (2009), "王伯庆: 经世之学的社会担当", *中共西南财经大学委员会校报* [Dong, Y., "Wang Boqing: A scholar with social responsibilities", *SWUFE Campus Newspaper*], 2 April, available at: http://swufe.cuepa.cn/show_more.php?doc_id=150396 (accessed 10 October 2010).

关义霞, 陈雅琴 (2006), "海归出书的初衷: 我要改变大学生就业难现状", *天府日报* [Guan, Y. and Chen, Y., "As an overseas returnee, I publish books so as to change the harsh employment situations among college graduates", *Tianfu Morning Post*], 31 August, available at: http://news.xinhuanet.com/overseas/2006-08/31/content_5029154.htm (accessed 10 October 2010).

Wang, Chaoyong (汪潮涌 b. 1965)

Wang Chaoyong knows how to make a name for himself in the financial world of China and in his free time as well. Wang is the founding partner and CEO of ChinaEquity International Holdings, and founder and cochairman of the first China Team to race in America's Cup sailing regatta – one of the world's oldest sporting events.

With such great achievements, one would not think he came from one of the most recent revolutions in China. When Wang was one year old, his parents were sent to a labor camp during the Cultural Revolution. He was then raised by "a peasant family in remote village in Hubei province" (Sellers et al., 2004), and was unable to reunite with his parents until he was 13 years old. He persevered through these hard times and was accepted into the top-ranked Central China University of Technology, where he graduated with a bachelor's degree in business management in 1984. In the following year, Wang studied as a postgraduate student in the charter class of the Management School at the elite Tsinghua University. Afterward, he traveled to the United States in 1985 with only US$50 in his pocket, which was the maximum amount of money China would allow an individual to exchange at the time.

At the age of 22, upon earning his master's degree in business administration from Rutgers University, Wang first worked in the investment bank and rating service in New York City. From 1987 to 1990, he was a business executive at Chase Manhattan

Bank, and in the next three years he became the first senior staff member from mainland China ever recruited by Standard & Poor's, responsible for investment rating services. In 1993, Wang was appointed a senior manager of Morgan Stanley Dean Witter in Hong Kong. Two years later, when offered to head the Beijing branch of operations, Wang returned to China, becoming the youngest chief representative of a major Wall Street investment firm. Shortly afterward, he had also served as an investment consultant to the state-owned China Development Bank.

Over a span of 12 years, Wang has gained valuable experience and expertise in investment banking, and has directly participated in and presided over overseas financing business for the Chinese Ministry of Finance, Bank of China, China Oriental Airlines Incorporated, Shanghai Properties, Beijing Datang Power Generation Corporation, Beijing Enterprise Holdings Ltd., totaling several billion US dollars. Throughout the years, Wang has served on several corporate boards: Rising Tech Co., Longshine Info. Co., Futong Science and Tech Co., and Infront Asia Ltd. He has been an independent director for Beijing Beida Jade Bird Universal Sci-Tech Co. Ltd. and E-Future Information Technology Inc. He is also an advisor to several government organizations and funds, and a member of Board of Governors and Secretary General of China Venture Capital Association.

In 1999, Wang decided to form his own company, ChinaEquity International Holdings Co. Ltd. Designed as one of China's "leading private merchant banks" (ChinaEquity, 2008), ChinaEquity is a leader in venture capital (VC), private equity (PE), and direct investments in high-tech companies spanning across China. ChinaEquity invests in technology-, media-, and telecommunication-based companies: Sohu, Baidu, and Huayi Brothers are among them. Some of the services offered by ChinaEquity include fundraising, mergers and acquisitions, and asset management. Between 2000 and 2001, Wang was "rated as one of the twenty most active venture investors in China," and his company, ChinaEquity was listed as "one of the top ten local venture investment companies in China" (*China Vitae*, n.d.).

Since then ChinaEquity has expanded its investments beyond the China borders. He wants the company to keep its "Chinese roots but [have] and international structure" (*Ibid.*). Wang invested in high-tech companies in Europe, Singapore, and South Korea. The company has over US$120 million in assets, and its long-term goal is to "be the Carlyle Group of China" (Sellers et al., 2004). Founded in 1987 in Washington, D.C., the Carlyle Group is one of the largest global PE investment firms in the world. The company has more than US$88.6 billion in assets and operates in 19 countries.

As Wang has set out to conquer the world financially, he hopes to do it by sea as well. Wang founded China Team, the first competition sailing team in China, to race in America Cup in 2005. Formerly known as the Royal Yacht Squadron Cup, the America's Cup is a sailing regatta match that has been around since 1857. The only international sporting event to challenge the age of America's Cup is the Olympic Games. The China Team is a 50-person team and represents the Qingdao International Yacht Club. The team has increased its strength by partnering with a French challenger, Le Défi. In 2007, TAG Heuer, a Swiss luxury watch company, partnered with China Team as well. One of China Team's greatest accomplishments is its first and only victory of Louis Vuitton Cup against BMW/Oracle, the powerhouse of the America's Cup.

With all of Wang's success, he has been estimated to "have a wealth of US$160 million and thought to be the fourth-richest venture capitalist in China" (Parker, 2009). His current ambitions for ChinaEquity include an agriculture fund, which will expand its natural resources fund. The company's main focus is on health care and green technologies. Wang has set his sights on New Zealand and Australia, and his natural resources fund is currently invested in mining and cattle farms in Australia and agriculture businesses in Brazil.

JENNIFER CROSSMAN

Sources

ChinaEquity (2008), "About ChinaEquity", 31 March, available at: http://en.chinaequity.net/newslist.aspx?sortid=26 (accessed 12 April 2010).

China Vitae (n.d.), "Wang Chaoyong", available at: http://www.chinavitae.com/biography/Wang_Chaoyong/bio (accessed 12 April 2010).

CrunchBase (n.d.), "Chaoyong Wang", available at: http://www.crunchbase.com/person/chaoyong-wang (accessed 12 April 2010).

Parker, T. (2009), "Rich-lister wants a piece of NZ", *New Zealand Herald*, 2 February, available at: http://www.nzherald.co.nz/business/news/article.cfm?c_id=3&objectid=10554629 (accessed 16 April 2010).

Sellers, P., Schlosser, J., Chandler, C., Kirkpatrick, D., Gunther, M., and O'Keefe., B. (2004), "The Aspen Seven you think radical change is daunting? Not to these folks. They're all pros at making it happen – or profiting from it", *Fortune Magazine*, 23 August, available at: http://money.cnn.com/magazines/fortune/fortune_archive/2004/08/23/379372/index.htm (accessed 16 April 2010).

Wang, Chunyan (王春岩 b. 1963)

Known to the West as Raymond Wang, Wang Chunyan is the general manager of energy of Alstom China and former vice president of Siemens China.

Wang Chunyan graduated from Shandong Institute of Engineering (now School of Engineering of Shandong University) in 1984 with a bachelor's degree in electrical engineering. Prior to his study abroad, he had worked at state-owned enterprises for seven years and had already enjoyed a position and an income level that was pretty high-rank relative to his young age. If there were any turning point in his pre-overseas history, it would be the year 1987 in which he was sent to Daya Bay Nuclear Power Station where he had an opportunity to witness for the first time in his life a giant project following international standards. He was shocked by the modernized technologies, management, and operations embodied in this US$5-billion project. He had always thought about the urgent need for reforming the state-owned enterprise system, and this experience, along with what he saw from his subsequent travels in Europe, made him determined to study abroad.

In 1990, Wang was admitted to the University of Arkansas in the United States. Unlike many other people who chose to study MBA programs, he majored in electrical engineering again, out of his strong belief that authentic management insights and skills can only come from real-world practice and are not obtainable from classrooms. His experience of studying in the United States was very enlightening, and he gained a vivid sense of the importance of developing abilities to process daily tasks in life as well as in work, independent of others. An interesting episode of his life in Arkansas is related to Bill Clinton who still held the position of associate professor at the University of Arkansas while being the Governor of Arkansas and campaigning for the post of US president in 1992. Wang remembers very well how excited he felt while listening to Clinton's speech and joining everybody else on campus to cheer up Clinton's race.

Upon obtaining his master's degree from the University of Arkansas in 1992, Wang did not choose to return to China. Instead, he decided to work in the United States. Back in 1991, when he was still a graduate student at the University of Arkansas, he had already started to work for IBM. Later he went to work at SVI, one of IBM's suppliers. He recalls that in those years he did not have a clear plan about his future career. When he first went overseas, he just wanted to learn something and then got a job. With the passage of time, however, Wang was inclined to have some change in life. In 1995, he made a business trip to Hong Kong, and met with some friends he made when he worked in China. One of them, a high-level executive at Alstom, invited Wang to join the company in expanding its business in mainland China. Wang accepted this invitation and returned to China at the end of 1995. With the help of his aforementioned friend, Wang was soon able to earn a series of promotions, and in 1997 he was sent to work in Wuhan as the general manager of the Greater Central South Region. This was the first time in Alstom's history that a Chinese national was appointed the general manager of a greater region. He would continue to work in this position until the end of 1998.

Although Wang had some prior experience before he started to work at Alstom, his focus used to be on technological support. His three years (1995–1998) at Alstom marked a new era of his career, where he transitioned from technological support to management. During this period, Wang was in his early thirties and was not accustomed to refraining from sharing his thinking with other people in a straightforward way. This personality proved to a double-edged sword. On the one hand, Wang stood out when he attended meetings and discussed issues with colleagues and higher authorities, which helped him accomplish some of his achievements. On the other hand, however, his straightforwardness also easily caused unnecessary misunderstandings and even conflicts with his French colleagues. In hindsight, Wang realized that what he thought was his support and care for his colleagues might well be interpreted by them as being excessively strict and imposing pressures on them.

When these misunderstandings and tensions accumulated to a certain point, Wang knew that it was time for him to leave Alstom. While he was planning to go abroad for a second time, for an MBA program this time, Siemens issued an offer to Wang. Initially Wang did not accept this invitation. After a second thought, especially due to the relatively unsatisfactory offers from US MBA programs, Wang decided to give up his effort in obtaining an MBA degree and chose to work at Siemens. In 1999, he joined Siemens China as the general manager of North China Region of its Grid Group. On the second day of his job at Siemens, Wang flew to the Three Gorges to start working on electricity projects with which he was most familiar. His predecessors had not made any major breakthroughs in this position, but Wang was able to accomplish some impressive successes thanks to his experience and connections in this field. In the nine years when he stayed at Siemens, Wang was eventually promoted to vice president of Siemens China, which represents the highest achievement a Chinese professional manager can accomplish in a foreign-owned enterprise. In June 2008, Wang returned to Alstom China to work as the general manager of energy.

Despite the notable achievements he has accomplished as a professional manager, Wang lives a very simple life. Neither is he interested in watching entertainment TV shows, nor does he enjoy going to bars or nightclubs. What he likes doing in his off-work time is reading news analysis and doing physical exercises. Between work and family, he puts family first. For this reason, even though he has been a professional manager for many years, he is not interested in starting his own business. "Starting your own business will make you busier, so I won't do that." Wang takes time spent with his family very seriously.

ZHAOCHANG PENG

Sources

Western Returned Scholars Association Chamber of Commerce (2005), "Wang Chunyan", available at: http://www.2005committee.org/english.php/member/ls/926 (accessed 19 October 2010).

冯嘉雪, 郭玉梅，郭俐君 (2007), "王春岩: 游走在平淡与执着之间", *巅峰职业: 10位海归职业经理人* (王辉耀主编), 中国发展出版社, 北京 [Feng, J. Guo, Y. & Guo, L., "Wang Chunyan: A smooth walk between tranquility and passion", in Wang, H.Y. (ed.), *Top Careers: Ten Overseas Returnees in Professional Management*, China Development Press, Beijing], pp. 1–21.

Wang, Lifen (王利芬 b. 1965)

Wang Lifen's career has been a varied one, to say the least. She has been an academic, a reporter and television host, a TV producer and director, and an entrepreneur. In recent years, she has focused on encouraging entrepreneurship through mass media, mostly through her popular television program *Win in China*, which pits Chinese would-be entrepreneurs against each other in a competition to see whose business plan is most deserving of a 10-million-yuan prize, and her new Internet television platform, Umiwi.com.

Wang was born in the Huangpi District of Hubei Province in Central China, to a family of intellectuals. Her interest in journalism was sparked as a child when her father read her the reportage of Xu Chi, a well-known Chinese poet and journalist. From 1982 to 1986, Wang attended Huazhong Normal University in Wuhan, where she received a BA in politics and law and studied literature on her own. She continued her graduate studies at the same university over the next three years and attained an MA in Chinese contemporary literature review. Between 1989 and 1991, she taught at Wuhan University before pursuing her PhD in Chinese contemporary literature at Peking University in Beijing. She was a prolific author in her graduate and doctoral programs, producing 29 scholarly articles on literature and two short novels between 1987 and 1994.

After earning her PhD in 1994, Wang spent the next six years working as a television journalist and anchorwoman for Channel One of China Central Television (CCTV). She contributed dozens of news segments and interviews on several different programs on CCTV1, including *Oriental Horizon*, *Focus*, and *News Probe*. In 1999, she published her scholarly book *Perspectives on Stability and Change: A Constructionist Review of Chinese Contemporary Literature from 1942 to 1994*. The next year, she originated the program *Dialogue*, a talk show that became one of the country's most-watched programs during her tenure. At 60 minutes long, *Dialogue* also has the distinction of being the longest studio talk show on Chinese television. Another thing Wang found significant about the program, which featured famous executives and high-profile Chinese artists and politicians, was that it caught the attention of teenagers first, followed by their parents; this model was the one she would later try to recapture in founding her own media platform. Wang conducted more than 300 interviews for *Dialogue* before moving on in 2003 to direct four live daily economic news programs for CCTV2.

Wang continued in that role until September 2004, and then began a year as a visiting scholar at the Brookings Institute and Yale University, where she studied American media. Only months after returning home, she launched what has probably been her most well-known television program internationally: *Win in China*, an award-winning Chinese take on the American reality show *The Apprentice*. In contrast to *The Apprentice*, however, victors on *Win in China* were judged by a panel of Chinese business leaders and by public votes. The winners received 10 million yuan (nearly US$1.5 million), while the runners-up and three finalists went home with seven million and five million yuan apiece, respectively; the prize money was provided by private investors in return for a 50% share in the business for which the winning contestant would use. A 15% share was awarded to some of the viewers who voted during the show's season. Wang served as executive producer and host of the show from September 2005 to June 2008. She credits the program with promoting entrepreneurship in China, since 400,000 contestants applied for the first season alone. During the success of *Win in China*, Wang was also the executive producer and host of *Us*, a talk show on CCTV1 that debuted in November 2007. She describes *Us* as a program that "analyzes and critiques what needs to be done to ensure a modern China ... we can all be proud of" (Wang, 2009).

After creating a national platform for so many aspiring entrepreneurs, perhaps it was only natural that Wang followed in their footsteps. In 2010, she announced her surprising decision to leave CCTV after 15 years and found Umiwi.com. "I believe many people will ask the reason for my resignation; in fact, it can be summarized in one sentence, which is: I want to start something new" she told readers of her Chinese-language blog (Wang, 2010).

Umiwi (from the English words "you, me, we," the people Wang says generate Umiwi's ideas), which first went live in March 2010, is an independent Internet television platform aimed at China's youth market. The Chinese-language site features self-produced talk shows and focuses primarily on such topics as entrepreneurship and innovation, aimed to appeal to young viewers. Its videos can also be watched via cell phones and on 30 local channels that have reached broadcast agreements. In addition to being Umiwi's founder, Wang is also its chief editor.

Wang said that the idea for Umiwi came to her after she realized a few years ago that when modern families are at home, it is now their computers, not their televisions, that they switch on after dinner – even television employees! She began to research online media content and in 2009 went live with a new website. However, Wang found that users were not willing to pay for content and quickly left. Although she has said she thinks this e-business model will become feasible within the next decade, she soon retooled and opened the free Umiwi.com within a few months of the first site's closing. Umiwi, which has about 70 employees and a studio in Beijing, derives most of its profit from advertising, although it has received initial support from investors. Wang has said her initial focus is on building the site's credibility, then continuing to work on its profitability in the future.

Wang used her experience in business-related programming to help develop the site's initial slate of programming, which she says will continue to expand in the future. A live show at 8:00 p.m. on weeknights asks industry experts about personal growth and development. Another program is focused on innovation – introducing viewers to everything from new inventions and experiments to developments in art to unique life experiences – while a third is aimed at aiding young job seekers with company interviews. Wang views yet another program as a sequel of sorts to *Win in China*: while that show sparked enthusiasm for entrepreneurship, Umiwi's show deals with the practical problems of sustaining a business.

Umiwi's most highly publicized venture to date has been a charity auction, modeled on Warren Buffet's lunch auctions, in which the highest bidder paid more than 200 million yuan (about US$29.5 million) for three hours with Shi Yuzhu, the billionaire president of Giant Interactive Group Inc. Umiwi has also solicited users' opinions about which celebrity's time should be auctioned off next.

"A person who has just started a business will face unimaginable difficulties. Because a business means looking for their own path, instead of walking a path other people have already paved. So the way ahead of me is not likely to be smooth," Wang told her readers in her resignation post (Wang, 2010). Nevertheless, she added, "If our future is to make a voyage, then everyone's feedback is our compass" (Wang, 2010). Although it remains to be seen how smooth Wang's road – and Umiwi's – will be, it is certain that people will be watching.

James P. Gilbert and Elisabeth K. Gilbert

Sources

Chen, E. (2009), "Win in China," *People's Daily Online*, 15 September, available at: http://english.peopledaily.com.cn/90001/90780/91344/6758267.html (accessed 30 August 2010).

China Daily (2010), "Seeking out the youth market online," 31 May, available at: http://english.sina.com/business/p/2010/0530/322170.html (accessed 30 August 2010).

Fallows, J. (2007), "Win in China! A reality show is teaching Chinese how to succeed in business", *Atlantic*, 9 April, available at: http://www.theatlantic.com/magazine/archive/2007/04/win-in-china/5700/ (accessed 30 August 2010).

Marbridge Daily (2010), "Ex-CCTV producer heads new online TV site Umiwi", 17 March, available at: http://www.marbridgeconsulting.com/marbridgedaily/2010-03-17/article/34302/ex_cctv_producer_heads_new_online_tv_site_umiwi (accessed 30 August 2010).

Rutledge, J. (2006), "Capitalism is alive and well in China", *Rutledge Capital*, weblog, available at: http://www.rutledgecapital.com/Articles/200610_wsj_win_in_china.html (accessed 30 August 2010).

Schafer, S. (2005), "The princess who woke the dinosaur", *Newsweek*, 6 June, available at: http://www.newsweek.com/2005/06/06/the-princess-who-woke-the-dinosaur.print.html (accessed 30 August 2010).

Women of China (2010), "Wang Lifen: Woman of action," 3 August, available at: http://womenofchina.cn/Profiles/Others/220915.jsp (accessed 30 August 2010).

曹栗 (2010), "王利芬: 离开央视不是个艰难选择", *鄂商* [Cao, L., "Wang Lifen: Not a difficult choice to leave CCTV", *Hubei Businessmen*], 7 July, available at: http://money.163.com/10/0707/10/6B01D4SH00253G87.html (accessed 30 August 2010).

工人日报 (2010), "央视名嘴王利芬: 辞职创办网站" ["Wang Lifen, CCTV host: Resigning to found a site", *Worker's Daily*], 25 May, available at: http://yesee.qianlong.com/3910/2010/05/25/2523@5742498.htm (accessed 30 August 2010).

王利芬 (2009), Personal résumé.

王利芬 (2010), "我已辞去央视公职创办优米网" [Wang, L., "I have resigned from CCTV to found Umiwi", Wang Lifen's Blog], 17 March, available at: http://blog.sina.com.cn/s/blog_498646b40100hdoq.html (accessed 30 August 2010).

薛芳, 寿立群 (2010), "王利芬离开央视", *南方人物周刊* [Xue, F. and Shou, L. "Wang Lifen Left CCTV", *Southern People Weekly*], 9 April, available at: http://business.sohu.com/20100409/n271412546.shtml (accessed 30 August 2010).

中国新时代 (2010), "王利芬: '创业教母'创业难" ["Wang Lifen: 'Godmother of Venture's hard start", *China New Time*], 15 July, available at: http://money.163.com/10/0715/09/6BKGFRLT00253G87.html (accessed 30 August 2010).

Wang, Shen (Sing Wang 王兟 b. 1964)

As a global partner of Texas Pacific Group (TPG), Wang Shen is among the most distinguished private equity executives in China. With a deep expertise in technology and a background in investment banking and capital markets, he joined TPG in 2006, where he was responsible for spearheading the firm's efforts in growth equity and venture opportunities in North Asia. Founded in 1992, Texas Pacific Group is one of the world's largest private equity firms; currently, it has more than US

$30 billion of assets under its management. The firm has extensive experience with public and private investments executed through leveraged buyouts, recapitalizations, spinouts, joint ventures, and restructurings; and its investment spans a variety of industries including health care, retail and consumer, media and communication, financial services, etc.

Born in 1964, Wang grew up in Kunming, Yunnan Province. He demonstrated special interest in collecting arts and playing sports like golf and tennis. Swimming and traveling were his other hobbies. Since the very beginning, he was always very hard at work and aspired to be on the top. In 1978, he was admitted to Yunnan University for pursuing a bachelor's degree in chemistry. During his college years, Wang demonstrated his exceptional verbal skills and the ability to network among students. He became so popular that he was elected as president of Student Union. In 1982, he graduated with top honors and was awarded the title of "Outstanding Student."

After graduating, he started working for the Chinese Academy of Sciences, specializing in soil properties of southwestern provinces. He soon realized that he was not fit to do research, but was more suitable for working with people. Following his heart, in 1984 he decided to enroll himself at Oxford University, restarting from the undergraduate program studying philosophy, political science, and economics courses. While in the United Kingdom, Wang closely interacted with students of diverse cultural background, and gradually he mastered the art of communication. After receiving his Bachelor of Arts, he opted for a master's program in land management, which he completed in 1989 with distinction. During this time, he also became the president of the International Society at Oxford University, and was awarded the Commonwealth Forestry Bureau Prize.

Altogether, Wang spent five years at Oxford, which was not only a great opportunity, but also a very important experience in his life. Nurturing literature and the impact of British social life changed his perspective toward life. At Oxford, he learned that political and economic philosophy is focused on logical thinking, reading, and writing, important skills that have been reflected in his decision making ever since. Another strong attribute of his decision making is the "Humanities" aspect, the credit for which is also given to his British education.

In 1989, after graduating from Oxford, Wang first worked briefly in the Chicago office of the global management consulting firm McKinsey & Company. In 1991, he founded Amerinvest Group, an investment firm focused primarily on real estate, natural resources, and early high-tech companies. A year later, Wang became an associate of Wardley Direct Investment Management based in Hong Kong. He then joined Goldman Sachs, where he spent seven years from 1993 to 2000. A founding member of the company's Asian private equity team, Wang also worked in the Equity Capital Markets and Corporate Finance Divisions; in 1999, he became the head of China High Technology Team. During his tenure at Goldman Sachs, Wang oversaw the investment in China Ping An Insurance Company and was appointed a member of its board. In addition, Wang initiated investment in Beijing Hua Yuan Properties, where he became director of both Hua Yuan and its Hong Kong listed parent company, China Resources Beijing Land.

From July 2000 to January 2006, Wang served as the CE
of TOM Group, a major media company in the Greater Chi
TOM, Wang hosted a series of acquisitions, which were sev
uncertain market conditions. However, in 2004, the market pro
In just over three years, TOM Group had evolved from an Int
premier Chinese-language media conglomerate commanding lea
media sectors: Internet, outdoor media, publishing, sports, televisi
ment. In all, Wang led TOM Group through more than 40 acquisiti
alliances, building a company of unparalleled scope and scale in
increasing its revenue 36 times in five years from US$11 million in
joined, to approximately US$400 million in 2005.

During this time, Wang's reputation soared as one of the most famous p
managers of China. His strategic vision and outstanding leadership was
reference to his Oxford style of thinking. Under his guidance, TOM Group's
flagship, TOM Online, was listed on the NASDAQ and GEM (Growth En
Market) Board of the Hong Kong Stock Exchange in early 2004. In the same
TOM Group migrated from the GEM Board and was successfully listed on the
board of the Hong Kong Stock Exchange, a milestone affirming the compan
success in expanding its business. TOM Group also scored an honor in corporate governance, being ranked fifth among all Hong Kong companies of the 2004 annual report on corporate governance by *BusinessWeek*.

Wang is one of Greater China's most experienced private equity investors with broad experience in investment banking, equity capital markets, and technology. For his professional accomplishment, Wang has been bestowed with a number of honors and awards, including China's Venture Capital Award for Outstanding Investor (1998–2008), the Top Ten China Media People Award (2005), the Executive Award (2004), and the Top Ten China IT Business People Award (2003). In addition, he was also named one of the "Young Global Leaders" by the World Economic Forum.

Wang's motto to success is "In Life, you do not solve problems, you survive them." With his Oxford education combined with deep Chinese cultural heritage, he firmly believes that business is an art, and the road to success is smooth if you are motivated, have commonsense, able to generate new ideas, be patient, and withstand failures.

KAWAL GILL

Sources

ACCA (2006), "Mr. Sing Wang", available at: http://www.hongkong.accaglobal.com/doc/hongkong/centenarybio/sing_wang (accessed 22 July 2010).

Business Wire (2006),"Texas Pacific Group and Sing Wang partner to make growth equity investments in Northern Asia", 29 May, available at: http://www.allbusiness.com/banking-finance/financial-markets-investing/5480874-1.html (accessed 22 July 2010).

互动百科 (2010), "王兟" ["Sing Wang", *Hudong.dom*], available at: http://www.hudong.com/wiki/%E7%8E%8B%E5%85%9F (accessed 22 July 2010).

160 王炜: 昆明走出的国际投资家", 云南日报 [Wang, W., "Sing Wang: An enture capitalist from Kunming", *Yunnan Daily*], 14 March, available at: ıdaily.com/html/20070814/news_93_48607.html (accessed 22 July 2010).

ɪg, Weijia (Victor Wang 王维嘉 b. 1958)

known as Victor Wang, Wang Weijia is a pioneer in the wireless data network rket and the president of MTone Wireless Corporation, the first company to pply mobile Internet service in China. Wang presided over the development of the ırst wireless data network in the world based on the cellular telephone network, a technology that evolved into the North America wireless data standard CDPD (Cellular Digital Packet Data) today. In addition, he proposed "Thumb economy," a concept that forecasted the popularity of the mobile phone messaging service, and formed the earliest partnership with China Mobile.

Ever since he was nine years old, Wang Weijia has been fascinated by radio. However, this pursuit was interrupted by the Cultural Revolution, when he was sent to the countryside to do hard labor after graduating from high school. In order to change his status and go back to the city, he had to be admitted to a university, which was extremely difficult during that chaotic period. What made it more challenging was his lack of basic knowledge in math and English due to school interruption during the Cultural Revolution. Born with a love for challenge, Wang spent every spare second of his time preparing for the newly resumed national college entrance examination with substantial perseverance and confidence. Even under very harsh conditions and a very limited timeframe, he managed to take the exam and was admitted to the University of Science and Technology of China, a prestigious institution of higher learning in the country and a very popular place for young ambitious students at that time.

Inspired by the successful stories of Apple, HP, Intel, and other IT companies thriving in Silicon Valley, Wang applied for Stanford University in 1985 and started his pursuit of a doctoral degree in electric engineering. Surrounded by elites in the IT industry and a rich atmosphere for innovation and entrepreneurship, Wang established substantial technical expertise as well as confidence during his study at Stanford.

After graduation from Stanford in 1987, Wang led the designation and implementation of the first metropolitan ATM experiment network of Pacific Bell, one of the top seven telecom companies in America. In 1992, he took charge of the research of the fourth generation personal mobile communication in Interval Research owned by Paul Allen, one of the co-founders of Microsoft. Even when working for these renowned companies and having owned multiple foundational patents on wireless network, Wang was still not content with his career, the passion of searching for something better constantly surrounded him.

A trip back to China in 1992 enabled Wang to realize what he had been searching for: starting his own business. Inspired by the popularity of one-way pagers in China, he began to develop his initial plan of combining wireless communication and the Internet to realize two-way message service. For Wang, it was a very lonely path to explore as an entrepreneur with such innovative ideas at that time. He had to work on every aspect of the project that required the state-of-the-art technology.

Apart from technology and blueprint, funding and management are also crucial in starting a new business. Wang's persistence and charisma enabled him to gather enough capital for the establishment of MTone Wireless Corporation in Silicon Valley in July 1994. Leading a unique team equipped with expertise in both wireless service and the Internet, Wang was very confident in the future development of his company. It was at that time that he decided to enter the Chinese market to contribute to the country's wireless communication industry and to explore what he believed the future largest wireless communication market in the world.

In 1996, MTone succeeded in developing the first set of wireless Internet products, leading China to be among the top in wireless Internet industry and enabling China to enjoy an advanced position in the IT industry for the first time in decades. In 1997, Wang invented the two-way mobile personal information machine, referred to as TFMIM (The Double Faces Individual Move Information Machine), which made MTone the first in the world to introduce two-way pagers and provide information services. Experts pointed out that this development symbolized the birth of a completely new industry with a future global market of up to US$1 trillion worth – the personal mobile information industry. Wang was therefore referred to as the "king of information." In 1998, MTone introduced business information services in China for the first time, making wireless stock exchanges a possibility and MTone the first in the world to develop handheld stock exchange equipment.

During the first several years of its establishment, MTone did not make a profit due to the underdeveloped market and environment. Full of ambition, Wang regarded these difficulties as only temporary and achieved rounds after rounds of successful financing. Being an entrepreneur brings tremendous risks and challenges. The first major setback for Wang took place in 2000 with MTone's investment in the Wireless Application Protocol (WAP)-related market. Not easily defeated, Wang started to turn his attention to Short Message Service (SMS) and realized its huge potential. In contrast to the setback in the WAP investment, MTone enjoyed a huge success in the SMS industry and became the largest service provider in China as of 2003. Faced with more and more competitors in the SMS market and the development of WAP compatible mobile phones, Wang saw the second chance for the WAP market and developed a series of WAP products from music ringtones to online games for mobile phones, thus generating huge profits to MTone.

A key factor behind Wang's success is his passion for work, to him a positive and enthusiastic work attitude is the most important for a business. He also realized that the management of Silicon Valley is not very suitable for China. Once constantly puzzled by how to provide an incentive system for employees and how to facilitate communications within the organizational structure, Wang learned from the lessons of some successful large hi-tech companies in China. He also acknowledged the need for adjusting his management system in accordance to the actual situations instead of simply following the successful experience of other Chinese companies.

In an effort to make MTone an industry giant like General Electric, Wang hopes that MTone's corporate culture consists of the following features: taking initiatives and responsibilities to do the job well, being detail-oriented, using facts and data as the basis for decision making, and having effective executions. When it comes to making hiring decisions, ethics is still the most important determinant. In contrast to more than 10 years ago when Wang just started his business and believed that technology was the only thing that mattered to a company's success, Wang no longer thinks it is the case nowadays; in his opinion the everyday management is more important than ideas and technology.

Accompanied by perseverance, confidence, and an incurable addiction to entrepreneurship, Wang pioneered the wireless data network market on his revolutionary yet lonely road to success. To Wang, being an entrepreneur is his only career and no challenges or failures can stop him from pursuing this passion.

MIAO CHI

Sources

胡冰 (2007), "王维嘉: 无限互联网的寂寞高手", 创业英雄: *10位海归创业先锋* (王辉耀主编), 中国发展出版社, 北京 [Hu, B., "Wang Weijia: A lonely expert in the wireless data network market", in Wang, H. (ed.), *Entrepreneurial Heroes: Ten Overseas Returnees in Entrepreneurship,* China Development Press, Beijing], pp. 49–72.

Stanford Asia Technology Initiative (2006), "Dr. Victor Wang, CEO and President, MTone", available at: http://ati.stanford.edu/ (accessed 5 October 2010).

Wang, Yafei (Jane Wang 王亚非 b. 1955)

Founder and chairwoman of Huice Capital Management, Wang Yafei is also a senior partner of Beijing Investment Consultants Incorporated (BICI), an associate professor at the Guanghua School of Management at Peking University, and a director of the Chamber of Commerce of the Western Returned Scholars Association.

In 1985, texts, newspaper articles and business magazines were rife with information on "Doing Business in China." It seems the world had finally realized the importance of this burgeoning economic power, not just as a potential market, but also as a new and powerful player in world finance. The recognition of China as a major global power was amplified by growing political and cultural interactions. In July 1985, President Li Xiannian traveled to the United States, the first such visit by a PRC head of state. This exciting period in China–US exchange also brought about a large increase in the number of young Chinese academics who were interested in broadening their understanding of the American culture and business environment. It was in this exhilarating year that Wang Yafei, known as Jane Wang, was offered an opportunity unique to Chinese university graduates: a visiting scholar position at the University of Maryland in College Park.

Wang was well prepared for her scholarly duties. As a 1981 graduate of the International Politics program at prestigious Fudan University in Shanghai, she had studied all aspects of global politics, international law, and cross-cultural communications. In addition, she was fluent in English. Yet her experiences in the United States provided her with an education of a different nature. Wang immersed herself in her new environment, living with a middle-class American family, and joining the family in social events and holiday celebrations. Viewing American television programs and reading local literature provided her additional insights into this new lifestyle. Her American experience culminated in a driving tour of the US Eastern Seaboard. From the nation's capital, Washington DC, to Key West Florida, the Southernmost City in the United States, Wang was able to experience this Western culture from many different perspectives.

In the fall of 1986, Wang bid adieu to her American friends and colleagues and returned to Beijing. Her homecoming reflected an important commitment to China, as many Chinese graduate students studying in foreign locales were not returning from their foreign host countries, creating a "brain drain" that was of special concern to the Chinese government. Yet her US experience was not to be Jane's last venture into Western studies. In 1987, chosen from more than 800 applicants, she was admitted to the Master of Business Administration program at the eminent Lancaster University in the United Kingdom. This was certainly a testament to her potential as a future Chinese business leader.

The MBA program at Lancaster University focused on knowledge and skill sets that were to serve Wang well in her rise in the Chinese business community. Here, she was able to study theory and application of business and management principles that would be applied to a variety of real world business situations. In addition, the degree provided her with enhanced personal skills such as critical thinking, team playing, time management, and networking abilities. She expanded her learning experience in Lancaster by touring Europe as well.

Importantly, Wang was dedicated to applying her newly honed business acumen to the growth and development of the Chinese economy and business community. Seeking just such an opportunity, she returned once again to China. First in Shenzhen, then in Beijing, she explored various business opportunities. Her quest for a business position was realized when, in 1991, she became the office manager of a joint venture shoe company comprised of five separate subsidiaries. Wang soon discovered that the company was suffering from some significant management challenges, and sales results were suboptimal. Her professional instincts, combined with her extensive training, led her to nurture new business relationships with customers in Eastern Europe and South America. Her efforts resulted in incremental sales of over 40 containers, and served to rejuvenate the firm financially.

In spite of her success, or perhaps because of it, Wang experienced a call to entrepreneurship. Along with two fellow returnees, she formed an independent consulting firm that leveraged her business experience in a wider array of industries, thus contributing to the overall growth and success of Chinese industry. During this time, it became clear to her that professional success in China was largely predicated on the development and maintenance of solid, long-term relationships, both with business partners as well as government agencies. These relationships, known as *Guangxi*, are often complex and take some time to foster. However, those who are successful in doing so are able to minimize the potential risks and frustrations inherent in Chinese business. Clearly, Wang was an expert in this area.

Moreover, that expertise led her to a position as assistant to the president of China Enterprises Fund Management Corporation in 1994. During that time, there was no better place to cultivate business opportunities. Due to its proximity, Hong Kong was considered the gateway to any firm hoping to conclude a business arrangement in China. Living in Hong Kong and traveling frequently to the mainland, Wang's job was to unite Hong Kong and China-based sources of investment funds with investment opportunities. Although challenged by a lack of foreign investment regulations, the firm realized several profitable transactions. Wang's success here did not go unnoticed. In 1996, she was offered a much-coveted role with BICI. Not coincidentally, the founder of BICI, Dr. Gao Xiqing, was also a returnee, having graduated from Duke University Law School in North Carolina, USA.

In no small measure due to Wang's contributions, BICI has become a renowned investment and consulting firm. BICI specializes in financial advisory services and is a leader in both domestic and international capital markets, guiding individuals and institutions through the process of issuing, trading, and managing equity shares, bonds, and investment funds. The firm offers assistance in corporate restructuring, mergers, and acquisitions, and is noted for its ability to enhance customer value creation.

BICI has benefited handsomely from its ability to leverage *Guangxi*, a lesson that Wang learned early in her career. Not only has the company has been granted investment advisor status by the Chinese Securities Regulatory Commission, BICI has also maintained excellent relationships with relevant government departments as well as investment banks, accounting firms, law firms, and other critical intermediaries. In fact, the firm's highly regarded managers have participated in the development and refinement of Chinese economic legislation. Wang herself was instrumental in writing Chinese bankruptcy law and regulation.

During her tenure as senior partner with BICI, Jane has worked directly with over 20 clients. Her customer list resembles a roster of some of China's most noteworthy organizations, including China Road and Bridge, Chinese Medicine Corporation, Beijing Bus Incorporated, Guangzhou Guangsheng Group, and Sichuan Hard Alloy Metal. Given her many responsibilities and obligations, it is remarkable to note that Wang has also engaged in a number of entrepreneurial investments. Industries as diverse as software, electronics, and engineered plastics have all profited from Wang's financial contributions and expertise.

Students at the Guanghua School of Management at Beijing University have been fortunate to learn first-hand the intricacies of business and financial management from Wang, who has served as associate professor since 1995. In addition, Wang serves on the boards of such august bodies as Shanghai Huice Investment Management Company, Beijing Huitu Technology Company, China Time Share

Media Company, and Li Ning Company. Her career thus far has culminated with the founding and chairmanship of Beijing Century Huice Capital Management, established in 2007.

With a life this full of accomplishment, one would think that Wang Yafei would be ready for a brief respite. Yet she feels that her contributions to China's economic growth are just the start of the nation's metamorphosis into one of the world's greatest economic entities. Quotes Wang (2010), "If we can tell in 10 or 20 years from now, I believe that what we have achieved so far is only a beginning! Uneven economic development and backward areas in China demand further tremendous creative work even with lots of dilemmas ahead of us."

There is no doubt that Wang will continue to champion this cause. Her unwavering commitment to professional excellence, devotion to her country and her ability to prosper in spite of challenging and ever changing business environment teach us all a valuable lesson: in every crisis, there is opportunity. As an ancient Chinese proverb states, "If you want one year of prosperity, grow grain. If you want ten years of prosperity, grow trees. If you want one hundred years of prosperity, grow people." Surely, Wang's students, her business protégés, her colleagues and her acquaintances have all grown considerably from having known her.

ROBIN E. KELLY

Sources

BICI (2010), *Beijing Investment Consultants Website*, available at: www.bici.com.cn/ (accessed May 25, 2010).

Bloomberg (2010), "Executive profile: Yafei Wang", *BusinessWeek*, available at: http://investing.businessweek.com/research/stocks/people/person.asp?personId=13753194&ticker=2331:HK&previousCapId=10877491&previousTitle=LI%20NING%20CO%20LTD (accessed 30 June 2010).

Fuqua (2007), "NCHS fall newsline", *Duke University Website*, available at: http://www.google.com/search?hl = en&rlz = 1T4HPIB_enUS311US311&q = BICI%2C + Dr. + Gao + Xiqing + Duke + University + Law + School&btnG = Search&aq = f&aqi = &aql = &oq = &gs_rfai = (accessed May 30, 2010).

Guanghua (2010), "January 2010 newsletter", *University of Peking Website*, available at: http://mba.pku.edu.cn/english/pdf/NewsletterJan2010.pdf (accessed May 25, 2010).

Lee, J. (2010), "The importance of *Guangxi* (relationship) when doing business in China", *China Window Online*, available at: http://www.china-window.com/china_business/doing_business_in_china/the-importance-of-guangxi.shtml (accessed 30 May 2010).

Maswana, J. C. (2008), "China's financial development and economic growth: Exploring the contradictions", *International Research Journal of Finance and Economics*, (19) pp. 89–101..

VisitFlorida (2010), *Website of VisitFlorida*, available at: http://www.visitflorida.com/video/video_id.266.

Wang, Y. (2010), "Yafei Wang, my brief story: West to East", personal publication.

WuDon, C. (1992), "Li Xiannian, China ex-President and rural economist, dies at 82", *The New York Times*, 23 June, available at: www.nytimes.com/1992/06/23/world/li-xiannian-china-ex-president-and-rural-economist-dies-at-82.html (accessed April 12, 2010).

Wang, Zhongjun (王中军 b. 1960)

An artist by training, Wang Zhongjun is the president and CEO of the Huayi Brothers Media Group. He and his brother Wang Zhonglei have grown their company from a small advertising firm in 1994 to a media conglomerate running film, television, music, advertising, and talent management operations in China.

Although a grade school student, Wang demonstrated a special interest in fine arts. Growing up in a military family, he also developed a strong will power at an young age. In the early 1970s, when he was not able to carry out his studies in his Beijing neighborhood school, Wang decided to enroll into a rural school in his father's hometown, enduring all kinds of hardship. During the latter part of the Cultural Revolution when there was no college entrance examination, joining the army had become the preferred choice for many young people. In 1976, through his father's connection, Wang became a reconnaissance scout in the elite 38th Army of PLA. He was among the first group of soldiers to join the Party, and was made a squad leader at age 18. The four-year military training had profound impact on him. Even today, Wang still hangs a portrait of Chairman Mao in his spacious office located at the Central Business District of Beijing, as he regards Mao a poet in politics, himself an artist in business.

Discharged in 1980, Wang secured a position at the Chinese National Commodities Bureau in Beijing, while enrolling into the evening school of the Chinese Central Academy of Craft Art to receive a systematic education in art design. Because of his talent, Wang was promoted to an art photographer and editor in the ministry press. However, unlike many Chinese of that time who were content with lifelong employment at government agencies, he soon quit his work because of strong personal interests in arts and photography. In 1985, Wang became a self-employed professional designer and photographer, first making children's pictorial books, commercials, and calendars, then managing a small marketing firm. Although he began to make 10 times more than before, he was still not satisfied with his life. In 1989, Wang sold his minivan and joined the wave of Chinese students to study in the United States.

For Wang, the overseas period was by no means a picnic in the park. As a self-sponsored student, he along with his wife endured a great deal of challenge and fiscal instability during the five years in the United States. Both of them worked in all kinds of odd jobs, typically laboring 13–16 hours each day during weekends. Remarkably, by the time Wang completed his study in mass communication in the United States in 1994, the couple had cumulated a personal saving of $100,000. Again, Wang demonstrated his ability for independent thinking. Unlike many other mainland Chinese students who usually settled for a comfortable living in America, Wang's heart was swirling with dreams of fame and success. He promptly returned to China in 1994, and spent all his money setting himself up as boss of a privately owned company that he believed could one day be the "Chinese Warner Brothers".

Nevertheless, the road to success was not easy and straightforward. At the beginning, Wang published a small magazine with commercials tailored for upscale clientele and foreign diplomats in Beijing. Although paddling a bicycle to sell advertisements across the city, Wang, based on his overseas experience, quickly realized that many large Chinese corporations did not have uniformed corporate images, which prompted him to present a proposal to the Bank of China (BOC) for its first standardized corporate image plan. After his winning design was implemented among 15,000 BOC branches across the country, other banks and large corporations quickly followed, and business began to boom. Within three years, Wang's Huayi Brothers Media grew to become one of the top 10 advertising firms in China, whose clients include the China State Power, the Agricultural Bank of China, and the Sinopec Group among others. Loaded with money, Wang traded his bicycle for a Mercedes Benz and BMW, and then tried to expand his business into the fields of medical and automobile sales without much success. His luck turned when a former colleague convinced him in 1998 to make a popular drama series for the massive Chinese television market. However, with no experience in TV production, Wang reaped 100% return to his investment due to a successful promotion campaign. On December 18, 2000, with a registered capital of 100 million RMB, the Huayi Brothers' Taihe Film and Television Investment Company was incorporated with Wang as president and CEO.

Out of his overseas experience, Wang became keenly aware that entertainment was the second largest industry in the United States after the military spending, and a billion Chinese with improved lifestyle would certainly be willing to pay more for their personal enjoyment. Following the commercial model of the Hollywood film industry, Wang brought talented Chinese directors and stars on board and made a succession of hit films. One of his primary partners and stockholders was *Feng Xiaogang*, a leading "Fifth Generation" director in China, whose films have been very successful both at the box offices and with critics. In 2004, Huayi Brothers' four films, *A World Without Thieves*, *Kung Fu Hustle*, *Kekexili Mountain Patrol*, and *Breaking News*, took in over 350 million yuan ($43.75 million) at the box office, a staggering 35 percent of total sales in the Chinese film industry that year and a record for a single film company in China. Other blockbusters by Huayi included: *Big Shot's Funeral* (2001), *Cell Phone* (2003), *Banquet* (2006), *Battle of Wits* (2006), *Assembly* (2007), and *If You Are the One* (2008). With a successful track record, Huayi Brothers became a market leader in the Chinese entertainment industry, the first film company to receive loans from banks without collateral, and among the most recognized brand names in China. As a private firm, Huayi competes with large film production corporations that have ample state funding and established distribution channel, and with Hong Kong and Taiwan companies that have rich experiences in media production and overseas distribution. Wang's secrets were to build a strong team under talented directors, and to implement what he called "industrialized operation model," which includes targeted intensive investment, scaled production, specialization, and high technology. Since the company only made a few productions each year, Wang and his brother personally reviewed and approved every plot, which all had clearly defined goals such as reaping commercial profits, building brand, or nurturing new talents. With tight fiscal control, Wang was able to apply his talent in arts and advertisement and diversify financial risks. Because of corporate sponsorship, some of his films such as *Cell Phone* were able to recover a large portion of investment even before the production began.

Although the Chinese commercial film and television industry is still relatively young compared with Hollywood, Wang is confident that "given the speed at which China's economy is developing, a world-class Chinese entertainment and media group is sure to emerge in the near future (Zuo, 2006)," and his ambition is to make Huayi Brothers "the largest private entertainment group in China. Then maybe we can become number one in Asia and even in the world (*Ibid*)."

WENXIAN ZHANG

Sources

Zuo, Y. (2006), "Man behind *Banquet* aspires to be China's Warner", *Xinhua News*, 6 October, available at: www.china.org.cn/english/features/film/183047.htm (accessed 28 November 2009).

侯亮 (2006), "王中军的职业幸福", *大众电影* [Hou, L., "Professional happiness of Wang Zhongjun", *Popular Cinema*], 15 September, pp. 12–17.

胡冰 (2007), "王中军: 潇洒投资的艺术家", *创业英雄: 10位海归创业先锋* (王辉耀主编), 中国发展出版社, 北京 [Hu, B., "Wang Zhongjun: An artist who makes graceful investment", in Wang, H. (ed.), *Entrepreneurial Heroes: Ten Overseas Returnees in Entrepreneurship*, China Development Press, Beijing], pp. 1–22.

Wang, Zhongwei (王中伟 b. 1966)

A well-known entrepreneur who started his business with only 200 RMB, Wang Zhongwei is the CEO of Longman Schools, a subsidiary of Pearson Group that now has more than 70 English learning centers in large cities across China.

Wang was born in 1966 to a medical family of several generations in Liaoning Province, Northeastern China. However, during the Cultural Revolution, his family was expelled to the remote northern wilderness because of his father's educational background. Growing up in a poor environment, Wang dropped out of school several times, doing farming, hunting, and at times begging. Nevertheless, the hardship in life made him a strong willed person, and he never gave up school and his education. Finally, in 1985, Wang was admitted to the Liaoning Medical University. After five years of study, he followed his family tradition and became a doctor in a local hospital, where he worked for another five years. When the economic reform finally reached the medical service field, Wang took the opportunity and transformed a community clinic into a private hospital. As a result, his salary jumped more to 30,000 RMB per month, more than 10 times of that of average people of the time.

Working in the hospital for several years, Wang saw enough patients suffering, which made him wonder about the truly meaning of life. After some soul searching, he decided to enrich himself instead. Therefore, he quitted his job and stayed at home while focusing on learning English. It was very difficult task because he only studied

Russian before, but he was able to master enough English skills in time to pass the TOEFL exam. In 1996, Wang had a chance to guide a Canadian group visiting the Forbidden City, where he bumped into his future wife, an American student in an internship program at Yunnan Normal University. They learned languages from each other and soon fell in love. After their marriage, Wang received his visa and went to the University of Minnesota for his MPA degree.

After his graduation, however, Wang found out it was not easy for him to make a good living in the United States, so he decided to return to China with his wife in 1999. First, he tried very hard to find a decent job in Beijing. However, without any success, he could only stay at home in a basement apartment feeling deeply depressed. Although Wang had nothing to make a living, his wife supported the family by teaching English at difference schools in Beijing. Working as a broker for her classes, the couple could earn about 20,000 RMB per month. Wang soon realized the huge market potential in English learning. Therefore, they used a friend's rental place, advertised on the local newspaper with only 200 RMB, and launched the Dell English School. With Wang in charge of marketing and promotion and his wife as English teacher, they quickly recruited 26 students for oral English and 84 students for learning TOFEL during the first month of operation. Though they faced fierce competition from the New Oriental Schools, clear leader in the domestic market, Dell English School soon made a name for itself because of its special teaching method, small classes, and opportunities for practice with native English speakers.

However, business was not all smooth, and Wang had to face many challenges. Space became an issue when the enrollment reached 2000. Because of its rising reputation, many schools did not want to rent out classrooms to Wang, as students would just go to Dell instead. Finally, Wang was able to find some office space in a business center and converted that into classrooms, which had the added benefit of attracting young white-collar workers. As a private company, Wang also struggled to keep a stable team of professional teachers during the quick expansion phase, as he often had to find replacement teachers on very short notices. In addition, Wang soon faced a legal challenge. Since the school was promoted and marketed as Dell English, the better-known American personal computer maker Dell filed a lawsuit, which forced Wang to rename his school to the Dellenglish International School and pay a fine of 200,000 RMB in 2006.

Nevertheless, Wang was able to overcome those hurdles and the business grew steadily. His philosophy about learning English is study by practice, simple yet practical concept that attracted many young people, and the total enrollment quickly reached 5000. Students of the Dellenglish International School came from different backgrounds, including not only university students but also staff members of international companies such as Intel, P&G, and Samsung. As China geared up its preparation for the Beijing Olympic Games, Wang's school expanded at even faster pace, with more than 20 learning centers set up in 2007, most of them located in Beijing.

Meanwhile, Pearson Group, a global leader in education, was seeking to expand its market in China, especially for its subsidiary brand Longman. During 2008–2009, Pearson acquired Dellenglish schools along with the Wall Street English School and 51 learning English Schools in Shanghai. After the acquisition, Dellenglish International Schools were renamed to Dellenglish Longman Schools, and Wang changed his career from an entrepreneur to a top-level executive. He is ready for another chapter of his professional career.

ZICHENG LI

Sources

财富故事会 (2006), "戴尔财情史", *央视国际* ["Dell's wealth and love story", *CCTV International*], 23 March, available at: http://www.cctv.com/program/cfgsh/20060323/101395.shtml (accessed 30 June 2010).
何悦 (2007), "我不贫穷但我仍要奋斗", *竞报* [He, Y., "I am not poor, but I still work hard", *The First*], 20 March, available at: http://www.thefirst.cn/141/2007-03-20/55668.htm, (accessed 30 June 2010).
纪春 (2005), "王中伟: 苦难的受益人", *中国广播网* [Ji, Q., "Wang Zhongwei: The man who benefited from hardship", *China National Radio Network*], 5 April, available at: http://www.cnr.cn/wcm/fortune/guest/t20050509_170641.html (accessed 30 June 2010).
罗燕 (2009), "王中伟: 传统教育的忧思者与革新者", *华人财富* [Luo, Y., "Interview with Wang Zhongwei: A thinker and reformer in traditional education", *Chinese wealth*], available at: http://bbs.newssc.org/thread-1558070-1-1.html (accessed 30 June 2010).

Wu, Ping (武平 b. 1961)

Wu Ping is the co-founder, former president, and CEO of Spreadtrum Communications Inc., a high-tech company based in the Zhangjiang Science Park of Pudong District, Shanghai. Founded in 2001, the company designs and markets baseband communications chips for the massive wireless telecom market in China. Its semiconductors, which are compatible with a range of international wireless standards, are sold to manufacturers of cell phones who incorporate them into their products.

At 49, Wu can look back at a solid experience of 20-plus years and a high-powered career in the telecommunications and semiconductor industry during which he acquired three integrated design circuit patents in his name. Before Spreadtrum, he held positions of senior director of VLSI designs at Mobilink Telecom from 1997 to 2001, and before 1997, served as design manager of Trident Microsystems, Inc. However, his success was not accidental. With a BS in electrical engineering from Tsinghua University, a MS and a PhD in electrical engineering from the China Academy of Aerospace Dynamics, Wu was well equipped for his ultimate brainchild.

Upon graduation, Wu went overseas, first working on the integrated circuit design in Europe, then relocated to the United States where he befriended three other fellow scientists from mainland China who were working in the semiconductor industry at the time. The idea for a new company of communications chips came over a meal in a Chinese restaurant in Silicon Valley back in 1999, when the four friends were discussing the development of the wireless communication market back home. Although China had the highest rate of growth and the largest wireless user group in the world, the core technology on cell phone chips was still controlled by a few large American and European companies. Since the chip counted about 50–70% of cell phone price, according to their estimates, if each chip cost $25 to $50, and if cell phone users in China reached over 200 million, the country would pay more than $10 billion each year on chip importing expenses. Astonished by their simple calculations, Wu and his friends also sensed the great market potential waiting to be explored. Although they all had comfortable lives in the United States, the four friends decided to launch a world-class company of communications chips aiming for the massive wireless telecom market in China. Later on, co-founder Chen Datong became CTO, Fan Renyong was the vice president of operations, and Zhou Chengyun the vice president of sales and the director of marketing.

In April 2001, Spreadtrum Communications was incorporated in California, and in July Wu returned to China along with 37 other Chinese scientists and engineers recruited from the Silicon Valley, and founded Spreadtrum Shanghai. Since more than half of the team members were also former graduates of Tsinghua University who went overseas for study and work, the company was able to combine the top talents from China with the operation management and capital structure of high-tech company in Silicon Valley. Under Wu's leadership, Spreadtrum was soon expanded from 40 employees to more than 200 people, with research and development taking place around the clock in both Silicon Valley and Shanghai. However, when its first chip design was about done and ready for final testing and production, September 11 terrorist attack occurred, which led to a major setback to the global economy and the venture capital market. At that critical moment, Wu and other senior management personnel decided to take 50% reduction in compensations, which inspired other employees to remain with the company, resulting no resignation during the three-month pay cut period. Fortunately, the second-round funding came through quickly with additional investment from Vertex and Pacific Venture Partners, and Spreadtrum emerged from the crisis and went on the fast track of development.

By 2003, based on his revolutionary and unique GSM/GPRS (2.5G) multimedia baseband integrated single-chip design, Wu and his friends had developed Spreadtrum into China's largest communications chip company. A year later, he followed-up the punch with an industry-first TD/GSM dual-mode baseband single core design, which was immediately put into mass production. That ultimately, and more importantly, earned him the NASDAQ listing in mid-2007 for Spreadtrum, a first for any Chinese 3G venture. Although the race for such advancements was fierce, Spreadtrum's advantage was that it proposed a far cheaper and less power-hungry solution, yet based on open-source philosophy and technology, which enabled its customers to quickly and efficiently develop feature-rich wireless solutions. Thus, the Chinese peer-production and collectivist-oriented information-technology advancements challenge and trump a more protectionist Western model on its own turf, ironically, but non-the less utterly constructively and effectively demonstrated by a successful Silicon Valley returnee.

Since the development of semiconductor and communication technologies was regarded as a pillar industry for China's modernization drive, Spreadtrum enjoyed strong support from the Chinese government. Not only it received the PRC National Science and Technology Advancement Award, but also both President Hu Jintao and Premier Wen Jiabao toured the company on separate occasions. The spreading use of cell phones means expanded profits for makers of wireless communications semiconductors like Spreadtrum Communications, which makes sales directly to customers through its representative offices in Shanghai, Beijing, Shenzhen, and Korea, whereas R&D are conducted in San Diego, Shanghai, and Beijing. By October 2009, Spreadtrum shipped out its 100 million units of communication chips.

For his accomplishment, Wu was named as a "Leading Entrepreneur in Science and Technology" in Shanghai in 2004, and was honored for "excellent contribution" during the award ceremony on the 10th anniversary of the development of the Chinese integrated circuit design industry. In the following year, he was named as an "Outstanding Entrepreneur in Science and Technology" in the new Pudong District, the "Most Vigorous Technological Entrepreneur" in Shanghai, and an "Outstanding Entrepreneur" among overseas Chinese professionals. In 2006, Wu was honored for his "Leading Role in China Semiconductor Enterprise," and was awarded as an "Outstanding Individual of PRC National Information Industry in Technological Innovation" by the Ministry of Information Industry. He was also given an innovation award during the 2007 China Management Forum, and the 10th "Shanghai Science and Technology Elite Selection" award in 2008. Meanwhile, Spreadtrum was named as a semiconductor enterprise with the greatest potential, and the "Enterprise of the Decade with Outstanding Contribution in China's Mobile Handset Industry."

Wu served as the president and CEO of Spreadtrum since its inception in April 2001. In October 2008, Li Yu was named president while Wu continued as CEO until February 2009; since then Wu has remained as the chairman of the Board. It is recently reported that he is leading the charge in a new 150-employee venture, the Zhangjiang-registered Shanghai Information Technology Co. Given his track record as a successful entrepreneur, it will be interesting to see Wu's next move.

JONATAN JELEN AND WENXIAN ZHANG

Sources

Chen, W. (2010), "Ping Wu, Spreadtrum Communications founder left", 10 June, available at: http://babyton.com/chanel672/2010/06/10/ping-wu-spreadtrum-communications-founder-left-an/ (Accessed 9 September 2010).

Forbes (n.d.), "Wu Ping, Chairman of Board, Spreadtrum Communications", available at: http://people.forbes.com/profile/ping-wu/38726 (Accessed 9 September 2010).

Spreadtrum (2010), "About us: Milestone", available at: http://www.spreadtrum.com/eng/about.asp?name=milestone (Accessed 9 September 2010).

李政 (2007), "武平: 缔造3G中国第一股", *叱咤华尔街: 10位海归上市公司领袖* (王辉耀主编), 中国发展出版社, 北京 [Li Z., "Wu Ping: Building the first 3G venture in China", in Wang, H. (ed.), *Movers on Wall Street: Ten Overseas Returnees Who Took Their Business Public*, China Development Press, Beijing], pp. 159–180.

Wu, Shangzhi (吴尚志 b. 1950)

Wu Shangzhi is the founding partner of CDH China Management Company Limited, or CDH, an international private equity fund manager with more than 2 billion US dollars of committed capital under management and with a focus on investments in China's leading companies.

Born in Beijing as the eldest child to a family with advanced educational achievements, Wu constantly found inspirations in his father, a thoracic expert once studied in the United States. Even during the extreme harsh period of the Cultural Revolution when his whole family was substantially impacted, Wu's father still encouraged Wu and his siblings to value the power of education and improve themselves through obtaining knowledge. From 1972 to 1975, Wu self-studied almost all the middle school and high school courses and built a good foundation of English. His hard work enabled him to get into a university, which was the only way to change one's status for most Chinese during that time. Very different from his peers who were used to waiting for instructions, Wu took a proactive approach and was admitted to Massachusetts Institute of Technology where he obtained a doctoral degree in mechanical engineering and a master's degree in management. His experience at MIT also exposed him to private equity (PE) fund for the first time.

From 1984 to 1991, Wu worked for the World Bank as an operations officer, specializing in investment projects for China and India; and from 1991 to 1993, he was a senior investment officer at the International Finance Corporation (IFC). With an increasing exposure to PE related projects, Wu's interests in PE became stronger and stronger, an initial blueprint to develop PE in China also began to form in his mind. After eight years at the World Bank, Wu could no longer feel a sense of accomplishment from work; he thus decided to quit his job at the IFC and return to China to start a PE focusing on investing in Chinese companies.

Even with substantial work experience from the World Bank and a deep understanding of China and Chinese firms, Wu's initial attempts ended up in failure due to the many hidden factors restraining the introduction of PE to China. After this initial setback, Wu decided to look for a job instead of hanging on to a good yet premature plan. From 1995 to 2002, he worked for China International Capital Corporation Ltd. (CICC), serving as the head of the direct investment department beginning in 1996. Having worked for the World Bank, Wu was very aware of the value of talents and teamwork, thus cherished the work and contributions from other partners of CICC. Although his first two years at CICC were filled with difficulties and challenges, Wu and his talented team quickly achieved success from investing in China Mobile, Sina and other promising businesses. Given the unique features of CICC and its earliest partnership with international investment banks in China, most of its projects could be regarded as "milestones" in the Chinese economy.

Just as CICC was enjoying a steady growth with an annual return rate of over 30%, an unexpected regulatory change from the China Securities Regulatory Commission in 2001 caused a sudden disruption of CICC's development. Faced with the resolution of splitting the direct investment department, Wu and his team decided to start their own business. In May 2002, five managing members from the CICC's direct investment department co-established Shenzhen CDH Management Co., Ltd. together with China National Investment & Guaranty Co., Ltd. The five members worked as general partners in charge of CDH management and operation. There were two funds under their management: one was an overseas fund with a total value of 100 million US dollars, and the other was a Chinese currency fund of RMB 135 million.

As Wu recalled, "CDH started from a very high platform with a mature credit system among investors and the market" (Xing, 2007). CDH's success does not lie in its capital holdings nor its international background, but rather in its particularly competent and localized team of which Wu is the most proud: president Jiao Zhen, partners Wang Lin, Hu Xiaoling, Wang Zhenyu, etc. Faced with an unpromising investment environment, Wu directs CDH to make the best use of its advantages and networks to attract and build partnerships with Morgan Stanley and Goldman Sachs, thus enabling CDH to create its own overseas IPO and obtain its leading position in the industry. With a well-designed strategy and a talented team, CDH experienced a steady stream of successes. From 2002 to 2005, CDH Venture invested nine projects, six of which were listed on the Hong Kong stock market and NASDAQ. Among these cases, the most widely known was with Mengniu Dairy Group while its investment in Focus Media Holding Ltd. returned a profit of over 21 times and became CDH's classical case featured by a small investment and a huge return.

With growing experience and investment successes, CDH aimed at attracting larger-scale funds to increase profit and reduce its dependence on overseas partners. In 2007, CDH's growth fund became the largest Chinese growth fund in Asia. In Wu's blueprint is an enormous and comprehensive investment organization consisting of venture capital fund, growth fund, stock fund, real estate fund, etc. In Wu's opinion, seizing every opportunity is crucial to CDH's future success.

The constantly changing PE market and favorable legislative regulations will contribute to an explosive growth in China's domestic PE fund, which has been playing an increasingly important role in the stock market over the recent years. Guided by Wu, CDH will likely maintain its leading status in China's private fund market in the near future.

MIAO CHI

Sources

邢学军 (2007), "吴尚志: 领跑中国PE", *财富裂变: 10位海归风险投资翘楚* (王辉耀主编), 中国发展出版社, 北京 [Xing, X., "Wu Shangzhi: Leading China's Private Equity Fund", in Wang, H. (ed.), *The Fission of Wealth: Ten Overseas Returnees in Venture Capitalism*, China Development Press, Beijing], pp. 81–99.

Forbes (2010), "Shangzhi Wu, Director", available at: http://people.forbes.com/profile/shangzhi-wu/20595 (accessed 10 October 2010).

Wu, Ying (吴鹰 b. 1959)

As the president and CEO of UT Starcom, Wu Ying was once known as a legendary developer of the Chinese telecommunication hardware sector, achieving amazing success during his career. When he was 48 years old, after a strategic failure, Wu had a dramatic turn-around. He then reinvented himself as a venture capitalist by joining CTC Capital in early 2008. After the rise and fall in UT Starcom, Wu has recently been utilizing his accumulated resources, experiences, and management skills toward the creation of more high-tech companies in China.

Born and grew up in Beijing, Wu attended Beijing Industry University, where he obtained his BS in electrical engineering. Soon after, Wu went to the United States in 1985 to pursue further studies at the New Jersey Institute of Technology. Starting with just $27 in his pocket, he worked his way through graduate study and gained an MS in electrical engineering.

For the next five years, Wu served as a consultant, member of technical staff and group leader for Bell Laboratories on personal communications services (PCS) and multimedia systems. In 1991, in cooperation with another overseas Chinese student in New Jersey, Wu founded a technological consulting company Starcom Networks, and returned to China in 1992 to launch his business.

Three years later, this company merged with California-based Unitech, also founded by overseas Chinese students, to form UT Startcom. In the first three years from its initial public offering from March 2000 to 2003, the company reached a market cap of more than US$3 billion, and reported 10 times an increase in revenue to $330 million in the first quarter of 2003 (Kuo, 2003). At the time, UT Starcom was considered one of the best Chinese technological stocks on the NASDAQ. The company's biggest success was the Personal Access System (PAS) handset, widely known in Chinese as "Xiao Ling Tong," translates to *Little Smart*. As the CEO of China operations for UT Starcom, Wu fine-tuned the "personal handy phone" technology that was popular in Japan and launched *Little Smart* in China in 1998. This caused something of a revolution by introducing the Chinese masses to an inexpensive alternative to the mobile phone in a fuzzy regulatory environment.

In China at that time, while the government allowed only two firms to provide cellular service, with his engineer background, Wu convinced telecom mandarins that cell phones are actually just a wireless extension of fixed-line phones. He then sold the system to the two Chinese fixed-line companies that were eager to share the huge mobile market but were restricted by government regulations. Citywide mobility and 75% lower prices compared to traditional carriers have made *Little Smart* popular among ordinary Chinese. According to UT Starcom, until March 2006, the number of *Little Smart* subscribers was nearly 90 million and UT Starcom enjoyed a 60% market share.

After enjoying rapid growth brought about by *Little Smart*, Wu initiated a digital TV solution called Internet Protocol TV (IPTV) as its new line of innovation (Yu, 2006). According to Wu, IPTV would deliver digital television service to subscribers via Internet Protocol over a broadband connection. Transmitting TV programs based on Internet Protocol breaks the bounds of fixed time and fixed channels of traditional TV programs. Although watching IPTV, customers are able to pause, rewind, and fast forward live broadcasts. They can also select programs broadcasted during the past 48 hours, or even one to two weeks earlier from the menu display. Wu has predicted that IPTV would dominate the market in the post-digital age.

This safe and inexpensive use of Digital TV technology has also gained the Chinese government's support. It had hundreds of thousands of customers in China by 2006. However, this time Wu did not turn IPTV into another killer product. The further development of IPTV was obstructed by the lack of industrial standards and strong supervision. At the early stage of product life cycle, it took time for IPTV to reach extensive use; meanwhile, *Little Smart* had matured in terms of its product life cycle, and started to experience rapid decline in market share. Accordingly, UT Startcom suffered from weak performance of both core products. Although he was a successful innovator, Wu sadly failed in the strategic launch of his new product line. Reluctantly, Wu resigned from the company in 2007, after a disagreement with the board.

Six months after his resignation, on January 3, 2008, Wu was back in the public limelight by announcing his new position as a general partner of CTC Capital. From an entrepreneur to venture capitalist, Wu accomplished a smooth transition by bringing over 20 years of experience in technology innovation and start-up enterprises. As a venture capitalist, Wu had previously made a few successful cases, including a joint-investment in Alibaba.com together with Sun Zhengyi, turning $5 million to $55 million in five years (Zhang, 2008). By utilizing his connection to government and other enterprises, Wu has been leveraging his resources and techniques for creation of future companies similar to UT Starcom. So far, Wu has helped CTC Capital invest in more than 10 companies with a total amount exceeding $50 million, with most of the funds going to high-tech related innovative projects (Xiao, 2008).

Within his new role, Wu is more than ready to contribute to the success of other Chinese companies. He is quoted as saying "There are too many opportunities in China; when you can catch several at one time, why stick to only one?"

XIAOTIAN ZHANG

Sources

China Tech News (2007), "Wu Ying leaves UT Starcom", 4 June, available at: http://www.chinatechnews.com/2007/06/04/5472-wu-ying-leaves-utstarcom (accessed 23 June 2010).

Kuo, K. (2003), "Tech survivor – UTStarcom: Wu Ying", *Time*, 4 July, available at: http://www.time.com/time/2003/survivors/wu.html (accessed 24 June 2010).

Xiao, X. (2008), "Wu Ying: Back to the market", *Business Man*, **2**, 34–35, available at: http://www.cqvip.com/qk/81291X/20082/26592968.0.html (accessed 23 June 2010).

Yu, S. J. (2006), "Telecom innovator: UT Starcom eyes new opportunity with IPTV", *Beijing Review*, 20 April, available at: http://www.bjreview.cn/EN/06-16-e/bus-2.htm (accessed 25 June 2010).

张刚 (2008), "吴鹰: 48岁的转身", *英才* [Zhang, G., "Wu Ying: A turn-around at 48 years old", *talents*], Vol. 2, available at: http://finance.sina.com.cn/leadership/mglgs/20080204/10434490302.shtml (accessed 24 June 2010).

Xiang, Bing (项兵 b. 1961)

Dr. Xiang Bing is one of the pioneers of executive education in China. Before becoming the founding dean of Cheung Kong Graduate School of Business (CKGSB), he was a member of the founding faculty for China Europe International Business School (CEIBS), and later went to Peking University where he developed the EMBA and Executive Education programs at Guanghua School of Management. He has also spent time as a faculty member at Hong Kong University of Science and Technology and the Chinese University of Hong Kong.

A top graduate of Xi'an Jiaotong University in 1983, Xiang received his PhD in accounting from the University of Alberta years later. As a well-respected scholar, he published research papers in leading international academic journals, and his research interests focus on comparative corporate systems, corporate governance, transition and management of state-owned enterprises, private enterprise business models, and corporate competition in emerging markets. In addition, he also serves as an independent, nonexecutive board member on a number of companies listed in both Hong Kong and mainland China.

Xiang has always had a global outlook himself, and a belief that a global mindset is of key importance to business leaders. When working at Guanghua School of Management, he approached the Li Ka-shing Foundation for funding to establish a satellite program for the school in Hong Kong. Li and the foundation were impressed enough by the proposal to invite him to start an entirely new business school in China under their sponsorship. In November 2002, Cheung Kong Graduate School of Business opened its doors as China's first private, nonprofit and independent business school.

Headquartered in Beijing, the school now also has campuses in Shanghai and Guangzhou, and offers MBA, EMBA and executive education programs. Its alumni include some of China's top business leaders across a variety of sectors, including Jack Ma, founder and CEO of Alibaba Group, Zhu Xinli, founder and chairman of Huiyuan Juice Group, Peng Xiaofeng, founder, chairman and CEO of LDK Solar, and Fu Chengyu, president and chairman of China National Offshore Oil Corporation (CNOOC).

As a leader on executive education, Xiang believed it was not enough just applying Western management theory and concepts to China and to Chinese companies, instead it is important to document the best management practices and innovations from China; some of them could be globally leading in the future. Also he believed it was not enough just developing students to be a very competent instrument to create value for shareholders, but how they look at some of the developments in China; for example, Xi'an, the ancient capital of China, might have had all the elements and ingredients to become the Florence of China, but that possibility has been totally destroyed because of narrow-minded pursuit of GDP and to be modern and have wider streets, etc.

Regarding the development of Chinese entrepreneurship, Xiang believed there were many limitations. One is they are too family oriented. Chinese people do business because they want to create wealth for themselves, for their sons, their daughters, their grandsons or granddaughters. That narrowly defined objective of doing business has been probably the most important driver of China's economic success. However, this could generate serious problems long term. First, they tend to make money every way possible, sometimes with no respect for rules or laws. Second, when they select their future company leaders, they tend to restrict themselves to their sons or daughters. Imagine if Bill Gates' son is automatically going to be the chairman of Microsoft. If you work at Microsoft, no matter how talented you are, you have no opportunity. Though not entirely impossible, he saw great difficulty for many Chinese businessmen to go beyond that; and if they could not, Xiang believed there was no possibility of a future IBM or GE in China, and the country could just end up with trading companies in non-mainstream sectors, such as shoes, ties, and lighters.

As to the globalization of Chinese companies, Xiang proposed alternative strategy for Chinese companies to engage in global business, not just by proactive management. Everything is global. He strongly believed that Chinese companies had to have board representation. Since many leading Chinese companies have a lot of cash on hand because of the strong currency reserves, equity participation would be an important way for China to be more global rather than just acquiring of foreign corporations.

As a well-known management consultant, Xiang has also done extensive work on the establishment of corporate internal incentive and monitor systems, corporate investment and mergers and acquisitions, corporate globalization strategy, and the training of corporate senior management. He has cooperated with many state-owned enterprises, private enterprises, and multinational corporations, helping them to improve their business strategy and globalization. The list included not only top companies in the world, but also some government agencies and nonprofit organizations in China.

In recent years, Xiang has actively proposed his perspective of "standing on the moon to see the Earth," and suggested using global vision to look at China's economy and national business opportunities and challenges. His thinking not only had great impact on the modern Chinese enterprises, his research on China's state-owned enterprises reform and family-oriented enterprises has also been listed as reading material for senior manager courses by Harvard Business School, Stanford Business School, and European Business School. In addition, Xiang has often been invited by mainstream media such as CCTV, Phoenix TV, CNN, The *New York*

Times, the *Far Eastern Economic Forum*, *Entrepreneur* magazine, Global Resources, and Voice of America to give speeches on the reform of Chinese state-owned enterprises, private enterprise development and management of family-oriented businesses in China, management education, and the globalization of Chinese enterprises and other issues.

JING BAI

Sources

Cheung Kong Graduate School of Business (2010), "Xiang Bing", available at: http://en.ckgsb.com:8080/faculty/XIANGBing/index.aspx (accessed 21 July 2010).
Coughlin, J. (2000), "Face to Face: Xiang Bing", *Chinese International Business*, No. 267 (March), available at: http://www.cibmagazine.com.cn/Features/Face_To_Face.asp?id=1241&xiang_bing.html (accessed 21 July 2010).
新浪财经 (2008), "长江商学院创办院长项兵" ["Xiang Bing: Founding Dean of Cheung Kong Graduate School of Business", *Sina Finance*], available at: http://finance.sina.com.cn/hy/20081219/09515658891.shtml (accessed 21 July 2010).

Xiao, Zhiyue (肖志岳 b. 1958)

Known to the West as Jeremy Xiao, Xiao Zhiyue is an accomplished corporate finance lawyer. Currently CEO of Cinda Capital Management Limited, Xiao has served as co-chairman of the China Investment Department of Credit Suisse, and before that the managing partner of the well-known English law firm, Herbert Smith's Beijing Office, and has advised on a number of groundbreaking transactions related to the Chinese economic development. He has particular expertise in debt and equity issues by mainland Chinese issuers, and the regulatory aspects of the Hong Kong and mainland Chinese securities markets. Xiao's career has been one full of initiatives and amazing accomplishments.

Xiao was born into an ordinary family in Ningbo, Zhejiang Province. Due to his diligent learning and excellent grades, he was always one of the teachers' favorite students in school. During the Cultural Revolution period, Xiao Zhiyue graduated from high school in 1974 and participated in the "Up to the Mountains and Down to the Villages" campaign by returning to his home village to farm. With the end of the Cultural Revolution in 1976, Xiao's fate was about to change. In late 1977, when China's national college entrance examination was revived, Xiao was among the first group of students taking the newly resumed test. However, due to very limited preparation time for the exam, Xiao did not perform well enough to accomplish his dream of getting admission to Peking University, the nation's leading institution. Nevertheless, he was not totally disappointed either: he was enrolled into Hangzhou University instead, a top school in Zhejiang Province.

With the excitement of starting a college life, Xiao went to the campus of Hangzhou University in March 1978 and began to study hard as a student majoring in economics. Upon graduation in 1981, Xiao decided to pursue the graduate program at the Institute of Economics of the Chinese Academy of Social Sciences in Beijing. Unfortunately, to his surprise, he failed to get the final admission even after a face-to-face interview. Therefore, at the end of 1981, Xiao took the job of working in the Department of Law of Hangzhou University as an instructor in economic law. The ups and downs of his life did not frustrate Xiao at all, and his fate would turn better soon after.

In 1982, out of concern that Xiao might not perform well in teaching economic law without a legal background, Hangzhou University decided to send him to Peking University to undertake specialized training in law. Interestingly, Xiao eventually accomplished his dream of studying at Peking University. He wasted no time to catch up on the subject knowledge of law and studied extraordinarily hard under the guidance of internationally well-known law professors such as Rui Mu and Wang Tieya. At the end of 1983, Xiao took a highly competitive qualifying exam for overseas study funded by the British Council and he succeeded this time. In 1984, he began his overseas study for his master degree in law at the London School of Economics and Political Science, University of London. His initial learning experience in Britain was by no means a smooth one. He was a student characterized by "three poors": poor at English, poor at legal studies, and poor at personal income. However, this was not the first time Xiao faced difficulties in life. Fueled by a strong desire to catch up, Xiao tried all he could to improve his English and law skills while doing small part-time jobs to make ends meet. His life started to get better when he obtained his master degree in Law in 1985.

In the rest of 1980s, Xiao built a strong basis for his career by studying toward a doctorate in law and working at law firm simultaneously. He got a job at Slaughter & May at the end of 1986 and obtained his doctorate in law in 1989 from King's College of the University of London. During these few years in Britain, what Xiao was most proud of was a project for training young Chinese lawyers that he and his colleagues initiated, which would later be named Lord Chancellor's Training Scheme for Young Chinese Lawyers (LCTS) and widely praised as the "Huangpu Military Academy (The Chinese counterpart of West Point) of the Chinese Legal Profession."

In January 1989, a senior partner at Slaughter & May returned from Hong Kong and encouraged Xiao to transfer to the firm's Hong Kong Office. To do so, however, Xiao needed to obtain a work visa from the Hong Kong government. The visa application process proved a protracted yet victorious battle for Xiao. Because all mainland Chinese people staying in Hong Kong at that time were personnel sent by the Chinese government, Xiao's special situation of holding a private Chinese passport constituted a barrier for him. The extended delay in Xiao's visa application was finally ended by the intervention of British Prime Minister Margaret Thatcher, who granted the visa to Xiao. Being the first person holding a private Chinese passport to receive a Hong Kong work visa, Xiao created an incredible precedent that opened the door of Hong Kong to many more mainland Chinese to come.

After arriving in Hong Kong in September 1989, Xiao soon found himself being regarded as a monster – he did not speak Cantonese and was the first lawyer in Hong Kong to speak Mandarin. This, however, would prove to be his unique advantage for attracting business from mainland China. He advised on the first mainland Chinese B-share international offering, which was listed on the Shanghai Securities Exchange in 1992 and the first mainland Chinese H-share international public offering and listing in Hong Kong in 1993. However, these groundbreaking achievements still did not entitle him to partnership at Slaughter & May. Therefore, he decided to leave Slaughter & May and for the two subsequent years, he worked at Johnson Stokes and Master. In 1996, Xiao joined Herbert Smith LLP as a partner. This again set a record – Xiao was the first People's Republic of China citizen to become a partner at the top 10 law firms in Britain.

With the business expansion of Herbert Smith into mainland China, Xiao started to think about coming to Beijing for further development. In late 2002, he made the move. In Beijing, while continuing to advise on landmark deals such as the multibillion IPOs of Sinopec, China Construction Bank and ICBC, he also became involved in the efforts of China's giant state-owned enterprises to acquire foreign businesses of strategic significance. In 2005, Xiao witnessed the failure of China National Offshore Oil Corporation to acquire Unocal of the United States due to the political intervention of US government. In 2006, he succeeded in assisting Sinopec in its acquisition of the Russian oil corporation Udmurtneft. Xiao's career development has not stopped at Herbert Smith. In November 2007, he joined Credit Suisse as the managing director of its China Investment Banking Department, where he initiated and executed Sinopec/Addax acquisition deal, the largest oil and gas acquisition China has successfully done thus far. In March 2010, Xiao took up the role of CEO of a PE firm-Cinda Capital. If there are any secrets to Xiao's success in legal advising, then his deep sense of legal responsibility for his clients is certainly a crucial piece among them. This is why people like to turn to Xiao for advising. He is the kind of legal adviser who can give his clients the peace of mind they need the most.

ZHAOCHANG PENG

Sources

Credit Suisse (2008), "Investment banking senior appointments in Asia", press release, 4 August, available at: https://www.credit-suisse.com/news/en/media_release.jsp?ns=40853 (accessed 18 October 2010).

Herbert Smith LLP (2010), "Jeremy Xiao: Consultant Beijing", available at: http://www.herbertsmith.com/People/JeremyXiao.htm (accessed 18 October 2010).

Lloyd, R. (2009), "Letter from London: Jeremy Xiao heading back to Herbert Smith", AM Law Daily, 12 March, available at: http://amlawdaily.typepad.com/amlawdaily/2009/03/herbert-smith-rehires-former-beijing-head.html (accessed 18 October 2010).

Taylor, M. (2007), "Herbert Smith's China boss quits for Credit Suisse", The Lawyer, 10 October, available at: http://www.thelawyer.com/herbert-smiths-china-boss-quits-for-credit-suisse/129304.article (accessed 18 October 2010).

冯嘉雪, 郭玉梅, 郭俐君 (2007) "肖志岳: 纵横资本市场的海归律师", *巅峰职业: 10位海归职业经理人* (王辉耀主编), 中国发展出版社, 北京 [Feng, J.X. et. al., "Xiao Zhiyue: A returnee lawyer soars over the capital market," in Wang, H.Y. (ed.), *Top Careers: Ten Overseas Returnees in Professional Management*, China Development Press, Beijing], pp. 103–28.

Xie, Guozhong (Andy Xie 谢国忠 b. 1960)

Considered an authority in the fields of economics and financial advising, Xie Guozhong is the director of Rosetta Stone Capital, an offshore venture capital company controlled and managed by Xie along with five other investors. With educational experiences and professional roles spanning both the United States and China, Xie has gained the necessary insights to be poised for success and regarded as a trusted contributor in his field. He has nurtured an illustrious career and diverse experiences that include consulting, corporate finance, and investment management, and his researches, speeches, and writings have made an indelible impact on the face of these industries and the Chinese economy as a whole.

Born in 1960, Xie attended the elite Tongji University in Shanghai from 1979 to 1983, and then went to the United States for his graduate studies, receiving an MS in civil engineering as well as a PhD in economics from the Massachusetts Institute of Technology in 1987 and 1990, respectively. After his graduation, Xie began to work for the World Bank and gained valuable professional experience in finance and investment management. During his five-year tenure in the Young Professionals Program, Xie worked closely with the finance industry in Indonesia and did additional work in the power and telecom sectors of other Asia-Pacific countries. In 1995, Xie left World Bank to become an associate director of Macquarie Bank. In this role, Xie was stationed in Singapore and gained valuable experience in the field of corporate finance. Two years later, Xie joined Morgan Stanley Dean Witter Asia as a managing director based in Hong Kong, which is a market leader in the financial services industry and maintains a broad global reach. Xie was dubbed a "star economist" in this role and remained with the company until 2006 (Chen, 2007).

Xie Guozhong currently works in Shanghai as an independent economist with a particular focus on Asia. He also holds a number of positions with diverse firms across the investment and financial services industries that include independent directorship at the Shenzhen Development Bank. Additionally, Xie is identified as a director for China Boqi Environmental Solutions, a company that completes environmental projects that include design, installation, and other services. More notably, Xie is the owner and manager of Rosetta Stone Capital Limited since 2007. This offshore venture capital company has made investments in companies including natural resource mining and collection firms. According to SEC documentation, Rosetta Stone Capital Limited was 32.5% owned by Xie, 29% by Keen View Investments Limited, and 29% by Sun Fortune Investments Limited.

Xie has gained a great deal of recognition as an economic expert. He has been writing regularly as a guest columnist for the *South China Morning Post* and *New*

Century Weekly, and publishing extensively on business finance and investment related to Chinese and Asian economies. Xie has been identified by his peers as one of the few economists to anticipate and preemptively report the critical economic bubbles of the 1997 Southeast Asian Financial Crisis and the devastating United States subprime financial crisis in 2008 (*Asian Venture Capital Journal*, 2010).

Xie is also a guest economist of *CAIJING Magazine*, China's most widely read business and finance publication with a top-level reader base that includes not only business leaders but also government officials. With his broad international perspective, Xie regularly shared his professional insights on the most important aspects of China's economic reforms, developments, and policy changes as well as major events in the capital markets. On the recent global recession, he noted that the G-20 summit had its successes, but it failed to generate a coordinated strategy for handling the economic crisis. According to him, monetary policy, not interest rate cuts, was the key to the efficient, equitable deployment of the stimulus package. Although the stimulus measures may make people feel good at the moment, but it would only delay necessary reforms. If the governments did not understand the situation and simply tried to bring back the "good times" of an asset-based economy, it could result in a decade of stagnation for the country.

As an economic personality with growing influence, Xie has been honored for his notable contributions to his field of work and to the Chinese economy as a whole. *Institutional Investor* magazine, a leading publication with a focus on global finance news and research, ranked Xie as the premier economist in Asia in recent years. Additionally in 2003, CCTV, the largest television network in China, in partnership with the World Economic Forum, identified him as one of the 10 future economic leaders in China. Xie was included in this group for the major contributions he has made to the study and development of the Chinese economy. More recently, Xie was ranked by *BusinessWeek* among the "China's Most Powerful People" in 2009 for his outspoken voices taking aim at policymakers at home and abroad.

Xie has served as an excellent example of a Chinese national gaining a strong educational foundation in the United States and returning to the Chinese economy to make significant, long-term contributions. Xie's contributions to the field are perceptible on a worldwide basis but have had a special significance in the Chinese market. In addition to his independent contributions as an expert in economics, his venture capital firm and his executive role in financial services firms have fortified Xie's place among Chinese returnees who are shaping the economic landscapes of contemporary China.

Ashley Snyder

Sources

Asian Venture Capital Journal (2010), "China 2010 speaker biographies", available at: http://www.avcjforum.com/static/biographies (Accessed 11 April 2010).

BusinessWeek (2009), "China's most powerful people 2009: Andy Xie", available at: http://images.businessweek.com/ss/09/11/1113_business_stars_of_china/31.htm (accessed 11 April 2010).
Chen, J. S. (2007), "China Natural Resources' wild ride", *Forbes*, 5 October, available at: http://www.forbes.com/2007/10/05/china-natural-resources-market-equity-cx_jc_1005markets2.html (accessed 11 April 2010).
Xie, A. (2009), "A decade to lose", *China Stock Analyst*, 4 March, available at: http://www.chinastockadvice.com/Article-48-A-Decade-to-Lose.html (accessed 11 April 2010).

Xie, Lina (谢丽娜 b. 1950)

A shareholder and counsel of the company, Xie Lina is the senior vice president, vice chairman, and patent and trademark attorney at China Sinda Intellectual Property Ltd. Her areas of expertise are patent and trademark prosecution and counseling and general intellectual property (IP) counseling, a booming business field that is closely associated with the rising Chinese economy.

Xie attended Beijing No. 2 Foreign Language Institute and graduated in 1975. From 1982 to 1985, she studied at the School of Journalism in the University of Regina, Canada. Coincidentally, in 1985, the same year in which Xie completed her education, China's first patent law was born. She then worked as a journalist and editor in the International News Department of the Xinhua News Agency. By sheer chance, she was recommended by the Personnel Bureau of the Science and Technology Commission to the State Council, and became the secretary of Wang Jiquan, who was a director of the Centre for Economic Development. Until then, none of her jobs had anything to do with the patent area. However, her position as a secretary became a turning point for her new career in the world of patents.

Wang Jiquan had always wanted to create a patent agency in Hong Kong, and with Xie as his assistant, that dream came true. Xie participated in the founding of the NTD Patent and Trademark Agency Ltd., and obtained her Patent Agent Qualification Certificate in 1987, after completing a training course sponsored by the China Patent Office. Shortly afterward, Xie joined NTD, one of the pioneering firms officially designated by the State Council and the State Administration for Industry and Commerce of the People's Republic of China to represent foreign clients in the field of patent and trademark. As one of the cofounders of the NTD Patent and Trademark Agency, Xie held the position of manager of the Application Department at its Hong Kong headquarters, handling a wide range of patent and trademark application cases. For Xie, the job was love at first sight, because she needed to deal with not only the legal aspects of IP, but also new technologies, foreign languages, and interpersonal relationships, which demanded both high intelligence and professionalism, qualities that she possessed. The work presented her new challenges on a daily basis, as she always had to face different cases, situations, and problems. Xie took advantage of this great opportunity, improving her professional skills as well as enriching her personal life. As she was one of the first people involved in the new IP system in China, she has witnessed the development of the IP protection system over the years, and the firm has since grown into one of the largest and leading law firms specializing in all areas of intellectual property law.

In 1988, Lina Xie was visited by several Taiwanese businessmen, who sought her assistance in the protection of their seven model patents in China. As she knew that the relationships between mainland China and Taiwan were strained, and as the case in her hands was not only a commercial act but also a political issue, she flew to Beijing to talk directly to the Patent Office and raised the awareness of the authorities regarding the legal situation of patents in China. Because of her efforts, Xie was assigned the task of handling the first Taiwanese patent application ever filed in mainland China.

In 1990, Xie put her career on hold and went to Canada to further her education. After receiving advanced training there, she briefly worked for a patent law firm located in Toronto. Meanwhile, in the early 1990s, China underwent a sweeping economic policy reform and began to allow private foreign patents and the establishment of trademark agents. In 1993, Xie returned home from Canada to set up China Sinda Intellectual Property Ltd. together with Mu Dejun, also a returnee. Both of them had a similar background in their qualifications, after having studied IP law for eight years, and they had their training and working experience in similar foreign law firms.

Shortly after its founding, China Sinda was granted by the State Intellectual Property and Trademark Office of People's Republic of China the right to submit applications for patents and trademarks in China and abroad on behalf of foreign and domestic clients. Xie and Mu endeavored to build a "*first-class international property firm*" by providing "*first-class service, first-class quality.*" When the company was first launched, it had a staff of fewer than 10 people; nowadays, the firm has over 200 employees in four offices.

In 1995, Xie represented China for the first time in the annual meeting of the International Trademark, in which around 2000 intellectual property lawyers took part. She had the opportunity of speaking about the changes in China's trademark law, anti-infringement, and antipiracy protection system. Nobody ever suspected that she was still recovering from spinal surgery and that she had written the speech for the meeting while she was in hospital. She was so enthusiastic about the great opportunity on behalf of her country, that it seems as if that alleviated her pain. Since then, due to her successful speech, she has been a guest speaker in a wide range of important academic conferences, IP organizations, and legal firm meetings such as the one held on April 18, 2005, where she was invited by the Intellectual Property Law Association of New York. There she participated in a forum on Procuring and Enforcing Intellectual Property Rights in the People's Republic of China, where she reminded her audience of the paramount importance of paying special attention to intellectual property rights in the information age of the twenty-first century.

By 2000, China Sinda had grown to be one of the largest private IP law firms in China practicing across the full range of intellectual property protection. Based in Beijing, Xie specialized in IP cases of difficult nature, especially those relating to domain name, trademark infringement, and unfair competition cases, on behalf of world famous companies like Motorola, Procter & Gamble, Google, Toyota, NEC,

LG, China Union Pay, among others. Under the leadership of Mu and Xie, China Sinda was a finalist in the Asialaw IP Awards of 2005 and 2007.

In the course of her professional career, Xie has set up two different intellectual property firms in China. Serving as vice chairman and vice president of China Sinda, she plays a major role in the firm's decision-making process and daily management. As an experienced patent and trademark attorney, Xie is well qualified to practice before all organizations in China with jurisdiction over intellectual property including the patent, trademark, and copyright offices, the People's Courts including appellate level, and administrative agencies and tribunals. She is able to provide overall legal services to clients in connection with technical research, antitrust investigation, and litigation and a variety of other areas. Xie has always been willing to face the hardest challenges in her strive to forward the development of IP rights. One of her main achievements was the first trademark lawsuit representing the Swedish company IKEA to legitimate their trademark rights, which is well known in the judicial process history as it set a precedent. Another outstanding case was the one in connection with Educational Testing Service (ETS) exams, where she was instrumental in stopping the copyright infringement of the exam, which helped promote the legitimate development of ETS exams in China.

As a professional of IP, Xie is a member of the All-China Patent Agents Association (ACPAA), International Federation of Intellectual Property Attorneys (FICPI), Licensing Executives Society (LES), International Association for the Protection of Intellectual Property (AIPPI), and International Trademark Association (INTA).

M. ELENA ARAMENDIA-MUNETA

Sources

China Sinda (2009), "Ms. Lina Xie", available at: http://www.chinasinda.com/people/linaxie.htm# (accessed 8 June 2010).

WRSACC Committee (2005), "Xie Lina", available at: http://www.2005committee.org/index.php/member/ls/650 (accessed 6 June 2010).

WRSACC Committee (2007), "谢丽娜, 作伴专利法22年", *海风窗* ["Lina Xie, 22 years in patent law", *Global Outlook*], 2 September, available at: http://www.2005committee.org/index.php/magazine/getMagazineContentInfo/170 (accessed 8 June 2010).

搜狐财经 (2007), "跨国公司在中国" ["Multinationals in China", Sohu Business], 26 January, available at: http://business.sohu.com/20070126/n247855081.shtml#08 (accessed 8 June 2010).

Xu, Changdong (徐昌东 b. 1952)

A chemist by training, Xu Changdong is the chairman of China Anda Travel & Resort Ltd., an international timeshare company specialized in China market. Xu also has ownership stakes and executive roles in several other Chinese and American organizations, including the US Universal Foundation, Schiller Aircraft Manufacturing Company, and the US–China Investment Center.

Xu was born into an academic family in Jiangsu Province in December 1952, and his elder brother was a graduate of the Royal College. Xu completed his undergraduate coursework in China. After the conclusion of the Cultural Revolution, he was among the first to take the national college entrance exam and apply for admission to colleges in the West. In 1983, at the age of 30, Xu decided that an American education was worth the emotional cost of being away from his wife and four-month-old son, so he relocated to New York and attended the graduate school at the City University of New York (CUNY). Arriving at the John F. Kennedy International airport with only US$40 in his pocket, Xu had to spend US $30 for a cab ride to campus, which quickly made him realize how expensive it was to live in the Big Apple. One day after his arrival, he was able to find part-time work at a local restaurant. For four years, Xu was not able to even look up at the moon without teary eyes, because in Chinese culture the moon symbolizes family reunion. Enduring the emotional strains, Xu graduated from CUNY with two master's degrees in four years, one in computer science and the other in chemistry.

In 1987, his family finally joined him in the United States, and a year later Xu launched his first business undertaking with a venture named Darcy International Trading Company (DITC). To begin, Xu risked all his life savings of US$27,000 to purchase fertilizer in the United States for exporting it to China for resale. The deal was an instant success, and Xu nearly doubled his money with US$50,000 in return. DITC's venture in the chemical and investment industries grew from there, and it was this endeavor that started Xu down an entrepreneurial path.

Xu's time in the United States spanned nearly 20 years, and while there he and his family were avid travelers. Xu quickly realized the benefits in cost sharing and flexibility of owning a timeshare property, thus purchasing a timeshare card of US $10,000. In 2000, China introduced its May first golden week holiday. Viewing it as a tipping point for the growing Chinese tourism market, Xu decided that the time was right to bring the timeshare concept to China. Thus, China Anda Travel & Resort was incorporated in 2001, and Xu and his family returned to China.

Xu is known as the godfather of China timeshares not only for his role in introducing the concept to Chinese consumers but also because he helped popularize leisure travel in the Chinese market. The overall strategy of Anda was that consumers purchased a timeshare card, which on average cost 30,000 RMB, to own the right to use a villa for one week every year for 20 years. Consumers then may choose which villa they wish to stay in from the company's diverse network of resorts across the country. By providing people with high quality yet affordable vacation packages, Xu believed that timeshare could benefit Chinese consumers and boost local GDPs. However, when he first introduced the timeshare concept, Xu faced the tremendous challenge that every global business has to deal with: how to transform a foreign product into one that would thrive in Chinese society. Although timeshare has remained popular for over 20 years in the United States, it was completely new to most Chinese consumers. There was a potential market out there, yet much consumer education needed to be done first. Moreover, no regulations had been made for this industry under Chinese law. To make the matter worse, in March 2003, CCTV produced a special episode on commercial fraud in timeshares. In the face of the negative publicity, Xu was very optimistic about the future of timeshares in China. To him, the episode generated large consumer awareness and provided education to consumers about the concept. The key was to find an effective way to rebuild consumers' confidence in the timeshare concept despite the lack of regulations that protect consumers as in the United States.

To reduce consumers' risk related to purchasing timeshares, Xu introduced vacation benefits insurance along with the purchase of Anda timeshare card. The insurance, provided by PICC Property and Casualty Co., was designed specifically for Anda customers and help ensure consumer rights. Xu also established a strategic partnership with China CITIC Bank to sell the Anda timeshare cards exclusively. These steps helped to ease consumer concerns, and thus have been labeled a revolutionary development in the timeshare industry in China.

As the largest timeshare company in China, Anda currently owns 16 resorts (some of which are still under construction); accepts memberships from Resort Condominiums International, the world's leader in vacation exchanges; partners with various real estate companies, vacation resorts, and hotels; invests 10 billion RMB in constructing two luxury cruise lines; and plans to raise 20 billion RMB to build a harbor city totaling over 1 million square meters. As one of the founders and the vice president of the China Timeshare Association, Xu has continuously searched for ways to promote timeshares, regulate business conduct, and create a healthy environment for Chinese timeshare consumers. The effort that Xu has dedicated into timeshare business is not simply developing a product or a company, but also building a new industry.

Ultimately, Xu's career has been filled with one success after another, with over 10 successful ventures to his credit and billions of dollars in revenues and profit. Today, he spends his time dabbling in many different business ventures and serving on the boards of several organizations including president of the Entrepreneur Alliance of the Western Returned Scholars Association (WRSA), vice president of WRSA Chamber of Commerce, and director of the New York chapter of the National US–China Peoples Friendship Association. Recently, Xu visited Minnesota State University to finalize a three-year, US$600,000 partnership to train 300 Chinese helicopter pilots annually.

YINGLU WU AND ERIC LIGUORI

Sources

柴松献 (2007), "徐昌东: 中国'分时度假'的坚定守望者", *华商人物*, [Chai, S., "Xu, Changdong: The watcher for China's timeshare", *Chinese Business Leader*], 8 January, available at: http://www.hszzs.com/renwu/13/xiucandong.htm (accessed 18 July 2010).

李德金 (2009), "引产UH-12直升机内幕", *人民网* [Li, D., "Behind the production of UH-12 helicopter", *People*], 8 March, available at: http://military.people.com.cn/GB/1076/52984/8925975.html (accessed 18 July 2010).

卢灿飞 (2008), "徐昌东谈要以审慎的态度对待旅游地产的新模式", *环球旅游*, [Lu, C., "Xu, Changdong talks about the need for a prudent attitude towards the new model in tourism real estate", *yooso.net*], 10 March, available at: http://www.yooso.net/cehua/lvlun/200803/20080310163706.html (accessed 18 July 2010).

商务周刊 (2005), "徐昌东，分享分时度假的乐趣" ["Xu, Changdong: The joy of timeshare travel", *Business Watch Magazine*], 9 December, available at: http://finance.sina.com.cn/manage/cfrw/20051209/19312187322.shtml (accessed 18 July 2010).

Xu, Tiantian (徐甜甜 b. 1975)

As the founder and chief architect of DnA, Xu Tiantian stands at the forefront of a new generation of Chinese architects who are leading the industry to new artistic and technological heights. Xu has blended the knowledge and skills that she acquired both in China and in the West to enrich her architectural tool kit. In each of her designs, Xu infuses a keen sense of a location's unique identity and experience to create functional yet evocative space. She has embraced diverse projects ranging in size and purpose, including a 29,000-square-foot art museum in Ordos, Inner Mongolia, a 20-unit housing residence for artists in Songzhuang, and even a small cluster of public toilets in Jinhua Architecture Park in Zhejiang Province. Before she was 35 years old, Xu had acquired numerous awards recognizing her creativity and innovativeness. In 2009, her design company, DnA: Design and Architecture, was selected as a Design Vanguard by the *Architectural Record* and was listed as an emerging designer firm by the Urban Land Institute.

Born in the Fujian Province, Xu's academic potential became apparent at an early age. Although most students begin university at the age of 18, Xu was recommended and enrolled in Tsinghua University, one of China's most prestigious science and engineering institutions, at the age of 16, bypassing the traditional *Gaokao*, the national college examination. Unlike many of her classmates, Xu was not born into the architectural profession. Instead, the field attracted her much like a moth to a flame. Architecture was appealing, she often said, because it gives one the opportunity to inculcate "inside feeling and inner experience" (*Designer and Designing*, 2007).

At Tsinghua University, Xu acquired a sound training in basic engineering and architectural skills but still hungered for additional learning. She decided to pursue a master of architecture in urban design at Harvard University in the United States to strengthen her theoretical knowledge about architecture and her technical design skills. After graduation, she continued her professional training in the States, working for three years at Leers Weinzapfel Associates, an architectural design firm owned and operated by Andrea Leers, one of Xu's former Harvard professors. She also worked at the Office for Metropolitan Architecture in Rotterdam, the Netherlands, for a year before returning to China. Although she enjoyed her educational experience in the West, she found the actual practice of architecture there artistically stifling, as Western clients often present preconceived notions of design to architectural teams.

In 2004, Xu decided to return to China and founded DnA: Design and Architecture in Beijing. As China's economy has grown, demand for architectural services has surged. After a long history of preference for foreign architectural firms, Chinese developers now demand the services of domestic architects such as Xu and her design team. Yet the number of local firms in the industry remains limited. According to a 2009 survey conducted by China's Ministry of Housing and Urban-Rural Development, there are only 47 large-scale engineering companies with comprehensive engineering design qualifications and a scant number of small and medium-sized engineering design companies with expertise in any one area. Xu is excited about the opportunities for DnA in the Chinese architectural design market. She has observed, "Modern Chinese architecture has been developing profoundly recently. It's not as mature as in Western countries – we're still learning on the technical side – but the initial ideas are originating from our own culture. By incorporating the old and the new we have great potential for creativity. In general I found what's happening in China now is probably the most creative in this nation's history" (Allen, 2007).

In a recent book, *On the Edge: Ten Architects from China*, editors Ian Luna and Thomas Tsang note that today's Chinese architects face the daunting task of defining the nation's modern identity and character in their designs. Doing so, the authors note, often requires making difficult decisions about what role China's rich past and current Western imagery and style might play in current Chinese architectural expressions. Interviewed by the authors for the book, Xu weighed in on this artistic controversy saying that her design team "aspires to architecture that can reflect China's uniqueness by neither rebuilding traditional symbols nor relocating a modern architecture from Berlin to Beijing" (Baker, 2007).

Xu seeks to express China's uniqueness in her designs by rooting them in the physical and functional characteristics of the locations themselves. Her designs not only take into account the current use and purpose of a space but they also envision the venue's potential, which is crucial in today's dynamic climate of economic growth and development. DnA's creations, the Songzhuang Art Center and the Songzhuang Artistic Residences typify Xu's particular approach. The structure of Art Center comprises 27,000 square feet of flexible gallery space within a bold, brick-clad structure that floats on a glass base. Xu notes, "while the urban context grows and its function program alters ... the building develops as well" (Hawthorne, 2008).

Outside of Beijing, Xu and her design team have created a 20-unit structure, which serves as living space for some of the city's leading artists. The building consists of a dynamic, random stack of 10- and 20-foot-tall concrete boxes, each housing separate living and studio spaces. What has been described as a "chaotic" design purposefully reflects the area's history of serving as a refuge for artists randomly expelled from the city by the authorities. The harshness of the concrete design evokes the sharp tensions of the past. "In such an artist community formed gradually after being expelled by the police, order and discipline have never been key characteristics. Rather, violence and anger are more expressed" (Chen, 2009).

Xu was one of China's first women to establish her own architecture design firm. She is also a mother, an experience that has not only been rich and rewarding personally but also has inspired her professionally. One of her most recent projects is the Xixi Leisure Center, one of twelve buildings located in an art and culture compound in Xixi National Wetland Park in Hangzhou. As Xu initially walked the space, exploring its presence and character, she immediately was reminded of the fairy-tale story Thumbelina, a book she often read to her two little girls. In the fairy tale, Thumbelina is born a tiny girl – smaller than a field mouse – in a wild forest, and she explores the natural wonders around her while often traveling on lily pads. To Xu, XiXi's wetland park is as richly overwhelming to the visitor as Thumbelina's forest. Wanting the visitor to fully experience and bask in the park's beauty as Thumbelina had done, Xu created a design that allows the visitor to gradually descend or ascend to discover its treasures. The structure includes an open space on the ground level and is further composed of several sunken "activity pools imitating paths and ponds of wetland topography." The upper level is divided into suspended, individual lookout spaces that are shaped like leaves supported by columns. The pathway of "leaves" creates an outdoor promenade through lily ponds up to a roof terrace, revealing a wide, panoramic view.

Xu is committed to sharing her passion and knowledge with the next generation of architects both at home and abroad. She has taught at School of Architecture of the Central Academy of Fine Arts in Beijing and has served as a guest critic at numerous schools, including Peking University and Tokyo Chiba Institute of Technology. However, for Xu, learning never ends: Only her classroom environment has changed. Reflecting on her future, she posited, "I think of what's happening now for me is a very intense training session, and I don't have to pay tuition .... Five to ten years? That's the next lifetime. Ask me about five to ten months!"

EVERLYNE MISATI AND LIESL RIDDLE

Sources

Allen, D. (2007), "China chasing an urban utopia", *Asia Times*, 18 May, available at: http://www.atimes.com/atimes/China/IE18Ad01.html (accessed 17 February 2010).

Baker, J. (2007), "New architects of China", *Architecture Week*, 19 September, available at: http://www.architectureweek.com/2007/0919/design_1-1.html (accessed 17 February 2010).

Chen, A. (2009), "DnA Design and Architecture DnA founder Xu Tiantian puts down roots in her native China", *Architectural Record*, **197** (12), 34, available at: http://archrecord.construction.com/features/designvanguard/2009/09DnA/default.asp (accessed 17 August 2010).

Designer & Designing (2007), "'我不能改变北京城' – 访DnA北京工作室主持建筑师徐甜甜" ["'I cannot change the city of Beijing' – Interview with DnA Chief Architect Xu Tiantian"], Vol. 3, available at: http://shfly.5d6d.com/viewthread.php?tid=15623 (accessed 17 August 2010).

Hawthorne, C. (2008), "Rising generation of Chinese architects thrives on innovation", *Los Angeles Times*, 6 August, available at: http://www.latimes.com/entertainment/la-et-youngbloods6-2008aug06,0,4399198.story (accessed 17 February 2010).

Howlett, A. (2009), "Recent trends in the Chinese architectural and engineering design industry and new opportunities for foreign designers", *Mondaq Business Briefing*, available at: http://www.mondaq.com/article.asp?articleid=81750 (accessed 27 February 2010).

Xu, Xiaoping (Bob Xu 徐小平 b. 1956)

With an estimated US$240 million of personal wealth, Xu Xiaoping may have only ranked 460th in the *Hurun Report*'s 2007 China Rich List, but that was certainly enough to catapult him to the top of the richest teachers in China, if not in the world, along with Yu Minhong and Qian Yongqiang, his fellow cofounders of Beijing-based New Oriental Education Group. This intriguing status was firmly cemented in the records of world education, due to the estimate of Xu Xiaoping's wealth, which was made possible by the very successful September 6, 2006 IPO of the company on the New York Stock Exchange (NYSE). Listed under the expanded name of New Oriental Education &Technology Group, and with the truly emblematic ticker symbol EDU, this is one of only two cases where the ticker symbol of one single company is representative of the entire industry (the other is "DNA" belonging to a biotechnology company).

Xu Xiaoping's early and academic career did not strike as particularly eventful, which was somewhat uncharacteristic compared to other, more typical Chinese foreign-educated returnee-entrepreneurs who mostly favor business studies abroad. Xu initially earned a bachelor's degree in music from China Central Conservatory of Music before he moved on to earn his master's degree in music from the University of Saskatchewan in Canada.

In 1993, together with Yu Minhong (Michael) and Qian Yongqiang, Xu cofounded the New Oriental School in Beijing. Initially, the school focused more narrowly on preparing students for overseas undergraduate and graduate study in North America through TOEFL and GMAT preparation support. Since its IPO on the NYSE, New Oriental Education & Technology Group has been offering programs targeting students as early as three years of age, including among others: foreign language training, test preparation, international study and consulting, private school education for up to grade K-12, and online education. As the largest provider of private educational services in China, New Oriental's services cover the full repertoire of educational content development and distribution today, accounting for a 75% of the mainland market share in TOEFL testing and 90% in the US graduate-admission GRE and GMAT tests.

According to its own statistics, New Oriental claims an enrollment of nearly nine million students to date, of which 1.8 million are for 2010 alone. It has a strong network of 367 learning centers, of which 48 have school status; it also operates 25 bookstores under the New Oriental brand and collaborates with over 5000 more on a third-party basis; finally, it employs more than 8100 teachers and instructors in 40 cities and maintains an online presence with over six million registered users.

Reflecting on the impressive accomplishment of New Oriental, Xu noted, "Any successful enterprise has a unique formula. New Oriental's formula includes its tenet of inspiring the students, a humorous teaching style, emphasis on the culture behind the language and prolonged study of exam techniques" (Xinhua, 2006).

New Oriental built its operation on the fundamental belief that millions of Chinese parents want their children to have a better education, as well as countless young students who desire to have a valuable overseas learning experience and rich career advancement opportunities. Xu, however, was not only concerned about proper preparation for overseas study, but was also a pronounced critic of what he often perceived as an unthoughtful and mindless approach to such overseas experiences by many Chinese students. According to him: "There is a long-standing mistaken idea about studying abroad in the Chinese public's mind; [...] most Chinese students have gone abroad without definite objectives, while some utilitarians are motivated only by vanity, desire to evade pressure or longing for a foreign diploma. Overseas studies are just a process of receiving education, which means nothing more than itself despite the employment of international resources" (Li, 2004).

Ironically, it was precisely this initial activity of New Oriental that led to some highly controversial exposure. In January 2002, a protracted copyright infringement lawsuit was initiated by the Educational Testing Service (ETS) and joined later by the Graduate Management Admission Council (GMAC), which resulted in New Oriental's dubious honor to be part of landmark litigation, and its outcome was intimately scrutinized due to it being the first such instance since China's joining the WTO. In a first verdict, New Oriental's argument that they had published the plaintiff companies' material in good faith and only in the belief of it being in the public domain was rejected. In September 2003, after more than a year of litigation, the Beijing No. 1 Intermediate People's Court handed down a judgment ordering New Oriental to pay compensation of RMB10 million (US$1.2 million) for copyright and trademark infringement. The appeal nevertheless brought some relief, as the Beijing High People's Court ultimately ordered a compensatory fine of RMB 6.4 million (US $775,000) on 27 December 2004, along with a public apology via the Chinese newspaper *Legal Daily*, but exempting New Oriental from the trademark infringement charges that was also part of the original lawsuit.

Notwithstanding this controversial setback, Xu and his partners subsequently led New Oriental to its successful IPO on the NYSE in 2006. Since then Xu has shifted his focus. Serving as vice president, dean of the Cultural Development Graduate School, and the director of international study and consulting at the New Oriental Education & Technology Group, Xu also chose a novel role for himself as an angel investor for selecting ventures of social entrepreneurial character. Among the recent projects was his involvement in cofunding the Chinese online matchmaking website Love21cn.com, together with Wang Qiang and Qian Yongqiang in April 2007, with a joint RMB 40 million injection.

Besides being an active philanthropist and devout social responsibility advocate, Xu wants to be remembered for his inspirational teaching style and his pioneering of international study and consulting in China. Having been awarded the top prize as one of "Outstanding Returned Students" by the government in 2003 and having been listed in the "Top 100 Celebrities in China" in 2004 by *Forbes* magazine, Xu maintains a high profile with regular contributions to various media channels and best-selling publications on life philosophy and career planning. Through his insightful guidance and encouragement, Xu Xiaoping has been recognized by many college students as legendary and someone who has touched and influenced the career and life choice of many Chinese youth.

JONATAN JELEN

Sources

Huang, L. (2009), "Xu, Xiaoping", in Zhang, W. and Alon, I. (Ed.), *Biographical Dictionary of New Chinese Entrepreneurs and Business Leaders,* Edward Elgar, Cheltenham, UK, pp. 215–216.

Li, Z. (2004), "Foreign study frenzy: Students going overseas to study are getting increasingly younger", *Beijing Review*, **35** (A), available at: http://www.bjreview.cn/EN/200435/Cover-200435(A).htm (accessed 9 August 2010).

New Oriental Education & Technology Group (2010), "Overview", available at: http://english.neworiental.org/Default.aspx?tabid=3481 (accessed 9 August 2010).

Xinhua News (2006), "'American Dream' in China: Yu Minhong goes from rags to riches", 30 October, available at: http://www.china.org.cn/english/MATERIAL/186776.htm (accessed 9 August 2010).

Xu, Xin (Kathy Xu 徐新 b. 1966)

Also known as Kathy Xu, Xu Xin is the founder and managing partner of Capital Today, one of the first independent private equity firms in China. Established in 2005 with a commitment to provide growth capital to small- and medium-sized Chinese companies and help them build sustainable businesses and better-known brands in China. Capital Today manages a dedicated China country fund of US$280 million and has 22 employees (two of whom are Xu's partners), all based in China.

Radiating a quiet intensity and a flair for free-market sloganeering, this tactful lady with a delightful smile was raised in Dazu, near Sichuan's provincial capital of Chengdu. Her father was the general manager of a state-owned auto factory who regularly hosted visitors from the plant to discuss business while Xu poured tea for the guests; these served as her first business lessons. In 1988, after graduating with a Bachelor of Arts degree in English literature from Nanjing University, Xu began to work as a clerk at the Bank of China's headquarters in Beijing, earning only RMB 78 a month, i.e., about US$10. Being enthusiastic and diligent, she soon secured a leadership position in the Communist Youth League. Xu spent her tea breaks teaching English to colleagues, and within 18 months, she was named the bank's best female employee.

Xu was ambitious to succeed in business and eager to see the world outside China, which prompted her to apply for an entry-level auditor's position with Price Waterhouse Coopers (PWC) as a Certified Public Accountant (CPA) of UK, and was appointed to its Hong Kong office in 1992. As a young woman from the once sleepy Sichuan Province, Xu had a tough transition; the working hours were longer, and she didn't speak Cantonese. However, this diligent lady was not fazed, she adopted PWC's Japanese clients, an orphaned portfolio of small-business owners who spoke reasonably good English, and kept herself busy.

In 1995, Xu joined Peregrine Direct Investment, the private equity arm of an upstart investment bank. Chinese capital markets were springing to life, and Xu divided her time between Peregrine's Hong Kong headquarters and mainland China. As a financial advisor, Xu helped facilitate the joint venture between Wahaha Group and Groupe Danone, a French multinational food-products corporation. Unfortunately, Peregrine fell victim to the 1997–1998 Asian Financial Crisis. However, Xu was immediately recruited by Baring Private Equity Partners and quickly rose as a formidable turnaround artist and a top Chinese rainmaker, crafting the debut of the group's mainland deals from 1998 until her departure in 2005.

In the wake of the collapse of the global dot-com bubble, Xu helped revive Guangzhou Internet service provider Netease.com, then a Baring portfolio company that was listed on NASDAQ in 1999. She worked closely with Netease's 28-year-old founder, William Ding Lei and turned the company into one of China's leading online gaming and advertising vehicles. Within two years, its stock was trading above $80 a share, up from a low of $0.60. Consequently, Ding was named the richest man in China by *Forbes* in 2003, and by that time, Xu had delivered Baring an eightfold return on its investment. Since then, three other companies that she has invested in through Capital Today have been listed among the top 100 companies by *Forbes*.

Another successful company helped by Xu is ChinaHR.com, an online recruitment website. At the start of ChinaHR.com, there were only five employees, a twisted business plan with very little success. However, Xu saw promise in Internet recruitment, and after the initial investment, she boldly replaced the founder with professional managers in 2004, and made alliance with Monster, the largest US-based online recruitment service provider, with US$50 million in 2005, then sold remaining 55% stake to Monster with US$174 million in 2008.

Known informally as "iron lady" of rainmakers, Xu has led Capital Today to invest in over 12 companies since early 2006. Under the leadership of Xu, the venture capital firm prides itself with three core corporate values: helping Chinese entrepreneurs establish Key Performance Indicator (KPI) frameworks, developing enterprise culture, and building the best brands. For any new business to succeed, Xu believes that the venture must have a focus, and the company cannot enter many fields at the same time. She gives candid advice to aspiring entrepreneurs that "no matter how able you are, if you try to run three kinds of businesses at the same time, you cannot make them all number one." Therefore, she often requires that the entrepreneurs invest 50% of their assets in the company.

Xu now has about 15 years of experience in private equity in China and has led multiple successful investments, including companies such as Netease.com,

ChinaHR.com, Kungfu Fast Food, 360buy.com, Tudou.com, Great Wall Auto, Noah Education, and Comba Telecom System, among others. In 2006, Xu injected US$11 million into 360buy.com, the biggest 3C online retailer of the B2C market in China. She also sunk US$11 million into Kung Fu, a fast-food company with 245 outlets, with no existing debt but an ambitious plan to replace Kentucky Fried Chicken (KFC) as China's most popular food-and-beverage chain within the next decade. In 2008, the sales of 360buy.com generated revenue of US$180 million for Capital Today from its initial investment two years earlier.

For her impressive accomplishment, Xu has won a number of accolades in recent years, including the Most Influential People in Asia – Stars of Asia by *BusinessWeek* in 2004, the Most Influential Venture Capitalist in China by *Capital Magazine* in 2005, and an award as one of the Top 10 Venture Capitalists by *Forbes* in 2006. She is currently serving as a governor of the China Venture Capital Association (CVCA), where she is leading the Public Policy Action Committee. Until recently, nearly all of the top dealmakers in the Chinese private equity industry were returnees who leveraged their heritage and MBAs for a share of a virgin market. Most of them were men who knew more about finance than they did about the business culture of mainland China. Xu's ethnicity and gender made her exceptional, and she is not perceived as a returnee who has come back in China to make US private equity firms rich. As a result of this authenticity, she is a natural spokeswoman for her industry.

EVERLYNE MISATI AND SUNNY LI SUN

Sources

Glain, S. (2008), "Rainmaker Kathy Xu, founder of Shanghai's Capital Today Group, bridges the gap between Beijing bureaucracy and China's private equity groups", *Forbes*, 20 March, available at: http://www.forbes.Com/global/2008/0407/050.html (accessed 20 April 2010).

Liberation Daily (2006), "Xu Xin: A discerning woman in control of two billion RMB", 10 April.

Zhou, Y. (2009), "Local VC firms hunker down, shift focus", *China Daily*, 30 March, available at: http://www.chinadaily.Com.cn/bizchina/2009-03/30/content_7628224.htm (accessed 20 April 2010).

Xue, Lan (薛澜 b. 1959)

An educator and researcher, Xue Lan is the dean of the School of Public Management and executive vice president of the Development Research Academy for the twenty-first century at Tsinghua University. Combining a strong educational background with a passion for research, Xue has established his presence as an authority figure in the fields of public policy analysis, management science, technology policy, and crisis management in China.

Born in China in 1959, Xue began his college education in 1977, earning his BS degree from the Changchun University of Science and Technology in 1982. Three years later, Xue traveled to the United States for his graduate study, first enrolled into the State University of New York at Stony Brook where he received his master's degree in system management, and then at Carnegie Mellon University in Pittsburgh, Pennsylvania, earning a PhD in engineering and public policy. Upon graduation, Xue served as an assistant professor in the Department of Engineering Management at George Washington University from 1991 to 1996. This faculty appointment represented Xue's first foray into teaching within an academic setting, a trend that continues throughout the years of his professional career.

In 1996, Xue Lan returned to China and began his teaching career at Tsinghua University where he continues his work and research till today, first as a professor and then the dean of the School of Public Policy and Management. Xue has also maintained a strong connection to his alma mater in the United States, serving as an adjunct professor at Carnegie Mellon University. While at Tsinghua, Xue focuses primarily on the study of public policy analysis and management, science and technology policies, higher education policy and crisis management, a discipline that has profound practical impact on contemporary China as the country is swiftly being transformed from a plan-based to market-oriented economy.

In 2002, Xue and three other scholars edited a book titled *China's Future in the Knowledge Economy: Engaging the New World.* Published by the Centre for Strategic Studies of Victoria University of Technology and Tsinghua University Press, the volume argued that in facing the challenges and opportunity created by the knowledge economy, China should make its own distinctive response to meet its own needs, and not copy the experiences of the Western developed countries indiscriminately. A year later, he also published *危机管理: 转型期中国面临的挑战* [*Crisis Management: Challenges Faces by China in Transition*]. In his strategic research, Xue not only focuses on the most important issues of China's economic reforms and domestic policy changes, but also scrutinizes the country's development from the global perspective of the twenty-first century. In a recent article published by *Nature*, Xue argued that pushing to globalize science must not threaten local innovations in developing countries such as China and India. In another IDRC public lecture in 2010, Xue Lan examined China's aid to Africa in the broad context of the country's involvement with the continent. He also analyzed the evolution of China's foreign aid policy and its potential for long-term engagement with Africa.

Xue's research work not only contributes to a better understanding of Chinese economy in theory, but also influences the course of the country's economic development in practice. In addition to his roles in academia, Xue has provided extensive consulting services to a number of NGOs and think tanks globally, including the World Bank, International Development Research Centre (IDRC), and Asia-Pacific Economic Cooperation (APEC). Within China, Xue serves on advisory boards for a number of government agencies that include the vice president of the China Association of Public Administration, vice president of the Chinese Association of Science and S&T Policy, and deputy secretary general of the National Steering Committee for MPA Education. In corporate arena, Xue has served as an independent director of the Neusoft Corporation since late 2009. He also held fellowship at the Brookings Institute and the University of Texas at Austin. Furthermore, he is a member of the Policy Committee on Developing Countries, International Council for Science Unions, and advisory member of Research on Knowledge Systems, and serves on the Board of Trustees of SciDev.Net, an international nonprofit organization aimed at promoting science and technology for international development. Those titles and affiliations are a clear indication of Xue's rapport among key players in the Chinese government and organizations within and outside of the Chinese market.

For his academic work, Xue has received a number of honors and accolades. In 2001, Xue received the National Distinguished Young Scientist Award and in 2009, the Chinese Ministry of Education named him a *Changjiang Scholar*. Admission into this program, sponsored by the Chinese Ministry of Education and the Li Ka-Shing Foundation, is regarded as a great honor for an individual who is an academic within China. As a representative of many Chinese natives who received solid educations from both Chinese and Western institutions, Xue is able to translate his personal preparations into a successful career upon return. With a strong emphasis on education, Xue has established himself as a recognized leader both within China and globally. His career choice of education in the fields of public policy and management will likely have a lasting impact on the development of future Chinese scholars, business managers, and public administrators. In this regard, Xue's impact on the Chinese economy will extend far beyond his individual research contributions.

Ashley Snyder

Sources

IDRC (2010), "Xue Lan: China's engagement with Africa — challenges or opportunities? For whom?", 22 March, http://www.idrc.ca/en/ev-152471-201-1-DO_TOPIC.html (accessed 11 April 2010).

Maastricht University (2010), "Prof. Xue Lan", available at: http://www.merit.unu.edu/about/profile.php?id=1055 (accessed 11 April 2010).

Tsinghua University (2009), "Dean Xue Lan appointed as Chang Jiang Scholar by the Ministry of Education of P.R. China", School of Public Policy and Management, 30 December, available at: http://www.sppm.tsinghua.edu.cn/english/news/26efe48925dd5b940125debd64070002.html (accessed 11 April 2010).

Xue, L. (2008), "The prizes and pitfalls of progress", *Nature*, **454** (24 July), pp. 398–401.

Yan, Wangjia (Jane W. Yan 严望佳 b. 1969)

Also known as Jane Yan, Yan Wangjia is the founder and CEO of Venus Information Technology Inc., a network security firm. Founded in 1996, Venustech is a leading player in China's information security industry; its clients have included large percentages of Chinese banks, telecom carriers, and other enterprises, as well as the 2008 Beijing Olympic Organizing Committee. The company has its headquarters in Zhongguancun, a Beijing technology hub often referred to as "China's Silicon Valley." Venustech also has a subsidiary in Shanghai, as well as five branches, 10 representative offices, and technical support centers, and a nationwide distribution network covering all major regions in the country.

Yan was born in the city of Kunming, Yunnan Province, in Southwestern China in July 1969. Her mother was a primary school teacher, father a doctor, and grandfather a well-known calligrapher, so the importance of scholarship was instilled in her early life. At just the age of 16, she was admitted to the prestigious Fudan University in Shanghai, where she received a bachelor's degree in computer science. Upon graduating four years later, Yan moved to the United States, where she received a master's degree in computer science at Temple University in Philadelphia, followed by a PhD – also in computing – at the University of Pennsylvania. For the first few months after she arrived in the United States, Yan did not have a scholarship, so she supported herself by selling packaged tofu and sausage. Later, she got some more relevant professional experience working for the University of Pennsylvania's Wharton School of Business's computer center, where her responsibilities included system management, security, data encryption, and hardware and software selection and customization. She returned to China and founded Venus in Beijing in June 1996, at the age of 26. She had spent a total of six years abroad.

The Internet was still a relatively new phenomenon at that time – worldwide, especially in China. Yan said that when she returned, she found that internal network security had no commercial interest or research institutions in China. Luckily, for Yan, the field was not only important and wide open, but she also felt it played to her strengths. She predicted that there would be a market for it – and she would turn out to be right.

In 1999, the company launched its first product, the "WebKeeper" website antidefacement system. In the same year, it also created the Active Defense Laboratory (ADLAB). ADLAB – the first institution of its kind in China – focuses on information security technology research, specifically anti-intrusion technology and the vulnerabilities of various operating systems and applications. To explain how ADLAB operates, Yan gave an example from the mid-2000s, when a hacker bot was targeting thousands of computers. The cracker was using a proxy server to hide its IP address, and thus, its location. Once, however, the cracker failed to use a proxy server. The lapse lasted for only a few seconds, but that was enough time for ADLAB to catch it – and then hand it over to the police, along with other information the lab had collected. The cracker was caught the next day.

The following year, Venus debuted its flagship product, an Intrusion Detection and Management System (IDMS). The IDMS finds records and analyzes security events (attacks and other abnormal network behavior) and provides management measurements and suggestions to help users deal with these events. According to a company statement, Venus is currently focused on three "core businesses." First, it provides security solutions – industry-specific network security solutions as well as a package called Venus Security Operation Center that works with customers' existing security to build a "real-time dynamic risk management system" to monitor and respond to threats. Second, it offers security service, including risk assessment, emergency response, and Certified Information Security Professional (CISP) certification and training. Finally, it has a series of network security products based on intrusion detecting, defending, and blocking technologies. Among the other products listed on Venus's website are Unified Threat Management, Vulnerabilities Scanning and Management System, and Network Security Audit System.

And the company remains active. In the summer of 2010, Venus participated in a nine-city touring forum on IT Development in China. Yan was elected the first president of the Beijing Junior Chamber of Commerce in June, and in August, Venus was awarded with the Ministry of Industry and Information Technology's 2010 Electronic Development Fund, which will provide monetary support for a new R&D project. Venus's English-language website (which refers to the firm as "Venusense") claims the firm has provided security for 30,000 users around the world and more than 30 of the world's top 500 companies – not to mention 80% of China's banking institutions, 60% of its large state-owned enterprises, and all of its telecom carriers. It also scored a coup during Beijing's hosting of the 2008 Summer Olympics, for which Venus was the largest information security service provider, offering around-the-clock technical support. Perhaps unsurprisingly given these facts, Venus has close ties to the Communist Party. Then-president Jiang Zemin and other leaders visited and praised the company in January 2000 and General Secretary Hu Jintao met with Yan in January 2003. Yan is also a member of the Chinese People's Political Consultative Conference (CPPCC), a political advisory body.

Yan has said she believes teamwork is the key to her company's success, and the basis for its innovation and development. She describes Venus's management style as "American-style Chinese-style strict management with human characteristics" (Wang, 2005). Though seemingly contradictory, this approach is intended to combine what Venus's CEO sees as the best of both worlds: Western management (which is effective, but can become mechanical) with Chinese-style management (a human-focused approach). News articles often touch on her relationship with her employees: recommending books to them, meeting over tea, keeping up with their lives, and offering condolences for their losses. Yan herself is frequently described in media reports as low-key and quiet, and says she has even been mistaken for a secretary at times. She says she does not let that faze her. "I stress professionalism," she has said, "not gender" (Hu, 2007).

Of the future of her business, Yan said in 2009, "The information security industry has entered a consolidation phase" (Huang, 2009). In an increasingly competitive market, she believes, there will be "labor pains" as some firms experience mergers, acquisitions, restructuring, and bankruptcy, but the businesses that succeed will have room for growth. Venustech will focus on integrating industry and technology, making customer-centric strategic decisions, improving its product maturity, and staying close to its large customers and partners in the long term. "If the past ten years have been the Chinese IT industry's golden years, then the next ten years will be the information security industry's golden years," Yan said (Huang, 2009). On June 23, 2010, Venustech landed on Shenzhen Stock Exchange.

James P. Gilbert and Elisabeth K. Gilbert

Sources

Minnick, W. (2009), "Chinese IT firm accused of links to cyberwarfare", *Communications of the ACM*, available at: http://cacm.acm.org/news/21731-chinese-it-firm-accused-of-links-to-cyberwarfare/fulltext (accessed 3 September 2010).

Venusense (2009), "Venustech Company information", available at: http://english.venustech.com.cn/About_249.html (accessed 2 September 2010).

胡菊芹 (2007), "严望佳: 冉冉升起的启明星", *科技日报* [Hu, J., "Yan Wangjia: The rising 'Venus,'" *Science and Technology Daily*], 19 September, available at: http://www.enet.com.cn/elady/itrw/cxhd/200709/20070919252701_1.shtml (accessed 2 September 2010).

黄智军 (2009), "严望佳: 信息安全下个十年更'黄金'", *计算机世界* [Huang, Z., "Yang Wangjia: Golden years of information security in the next decade," *Venustech (Chinese-language company website)*, 3 November, available at: http://www.venustech.com.cn/NewsInfo/13/5591.Html (accessed 3 September 2010).

梁国胜 (2007), "严望佳：温柔女子挑信息安全产业大梁", *中国青年报* [Liang, G., "Yan Wangjia: The gentle lady who lifts the beam of the Information Security Industry", *China Youth Daily*], 10 April, available at: http://finance1.jrj.com.cn/news/2007-04-10/000002135254.html (accessed 2 September 2010).

启明星辰 (2010), "启明星辰CEO严望佳女士当选北京青年商会首任会长" ["Venus CEO Ms. Yan Wangjia elected the first president of the Beijing Junior Chamber of Commerce", Venus press release, 14 July, available at: http://www.venustech.com.cn/NewsInfo/4/7613.Html (accessed 3 September 2010).

商务周刊 (2005), "严望佳: 技术创新是留学生的重要责任", ["Yan Wangjia: Technological innovation is an important responsibility of students", *Business Watch*], 8 December, available at: http://tech.sina.com.cn/i/2005-12-08/1614786660.shtml (accessed 2 September 2010).

王厉子 (2005), "'网络卫士'严望佳", *投资北京* [Wang, L., "Yan Wangjia: 'Network Guardian'", *Invest Beijing*], 17 November, available at: http://www.bjinvest.gov.cn/tzgc/rwft/200511/t98256.htm (accessed 2 September 2010).

温星 (2008), "CEO严望佳: 中国网络安全女神", *生活新报* [Wen, X., "CEO Yan Wangjia: China's goddess of network security", *New Life*], 4 January, available at: http://www.shxb.net/html/20080104/20080104_77644.shtml (accessed 2 September 2010).

赵民 (2007), "严望佳赵民对话录" [Zhao, M., "Yan Wangjia – Zhao Min Dialogue"], 19 November, available at: http://blog.ce.cn/html/50/102550-53789.html (accessed 2 September 2010).

Yan, Yan (Andrew Y. Yan 阎炎 b. 1957)

Yan Yan is a managing partner of SAIF (Softbank Asia Infrastructure Fund) Partners III and SB Asia Investment Fund II, to whom the management at Softbank, Cisco, Lee Ka Shing, Princeton, JP Morgan, Carnegie Mellon, and Rockefeller are all eager to hand money from their investment funds. Yan's credential as an outstanding venture capitalist was earned and proven. Under his leadership, SAIF was voted as "Venture Capital firm of the Year" in 2004 and 2007. It was also named as "The Best Performing Fund in Asia" by *Private Equity International* in 2005 and

2006. IPO successes such as Acorn International, Perfect World, and Digital China Holding returned unprecedented multiples for SAIF. Twice named "The Venture Investor of the Year" by China Venture Capital Association – in 2004 and 2007, Yan was also voted as one of the "Fifty Finest Private Equity Investors in the World" by the *Private Equity International* in 2007.

So what were the ingredients in his investment recipe? Yan cited partnering with the right entrepreneurs as a key element. He looked for entrepreneurs who possessed these character traits-honesty, passion, tenacity, depth, perseverance, and endurance. In addition, as a successful venture capitalist, Yan believed that one must have a good business sense coupled with uncanny intuition in choosing a winner. Born in an army family of five children in Anhui Province, Yan's sense of independence and burning desire to succeed were developed since childhood. He often skipped school and involved in fights while his parents were too busy earning a living. Defying the book-burning era during the Cultural Revolution, he developed his love for literature, and scrambled for all kinds of books and magazines he could laid his hand on from local libraries throughout his childhood.

Athletic by build and devoted by nature, Yan excelled in sports, and became a volleyball captain representing his province. Surprisingly, he later turned down a volleyball coaching position and settled in countryside as an "educated youth." The farming salary was meager and lifestyle mind numbing, which Yan endured as he began to set his eyes on pursuing higher education. In 1977, opportunities arose when Deng Xiaoping reinstated the nationwide university entrance exam, and Yan's high score in arts earned him a second place in Anhui. Upon realizing that his dream as a movie director was not going to be materialized, he opted for his second ambition – a pilot, and entered the Nanjing Aeronautic Institute. However, upon enrolling, that aspiration was shattered too, as the institute was actually an engineering school. Within a few months, Yan began to divert his attention to volleyball again to compensate for the lack luster engineering courses. As the captain, he led the Nanjing Aeronautic Institute's Southern Airline men's volleyball team to victorious championship three years in a row. He was devastated after losing the final game in his senior year, as his severe right arm injury prevented him and his team to round up a straight fourth championship.

After earning his Bachelor degree, Yan worked for three years as an engineer at the Jianghuai Airplane Corp. Dissatisfied with the way the management ran the firm, and ambitious to become a corporate CEO later on, Yan in 1984 nailed the entrance exam for a graduate study program at Peking University. Yan thrived in the intellectually stimulating yet challenging environment of Peking University during the early days of the reform era. As the deputy president and secretary of the student body, he led a team of four in research on social economic reform and presented the results to the government. Till today, Yan contended that graduate education at Peking University was among the most important factors that contributed to the success in his life.

While at Peking, Andrew befriended Roger Michiner, a Princeton visiting professor. Armed with a recommendation letter from Michiner and an impressive TOEFL score, Yan was granted a full scholarship from Princeton, and went to the

United States in 1986. In an effort to improve his English, Yan made a conscious decision to live with an American couple in the first 10 months of arriving to New Jersey. During semester breaks, he would drive his used car of $600 to marvel at the majestic campuses of the world-renowned universities, such as Harvard, Stanford, and Pennsylvania. After the first six months at Princeton, he changed his major from sociology to international political economy. Upon completing his master degree from Princeton in 1989, Yan landed a six-figure income position working for the World Bank at its Policy, Planning and Research Division, with primary focus on the reform of Chinese enterprise and welfare systems. However, discontent with the laid-back atmosphere at the World Bank, Yan soon took a pay cut to join the Hudson Institute, where he was the first research fellow from mainland China. His research covered the US foreign policy issues on China, Japan, and Korea.

Two years later, while disillusioned by the results of his research publication, Yan received an invitation to join the newly created Asia Infrastructure Fund (AIF). Jointly funded by AIG (American Insurance Company) and GIC (Singapore Government Investment Corporation), AIF was designed to be an early mover by investing in the Asian emerging markets, primarily China. Exhilarated by the prospect of learning something new every day, Yan joined AIF in 1995. At that time, the investment fund concept was still new to China. In addition, political risks still loomed before China's joining WTO. However, Yan soon made a name for himself by investing in the troubled China Offshore Oil Service and successfully facilitating its listing on the NYSE. This resounding success led Hong Kong's richest man, Lee Ka Shing, to make an exception to his investment policy by investing with Yan's SAIF later on.

Naturally, headhunters started knocking on his door. This led to his appointment as the CEO for Softbank Asia Infrastructure Fund in 2001. His tenure at SAIF was not without struggle, especially his recommendation to invest in Shanda Networks. Nevertheless, when Shanda was listed on NASDAQ on May 13, 2004, Yan was able to generate a record-breaking return of 16 multiples for SAIF within a year of investment. By the end of 2004, all of the initial capital with SAIF was fully invested. As of 2005, with the support of Cisco, Yan formed SB Asia Investment Fund and continued to act as managing director for SAIF II. Another record-breaking return was achieved with the IPO of Perfect World, reaching 50 times in 2007. Because of his series of successes, the SAIF III Fund attracted unsolicited partners such as investment funds from Cisco, AIG, Lee Ka Shing, Princeton Endowment, Carnegie, Rockefeller, etc.; and now, the world is awaiting Yan's next move.

KIRSTY S. F. TAN

Sources

SB Asia Investment Fund (2010), "Andy Yan", available at: http://www.sbaif.com/team_hongkong_andyyan1.htm (accessed 28 April 2010).

Wang, H. (2010), "Chinese returnees: Impact on China's modernization & globalization", Brookings Institute, 6 April.

Wharton Global Alumni Forum (2009), "Private equity in China: IPOs are out for now, but opportunities exist", available at:http://www.knowledgeatwharton.com.cn/index.cfm?fa=viewArticle&articleID=2063&languageid=1 (accessed 30 April 2010).
新财富 (2008), "阎焱: 亚洲最大的风险基金掌门人,软银赛富主管合伙人阎焱档案" ["Andrew Yan: Managing partner of SAIF and chief of the largest VC fund in Asia", *New Fortune*], 3 April, available at:http://www.sunwukong.ws/economic_cooperation/venture_capitals, 2114.aspx (accessed 30 April 2010).
邢学军 (2007), "阎焱: 挑起独立大旗", *财富裂变: 10位海归风险投资翘楚* (王辉耀主编), 中国发展出版社, 北京 [Xing, X, "Yan Yan: Raising the flag of independence", in Wang, H. (ed.), *Wealth Creation: Ten Overseas Returnees in Venture Capital Investment,* China Development Press, Beijing], pp. 207–235.

Yang, Lan (杨澜 b. 1968)

Ranked among China's 50 most successful entrepreneurs and one of the China's wealthiest self-made women, Yang Lan is a well-known broadcast journalist and talk show hostess, one of the China's best-known media personalities, and is often referred to as the "Oprah Winfrey" of China. Yang is also the co-founder and co-owner with her husband Bruno Wu Zheng of Hong Kong-listed Sun Television Cybernetworks (Sun TV), one of the China's most prominent private-media groups.

Born in 1968 in Beijing, Yang came from an intellectual family. Yang's mother was an engineer, and her father taught English literature at Beijing Foreign Studies University and sometimes served as the official translator for former Chinese Premier Zhou Enlai. Although a college student, Yang demonstrated her amazing talent. In 1990, she won national fame by hosting the Zheng Da Variety Show on China Central Television (CCTV). She was only 21 in her last year as an English language and literature major at the Beijing Foreign Studies University when she won the audition for the host position of the Zheng Da Variety Show on CCTV, after giving a confident performance, explaining that she wanted to be more than a pretty face agreeing with her male counterpart. Within a year, this prime-time-Saturday celebrity quiz and talk show was China's top-rated TV program, with an audience of 220 million. Shortly after, she won China's most prestigious honor for the television industry, the Golden Microphone award in 1994.

Despite her rising celebrity status, Yang Lan quit the show after four years to go to New York, where she spent two years pursuing a master degree in the School of International & Public Affairs at Columbia University. In 1994, she met Bruno Wu Zheng, the scion of a prominent Shanghai family – his grandfather was China's former ambassador to the League of Nations – who was running an Internet consulting firm at the time. Although in the United States, she also shot her next project, *Yang Lan Horizon*, to introduce Chinese viewers to American culture and society. *Yang Lan Horizon* was syndicated to more than 50 affiliate channels in China, attracting millions and millions of Chinese audience at home.

Upon graduation, she headed back home. In 1996 while Yang commuted between Hong Kong and Shanghai, she published a book of essays, travelogues and sketches compiled during her time at Columbia, and half million copies were sold. The following year, Yang landed at the Phoenix Chinese Channel in Hong Kong, where she produced and starred in two new shows: *These Hundred Years*, a nonfiction series about the twentieth century China; and *Yang Lan Studio*, which featured pointed interviews with business and media luminaries.

In 1999, Yang left the company, seeking more independence and creative control. She and husband Bruno Wu Zheng founded, acquired, and renamed a listed company in the Hong Kong stock market, and set up the Sun Cybernetworks Holding Limited. Under the holding, Sun TV started its operation via satellite Asia 3S since August 2000. Sun TV brands itself as the first history and biography channel in the greater China region, designed to bring culture and learning to the massive Chinese audiences.

Sun TV later became part of a much bigger operation, Sun Media Investment Holdings Limited (SMIH), which has holdings in several different arenas of the media, including television, publishing, and advertising. In 2001, *Forbes* magazine named SMIH one of the 200 best small capital companies, and thanks to the acquisition of a Hong Kong-based newspaper network, the corporation later owns more than 30 magazines and several newspapers, the economics-focused *Observer Star* among them. In 2004, the *Observer Star* became the first Chinese-language financial paper released simultaneously in the world's largest Chinese markets outside of mainland China: Taiwan, Singapore, Malaysia, and North America.

However, Sun TV faced some financial difficulties in 2004, and Yang and Wu sold 70% of the Sun TV. In 2005, they founded a nonprofit Sun Culture Foundation that holds 51% of their holding company for Sun TV, and completely retreated from the management of the TV network. Sun TV was first under control of Xinmei Media and its affiliated Strategic Media International, and then transferred to a Hong Kong-listed company TideTime.

After this business transaction, Yang wants to focus more on culture production, TV programming and charity. She is still producing her renowned talk show program, *Yang Lan One On One*, for which she has interviewed more than 500 world leaders, and is vastly popular with Chinese audiences around the world. Since 2006, her talk show, *Her Village*, has opened new horizons for Chinese women professionals, and has now expanded into the leading cross-media community for Chinese working women.

These years, Yang found herself actively involved in charitable work. According to *Hurun Report*, Yang Lan and Wu Zheng were among the top 10 China's most generous in 2009, who donated US$47 million to the causes of education, culture, and sports in China. She also actively serves as a goodwill ambassador on several national charity foundations, promoting environmental protection, education, disaster relief, and capacity building for NGOs. For her contributions to the development of the civil society in China, she won a National Charity Award in 2008.

At the end of 2009, Yang Lan and COFCO (China National Cereals, Oils and Foodstuffs Corporation) co-founded a world's leading high-end private club, "Junding Elite Club" in Beijing. The founding members include not only some dignitaries from around the world such as former prime minister, leading business leaders, entertainment stars, Nobel Award winners, top billionaires, but also the Bill

Gates Foundation, the Prince Charles Foundation, as well as important domestic companies such as China Life Insurance, Lenovo, China Merchants Bank, and China Unicom.

As early as 1999 and 2001, Ms. Yang was named by *Asia Week* magazine as one of the "Leaders in Society and Culture in Asia," and one of the "Movers and Shakers of the 21st Century China." In addition, she was honored with the Chinese Woman of the Year award in 2001 and the Top Ten Women Entrepreneurs award in 2002. Yang also served as a goodwill ambassador for Beijing's bid for the 2008 Olympic Games, joining the Ping-Pong World Champion Deng Yaping, the film actress Gong Li, and Sang Lan, the gymnast who was paralyzed in 1998 as she represented China at the Goodwill Game in the United States, to campaign for the Beijing Olympic Games bid. She served as one of the speakers in the final presentation to the International Olympic Committee in Moscow, where Beijing won the bid.

Since 2007, Yang has been serving as a director of the International Academy of Television Arts & Sciences. In that same year, she was honored by the Paley Center of Media (formerly the Museum of Television and Radio) with the "She Made it" Award. Since 2005, she has also served as a member of the Columbia University International Advisory Council (IAC); and in 2008, The School of International and Public Affairs of Columbia University honored her with a Global Leadership Award. Socially active, Yang also serves as a member of the National Committee of the Chinese People's Political Consultative Conference and as United Nations Children's Fund (UNICEF) Ambassador in China in 2010.

WEIDONG ZHANG

Sources

Forbes (2001), "Yang Lan: #56 of China's 100 Richest Business People", 12 November, available at: http://members.forbes.com/global/2001/1112/032_61.html (accessed 4 June 2010).

Fung, A. Y. H. (2008). *Global Capital, Local culture: Localization of Transnational Media*. New York: Peter Lang Publishing.

Hurun Report (2009), "2009 Hurun Philanthropy List", available at: http://www.hurun.net/listen153.aspx (accessed 20 July 2010).

Mo, X. (2009), "Yang Lan", in: Zhang, W. and Alon, I. (eds), *Biographical Dictionary of New Chinese Entrepreneurs and Business Leaders*, Cheltenham, UK: Edward Elgar, pp. 223–224.

Paley Center for Media (2008), "Yang Lan: Television journalist, executive", available at: http://www.shemadeit.org/meet/biography.aspx?m=161 (accessed 4 June 2010).

Wall Street Journal (2007), "Chinese TV celebrities go on Internet", 28 August, available at: http://dalian.neworiental.org/publish/portal79/tab6504/info178338.htm (accessed 4 June 2010).

Xinhuanet (2003), "Famed Anchorwoman Yang Lan", 13 August, available at: http://news.xinhuanet.com/english/2003-08/13/content_1024117.htm (accessed 4 June 2010).

胡媛 (2009), "杨澜的商业复兴", *商业价值* [Hu, Y., "Yang Lan's business revival", *Business Value*], 5 November, available at: http://content.businessvalue.com.cn/post/17.html (accessed 20 July 2010).

Yang, Lijun (杨丽君 b. 1957)

Known to the West as Lily Yang, Yang Lijun is the China chief representative of ING Insurance, a global financial institution of Dutch origin. Yang's name has entwined with ING and China, as she is one of the pioneers in introducing the Dutch three pillars pension system, the LOMA training and education system, housing mortgage system, and compliance policy, among others, to China. Coincidentally, since the symbol of the company is a golden lion and Yang's horoscope is Leo as well, she shows great empathy with ING.

After two and a half years in the Investment Promotion Section (IPS) of UNIDO Zurich office from 1986 to 1988, Yang joined Edward Keller, one of the world's leading international trading and investment companies, and held the position of chief representative in China for nearly 10 years. In 1994, Yang obtained her master degree in international business from the Fletcher School of Law and Diplomacy at Tufts University in Medford, Massachusetts. Since August 1997, she has been working as chief representative of ING Insurance in China, and is actively involved in numerous business promotion activities across the country.

In 2000, China's entry into the WTO meant a great deal for Yang as an insurance professional. She welcomed the announcement, as she had been striving for years to obtain a life insurance operating license in China. However, based on her experience, Yang warned ING, her company, that the process of opening up the Chinese market should be undertaken step-by-step, and large foreign companies should not expect too much from China's membership of the WTO. The market development later proved that she was right in her predictions. In 2002, ING established its first joint venture (JV) fund management in China. Although the Pacific Insurance had the final say, Yang strongly recommended the Bank of Beijing as the ideal partner for her company. Eventually, she was able to convince the upper management, and in 2005 the firm acquired 19.9% of the shares in the Bank of Beijing, which enabled the company to enter strategic partnership agreements in the retail banking business in China. Since then, the company she represents has been the largest shareholder of the Bank of Beijing.

In 2006, Yang was appointed to the Board of Directors of ING-Pacific Life Insurance Company and ING-Capital Life Insurance Company, two licensed ING joint ventures in China. Due to her tireless efforts, ING Insurance has made great progress in China in recent years. Currently, it is the only life insurance JV in China that has two licenses to operate there, a feat which no other foreign company has so far achieved. As she pronounced, "There is no competition in the Chinese market there is no need for the two ventures to get together… China is so large a market that we can expand further with the two units (Cornhill Direct, 2000)."

Besides her corporate responsibilities, Yang is very sensitive to the potential on how her company can help the people and local communities. Under her leadership, the ING has sponsored a water project in China, building the infrastructure for providing clean water for 5000 people. At the opening ceremony for the building of the first facilities in Jiaoliudao Township of Liaoning Province in August 2005, Yang remarked: "The Dutch have a long tradition of dealing with water, and ING hopes that this tradition will help improve the lives and hygiene conditions of the villagers through this project (ING, 2005)." In the following years, in a partnership with the Red Cross Society in China, the company completed two other projects to provide drinking water and sanitation infrastructure in a poverty-striking area of Northeastern China, and it was particularly moving for Yang to see how grateful the locals were to have running water and proper sanitation facilities at home. In 2008, Yang represented her company at a ceremony held at Peking University, where students were given grants by the Peking University Education Foundation sponsored by ING. Above all, she is very proud the fact that with the backing of financial institutions operating in China, she is able to help less fortunate people by adhering to the basic tenets of a sustainable development.

Apart from her regular job, Yang served as the vice chairperson of the Security Working Group of the European Chamber of Commerce from 2001 to 2003, and she was the chairwoman of the Insurance and Fund Management Working Group of the European Chamber of Commerce from 2003 to 2007. In March, after a recommendation by the China Insurance Regulatory Commission, Yang was made a member of the council of the China Society for Finance and Banking, becoming its first member working for a foreign company. In addition, she is also a member of the influential 2005 Committee of China Western Returned Scholars Association, Chamber of Commerce (WRSACC).

Given her expertise in insurance and funds management and her rich international experiences, Yang has been invited to participate in different meetings and conferences such as the Forum on Management of Insurance Funds sponsored by the Hong Kong Special Administrative Region in March 2004, and Boao Forum for Asia Annual Conference in April 2007 and April 2008. In June 2010, she took part at the XII Saint Petersburg International Economic Forum (SPIEF), working together with other intellectuals to identify the key challenges facing emerging markets around the world and to find common purposes and frameworks to forge solutions.

Since 2007, Yang has served as a visiting professor at Guangxi Normal University. Although Guangxi is located in China's remote southwestern region, she feels that there she is closer to her students and has really grown fond of them. As a result, she has promoted a program to grant scholarships to students at that university. In 2008, largely due to her leadership efforts, ING was recognized among the most valuable brands in China during the Sina Network Festival held in Beijing's Chang'an Grand Theatre.

M. ELENA ARAMENDIA-MUNETA

Sources

Cornhill Direct (2007), "ING link-up not happening", 27 December, available at http://www.cornhilldirect.co.uk/news/18407513-ing_link_up_not_happening.htm (accessed 9 June 2010).

ING (2005), "Fulfilled promises: Water projects in China and India", 16 September, available at: http://www.ing.com/group/showdoc.jsp?docid=124380_EN (accessed 9 June 2010).

WRSACC Committee (2005), "Li-Jun Yang (Lily): Chief Representative of ING Insurance in China", available at: http://www.2005committee.org/index.php/member/ls/716 (accessed 9 June 2010).
北京大学教育基金会 (2008), "北京大学ING助学金签字仪式暨学生见面会举行" ["Peking University students met with ING during the grant ceremony", Peking University Education Foundation], 5 November, available at: http://www.pkuef.org/newdetail2.php?id=924 (accessed 9 June 2010).
人民网 (2008), "ING保险中国首席代表杨丽君向海内外网友拜年", ["Yang Lijun, chief representative of ING China, sends new year greetings to all netizens", People.com.cn], 11 January, available at: http://finance.people.com.cn/GB/8215/113604/6764042.html (accessed 9 June 2010).
新浪财经 (2007), "杨丽君聊金融巨头ING的中国之路实录" [Lily Yang on the development of finance giant ING in China", Sina Finance], 27 December, available at: http://finance.sina.com.cn/money/lczx/20071227/13544343294.shtml (accessed 9 June 2010).
新浪娱乐 (2008), "ING中国首席代表杨丽君专访: 谈可持续发展战略" [ING China Chief Representative Yang Lijun on strategies for sustainable development", Sina Entertainment], 17 January, available at http://ent.sina.com.cn/s/m/2008-01-17/21401881743.shtml (accessed 9 June 2010).
张晓晨 (2009), "审慎风险管理, 强化自身建设" 价值中国 [Zhang, X., "Carefully examining risk management, while strengthening self-development", China Value], 25 September, available at: http://www.chinavalue.net/figure/show.aspx?id=1467 (accessed 9 June 2010).

Yang, Ning (Nick Yang 杨宁 b. 1975)

Ask Yang Ning for an explanation of what he does, and he is quick to emphatically state that he is a professional entrepreneur: "That's my job – an entrepreneur" (Bye, 2009). The youthful Yang has accomplished more in his first decade out of college than most people dream of accomplishing in a lifetime, with two highly successful startup companies under his belt and a third on the way: ChinaRen, KongZhong, and Monkey King Search. Hundreds of millions of people use the services he has created.

Colorful with enthusiasm and energy, Yang communicates in passionate metaphors. He describes China in the late 1990s as the brink of a tsunami, and he and his partners as surfers always searching to ride the next giant wave. His favorite role models, not surprisingly, are Bill Gates and Steve Jobs, but he enjoys Confucian works and has been fascinated with Leonardo Da Vinci since childhood. Yang enjoys golf, art collecting, and photography; he limits his work to eight-hour days and spends his spare time with artist friends in Beijing's 798 Arts District or wandering with his camera in hand.

Born in 1975 in Xi'an, Yang's family moved to Michigan when he was in primary school, sent by the Chinese government for his father to pursue further training for his engineering career. From 1993 to 1997, Yang attended the University of Michigan for his Bachelor degree in electrical engineering, and went to Stanford for graduate studies in electrical engineering, completing a master degree with honors in 1999.

It was at Stanford that Yang's future would be changed forever. After listening to entrepreneurial speeches by highly successful Stanford alumni, Yang and two of his classmates, Zhou Yunnan (MBA) and Chen Zhou (Engineering) were inspired to dream big. Together they would partner to build their fortunes, earning them the moniker of the Three Stanford Musketeers.

One year before graduation, Zhou Yunfan had a potential job lead in China, so the three friends traveled back to their homeland together. What they saw inspired them. They felt the tsunami of economic growth coming and wanted to be ready for it, to ride the wave. So while most of their graduating class headed to Silicon Valley in the midst of the dot-com boom (soon to be bust), these three musketeers perplexed their families and friends with a move to Beijing instead to found ChinaRen.

Without the typical family wealth and sophisticated network that many new entrepreneurs benefit from, Yang forged his way through his Stanford connections, gathering a total of $250,000 from 20 classmates. When Yang sold ChinaRen to Sohu the following year, the price tag was $33 million in Sohu stocks. Those Stanford classmates eventually cashed out with returns up to 50 times their initial investment.

In 1999, the Stanford Musketeers launched ChinaRen, Yang's first startup, when he was only 24 years old. The name ChinaRen is made up of the English name for China plus the Chinese word for people, an apt moniker for a community website built on a Western model adapted to meet Eastern culture. With limited seed money, they were forced to start with cheap office furniture, old computers, a dilapidated office rental space, and hired student labor – young engineering talent from Tsinghua University's Computer Science department. However, success came quickly. In March 2000, ChinaRen reached the milestone of 1 million registered users. A few months later ChinaRen merged into Sohu for $33 million, just an year after its formation and just a month away from running out of cash. Yang then served on Sohu's board for the next two years before he felt the pull to start something new again.

Believing that mobile Internet was the next big wave, Yang developed KongZhong in 2002 when he was 27 years old. KongZhong, whose name refers to the wireless services and content that are delivered through the air, quickly became China's top mobile Internet company with room for exponential growth: of the hundreds of millions of mobile phone users in China, only a small percentage has started to use wireless Internet, and most of them are using KongZhong.

KongZhong's services include wireless application protocol, interactive voice response, premium short messaging services, multimedia messaging services, Java, and color ring back tone, as well as a plethora of media and entertainment such as games and image downloads accessed by mobile phones from Kong.net, one of the nation's leading wireless Internet portals. KongZhong also hosts other websites, including the official mobile website of the CBA (Chinese Basketball Association), as well as being the official mobile web partner of the NBA, creating what Yang calls a "one-stop mobile portal for basketball… to give fans in China access to basketball anywhere, anytime" (Bye, 2009).

With just one round of fundraising that surfaced only one leading venture capitalist, KongZhong went public after just two years. At its landing on the

NASDAQ in 2004, Yang became the youngest president of a listed company at a mere 29 years old. In 2005, the company was number two in the Asia Pacific Deloitte Technology Fastest 500 list, having grown from $200,000 to $47 million in just three years. In 2009, Yang resigned as president and chief technology officer of KongZhong, ready for a new adventure.

At the age of 34 Yang started his third company, Monkey King Search, following his longtime passion to create a concept-based search engine. Yang's strategy is to start with a mobile search engine to gain quick market recognition as a predecessor to grander ambitions. His goals are to upset the dominance of Baidu and Google, an ambitious task. Though it has been tried unsuccessfully by many before, Yang is determined to be the one to pull it off. To him, search engines are as fundamentally important as tap water, and none have yet succeeded in truly quenching people's thirsts. The key, according to Yang, is to follow what he wants, as a so-called passionate user of the services he creates, as well as understanding what the nation wants. And he is one who can claim to know what China wants: between ChinaRen, KongZhong, and Sohu, he has created products that are used by hundreds of millions. Yang does not bother with fickle market research, surveys, and focus groups; he relies confidently on his own knowledge, intuition, and understanding of the market.

Yang has used a fusion of Western education and Chinese cultural perspective to his advantage, crediting this way of thinking as one of their original competitive advantages before the Internet abolished the information asymmetry between the United States and China. Yang explains, "We saw how things were done in the West, adopted it to China, and did really well" (Bye, 2009). Yang is now on the search for new opportunities and innovations as an angel investor. He is especially keen to find new technology and media with exciting potential. In the words of Yang himself, "Remember, we're surfers. Whenever there's a wave, you can be sure we're going to get in front of it" (Bye, 2009).

BARBARA L. STROTHER

Sources

Bye, A. (2009), "Nick Yang from KongZhong Corporation", *Meet Innovators*, 8 October, podcast available at: http://meetinnovators.com/2009/10/08/nick-yang-from-kongzhong-corporation/ (accessed 22 July 2010).

PR Newswire (2008), "Kong.net becomes one-stop mobile portal for basketball fans", 14 January, available at: http://en.prnasia.com/pr/2008/01/14/08021411.shtml (accessed 22 July 2010).

百度百科 (2010), "杨宁: 空中网总裁兼首席技术官" ["Yang Ning: President and CTO of KongZhong.com", *Baidu Encyclopedia*], available at: http://baike.baidu.com/view/171802.htm?fr=ala0_1#3 (accessed 22 July 2010).

中国移动 (n.d.), "斯坦福三剑客之一杨宁" ["Yang Ning: One of the three musketeers from Stanford", China Mobile], available at: http://dev.10086.cn/upload/subject/201003/yangning/index.html (accessed 22 July 2010).

Yang, Zhuang (John Yang 杨壮 b. 1954)

As the international dean and professor of management, Beijing International MBA (BiMBA) Program at Peking University, Yang Zhuang focuses primarily on subjects such as management fundamentals, human resources, comparative management, and corporate culture, critical success factors for multinational corporations operating in China, and leadership and organizational behavior. With insights and hard work, he has made some significant contributions to the Chinese understanding of those critical disciplines.

Both Yang's parents were graduates of the private Yanching University in China, which later merged into Peking University. Growing up during the Chinese Cultural Revolution, Yang was able to pull him through the social chaos and made into Peking University, where he received his BA in English from the elite Chinese institution in 1974. In 1978, he enrolled into the graduate program at the Chinese Academy of Social Sciences, where he received his master degree in journalism three years later. Upon graduation, Yang went to the United States to pursue additional studies, first at Princeton University where he earned an MPA in international relations in 1984, then an MA in sociology from Columbia University a year later, and finally his PhD in business administration in 1991 also from Columbia University.

Summer breaks in the United States provided Yang with excellent opportunities to gain applied experience with some top organizations in the world. He completed internships with the World Bank, the *Wall Street Journal*, and the *Washington post*, which provided him unique insight into economics, finance, and American cultures and society. His desire to learn about basic social behaviors and fundamental business skills imbued in him a keen interest in the corporate organization and greatly influenced his future studies and career aspirations. Going beyond simply obtaining a personal education, Yang spent 12 years in the United States and developed a deep understanding of American culture and the dynamics of business organizations.

However, an urge to return to China soon arose. With a sense of responsibility and desire to make a difference, Yang returned to his homeland in 1994. Initially he worked as an advisor in investment banking and focused on corporate reforms; nevertheless, he remained unsatisfied and felt the need to change directions professionally. Although he was compensated handsomely, the high pressure from the cutthroat financial industry really made him wonder about the purpose of his life. It was at this time that Yang decided to return to the United States and begin working in academia. He was able to secure a position as a professor at Fordham University, where he would remain for a good deal of time, ultimately earning tenure.

In 1998, the China Center for Economic Research at Peking University launched a plan for an MBA program with an international focus, which is co-sponsored by the Alliance for International Education and Fordham University. This presented a unique opportunity for Yang, who returned to China and resumed his academic career with BiMBA, whereas remaining its US dean since the program inception in the late 1990s. This post has allowed Yang to continue research and teaching while fulfilling his ambitious goals of contributing to the country's economic development more directly.

At Peking University, Yang devoted himself wholeheartedly in educating the next generation of China's leaders. According to him, the success of entrepreneurship should not be mystified in China. An entrepreneur must have knowledge and culture as well as passion, who should not only be a good executive but also a detective with sharp senses and a psychologist with great social skills. The power of a true leader comes from his noble character, which should be based on the notions of duty, integrity, and confidence. As a well-respected educator and an authority figure in management science, Yang's teaching has had a profound impact on the intellectual growth of many young Chinese students. Under his direction, the BiMBA has recently being recognized by the Chinese edition of *Fortune* magazine as one of the graduate MBA programs with most market value in China.

In addition to his administrative work on the MBA program and teaching, Yang has published extensively in academic journals and mainstream business publications both within China and internationally, revolving primarily around issues of human resources, management, and other organizational behaviors. Some of his research papers appeared in leading scholarly journals such as *Harvard China Review*, *Comparative Economic and Social Systems*, and *Journal of International Business Studies*. Yang was also a featured speaker during the 2005 Global Forum: China and the New Asian Century that was sponsored by *Fortune* magazine. Besides his academic undertakings, Yang has served as an independent director of the New Oriental Education and Technology Group, ChangYou.com and Tristate Holdings Limited.

Yang has made a clear impact on his field of studies and is notable for his research on the Chinese economic development. In recent years, with large growth in the presence of multinational corporations in China, the acquisition of global visions among the Chinese people is particularly critical. Yang's training in the United States has provided him such a foundation for research, instruction, and the development of future managers and business leaders. His deep understanding and appreciation for a global focus has influenced the standards set for Chinese MBA programs, which when fully implemented, will likely prepare students for the rigors of competing and doing business in an increasingly global economy.

Ashley Snyder

Sources

BiMBA (2007), "Yang, John Zhuang", National School of Development, 9 December, available at: http://en.bimba.edu.cn/article.asp?articleid=2671 (accessed 11 April 2010).

BiMBA (2009), "Dr. John Yang, A journey from an undergraduate at Peking University to US Dean at BiMBA", National School of Development, 29 July, available at: http://en.bimba.edu.cn/article.asp?articleid=3988 (accessed 11 April 2010).

华夏时报 (2008), "北大国际MBA杨壮：中国企业需要新型领导者", ["Yang Zhuang of BiMBA: Chinese enterprises need new generation of leaders", *China Times*], 30 June, http://www.mbahome.com/newss/Article/infoCenter/MBAcharacter/200806/29733.shtml (accessed 25 July 2010).

Yao, Naxin (Max Yao 姚纳新 b. 1970)

Also known as Max Yao, Yao Naxin is the co-founder and CEO of Focused Photonics (Hangzhou) Inc. (FPI). Ever since the founding of FPI in 2001, Yao's career has been closely linked to the rapid growth and expansive success of his company – a triumphant story made possible by a leadership that combines strong business acumen, total commitment, and incessant pursuit of excellence.

FPI is a high-tech company committed to the research and development of advanced photoelectric measurement, processes analysis, and laboratory analysis technologies, with the aspiration to become the world-leading supplier of high-end analysis and monitoring equipment. From the very beginning, FPI has ingeniously introduced the management system of the IT industry – key to FPI's dynamism and competitiveness. Followed by its peers, FPI has in fact revolutionized the way China's instrument manufacturers administer their businesses.

Yao was born in September 1970 in a small coast town near Ningbo in Zhejiang Province of Eastern China, a place well known for its tradition of commerce. Yao began his business experience in his childhood, carrying a basket to sell eggs in his neighborhood. Excelled academically, Yao was admitted into the biology department of Peking University in 1988. Although a college student, with the genes of a native Ningbo, he continued with his small trading activities such as selling teaching materials, thermo glass liners, calculators, etc. Four years later, Yao graduated with an assigned job in a state-owned hospital in the outskirt of Beijing. However, working there less than a year, he left and went door to door on the electronic street in Zhongguancun, Beijing pursuing a job with his resume, until finally a company selling scientific instruments took him in. Soon, due to his outstanding sales results and remarkable marketing capabilities, a Hong Kong Instrument Company hired Yao as its chief representative in mainland China. In 1995, three years after graduation from college, Yao went to the United States and enrolled at the University of California, Berkeley majoring cell biology. After obtained a master degree, he could have gone further down the road pursuing a doctorate, but for him it seemed too long a journey. He quit academics and followed his heart, jumping into the business world. He first worked as a manager in a biological company for DNA testing, and then served as general manager for Alibaba US.

Before officially undertaking of his own business, Yao participated in the MBA program at Stanford University for a year. In 2001, he founded Focused Photonics Inc. in Hangzhou, the capital city of Zhejiang Province, in partnership with Wang Jian, a Stanford PhD who was in charge of the technological aspects while Yao himself concentrated on sales and marketing and strategies.

Since its formation, FPI has developed about 10 series of photoelectric measurement and environmental monitoring and analysis products, applying independent research results in the fields of optoelectronics, precision instruments, industrial automation, semiconductor physics, electronic materials, and software engineering.

To bring this wide range of products to the market, FPI has built up a comprehensive distribution network all over China through the innovation of traditional marketing channels. Under Yao's leadership, FPI's sales force is characterized by its strong customer and service orientation and technical expertise. As a result, within a few years FPI has managed to enter the metals, chemical, petrochemical, and power industries as well as to successfully expand into the areas of environmental protection and surveillance, food safety, and aerospace.

In the domestic metallurgy industry, FPI has successfully eliminated multinational rivals such as ABB and Siemens to hold a dominant market share of 75%. Its sales of online gas detection and analysis instruments share 25% of the domestic market, and its online laser and UV instruments have been able to displace foreign products completely. FPI instruments are increasingly exported to overseas markets, such as the United States, the United Kingdom, Japan, India, Korea, Algeria, and Taiwan. In 2009, the total sales of FPI reached approximately 10 billion CNY.

Since 2001, FPI has been continuously investing 15% of its annual income into research and development. The R&D department accounts for 400 employees out of the company's total of 1,300. The highly qualified work force releases two new technology platforms each year, while keeping stock of technological innovations in preparation for future development. In 2009, FPI invested 200 million CNY to launch the FPI Research Institute for Internet in Wuxi, China. To date, FPI has become the proud holder of 158 national intellectual property rights items, including 76 patents for invention, 60 software copyrights, and other certificates. It has drafted six national industrial standards, and in 2008, the International Electro-technical Commission (IEC) officially approved the industrial standard for laser gas analysis instruments drafted and submitted by FPI on behalf of China.

For his key role in the areas of environmental protection and technical innovation of analytical instruments, Yao was elected to be a member of industrial associations and professional societies. He is the executive director of China Association of Environmental Protection Industry, president of Zhejiang Association of Environmental Protection Industry, executive director of China Instrument Manufacturers Association (Analytical Instrument Branch), and member of the Expert Committee of China Instrument Society (Analytical Instrument Chapter).

Yao was a vigorous student leader at Peking University as well as at Berkeley. His care for the community and sense of social responsibility now find expression in the various voluntary posts he has taken up. He is a mentor to the student entrepreneurship program at Zhejiang University, president of Hangzhou Overseas Returnees' Club, and host of the "Silicon Valley Elite Salon." He is generous in sharing his experiences as an entrepreneur and returnee with young Chinese talents home and abroad.

XIAOWEI SUN

Sources

钱江晚报 (2009), “新一代浙商姚纳新: 从硅谷到天堂‘牛仔’很忙” [*Qianjiang Evening News*, “New generation Zhejiang businessman Yao Naxin: “The busy ‘cowboy’ from the Silicon Valley to heaven”], 19 November, available at: http://xueyuan.cyzone.cn/gushi-gushi/125076.html (accessed 20 July 2010).

王德禄 (2009), “访聚光科技公司CEO姚纳新” [Wang, D., “Interview with FPI CEO Yao Naxin”], 27 February, available at: http://gei-wangdelu.blog.sohu.com/111152722.html (accessed 20 July 2010).

姚仲三 (2009), “姚纳新: 创新的冲动”, *新华商* [Yao, Z., “Yao Naxin: Innovation impulsion”, *New Chinese Businessman*], 18 September, available at: http://www.chbhr.com/article/show.asp?id=4055 (accessed 20 July 2010).

Yuan, Yue (Victor Y. Yuan 袁岳 b. 1965)

Yuan Yue is the founder and chairman of Horizon Research Consultancy Group that conducts survey, research, and consulting services as its core businesses. Founded in 1992, Horizon Research is a leader in China that integrates data-based market research findings with consulting to provide clients customized solutions for strategic directions. Under Yuan's leadership, currently there are four companies within Horizon Research Consultancy Group: Horizon Research (full-service market research), Progress Strategy (marketing and management consulting services), Horizonkey (omnibus), and Vision (investment project selection).

Yuan was born on April 27, 1965 in Dafeng, an agricultural village in northeastern Jiangsu Province. Originally named Yuan Hao, he changed his given name to Yue as he enjoyed reading the story of a great Chinese ancient army general from the Song Dynasty named Yue Fei. Growing up in a large family, Yuan has over 10 siblings, and his father was a farmer who suffered from a critical illness. Understandably, he can only have a very humble level of lifestyle during his teenage years. In his later writings, Yuan often reflects his affection and care to those underprivileged farmers.

In 1985, Yuan received his bachelor degree from the Law School of Nanjing University. With a scholarship, he was then admitted to Southwestern University of Political Science and Law, earning a master degree in law three years later. Between 1988 and 1992, Yuan worked with the Ministry of Justice, People Republic of China. He founded the Horizon Research (market research and index studies) in 1992, Horizonkey.com (online studies) in 1999, Progress Strategy (strategic consulting) in 2000, and Vision Investment (investment consultancy) in 2002. Under Yuan's leadership, the Horizon Group became a celebrated local brand on marketing and sociology research consultancy, and was one of the first companies certificated by the State Statistical Bureau eligible for engaging international research projects in China. In 2000, Yuan went to Harvard's Kennedy School to study for his Master in Public Administration and graduated in the following year. In 2004, he received a PhD in sociology from Peking University. As the host of the popular Brain Storm TV program on the Chinese Business News (CBN), he has unique communication skills that win fans of all ages across China.

Yuan's main contribution to the Chinese economy is the establishment of Horizon Research Consultancy Group, which marks the pioneer local establishment that conducts scientific marketing research and survey with international knowledge orientation in China. Headquartered in Beijing and has branches in Shanghai, Guangzhou, and Wuhan, Horizon Group have the following key services: marketing research, public opinion poll, management consulting, financial advisory, and online survey. Horizon's clients include multinational corporations, established Chinese enterprises, Chinese governmental entities, foreign academic institutions, and United Nations. For instances, Hutchison Whampoa, Lenovo, Li Ning, China Construction Bank, BP, LG, Microsoft, Coca-Cola, World Bank, Philip, Ericsson, Shell, and Cornell University have all engaged the services of Horizon Research in recent years. In addition, Horizon Group has also conducted several topical research assignments requested by some Chinese and international organizations and corporations such as Ericsson, Motorola, China.com, and China Unicom.

Led by Yuan, the major research undertakings of Horizon Group include the followings: the study on the Chinese private economy (1992–1995), co-sponsored by the United Front Work Department of the Centre Committee of the Chinese Communist Party and All-China Federation of Industry & Commerce; the mobility study of Chinese population (1994–2000), sponsored by American funding; the psychological readiness toward inflation of China's urban occupants (1996), sponsored by China National Bureau of Statistics; the investment environment appraisal of Chinese cities (1994–1999) co-sponsored by Hong Kong and Japanese enterprises; the evaluation report of the aid projects to China by the United Nations Children's Fund (UNICEF); research on the career evolution history of Chinese cities (1992–1996) sponsored by the World Bank; and China telecommunication market research (1994–1999). Together these reports have had a profound impact on China's transition process from planned economy to market economy, as data and findings from the Horizon research projects become instrumental for key decision makers both in and outside China.

As a highly qualified individual with local and international horizons, Yuan received key appointments in some influential Chinese and global research organizations that include China Association of Market Information and Research, Beijing Technology Consulting Industry Association, European Society for Opinion and Marketing Research (ESOMAR), American Marketing Association, American Political Advisory Panels, and American Association for Asian Studies. In addition, Yuan also holds visiting academic positions at Tsinghua University, and in the Business School of Nankai University.

Apart from hosting TV programs and managing his full-time responsibilities, Yuan is also an active writer. Among others, one of his books entitled *Yuan Yue's Handbook to Youngsters* compiled many of Yuan's exciting speeches during his road shows at high schools around China. The handbook provides insights on multidimensional aspects of a youth's life such as growing up process, socialization and career management, and how young people shall manage themselves to achieve self-actualization. In his leisure time, Yuan loves to play basketball and traveling. If he would have gotten an opportunity again, he wishes that he can bring his parents to travel around the world.

LOI TECK HUI

Sources

Yuan, V. (2007), "Act locally, think globally, grow together with our clients", Horizon Research Consultancy Group, available at: http://www.horizon-china.com/Page-Node=8724.htm (accessed on 26 May 2010).

Zhou, D. (2007), "情趣袁岳", *商界时尚* ["The interests of Yuan Yue", *Bizmode*], 14 June, available at: http://www.cnbizmode.com/people/coverpeople/301.shtml (accessed 26 June 2010).

百度百科 (2010), "袁岳" ["Yuan Yue", *Baidu Encyclopedia*], available at: http://baike.baidu.com/view/801470.htm?fr=ala0_1 (accessed 26 April 2010).

海平 (2006), "话说袁岳: 生于苦艰, 所以遥远", [Hai, P., "About Yuan Yue: Because of hardship, so that he can reach far"], 1 August, available at: http://blog.sina.com.cn/s/blog_4902f91d010004gq.html (accessed 26 May 2010).

尚品人生 (2008), "真情真性真袁岳" ["Truth about Yuan Yue", *Elegant Living*], 7 August, available at: http://elegantliving.ceconline.com/ART_6000002266_390200_EL_01.HTM (accessed 26 May 2010).

Zhang, Chaoyang (Charles Zhang 张朝阳 b. 1964)

Also Known as Charles Zhang, Zhang Chaoyang is a Chinese Internet guru, businessman, investor and the founder, chairman, and current CEO of Sohu.com (NASDAQ: SOHU), the second largest Internet portal and the first Chinese-language search engine in China. A leading Internet pioneer in the country, Zhang has been named as one of the richest men in China by *Forbes*, *as* well as one of the 50 Cyber Elites by *Time* magazine in recent years.

Born to a very humble family, Zhang's parents were residential physicians at a small arsenal near Xi'an, the ancient capital in Western China. Zhang has been interested in science from a very young age. As he excelled at school, he was accepted to study physics at the prestigious Tsinghua University in Beijing. Upon graduation, Zhang received the prestigious Tsung-Dao Lee Scholarship (a prize named after the Chinese Nobel Prize winner in physics) under the China– the United States Physics Examination and Application (CUSPEA) program, and traveled to the United States in 1986 at the age of 22, with a dream of winning a Nobel Prize for himself one day.

Things have changed. After receiving his PhD in experimental physics from Massachusetts Institute of Technology (MIT) in 1993, he continued his post-doc research at MIT. A year later, Zhang was appointed by MIT provost as its Asia-Pacific region liaison officer. Sensing the growing opportunities, he returned to China in 1995 and served as the chief representative of Internet Securities Inc. (ISI) in China. Although at ISI, Zhang quickly envisioned an Internet search engine company. In 1996, he launched his own company, Internet Technologies China (ITC) with an initial investment of $225,000 funded by two professors: MIT Media Lab Director Nicholas Negroponte and Dr. Edward B. Roberts of MIT Sloan School of Management. ITC became China's first Internet company funded with venture capital.

In 1998, Zhang led ITC in developing Sohu.com, the first Chinese search engine and important Internet portal. Subsequently the company was renamed SOHU.com Inc. "Sohu" stands for "search fox" in Chinese. Listed on the NASDAQ in 2000, Sohu.com provided corporate services such as online advertisement, web site design, and technical assistance. Sohu.com also allowed its customers to shop online and send text messages from their mobile phones. The company was soon regarded as having one of the best-known brands in the Chinese Internet world.

However, during the dotcom crash in the early 2000s, Sohu's stock dropped below US$1, and as a result many board members and investors wanted to replace Zhang, but his nonconfrontational style helped him hold on. Shortly after, Internet Community blogging and short-messaging service helped the company turn around and generated total revenues of $750 million in China in 2002, which later grew to account for 48% of company's revenues in 2004 and 2006.

Now Sohu.com has become China's premier online brand and indispensable to the daily life of millions of Chinese, providing a network of web properties and community-based web 2.0 products, which offer the vast Sohu user community a broad array of choices regarding information, entertainment and communication. Under Zhang's leadership, Sohu has built one of the most comprehensive matrices of Chinese language web properties and proprietary search engines, consisting of: the mass portal and leading online media destination, sohu.com; an interactive search engine, sogou.com; number one game information portal, 17173.com; a top real estate web site, focus.cn; the best-known online alumni club, chinaren.com; a wireless value-added services provider, goodfeel.com.cn; a leading online mapping service provider, go2map.com; and a developer and operator of online games, changyou.com. Sohu's total revenues for the fiscal year 2009 were US$515.2 million, up 20% compared to 2008.

In 2010, Zhang and his team are striving to "reshape Sohu." The company's year-over-year increase in revenue was mainly driven by an advance in online game revenue and advertising revenue. Zhang sees search engine Sogou as another pillar for Sohu's revenue increase. In early 2010, citing censorship concerns, Google announced it would no longer offer Chinese language-base search services from its mainland headquarters, effectively retreating from the mainland Chinese search market. Sohu decided to carve out a niche in the market boasting more than 200 billion search requests and 10 billion RMB ($1.46 billion) in revenue annually, Sohu updated its Sogou Pinyin, input software that facilitates fast and convenient input of Chinese into computer documents, to the latest 5.0 version. The new version, embedded with Sogou's search technologies, is supposed to help the search engine intelligently analyze the behaviors of Internet users while composing texts online.

The launch of Sogou Pinyin 5.0 helps expand the company's share of the search engine market on Mainland China.

Zhang is very outspoken person, often commenting on government policies and providing different voices in the country, ranging from intellectual property protection to economic reform in China. Along with being a technology entrepreneur, Zhang also has a colorful life and is an avid outdoorsman and environmentalist. Never married, Zhang is said to enjoy himself appearing in public and showcasing his success. In front of the Beijing Modern Plaza, he stepped into a pair of roller blades with a group of teenagers to promote a new Sohu product. He was also featured on the cover of a *Men's Health China* magazine, and is one of the first entrepreneurs in China to own a yacht. Zhang also enjoys mountain climbing. In May 2003, he joined the SOHU-sponsored China Mount Everest team to a height of 6666 meters in an expedition celebrating the 50th anniversary of human conquest of the tallest mountain on earth.

For his contribution to the Internet and information technology development, Zhang has received numerous honors. He was named as one of the Time Digital Cyber Elite Top 50 by *Time* in 1998, listed as one of the Top Ten Information Technology Men of the Year by *China Youth Daily* from 1999 to 2001, and selected as a cover figure by *Asia Week* in 1997. In addition, *Fortune* named Zhang one of the Top 25 New Corporate Stars in 2001, and in July 2003 *Time* also featured him as one of the15 Global Tech Gurus. Besides being recognized by the World Economic Forum as a Global Leader of Tomorrow, in December 2001, upon the invitation of former US Secretary of State Madeleine K. Albright, Zhang joined the international Advisory Board of the Pew Global Attitudes Survey as an inaugural member.

WEIDONG ZHANG

Sources

China Vitae (2009), "Zhang Chaoyang", available at: http://www.chinavitae.com/biography/Zhang_Chaoyang/bio (accessed 4 June 2010).

Huang, L. J. (2009), "Zhang, Chaoyang", in: Zhang, W. X. and Alon, I. (eds), *Biographical Dictionary of New Chinese Entrepreneurs and Business Leaders*, Cheltenham, UK: Edward Elgar, pp. 239–240.

Sohu (2010), "Charles Zhang, Chairman", available at: http://corp.sohu.com/20090617/n264590183.shtml (accessed 4 June 2010).

Sohu (2010), "Company profile", available at: http://corp.sohu.com/companyprofile-en.shtml (accessed 4 June 2010).

Zhang, Fan (Jack Zhang 张帆 b. 1970)

Founder of Zhanzuo.com and eYou Corporation, Zhang Fan has his thumb on the pulse of the Chinese university scene. Both of his companies cater to the communication needs of the university environment, eYou as a provider of email and related software systems and Zhanzuo as a social networking site for university students. It's no surprise that Zhang has done well with his target market; he grew up on Chinese campuses as the son of two university professors. Zhang believes universities are the market with the highest potential in China, but that is not the only reason he finds this demographic appealing: with users who are young, passionate, and full of enthusiasm about the future, Zhang confesses that they are what keep him energized.

Zhang has a rational and calm demeanor, yet he favors fast cars, competitive golfing, and rock climbing. His rugged good looks hint at his healthy vigor, and he tells of his transformation from a wild youth of drag racing to a more reasonable adult pace that focuses on inner contentment. He recounts with fond nostalgia his purchase of a classic American sports car with the first money he earned in the United States, which he drove half way across the nation on a classic American road trip. Those who know him well claim that he can see opportunities that others do not, a visionary by nature.

Born in Xi'an in 1970, Zhang spent his formative years growing up on college campuses in China but left the country in 1991 to follow his own educational pursuits, completing a bachelor degree at the University of Minnesota before attending Yale for an MBA. Zhang also worked at Harvard in a genetics lab for five years, an experience that provided a stepping-stone into the field of high-tech entrepreneurship. In 1999, Zhang started a software business in Boston focused on email systems, a precursor to his return to China and subsequent founding of eYou.

With a rich American education, epic American road trips, a fortunate introduction to high-tech entrepreneurship, and nearly 10 years in the States behind him, Zhang returned to his homeland to start eYou, a software provider focused on universities and enterprises in China. Starting with the school market before expanding to the mass market, it took some time to get the product right and lay the groundwork in its brand and customer base. Nevertheless, after the initial struggles, eYou enjoyed quick growth with high-profit margins. The company has appeared on the list of the top 50 fastest growing high-tech companies in China and one of the top 500 in Asia. Within six years of its inception, nearly 80% of China's large enterprises and more than 800 colleges and government agencies were using eYou products, including Tsinghua University, Zhejiang University, and the National People's Congress.

Zhang's initial success with eYou fostered the creation of Zhanzuo in 2006, China's leading social networking service focused on college students, utilizing his experience and knowledge of the university market. The name Zhanzuo refers to grabbing a seat, a term used in a classroom among students. On Zhanzuo.com users write blogs, post photos and updates, and stay in contact with friends. The site is similar to Facebook but falls within the necessary Internet compliance regulations in China. In fact, Facebook's frequent inaccessibility in China has provided room for growth of Zhanzuo and its regional competitors.

In 2007, Zhanzuo acquired www.yoolin.com, the largest website in the world for Chinese students studying abroad. Yoolin has kept its name and functionality intact as an overseas division of Zhanzuo, making the parent company the biggest communication platform for all Chinese students, whether at home or abroad.

Zhanzuo is also growing among the young professional demographic. Once they were hooked as college students, those habits are not likely to disappear after college when it becomes both more difficult to stay in touch with college friends as well as even more important for the sake of building career connections.

In China's unique cultural atmosphere for Internet-based social networking, Zhanzuo has huge potential. Its history backs this up. Zhanzuo surpassed one million users in just a few short months, and hit seven million in its second year. In China's one-child-family households, connecting with others over the Internet plays an important social role. With no siblings, they need their friends all the more – and they are likely to find them on Zhanzuo. According to Zhang's views, social networking has greater potential and significance for young adults in China than in the United States, since China's youth typically do not have institutions like church or sports groups that can bring them together outside the classroom. In fact, studies show that 30% of young adults in the United States use the Internet to make friends, the number is closer to 75% for Chinese young adults (Lee, 2008). The Internet has become a vital communication tool for this generation.

The purpose of Zhanzuo is to maximize people's communication, an especially important need as society is drawn deeper into technological interaction instead of face-to-face interaction. Zhang is passionate about his business, not just because of the product itself, but because of the way it can help individuals meet some of their deepest needs. Zhang feels that online communities such as those on Zhanzuo give the Chinese the vital spiritual support they need that comes through social connection.

It is perhaps Zhang's passion for the purpose behind his product that has made Zhanzuo so successful. Zhanzuo is the most popular real-name social networking service in China, and the firm has received multiple awards and recognitions for its growth, brand, and performance since the inception. In 2007, Zhang was recognized for his contributions to the field as one of the top 100 most influential in Internet-related enterprise.

BARBARA L. STROTHER

Sources

Clark, D. and Zhang, J. (2008), "Can we educate entrepreneurs?" Going Global Conference, December 3-5, British Council, available at: http://www.britishcouncil.org/goingglobal-gg3-proceedings-4b.htm (accessed 22 July 2010).

Lee, E. (2008), "China's young people connect online", *San Francisco Gate*, 4 August, available at: http://articles.sfgate.com/2008-08-04/business/17121816_1_social-networking-china-s-internet-one-child-per-family-policy (accessed 22 July 2010).

中国新闻人网 (2009), "张帆: 占座网CEO" ["Zhang Fan: Zhanzuo Net CEO", China News Network], 23 May, available at: http://renwu.xinwenren.com/2009/0523/2216.html (accessed 22 July 2010).

Zhang, Fan (张帆 b. 1972)

Known as an "entrepreneur behind the entrepreneurs," Zhang Fan is a private investor and former founder of Sequoia Capital China. Along with Shen Nanpeng (Neil Shen), Zhang co-founded Sequoia Capital China, and was named one of the "Top 10 Most Active Venture Capitalists" in 2004 and 2005 by zero2ipo Group, the leading venture capital consulting and research firm in China, and in 2006 was selected as one of the "Top Venture Capitalists in China" by *Forbes*.

Born in Jiangsu Province but grown up in Shijiazhuang, Zhang's childhood was relatively unadventurous. A dedicated student, he consistently excelled in schools, and later developed a keen interest in computer science while at Tsinghua University. In 1992, during his third year at Tsinghua, his university life in China was interrupted by his family's decision to move to San Francisco, USA. While in the US, his first job as a waiter did not last even a day. After three jobs in three months, he found a minimum wage position at a photo lab. Realizing that he could be more than a good technician, Zhang decided to attend a local community college at night, during which he studied English literature, philosophy, American history and politics. "Failure is the foundation for success," he emphasized. Through multiple setbacks and bitter taste of unemployment, he learned empathy and humility. Zhang later conceded that he would not be a good venture capitalist without being sympathetic, considerate and appreciative of the immeasurable pressure the entrepreneurs felt during the startup and IPO phases.

Zhang was keenly aware that education was the only viable way for him to move forward. With credit transfer for courses taken at the community college and Tsinghua, Stanford University offered him a full scholarship in economics. Soon after, his three-month summer internship at Smith Barney in New York exposed him to what would be a brand new chapter of his life, the capital market. As a trainee, he provided market analysis to the portfolio managers, many of whom worked more than 12 hours a day. Upon graduation from Stanford, Zhang joined the Investment Banking Division as a financial analyst at Goldman Sachs Asia, a major firm with a long-standing relationship with many local governments and successful investment deals in China, Singapore, the Philippines, and Australia. Greatly benefiting from this experience in the investment arena, Zhang learned that finance was not only one of the cores of a modern enterprise, its accessibility was also imperative for future growth of a company. Since at the time China did not have any large international corporations, Zhang realized that small and medium size enterprises in China would need investment financing to boost their growth globally.

Living in Hong Kong after the 1997 takeover, he witnessed the continuing boom throughout major cities in China. Many fundamental changes began to take place at large Chinese corporations, such as China Offshore Oil Service, which was listed successfully on the NYSE. Despite Goldman Sachs' ideal platform for learning M&A and financial transactions, Zhang returned to Stanford to pursue an MBA, which became yet another turning point in his life, where he met Tim Draper, the founder of DFJ (Draper Fisher Jurvetson ePlanet Ventures). Over the span of its

20 years history, DFJ has invested over 200 companies including Hotmail, Overture and Skype. In 2001, Zhang joined DFJ as the vice president of Asia and established DFJ Beijing office, focusing on foreign direct investment in China.

To his surprise, the path to recovery from the Internet Bubble was tougher than expected, as share prices for once successful Internet portals such as Sina, Sohu, and Netease dropped to US$1 and many Chinese Internet websites disappeared overnight. Some venture capitalists and investors counted their losses and returned home empty handed. However, a contrarian Zhang foresaw decades of prosperities and opportunities in this down market. Having witnessed the enthusiasm in the entrepreneurs and employees in many Chinese startups across China, he was confident of his decision, given majority of his investment decision lied on the entrepreneurs – their leadership, tenacity, dedication, expertise, perseverance and ability to attract and retain talents. By chance, Zhang met two entrepreneurs who founded ChinaRen, which was later sold to Sohu. Those entrepreneurs' dynamics, technical knowledge, and business propositions were so compelling, Zhang lobbied DFJ to invest US$800,000 in KongZhong Net, a leading Internet and mobile service content provider. In two and a half years, KongZhong completed its IPO successfully on the NASDAQ, generating a return of 25 times for DFJ's initial investment.

Unlike the return on investment in Silicon Valley that often hinged on the startup's innovative technology or competitive business model, Zhang believed the opportunities in the Chinese market were centered around perceived value-add for its existing consumers. After Softbank provided the first round of financing to Focus Media Zhang joined Dinghui Venture Capital, TDF and Milestone Capital etc., in investing a total US$12.5 million and US$30 million in Focus Media in the second and third rounds of capital financing. A year later, Focus Media became the first Chinese "media" firm to successfully list on the NASDAQ. It raised US$172 million, returning another 20 multiples for DFJ.

As the saying goes, like attracts like. During Focus Media's financing frenzy, Zhang got acquainted with Neil Shen, an individual investor who also founded Ctrip.com, the so-called Expedia of China and Home Inns and Hotels Management. The well-respected Shen and confident Zhang decided to co-launch a venture capital firm with a primary focus on Chinese companies. Upon approaching the well-established venture capital firm, Sequoia Capital in Silicon Valley, they set their first criterion in autonomous decision making. Sequoia Capital, a firm that had a global network and 30 years of capital financing successes such as Apple, Cisco, Yahoo, PayPal, Oracle and Google, agreed to their terms. In August 2005, Sequoia Capital China was born, with Zhang and Shen being Limited Partners (LP) in the first round of capital funding. The other LPs consisted of an impressive list from university endowment funds and renowned foundations such as Rockefeller, Carnegie, and Ford. The first round of US$200 million was raised in less than two months.

Shortly after he co-founded Sequoia Capital China, Zhang invested in Asia Media Company, which in 2007 became the first Chinese company to be listed on the Tokyo Stock Exchange. Under Zhang's leadership, Sequoia Capital China had invested in more than 50 companies in the technology, insurance, agricultural and automotive industries that include Youshi net, Qihu net, Dazhong net, 51.COM, Zhanzuo net, and HongMoong Cartoon. Since Zhang's resignation in early 2009, Neil Shen reins Sequoia Capital China to date. However, is this the beginning of an end for Zhang? Now a private investor, the venture capital world continues to monitor his "next big move."

KIRSTY S. F. TAN

Sources

Chen, G. (2009), "Sequoia Capital China founding partner Zhang resigns", *Reuters*, 2 February, available at: http://www.reuters.com/article/idUSHKG27937920090202 (accessed 30 April 2010).

Lacy, S. (2009), "Is Sequoia China in trouble?" *TechCrunch*, 15 May, available at: http://techcrunch.com/2009/05/15/is-sequoia-china-in-trouble/#ixzz0mu6hwDvI (accessed 1 May 2010).

Wang, H. (2010), "Chinese returnees: Impact on China's modernization & globalization", Brookings Institute, 6 April.

邢学军 (2007), "张帆: 红杉中国梦想者", *财富裂变: 10位海归风险投资翘楚* (王辉耀主编), 中国发展出版社, 北京 [Xing, X, "Zhang Fan: Dreamer of Sequoia China", in Wang, H. (ed.), *Wealth Creation: Ten Overseas Returnees in Venture Capital Investment*, China Development Press, Beijing], pp. 128–154.

Zhang, Hongjiang (张宏江 b. 1960)

As Microsoft's chief technology officer of Asia-Pacific R&D Group and director of Microsoft Asia Academy of Engineering, Dr. Zhang Hongjiang is responsible for technology, products, business development, strategy, and innovation, especially in the emerging markets of China. Under his leadership, Microsoft Asia Academy of Engineering has more than 400 technology experts, and leads product development in Internet technology, mobile technology, and digital entertainment.

Zhang was born in Yexian County, Henan Province. In 1977, he and his elder brother were admitted to universities at the same time, which became a major news item in his small hometown. At that time, he attended Zhengzhou University and worked on his bachelor degree in electrical engineering. As the youngest student in his class, Zhang enjoyed all kinds of sports activities, and he was especially good at basketball and long-distance running. Despite his engineering major, whenever he had time, he went to the library and read books on literature and history. All the knowledge he learned during the four years of college helped him develop a strong interest in science and the scientific way of thinking. Through searching the library collections, he also became very interested in bibliographic classification, which determined his future research direction.

Upon graduating with his BS degree, Zhang started to work in a national electronics research institution located in Shijiazhuang, Hebei Province. The organization has more than 4000 research staff members and an outstanding record in high-level scientific research on defense communication. Zhang devoted himself to his work assignment and soon made impressive contribution to the development of China's first two sets of road microwave communication system, an achievement highly regarded by the leadership team at the research institution he worked.

Because of his outstanding performance, after four years of work in Shijiazhuang, Zhang was recommended to go to Denmark Technology University for two years of advance study. Because of his hard work there, he was directly admitted into a PhD program during the second year of his graduate study. After careful consideration, Zhang selected remote-sensing image processing as his research concentration. Since then, he started his journey in image processing and content-based video retrieval, and eventually became a renowned expert in the field.

After five years study in Europe, Zhang left Denmark and went to the National University of Singapore to join the System Science Institute. In the early 1990s, with the popularization and application of a large number of computers and modern computer technology, multimedia technology became a hot topic. However, researchers struggled to create an effective multimedia search system that would help people quickly find the information they need. Recognized the importance of this issue, Zhang devoted himself to find a solution. After numerous attempts in design and testing, he proposed a new method for multimedia searching, and in 1993 published the first paper in this field in *Multimedia Systems Journal*, which established the foundation for the development of modern video search technology. A year later, he summarized his research outcomes and co-authored the *Video and Multimedia Systems in Image Processing* with two other scholars. Published in 1995, the book was the first scholarly work in the field and had a significant impact on future research. Zhang did not stop there. Based on the theory, he further developed a system used for video classification. Consequently, Eastman Kodak, Intel Corporation, Singapore International Science Research Institute, Singapore Television Company, and Digital River Company all purchased his patent and applied the technology to a wide range of product research and development practices.

After more than three years in Singapore, Zhang was attracted by the rapid advancement in computer technology and software development in Silicon Valley. Therefore, in 1995 he left for the United States, where he worked in the HP Lab as a research manager, responsible for multimedia content retrieval and management, intelligent image processing and video coding research projects. In 1997, he developed a new technology in video image analysis. Specifically, he proposed a machine-learning method, using the relevance feedback principle, which significantly improved the efficiency of content-based image retrieval method. Within three years, Zhang won 10 patents and successfully transferred them to the products. For his impressive accomplishment, at the end of 1998, he was invited as the technical committee chairman in the ACM (Association for Computing Machinery) Multimedia World Conference, the first Chinese to hold the position.

It was a sunny Saturday afternoon, after a week of intense work, the whole family went out to have some fun and relax. Zhang rent one Chinese TV series, *Deep Love*, and went home and started to watch them; suddenly he found he could not put them down. In the next couple of days, he watched more than 30 episodes. The program brought him such a shock. After so many years of life overseas, he became a stranger of his beloved homeland. Realized great changes taking place in China in the past decades, he was deeply attracted by the familiar accent and modern urban living in China, which he did not experience for a very long time. Two months later, when Microsoft set up its new research institute in Beijing, Zhang decided to return to China and contribute his effort to his country after living 15 years overseas. Back in Beijing in 1999, he managed a team of talented staff and focused on the use of Internet search engines for Chinese and multimedia-based resources. Soon he developed a new generation of intelligent, content-based video browser, which enabled real-time, automatic cataloging of news television programs, and searching and editing large amounts of information within shortest possible time.

Because of his outstanding research contribution in video and image content analysis, retrieval and browsing method, Dr. Zhang Hongjiang has been regarded as a pioneer and expert in the world of multimedia analysis. He was also recognized by the International Computer Association and the Institute of Electrical and Electronics Engineering (IEEE). As a leader in software development, Zhang was named an "Outstanding Asian-American engineer" in 2008. Besides holding more than 60 US patents, he has also published four academic books, more than 350 academic papers and 10 editorial articles in the field of media, Internet, and multimedia content retrieval, and many of his research studies have become classic references and applied to the relevant fields.

JING BAI

Sources

百度百科 (2010), "张宏江" ["Zhang Hongjiang", *Baidu.com*], available at: http://www.baike.baidu.com/view/287569.htm (accessed 21 July 2010).

IT人 (2009), "张宏江" ["Zhang Hongjiang", *IteeR*], available at: http://www.iteer.net/modules/people/singlelink.php?lid=1560 (accessed 21 July 2010).

微软中国研究院 (2001), "微软张宏江博士的故事", ["Story of Dr. Zhang Hongjiang", Microsoft Research China], available at: http://www.cad.zju.edu.cn/chinagraph/chinese/FreeTALK/Freetalk_ZhangHJstory.htm (accessed 21 July 2010).

Zhang, Lan (张兰 b. 1958)

Zhang Lan is the founder of one of China's most successful restaurant chains, South Beauty. As board chairperson and CEO of the South Beauty Group, Zhang aims to make her Sichuan cuisine the Louis Vuitton of Chinese food (Gong, 2008). Her bold decision in 2000 to create a luxury brand of Chinese food in China veered sharply away from tradition, but over the last decade Zhang has strategically maneuvered her way into the hearts and stomachs of China's business elite. In 2006, Zhang was named one of the Ten Most Influential Entrepreneurs in China's Food and Beverage Industry and one of the Top Ten Business Executives in China. In 2008, the *Wall Street Journal* listed Zhang as one of the Ten Women to Watch in Asia. One year later, Zhang was awarded one of the ten coveted spots on The Honor Roll of China Elite Business Women list, jointly issued by more than 100 Chinese and international media sources with feedback from the general public. The Honor Roll is highly regarded by the business world, reflecting a model for businesswomen in terms of corporate philanthropy, social responsibility, public influence, and leadership in commerce, among other things.

Zhang's ambition and conscientiousness – characteristics that have certainly contributed to her business success – were fostered as she navigated a difficult childhood in Beijing. Due to the political climate of the time, she grew up without her father, a university professor; by the time Zhang was born, her father had been shamed as a rightist and was forced to live in a shed (Newcomb, 2005). Ten years later, her mother, a public official, was labeled an intellectual, so they were relocated to the Hubei countryside for "reeducation" and very challenging living conditions. Today Zhang believes that these experiences provided her the determination to overcome obstacles along her career path.

First, Zhang pursued higher education, graduating from Beijing Technology and Business University in 1987 with a degree in business administration. Two years later, she moved to Canada, where she continued her studies and worked at a cousin's restaurant in Toronto's Chinatown. She eventually saved $20,000 and made the life-changing decision to return to China, starting her own business and investing in China's future. In 1991, Zhang opened her first restaurant, called A Lan Restaurant – a small Beijing restaurant seating 96 people. At the time, few Chinese women owned their own business, but Zhang completely recouped her investment within three months of opening. She realized that this line of work suited her well. Even before founding South Beauty, Zhang was always focused on changing people's minds about food. She notes, "At the time, not that many people were eating out. People were quite conservative in their concept of dining. So I focused on the cleanliness of the restaurant and the quality of the dishes. That was a big difference from others" (Newcomb, 2005).

The growing success of A Lan Restaurant enabled Zhang to save six million yuan ($877,000) in order to open her first South Beauty restaurant in 2000. Zhang not only bet on the idea of a luxury restaurant brand in a country where this was uncommon, but she also selected one of Beijing's most upscale and expensive buildings – the China World Trade Center – as the site for this restaurant. Zhang was confident that her gamble would pay off, saying, "What we promote is not meals, but a culture" (Gong, 2008). Although South Beauty is known as the best Sichuan cuisine restaurant in China, Zhang believes it was the culture of South Beauty – "the perfect combination of space and art, classics and extravagance" (All-China Women's Federation, 2007) – which helped her cultivate such a strong following among businesspeople and expatriates. As she notes, "Chinese cuisine offers everything, including nutrition and taste, but what has been lacking is the packaging. People in China didn't know how to present the food. I have changed that" (*Ibid*).

Zhang has also revolutionized restaurant service in China. She mandates a rigorous three-month training program for all wait staff, requiring them to master tasks such as setting a table within three minutes. Restaurant managers – some of whom are hired from McDonalds, Coca-Cola, and other international companies in order to benefit from their expertise of the global market – face two years of on-the-job training, and Zhang incentivizes them to do well. The best performers receive a car as well as the opportunity to earn an executive MBA at Changjiang University in Beijing – where Zhang herself completed the executive MBA in 2006. Zhang also sends top managers to tour restaurants in Europe, the United States and Asia for two weeks per year, with the aim of comparing service levels and bringing back fresh ideas.

It is this combination of global quality and Chinese style that contributed to the growth of South Beauty since the early 2000s. Zhang began to expand past Beijing, opening new South Beauty restaurants in Shanghai and Chengdu. In 2006, South Beauty was named a "Future Star of 2006 – one of China's mid-sized companies with the most potential." Zhang wanted to realize this potential, establishing the South Beauty Management company in 2006 to facilitate franchise operations. In 2007, South Beauty officially became a "China Well-known Trademark"; it is the only Chinese catering service with international legal protection.

For the past few years, Zhang has been working to make South Beauty an internationally recognized brand. She has accomplished this goal. Today there are nearly 50 South Beauty restaurants in 15 cities, including Jakarta, Indonesia, and within the next two years, South Beauty will be in London, Zurich, and Moscow. Zhang has her eye on New York, Paris, and Milan as well, noting, "We really want to be the number one Chinese restaurant brand, so we will focus on quality over quantity. We are not willing to do 10 to 30 restaurants in New York, but for that one project we do, the focus will be on high-end quality and culture" (Robertson, 2010).

In addition to increasing the number of South Beauty restaurants, Zhang also wants to increase the number of brands she offers to consumers. Currently, she has three brands in the South Beauty Group: South Beauty, LAN Club, and SUBU. LAN Club, the most premier brand, opened in Beijing in 2006 as an ultra-chic, exclusive restaurant and lounge designed by the world famous Philippe Starck; LAN Club Shanghai opened in 2008. SUBU, which caters to a young, style-conscious clientele, opened in Beijing in 2007; it offers futuristic modern style and healthy fusion cuisine. Zhang is considering new brands to attract the weight-conscious, among other groups.

Yet Zhang has not stopped there. She has also focused on catering opportunities for South Beauty. Since 2007, South Beauty has provided meals for select Air France and KLM Royal Dutch Airlines flights. At the Beijing Olympics in 2008, South Beauty catered to 31 Olympic venues. It is performing the same function at the 2010 Shanghai World Expo. In 2012, South Beauty will be providing Chinese food at the London Olympics.

With all these endeavors, an outsider might wonder whether Zhang is overextended. Yet Zhang is known for her keen understanding of the food and beverage industry; as she notes, "knowledge is power" (Newcomb, 2005). She has also kept South Beauty Group in great financial shape; it is completely free of any loans or debts. In exchange for selling a small stake (less than 10%) of the restaurant chain, Zhang negotiated an investment of 300 million yuan in 2008 from a private equity fund and a mainland investment bank, which she is using to accelerate the expansion of South Beauty in foreign markets. Setting her sights on the global market, Zhang confidently remarks, "Isn't it great to expose the whole world to the charms of Chinese food?" (Shu, 2006).

TONIA WARNECKE

Sources

All-China Women's Federation (2007), "Zhang Lan: a successful restaurant owner who loves Chinese cuisine", available at: http://www.womenofchina.cn/Profiles/Businesswomen/17354.jsp (accessed 16 June 2010).

Chao, L. (2009), "Zhang isn't dismayed by economic downturn", *Wall Street Journal*, 28 January, available at: http://online.wsj.com/article/SB123308840845720949.html (accessed 16 June 2010).

Chen, Q. (2008), "South Beauty receives 300 million yuan investment", *Caijing Magazine*, 17 December, available at: http://english.caijing.com.cn/2008-12-17/110039888.html (accessed 13 June 2010).

Gong, Y. (2008), "A tale of two restaurants", available at: http://www.china-embassy.org/eng/zt/t515971.htm (accessed 16 June 2010).

Jing Daily (2010), "South Beauty's plan for global (culinary) domination", 27 May, available at: http://www.jingdaily.com/en/luxury/south-beauty-plans-19-restaurants-globally-in-next-two-years/ (accessed 10 June 2010).

Liao, J. (2009), "Zhang Lan, President of South Beauty", interview available at: http://english.cri.cn/4406/2009/03/13/1701s464170.htm (accessed 4 April 2010).

Newcomb, A. (2005), "Four women who shape Beijing", *Christian Science Monitor*, 16 August, available at: http://www.csmonitor.com/2005/0816/p10s01-woap.html (accessed 13 April 2010).

Robertson, B. (2006), "Dishing it out", *Forbes*, 13 November, available at: http://www.forbes.com/global/2006/1113/098.html (accessed 17 June 2010).

Shu, S. (2006), "First person: Zhang Lan", *SH Magazine*, 1 December, available at: http://www.shmag.cn/feature/first_person_zhang_lan (accessed 16 June 2010).

Zhang, Ligang (Lee Zhang 张黎刚 b. 1971)

Also known as Lee Zhang, Zhang Ligang is the chairman and CEO of iKang Guobin Healthcare Group, one of the largest healthcare management companies in China. As a successful entrepreneur and businessman, he has also been the head of several successful websites such as eLong.com.

Born to an ordinary peasant family in Jiangyin County, Jiangsu Province, Zhang in 1988 passed the national college entrance examination and was admitted into the elite Fudan University in Shanghai majoring in biology. At Fudan, Zhang concentrated on improving his English skills, with a clear goal of going to the United States for his graduate studies. However, in a measure to curb the low returning rate of Chinese students overseas at the time, the central government issued a policy that only allowed those to go abroad with a five or more years of service requirement after receiving their undergraduate degrees. Unwavering by the policy change, Zhang promptly withdrew from Fudan during his junior year, and went to the United States and enrolled in Concordia College, a liberal arts institution in Minnesota. There, Zhang washed dishes in the school cafeteria and earned his Bachelor of Arts in biochemistry in 1992. He then worked at the Medical School of Columbia University as a research associate while applying for graduate studies.

After three attempts and bypassing a full scholarship offer from another institution, Zhang made into Harvard University, where he eventually received his master degree in biomedical science in 2001. Although everything proceeded smoothly in his academic work, Zhang was soon emotionally disturbed. During the 1996 Summer Olympic Games in Atlanta, he and many other Chinese students were offended by a casual remark from a NBC commentator, who implied a wide usage of banned substance among Chinese athletes. With rediscovered love for his homeland, Zhang organized a large initiative that raised funds among Chinese students from Harvard, Stanford, UC Berkeley and others schools across the country to publish a full-page ad in both *New York Times* and *Washington Post*, criticizing the irresponsible behavior of the NBC reporter. This event had a profound impact on him, and helped Zhang make the decision to return to China after his study. During his time at Harvard, Zhang also founded the *Harvard China Review*, a nonprofit organization that produces journal publications and sponsors conference series dedicated to issues involving China. This venture marked the start of his entrepreneurial career.

Although pursuing a PhD in genetics at Harvard Medical School, he befriended Charles Zhang, the founder of Sohu.com, who received his PhD from MIT in the 1990s. Through this personal connection, Zhang worked for Sohu.com as the head of product development, and helped develop Sohu.com into a major portal for China. His experience at Sohu.com inspired him to create his own website. For him, Internet revolution has created many unprecedented opportunities for those who had vision to spot them and the courage to seize the moment. If others can do it, be believed he could as well. To pursue this passion, he withdrew from Harvard, the school he worked so hard to get into, and moved back to Beijing in 1998.

A year later, Zhang created eLong.com with three other partners, which has since become a leading online travel service company in China. Headquartered in Beijing, eLong soon developed a national presence across China, and used web-based distribution technologies and a 24-hour call center to provide consumers with travel information and booking services. Targeting the rising middle-class in China, eLong aimed to deliver value and worry-free booking services to leisure and business travelers, empowering consumers to make informed decisions by providing convenient online and offline hotel and air ticket booking services as well as travel tools such as maps, destination guides, photographs, virtual tours and user reviews. The success of eLong.com quickly attracted buyers such as Expedia.com and Mail.com, a US messaging service company. With Zhang retained as CEO, Mail.com and Expedia.com acquired eLong.com in 2002 for over US$65.2 million. Since 2004, it has been listed on NASDAQ (long). Today the company holds a selection of more than 11,200 hotels in over 470 cities across China, eLong also offers consumers the ability to make bookings at over 100,000 international hotels in more than 100 countries worldwide, and can fulfill domestic and international air ticket reservations in over 80 major cities across China.

With a biomedical background and a successful Internet venture under his belt, Zhang set out to change the world. To improve healthcare in China, he envisioned an integration of information technology with healthcare service. His next venture was iKang Healthcare, "China's largest private and independent full-service healthcare management services company," designed to improve "medical care and quality of life in China (ePlanet Ventures, n.d.)." In 2005, a merger between iKang Healthcare and Guobin Physical Checkups Service occurred, resulting in the current iKang Guobin Healthcare Group. Under iKang is a network of affiliated hospitals and medical centers in Beijing, Shanghai, Guangzhou, and Shenzhen. The services in which iKang is involved include health insurance coverage, medical management, individual health screenings, and primary care. It also participates as a third-party administration service for large corporations in China.

In 2008, ChinaCare Group, the only international healthcare consulting firm in mainland China, signed a management contract with Bayley and Jackson Medical Center, a private, for-profit health center in Beijing. Bayley and Jackson are owned by iKang and offers services such as family medicine, dentistry, ophthalmology, and pediatrics. The vision of this contract is to create a highly reputable medical center that competes with international standards of quality healthcare (Jia, 2008). With the pleasant ambience of a traditional Chinese courtyard, the newly acquired medical facility is designed to ensure a comfortable and relaxing patient experience in a caring and friendly environment at all times. As chairman of the Board of Bayley and Jackson, Zhang is excited to see what the future may bring.

JENNIFER CROSSMAN AND WENXIAN ZHANG

Sources

Bayley & Jackson Medical Center (2007), "Board of Management: Lee Ligang Zhang", available at: http://www.bjhealthcare.com/aboutour_05.html (accessed 12 April 2010).

ePlanet Ventures (2008), "ePlanet Venture invests in iKang", 28 January, available at: http://www.chinaretailnews.com/2008/01/30/1013-eplanet-ventures-invests-in-chinas-ikang/ (accessed 12 April 2010).

Jia, X. (2008), "ChinaCare Group announces management contract", *ChinaCare Group*, available at: http://www.chinacaregroup.com/publications/PressReleases/Feb08CCG.html (accessed 12 April 2010).

WRSACC 2005 Committee (2005), available at: http://www.2005committee.org/english.php/member/ls/849 (accessed 12 April 2010).

百度百科 (2010), "张黎刚" ["Zhang Ligang", *Baidu.com*], available at: http://baike.baidu.com/view/807947.html?fromTaglist (accessed 26 July 2010).

Zhang, Weiying (张维迎 b. 1959)

Dr. Zhang Weiying is an Oxford-trained economist and a reformist administrator of the Guanghua (Reviving China) School of Management at Peking University, the oldest and most prestigious university in China. A disciple of American economist Milton Friedman (1912–2006), Zhang has written a dozen books on ownership, incentives and corporate governance, promoting marketization in terms of "citizens advancing while the state retreating." A professor of economics known for his rejection of Keynesianism, Zhang has participated in China's transitional policy-making and is credited as the first to introduce the emergent dual-track price system reform in 1984. As executive associate dean (1999–2006) and now dean (2006–), Zhang was the chief designer behind Peking University's 2003 faculty retention system reform. He has instituted a radical reformist agenda since 1999, ending decades of academic inbreeding practices in the Guanghua School of Management, but the restructuring has also earned him wrath from his colleagues.

Born into a poor peasant family in Shaanxi Province in 1959, Zhang graduated from the Xi'an-based Northwestern University with a BA and MA in economics in 1982 and in 1984, respectively. Afterwards, he was employed as a research fellow at the Economic System Reform Institute of China, an institution under direct control of the then State Council Office for Restructuring the Economic System (SCORES), predecessor of the National Development and Reform Commission. There as a junior economist heavily involved in the nation's economic transitional policy-making, Zhang spent the "most exciting" five years of his life (Chen and Fu, 2007). He briefly studied at Oxford University as a visiting student from October 1987 to December 1988, and then returned to Oxford two years later on a World Bank scholarship to study under Nobel Laureate Sir James Alexander Mirrlees. He received his MPhil in economics in 1992 and PhD in economics in 1994. Upon return from Oxford in 1994, he served as associate professor at Peking University and co-founded the China Center for Economic Research (CCER).

Zhang has maintained an impressive record of publications, mostly in Chinese. His numerous papers have appeared in top Chinese and international economic journals including *Economic Research Journal*, *Journal of Reform*, *Journal of Economic Behavior and Organization*, and *Journal of Comparative Economics*. He has published a dozen books on China's transition and economic principles, including the recent *Logic of the Market* (2010), *Thirty Years of Chinese Reform* (2008), *Price, Market and Entrepreneurship* (2006), *Ownership, Incentives and Corporate Governance* (2005), and the *Entrepreneurial-Contractual Theory of the Firm* (1995).

As is well known, the pursuit of "industrialization" of Chinese education has resulted in an unfortunate hybrid of daily institutional operation following both outdated government planning and market-oriented approaches. The coexistence of the dual mechanism has caused considerable distortion in students' academic careers, from recruitment to education to graduation. As a senior administrator, Zhang is critical of the internal contradictions within China's higher-education system and has been an enthusiast of radical reform in Peking University and elsewhere. His popular 2004 book *Logic of the University* detailed a vision for quality education while mapping out rationales for reforming lifetime employment in China's universities.

Zhang is considered daring and forthright, and occasionally controversial. As a graduate student, his first article, "Rectifying the Name for Money" appeared in 1983's *China Youth Daily*. At that time, few in China dared to publicly declare faith in a market-based economy; accordingly, this piece earned Zhang national condemnation (Mao, 2009). Twenty years later, his comment that "government officials suffered most material loss in Chinese reform" made him infamous overnight. Other remarks such as "the fundamental premise of reform is to respect the vested interests" and "poor people can't afford university because the tuition is too low" won him the outrageous title "a spokesman for power and money." These and other notorious statements are widely accessible online under "Zhang Weiying Quotations." However, Zhang is on record that his original meanings were distorted by the media.

Still controversial, he is bold in his criticism of the current system. On a recent Sino-Swedish Forum held in May 2010, Zhang lamented the deterioration of quality education by concluding that today's higher education in China is worse than it was 60 years ago. According to Zhang, the current faculty management system needed to be reformed due to the deep-rooted problems of academic inbreeding, a distorted tenure system, and weak links between faculty research and enterprises. According to Zhang, problems under the current educational system include the student "products" of higher education lack adequate humanity edification, the flawed multiple-choice-with-only-one-correct-answer approach to examinations and education evaluation, and a coupling of those with the communist education of "unifying thoughts" treatment. In his view, these entire negative attributes work together to curb students' creativity.

Known for his research on enterprise theory and entrepreneurship studies, Professor Zhang has taught courses on Theory of the Firm, Managerial Economics, Game and Society, Incentive and Corporate Governance, and others. He helped to transform business education in China by creating the MBA and EMBA in Peking University. He was an awardee of the National Science Fund for Distinguished Young Scholars in 2000 by the Natural Science Foundation of China. In 2002, Zhang was selected as one of the ten "Man of the Year in Chinese Economy" by Chinese Central Television.

Zhang was among the advocates that economic marketization should precede political democratization. In his speech on China's Reform Annual Meeting in 2009, Zhang predicted that China would need 30 more years to reform its political system. He viewed the Middle Kingdom's transformation as starting from 1840 when the British defeated her in the infamous Opium War. One of his prophecies is by 2040, China would have completed both its economic and political reforms.

In addition to his administrative and teaching positions, Zhang has also worked as a consultant with governmental agencies as well as business firms; this provides a basis for why some of his comments have angered so many. Among the government agencies he has served and is currently working for are the State Commission for Restructuring Economic System, the Department of Enterprises of the State Economic and Trade Commission, the State Informatization Committee, and the Telecommunication Law Drafting Committee. He has also served as senior advisor to a dozen firms.

CHUNJUAN NANCY WEI

Sources

Wharton Global Alumni Forum (2009). "Zhang Weiying. Dean of Guanghua School of Management, Peking University", available at: http://www.whartonbeijing09.com/bio-zw.html (Accessed 17 August 2010).

Zhang, W. (2010), "The main focus for the next thirty years is political reform" (translated by Rose Scobie), *China Elections and Governance*, 27 January, available at: http://chinaelectionsblog.net/?p=158 (accessed 15 August 2010).

北京大学光华管理学院 (2010), "张维迎" ["Professor Zhang Weiying", Guanghua School of Management, Peking University], available at: http://www.gsm.pku.edu.cn/faculty/zhangweiying.aspx (Accessed 17 August 2010).

陈东, 付小勇 (2007),"评北大教授张维迎: 从为钱正名到成 '人民公敌'", *南方人物周刊* [Chen, D. and Fu, X., "Commenting on Peking University Professor Zhang Weiying: From 'Rectifying the Name for Money' to 'Enemy of the People'", *Southern People Weekly*], 6 July, available at: http://news.qq.com/a/20070706/003155.htm (Accessed 17 August 2010).

茅于轼 (2009), "忆峥嵘改革岁月中的张维迎", *天益* [Mao Y., "Reflecting on Zhang Weiying during rough times of reform", *Tianyi Net: Leaders in a Learning Society*], 4 February, available at: http://www.360doc.com/content/09/0224/17/72154_2633622.shtml (Accessed 17 August 2010).

张程 (2009), "好与左派斗的张维迎：会等到他们向我道歉的一天的" *新财经* [Zhang, C., "Zhang Weiying, who enjoys fighting with leftists, says: Will wait till the day when they apologize to me", *New Finance Economics*], 7 April, available at: http://finance.ifeng.com/news/history/rwpz/20090407/515458.shtml (Accessed 27 August 2010).

张维迎 (2010), "高等教育比60年前还要差", 中瑞创新论坛 [Zhang, W., "Higher education is worse than it was sixty years ago", 2010 Sino-Swedish Creativity Forum], 21 May, available at: http://zhangweiyingblog.blog.163.com/blog/static/48120469201042122843360/ (accessed 15 August 2010).

张维迎 (2010), "体制改革与中国未来", *中国日报* [Zhang, W., "Systemic reform and China's future", *China Daily*], 29 January, available at: http://www.chinadaily.com.cn/zgrbjx/2010-01/29/content_9393815.htm (accessed 15 August 2010).

Zhang, Xin (张欣 b. 1965)

Zhang Xin is the CEO of SOHO China, a leader in real estate industry in China and the largest developer in Beijing. Zhang and her husband, Pan Shiyi founded the company in 1995, which focuses on acquiring properties in Beijing's Central Business District, and has completed the construction of approximately 2.3 million square meters of gross floor area (GFA) in central Beijing, with another 1.3 million presently under development.

Zhang was born in Beijing in 1965. In 1979, she and her family migrated to Hong Kong. She used to work as a factory worker and office assistant before she found the funding to undertake college education in the United Kingdom. Zhang first studied at University of Sussex, and in 1992 she received her master degree in development economics from Cambridge University. For the next three years, she joined Goldman Sachs and Travelers Group in the United States. Although overseeing the foreign direct investment transactions in China, Zhang often traveled to mainland China, and through her job assignments, she get acquainted Pan. After their marriage in 1994, she returned to Beijing and co-founded SOHO China with Pan in 1995.

The entrepreneurial career of Zhang was not all smooth in the early years. She and Pan have different strengths and ideologies. Basically, Zhang has additional exposure to the Western culture that emphasizes logical reasoning. Pan, on the hand, prefers natural, integration and harmony. They both had some difficulties in getting consensus on many aspects of project design, development and financing. Eventually, they managed to find convergent points in the aspect of understanding on commercial real estate business, and she gradually reconciled with his a sense of business intuition. Zhang and Pan agreed that the city planning of Beijing should embed rich contents and intellectual aspects that reflect it as a great city of the world and with Chinese identity. Therefore, the rational aspects of Zhang and the sensational aspects of Pan ought to be balanced in architectural designs of SOHO China's projects. As an entrepreneur, not only Zhang understands that profit is important for a business organization, but she further realizes the project architectural designs that embed rightful amount of art and cultural elements will be part and parcel in ensuring the sustainability of SOHO China.

SOHO China was incorporated in Cayman Islands and headquartered in Beijing. Under the mission of "building city center prosperity," it collaborates with internationally recognized architects in designing iconic real estate with strong appeal to the unique customer bases that it serves. Since the 1990s, Internet has profoundly affected the lifestyles of ordinary Chinese citizens. There was also rapid rise of large number of small and medium size enterprises in China. Realized the phenomenon, Zhang and Pan incorporated in their first project Japanese's SOHO concept of "Small Office, Home Office" with homes doubling as offices. The project has strong appeal to the young professionals and small to medium size enterprises, as the SOHO conception provides flexible and multifunctional space. Hence, when the project became available on the market, it was an instant success.

Under the visionary leadership of Zhang and Pan, SOHO China has played a key role in the urbanization initiatives in China. The success of SOHO China is in part due to its ability to produce products that match the taste of high net-worth customers in China. As a leading private company in the country, SOHO China undertakes several CSR initiatives in sustaining the growth of the Chinese economy, and to improve the quality of life amongst Chinese societies. For instances, as the top 10 taxpayers in China's real estate industry since 2003, Zhang and Pan have set up SOHO China Foundation with a mission of promoting social progress while enhancing spiritual advancement. For four consecutive years from 2006 to 2009,

Fortune China has named the company as one of the "Most Admired Companies" in the country.

On October 8, 2007, masterminded by Zhang, SOHO China went public on the Hong Kong Stock Exchange, raising HK$12.8 billion, becoming the largest ever IPO from a private enterprise in China and the largest ever commercial real estate IPO in Asia. In the same year, Zhang was ranked seventh by *Forbes* among the richest people in China. The celebrated projects that SOHO China has undertaken include SOHO New Town, Jianwai SOHO, SOHO Shangdu, Chaowai SOHO, Guanghualu SOHO, and Boao Canal Village in Boao, Hainan. Through acquisition of the Exchange – SOHO in 2009 and the Bund 204 land in Shanghai in 2010, these marked the expansion of SOHO China's operation to the prime locations in Shanghai, and the gaining of stronger footing for competition there.

In the booming real estate world of China, Zhang is known for her masterpiece design entitled "Commune by the Great Wall," which received the Architecture Promotion Prize at the eighth Biannual International Architecture Exhibition held in Venice. In 2004, *BusinessWeek* named Zhang as one the Top 25 Asian Stars. In the following year, the World Economic Forum in Davos considered Zhang a "Young Global Leader" in view of her potential in making contribution with impact to the world. In recent years, Zhang continues to receive similar recognitions in the media, such as the honor among the "Top Ten Women to Watch in Asia" by *Wall Street Journal* in 2007, the "World Top 100 Most Influential Women" by *Forbes* in 2008, and the "World Top 50 Most influential Business Women" by *Financial Times* as in 2009.

LOI TECK HUI

Sources

SOHO China (2010), "Corporate overview", available at: http://www.sohochina.com/en/about/index.asp (accessed 8 June 2010).

Wikipedia (2010), "SOHO China", available at: http://en.wikipedia.org/wiki/SOHO_China (accessed 18 June 2010).

百度百科 (2010), "张欣: SOHO 中国首席执行官" ["Zhang Xin: CEO of SOHO China", *Baidu Encyclopedia*], available at: http://baike.baidu.com/view/85663.htm#5 (accessed 9 June 2010).

MBALib (2009), "张欣: SOHO中国有限公司总裁" ["Zhang Xin: SOHO China's CEO"], available at: http://wiki.mbalib.com/wiki/%E5%BC%A0%E6%AC%A3 (accessed 9 June 2010).

偶社 (2009), "张欣生平简介" ["About Zhang Xin", *Oushe*], 4 October, available at: http://www.oushe.cn/intro/10692 (accessed 9 June 2010).

Zhang, Xingsheng (张醒生 b. 1955)

As the managing director of the Nature Conservancy's North Asia Region, Zhang Xingsheng holds an important position while facing mounting challenges in the environmental protection for one of the fast growing regions in the world. Before his association with the environmental NGO, Zhang also had a successful career in the Chinese telecom industry, and was one of the most active venture capitalists in the country.

Zhang's career advancement is in sync with the era of Chinese economic reform. After graduating from the Beijing University of Posts and Telecommunications in 1977, he worked in various engineering and management capacities at several different organizations of the Beijing Telecom Bureau, Beijing Telecom Administration and China International Telecom Construction Corporation under the Ministry of Posts and Telecommunication, known today as the Ministry of information Industry.

When Ericsson established its branch office in Beijing in 1990, Zhang was among the first group of Chinese hired by Western-based, multinational corporations in the country. Beginning as marketing manager, he went on to become the director of business development in 1994, vice president and head of mobile phones in 1996, and executive vice president and general manager of National Network Operators in 1997. Zhang earned his MBA from the Norwegian School of Management BI in 1999. His last position as chief marketing officer of Ericsson China left him in charge of the creation and implementation of strategies in business, sales, and marketing. These strategies were of vital importance, as they promoted systems and products valuing over US$2 billion in revenues for the company.

On April 1, 2003, Zhang was named president and CEO of AsiaInfo, who succeeded James Ding, co-founder of the company as well as president and CEO since 1999. A producer of elite level software and solutions to China's telecom carriers, AsiaInfo provides a variety of network infrastructure services such as design, implementation, operation and optimization, customer management and billing solutions, decision support systems, and service applications like messaging, broadband, and wireless. Zhang already had 20 years of experience in the Chinese telecommunications industry before joining AsiaInfo. Although his tenure there was only two years, Zhang was credited for the quick turnaround of the company, which under his leadership began to generate profit within a year.

Upon departure from AsiaInfo, Zhang became involved in venture capital investment and was credited with several successful ventures. In December 2006, Zhang joined an elite group of 31 Chinese entrepreneurs, economists, and commerce leaders to form the China Entrepreneur Club, which has since become one of the most influential business organizations in China, and aspires to become one of the top non-profit organizations in the world. By bringing together the country's top business leaders, the organization seeks to provide support to the private economy of China, whereas diligently pursuing common human values, creating new inspiration for entrepreneurs, and offering guidance for future business development.

Through his venture capital business and active social networking, Zhang became deeply interested in the environmental impact of the country's economy in swift transition. Back in 2002, as a part of the "Return to the Nature" movement in China,

Zhang organized a group of Chinese entrepreneurs on a tour of the remote western region of China. Although amazed by the striking natural landscape of the Qinghai-Tibet Plateau, he was alarmed by the rapid desertification in western China, and was shocked to find the poor conditions of Tibetan antelopes that have been hunted to near extinction. Upon returning, Zhang made up his mind that he would have to devote himself to the cause of environmental protection. He regarded his life in three stages: during the early years, he struggled to make a living; then at the second stage, he worked hard to build his business career; now it was time for the third stage of his life – doing something meaningful for the common good of human beings.

In October 2008, Zhang joined the Nature Conservancy, taking on the role of managing director of North Asia Region. With over a million members in the United States and over six million hectares of land under its protection, the Nature Conservancy is one of the world's largest environmental organizations, which first entered China through a succession of conservation projects in the northwest Yunnan Province in 1998. Backed by 60 years of experience, the organization successfully oversees projects in more than 30 countries throughout the world.

Since joining the Nature Conservancy, Zhang has become an outspoken advocate of green economy in China. He attended the recent Annual Summit of China Green Companies centered on sustainable development. In 2009, Zhang was appointed vice chairman of the 3rd Yangtze Forum sponsored by the Shanghai municipal government in coordination with the Changjiang Water Resources Commission of the Ministry of Water Resources. At the Horasis Global China Business Meeting in Portugal, Zhang discussed the possibilities for the Chinese corporate sector to utilize globalization strategies while remaining socially responsible and environmentally friendly. The quickly dilapidating state of the environment is a matter of great consequence, not only for this generation but also for those to come. As time passes the situation worsens, and it becomes more difficult and costly to repair the damages caused by human activities. In order to find timely solutions, the greatest minds of the world are turning their attentions to the protection and revitalization of the global environment, among them is Zhang.

Syntia Zeni

Sources

Business Wire (2003), "Telecommunications veteran Xingsheng Zhang named Chief Executive Officer of AsiaInfo", 24 February, available at: http://www.allbusiness.com/company-activities-management/board-management-changes/5715364-1.html (accessed 3 April 2010).

Chinese Entrepreneur Club (2007), "Launching", available at: http://www.daonong.com/english/launching.html (accessed 3 April 2010).

新浪科技 (2008), "张醒生：人生第三阶段的环保愿景" ["Zhang Xingsheng: Wishes of environmental protection for the third stage of in life", *Sina.com*], 23 Ocotober, available at: http://tech.sina.com.cn/it/2008-10-23/22042531008.shtml (accessed 25 July 2010).

Zhang, Yan (章彦 b. 1981)

Zhang Yan is a stunning example that age does not need to be a predominant factor in achieving your dreams and being successful. In 2007, when he was only 26 years old, Zhang and a friend co-founded an Internet start-up Meiloo.com. Since then, the company has enjoyed a great amount of success, and has been featured in CNN, *Forbes*, *Men's Health China*, *TechCrunch* and a variety of other publications both domestic and international. Zhang himself was featured in *Forbes* as one of the nine young entrepreneurs to watch in 2010.

Zhang Yan was born in Nanjing, China, and lived there until he was 10 years old. His mother was an OB/GYN and incorporated both traditional Chinese methods with those of the Western practices. Later on Zhang moved to Abu Dhabi, the capital of the United Arab Emirates, and then to San Diego, California. Although in the United States, Zhang excelled in academic work, graduating from the elite Princeton University with a degree from the Woodrow Wilson School of Public and International Affairs. He then worked for some time as an investment-banking analyst at the Lehman Brothers' consumer and retail group located in New York City, where he learned and practiced his skills in handling numerous transactions concerning household products and apparel. In 2004, Zhang left the Lehman Brothers to accept a position with the media powerhouse Bertelsmann as Random House's chief representative in China.

Part of Zhang's success can be attributed not only to his intelligence but a little bit of luck as well, and perhaps some personal charm. Zhang's high school in San Diego hired a prestigious alumnus to speak at his graduation. Determined and confident, Yan approached the speaker and managed to land himself an internship with the Chinese bookseller Dangdang, which is one of the biggest online retailers in China. Although he was given an internship, Zhang never saw the speaker again and thought he never would. Seven years later, in an incredible stroke of luck and chance, the two ran into one another in Beijing. Not one to miss an opportunity, Zhang described his business plan to his potential sponsor so convincingly that he was given enough capital to set up Meiloo.com. Even now Zhang still only refers to the angel giver as "Jim" and refuses to detail exactly how much capital he was given (Chao, 2008).

In founding Meiloo.com, Zhang has collaborated with his friend Jeffrey Wu. It was Wu who had first taken notice that advertisements for private hospitals and elective medical services (i.e., teeth cleaning, orthodontia, laser eye surgery, cosmetic surgery, and infertility treatments) had increased rapidly along with rising income levels in China. Wu then came to two important realizations: first, there was a growing need for elective medical service providers to advertise, thus creating a large potential market; second, there was not effective means or focused venue for them to market their services, as their ads were so randomly scattered about. With such a clearly defined customer-based discovered by two brilliant minds, it was not long before a business venture was dreamed up and materialized.

It was then that Meiloo was born, a website dedicated to informing consumers about nonessential medical services and connecting them with the right providers. Previously it was difficult for Chinese consumers to compare medical services from one hospital to the other. Information was neither transparent nor easily accessible without personally visiting each location for services and costs. One example is double eyelid surgery, which is one of the predominant cosmetic procedures in Asian countries. The disparity in prices is almost unbelievable, ranging from USD$425 to USD$1,418. Providers would also try to confuse patients by using names that were difficult to differentiate from one another, such as "Korean style" or "European style." Another complication lies in the structure of the medical industry in China, as the market is not mostly owned or controlled by HMOs or private insurance companies such as in the United States. Therefore, the industry grows quickly and fragmented, making it much harder to find reputable doctor at a reasonable price.

Zhang sees his Meiloo as a beacon of light in the fog of medical services and providers in increasingly prosperous yet still less regulated China. Meiloo.com provides a way for educated consumers to research the services from different hospitals by listing detailed descriptions as well as reviews from previous customers. Through using the site, Chinese consumers can now comprehend the differences in services and providers, make a price comparison, and share their experiences with others on Meiloo's bulletin board system. Customers can even find discounts on Meiloo, from which the company earns a commission. According to Zhang, the company's biggest accomplishment is that patients do not just use the site for research, but also book it through Meiloo, which allows the company to be compensated financially. The private clinics on the site are carefully screened, and Meiloo continues to follow up with the providers and the patients after their medical procedures were done. The company then uses this information at the end of the year to reevaluate whether or not any given clinic should be included in the site, therefore ensuring the quality of its services.

Zhang believes his website provides a benefit not only to consumers, but to the medical service providers as well. As more people feel comfortable with their decisions, they are more willing to undertake the procedures than before. In China, the drive for such selective medical procedures is primarily focused on self-improvement, not anti-aging as in the West. Due to a booming economy, ample supply of working population and a loosely regulated social environment, it is not illegal in China to require someone to be attractive for a job. This is why the company's name in Chinese is Meile (美乐), which translates to beautiful and happy, and ties to the company's belief that beauty, happiness, and health are intertwined. Looking forward, the market potential is huge for Meiloo, and with a vision and entrepreneurial spirit, Zhang is happily finding his niche in one of the fastest growing economies in the world.

SYNTIA ZENI

Sources

Chao, E. (2008), "Health and happiness", *China International Business*, No. 244 (April).

DeNoble, D. (2009), "Meiloo.com: China's future Webd 2.0, proto-HMO", *Asia Healthcare*, 31 March.

Lacy, S. (2009), "Healthcare reform, Chinese startup style", *TechCrunch*, 19 October, available at: http://techcrunch.com/2009/10/19/healthcare-reform-chinese-startup-style/ (accessed 25 July 2010).
Seligson, H. (2010), "Nine young Chinese entrepreneurs to watch", *Forbes*, 28 February, available at: http://www.forbes.com/2010/02/26/young-chinese-entrepreneurs-to-watch-entrepreneurs-technology-china.html (accessed 27 April 2010).

Zhang, Yaqin (张亚勤 b. 1966)

Zhang Yaqin is the corporate vice president of Microsoft Corporation and chairman of Microsoft Asia-Pacific Research and Development Group. In this role, Zhang is responsible for driving Microsoft's overall research and development efforts in the Asia-Pacific region. Under his leadership, Microsoft Asia-Pacific Research and Development Group has become Microsoft's largest R&D center outside of the United States with more than 3000 engineers and scientists engaged in basic research, technology incubation, product development, and strategic partnership and investment. Zhang has served as the chairman of Microsoft China Limited, with oversight across all of Microsoft's organizations in China.

Zhang's background has been marked by success and talent from an early age. He was born in Shanxi Province, China in 1966. At the age of 12, he was enrolled in the Gifted Program at the elite USTC (University of Science and Technology of China) as the youngest college student that year. In 1986, he went to the United States to pursue doctoral studies, and received his PhD in electrical engineering from George Washington University three years later.

Upon graduation in 1989, Zhang first conducted research at the GTE (General Telephone and Electronics) Laboratory as a senior scientist, before being recruited by the Sarnoff Multimedia Laboratory in 1997. At Sarnoff, Zhang held the positions of project manager, department chief and lab director. In that same year, he became the youngest-ever fellow for the Institute of Electrical and Electronics Engineers (IEEE), and has served as editor-in-chief for the influential IEEE journals and publications.

Respected and lauded by his peers as a world-renowned researcher and scientist, Zhang joined Microsoft in January 1999, bringing with him a wealth of technical knowledge in wireless and satellite communications, networking, digital video and multimedia technology. He has been granted more than 50 U.S. patents, and has authored more than a dozen books and 500 influential technical papers and journal articles. Many of the technologies he has singly or jointly developed have become the basis for start-up ventures, commercial products, and international standards. In 2000, he entered mobile network research, an area in which he had foresight in accurately predicting as an area of future significance. After three years, he and his colleagues received corporate funding, thereby creating a revenue-generating division. For his outstanding work, Zhang was soon promoted as corporate vice president of Microsoft's Mobile and Embedded Devices Division, where from 2004 to 2006, he oversaw research and development of Windows mobile software for pocket PCs and smartphones and Windows embedded operating systems, including Windows CE.

Zhang is one of the founding members of the Microsoft Research Asia Lab, where he served as managing director and chief scientist. He also founded the Advanced Technology Center (ATC) in 2003.Under his leadership, Microsoft Asia-Pacific R&D Group has become a regional research powerhouse and a major and regular contributor to Microsoft's core technology development. More than 100 innovations have made their way into critical products including new generations of the Microsoft Windows desktop operating systems, Windows Vista and Windows 7.

Zhang has served as Microsoft's corporate vice president since 2006. Together with his team, he is driving and shaping the company's next wave of evolution in Asia. In this role, he works as a key advisor to government and academia in the region. Zhang is an adjunct or visiting professor at approximately 20 universities in China, Australia, Hong Kong and the United States; and is an advisor to five provinces and central government agencies in China. He is also a member of the Malaysia government's International Advisory Panel and International Advisory for National Information and Communication Technology of Australia (NICTA).

As a scientist who benefited from both Chinese and American educations, Zhang has a personal interest in cultivating cooperation between China and the United States. He is a member of the influential "Committee of 100," which seeks to promote Sino-US political, economic, technological, and cultural exchanges.

Zhang has won many prestigious awards, including the IEEE Industry Pioneer Medal, IEEE Centennial Medal, IEEE Fellow Award, and the 2004 Young Engineer of the Year for his pioneering contributions on digital video, mobile communications, and Internet technology and industry. He is one of the most visible industry leaders in China with distinctions including being named one of the top 10 CEOs of 2007, IT leader of the year in 2005 and the top 10 innovators of the year in 2007.

When queried about his professional accomplishments, Zhang attributes his success to his curiosity. After listening to several Nobel Prize winners, he once observed: "Some of them are 90 years old, but they still retain the eyes and mind of a child. Curiosity is not weakened because of age." As a well-known young scientist, he also employed a unique research methodology, stating that one "must be willing to cooperate with luminaries from different fields, as this form of interdisciplinary cooperation is the most effective." Zhang's achievements reflect this philosophy. When engaged in research on video communication systems, much of his inspiration came from a friend who specialized in wireless communication; and they went on to jointly invent the first wireless video transfer system in 1993.

As a technology leader and visionary, Zhang is helping push Microsoft, as well as the industry, forward to make cloud-computing mainstream. At the same time he also advocates that pure cloud computing is not the "master key" to the future. Instead, he predicts that the coexistence of Cloud and Client, and the interaction between them will shape future computing trends. He also points out how the world of Web and the world of devices will converge. Looking forward, Zhang envisions an IT industry landscape that will be redefined through three areas of competition: the competition between cloud computing platforms; the competition between PC and mobile platforms; and the competition among mobile platforms and mobile devices. Given their successful track record, it is likely that Zhang and his colleagues at Microsoft Asia-Pacific Research and Development Group will continue to play a major role in shaping these developments.

YING HUANG AND MIAN WANG

Sources

Committee of 100 (2010), "Members in action", available at: http://www.committee100.org/media/media_members_inaction.htm (accessed 9 September 2010).

Microsoft (2006), "Ya-Qin Zhang, Corporate Vice President", news release, 10 February, available at: http://www.microsoft.com/presspass/exec/yzhang/ (accessed 4 September 2010).

刘书 (2002), "张亚勤推导天才方程式", *北京晨报* [Liu, S., "Zhang Yaqing reveals the genius formula", *Beijing Morning Post*], 29 July, available at: http://news.xinhuanet.com/it/2002-07/29/content_501789.htm (accessed 4 September 2010).

齐鹏 (2010), "张亚勤: 瞄准下一个兴奋点", *数字商业时代* [Qi, P., "Zhang Yaqin: Aiming for the next point of excitement", *Business Times*], 4 August, available at: http://d1.it168.com/show/68764.html (accessed 4 September 2010).

徐仁全 (2008), "张亚勤华人科技金头脑", *远见杂志* [Xu, R.Q., "Zhang Yaqin: The Chinese gold brain of technology", *Global View Monthly*], 1August, available at: http://www.committee100.org/media/media_eng/Ya-qinZhang%2808%29_092608.pdf (accessed 4 September 2010).

Zhang, Yichen (张懿宸 b. 1963)

Born in an ordinary Chinese family in Northern China, Zhang Yichen began to shoulder a large share of family responsibility at a young age, when he lost his father at age thirteen. But it is this plain and ordinary boy, who was supposed to be a violinist in a local chorus that worked as the managing director of Merrill Lynch and is now the CEO of CITIC Capital.

A major event in his life, Zhang Yichen lost his father to liver cancer in September 1976, when he just started his junior high school and his youngest brother was only five. Originally learned to play violin from his father, Zhang applied for a part-time job in the local chorus where his father used to work, with a monthly payment of 18 RMB. Though not much, it was critical for the whole family's livelihood. In order to keep the job, Zhang left school and focused on practicing violin at home. In addition, he carried bricks at a construction site to earn extra money.

Six months into violin practice at home and hard labor at the construction site, Zhang's fate changed for better. In 1977, the reinstitution of the national college entrance exam sparked the flame in his heart. After some struggles, Zhang discuss his thoughts of returning to school with his mother. Though surprised, she supported his decision. In September, Zhang was admitted into No. 3 Middle School in Harbin and resumed his junior high school study. Being naturally brilliant, Zhang still worked hard. He was constantly ranked at the top of his grade and was elected the class president, Youth League cadre, and later named the Provincial Outstanding Student several times. In 1981, Zhang took the nationwide college entrance exam and ranked third in the whole Heilongjiang Province. Without any hesitation, he applied for the economic management program at Tsinghua University. Meanwhile, the University of Science and Technology of China tried to persuade him to study there, and the Harbin Institute of Technology (HIT) invited him to join its exchange program in the United States. Being the oldest son and thinking of his family, Zhang refused both offers. However, his mother took the offer by HIT seriously and went to find the details of overseas studying. After learning about the program, she decisively modified Zhang's plan for college and sent him to America. A bit unwilling, Zhang followed his mother's decision.

While in the United States, Zhang continually excelled academically. After one year of senior high school study in Phillips Academy, Zhang received letters of admission from Harvard, MIT, and Stanford University. Unsure about his options, Zhang finally accepted the offer to attend MIT. While enjoying the stimulating atmosphere of MIT, he quickly had his first reality check, as his ability was questioned by some of his fellow foreign students. Driven by self-esteem, Zhang made an astonishing decision by taking double majors in both economic management and computer science. Though initially doubted by both his teachers and fellow students, Zhang successfully completed the requirements for both majors and earned him the admission into the Sloan School of Management at MIT. In 1986, while preparing for his thesis, Zhang began to work for Professor Huang of MIT on his cash flow model project entrusted by Greenwich Capital Markets. After months of hard work, they finished the project on time, and when implemented, the model design earned Greenwich a large sum of money in its first deal. Hence, Greenwich's director decided to offer Zhang a job in the company. Initially Zhang refused the offer, with the belief that he would just finish his PhD and go back to China soon. Persuaded by his professor, Zhang agreed to work two years in Greenwich, and gradually he fell in love with the job while getting to know the debenture market. Six years later, Zhang grew to become a Wall Street veteran, disciplined and sharpened in both theoretical analysis and practical deal making. In the early 1990s, he left Greenwich and became Bank of Tokyo's Head of Proprietary Trading in New York.

While working on Wall Street, Zhang never stopped thinking about going back to China and launching a new career; the right opportunity came when Chen Qizong, Chairman of Hong Lung Group presented him with an attractive offer. While doing investment banking for Hong Lung Group, Zhang also designed treasury bond futures for the Shanghai Stock Exchange. After discussions with Gao Xiqing and other friends, who also returned to China to work, Zhang resigned again and went to work for the Chinese Ministry of Finance. In 1996, Zhang was recruited by Merrill Lynch to be its managing director, responsible for debt capital market activities for the Greater China region. During his four years in Merrill Lynch, Zhang set an impressive investment record. In 1999, he simultaneously won four bond projects from the Ministry of Finance, China Development Bank, the Export-Import Bank of China, and China Telecom.

Just when everyone thought his career reached its summit, Zhang again handed in his resignation. In 2002, he was invited by Rong Zhijian, Chairman of CITIC Pacific, to join CITIC Group. With the development of investment banking business of CICC and BOC International, CITIC Group realized the importance of setting up a cross-border investment bank as the bridge for Chinese companies to list overseas. In 2002, CITIC Capital was founded, and Zhang was back to his investment banking game, serving as the executive director of CITIC Pacific and president of CITIC Pacific Communications. Working over 10 hours every day, he scouted for talents, developed strategies, and balanced relationship between shareholders and management team.

During his trips back home, Zhang learned about the vexing development strategy of Harbin Pharmaceutical Group. Being a publicly listed company, the group poured 90% of its top-quality assets into its joint stock company, which resulted in the unbalanced development of the company and the group. After detailed assessment of Harbin Pharmaceutical, Zhang decided to acquire the group. On December 14, 2004, Harbin State-owned Assets Supervision and Administration Commission, Harbin Pharmaceutical, CITIC Capital, Warbury Pincus, and Heilongjiang Chenergy HIT High-Tech Venture Capital jointly signed a restructuring and capital investment agreement. CITIC Capital's landmark buyout of Harbin Pharmaceutical, one of China's most profitable pharmaceutical companies, remains the largest closed buyout in China to date. In 2006, Zhang completed the assets and business restructuring of CITIC. In the following year, CITIC Capital Partners announced the final closing of CITIC Capital China Partners, its maiden China private equity fund. The fund closed at US$425 million, well above the US$250 million target size. Within five years, CITIC Capital grew from a US$250-million capital to a fund management company that controls more than US$1.5 billion in Zhang's hands.

Despite his successful career, Zhang never boasts himself in front of anyone. He is considered modest, firm, and stable by all his friends, and his deep love for his family is well known among his colleagues. According to him: "Set up the CITIC Capital platform was the biggest success of my career, but being a qualified husband and father is my greatest happiness."

WEI QIAN

Sources

CITIC Capital (2010), "Yichen Zhang, Chief Executive Officer", available at: http://www.citiccapital.com/team_e.aspx?i=39 (accessed 12 July 2010).

Forbes (2010), "Yichen Zhang, Independent director, SINA Corporation", available at: http://people.forbes.com/profile/yichen-zhang/7760 (accessed 12 July 2010).

王红茹 (2007), "张懿宸: 建设中国黑石", *资本推手: 10位海归投资银行家*, 中国发展出版社, 北京 [Wang H.R., "Zhang Yichen: Building China's Blackstone", in Wang, H. (ed.), *Capital Movers and Shakers: Ten Overseas Returnees in Investment Banking*, China Development Press, Beijing], pp. 106–129.

Zhao, Yang (赵阳 b. 1963)

During the global financial crisis of 2008–2009, when many companies were struggling in the deep recession and great financial difficulties, MEMSIC Semiconductor, located in Wuxi High-Tech Development Zone, was busy processing an ongoing acquisition of a foreign company. Zhao Yang's life as chairman, president, and CEO of MEMSIC is a successful story about a returnee entrepreneur and the pursuit of innovative business development.

Born in Northeastern China, Zhao Yang grew up in Beijing. With a height of 1.98 m, he was one of the players in the national youth basketball team. After graduating from Peking University with his BS in physics in 1985, he went to United States and enrolled at Princeton University in New Jersey, under the supervision of Dr. Daniel C. Tsui, who later became a Nobel Prize winner in physics in 1998. After receiving his PhD in electrical engineering, Zhao worked in the research and development at Analog Devices for the next seven years, which turned out to be a very valuable experience. He not only received 26 US patents on circuit design and manufacturing processes, but also developed his wisdom, sophistication, and a sense of humor.

When China's economic reform shifted into higher gear in the 1990s, Zhao Yang, like many overseas students, was attracted by the great changes and wanted to explore more challenges and new opportunities. Based on his professional knowledge, he believed that sensor technology would have a huge potential in the coming years. After studying the wide range of applications and researching on the product marketing, he realized China was a better place for him to develop his business because the great opportunities and growing market generated by the country's rapid economic growth. Therefore, he left the United States and returned to China in 1999. After careful consideration, he finally chose Wuxi New District to set up his company MEMSIC Semiconductor. Since then, Zhao embarked on the journey of leading and managing a company in the development, manufacturing, and marketing integrated MEMS (Micro Electro Mechanical Systems) chip products. His technological innovation and entrepreneurial spirit has become a remarkable story in the history of Chinese semiconductor industry over the last 10 years.

Under Zhao's leadership, MEMSIC Semiconductor has grown from fewer than 10 people to the world's first company that combined signal processing systems and microelectronic circuits integrated on single chip inertial sensors, and its electronic microelectronics, microprocessing technology also holds a leading position in the world. As one of the largest manufacturers of accelerometers in the electronics market, the high productivity and the product reliability made MEMSIC stand out among many suppliers. With top product performance and low price, MEMSIC was able to steadily gain market shares. Since 2001, the company has achieved rapid development, and all the products have been exported worldwide. In December 2007, MEMSIC was successfully listed on the NASDAQ in the United States.

More recently, Zhao has promoted the development of micronanoelectronic sensor technology in Wuxi. A few years ago, he and several experts had a discussion on the concept of "micro-inclusive." Zhao thought that instead of building another "Silicon Valley" to face strong competitions, it would be better to build a "Nano Park" to develop the Nano industry. With strong support from the local government, the Nano Research Park was soon established in Wuxi New District. Consequently, Zhao has developed a CMOS process, which is the first micro-mechanical system in the world to integrate the manufacturing process and testing technology. In addition, the company has also engaged in the research and development, and production of more than 20 models of accelerometer sensor IC products, which are mainly used in notebook computers, PDA, and LCD projectors.

"Innovation is a way of life, scientists use the wisdom to change people's lives", often said Zhao. With this belief, he put a great effort on new technology research and development. He encouraged innovative ideas and opened discussions between departments to help employees understand each other from different perspectives. With dedication and hard work by Zhao and his team, MEMSIC Semiconductor and its products have been recognized by various awards in recent years, such as EDN Innovation Award, Hong Kong Electronics Innovation recognition, Canada Industrial Electronics Invention winner, the Best Sensor Product Award, Sony Green Partner designation, and the China Chip Best Market Performance Award. Zhao himself was also named by the leading industrial magazine *Small Times* as one of the "outstanding business leaders" in 2003.

For all the achievements of MEMSIC in recent years, Zhao was extremely modest. He thought the company's success came from the great efforts from all employees and credited the strong support from the Wuxi municipal government. Known as a technical genius himself, Zhao is always trying to attract the world's top talents to join his team, and he encourages his employees to respect each other's culture and to learn from each other's experience. He believes that the future development of MEMSIC will be better and faster.

JING BAI

Sources

MEMSIC (2010), "Management team: Yao Zhao", available at: http://www.memsic.com/company/about-memsic/management-team.html (accessed 21 July 2010).

古月 (2010), "美新董事长赵阳看好传感器技术发展潜力", *无锡日报* [Gu, Y., "MEMSIC Chairman Zhao Yang in favor of the growth potential of sensoring technology", *Wuxi Daily*], 28 May, available at: http://news.thmz.com/col58/2010/05/2010-05-28765902.html (accessed 21 July 2010).

中国青年报 (2009), "美新半导体CEO赵阳: 一位海归创业者新追求" [MEMSIC Semiconductor CEO Zhao Yang: New undertaking of an overseas returnee entrepreneur", *China Youth*], 5 January, available at: http://www.mcuol.com/News/226/31559.htm (accessed 21 July 2010).

Zhen, Ronghui (Rick Yan 甄荣辉 b. 1962)

It may be no coincidence that Zhen Ronghui was born in 1962, the golden year of the tiger. In Chinese folklore, tigers are born leaders, fearless, daring fighters, and always in a hurry. Zhen Ronghui, known throughout the business world as Rick Yan, is the founder and CEO of 51job, Inc., a NASDAQ-listed HR services provider. 51job offers a range of services through a network of sales offices spanning 25 cities across China. With more than 140,000 business customers and 30 million resumes posted online, its recruitment portal 51job.com maintains a leadership position in a highly competitive industry.

Tiger attributions notwithstanding, the journey of Rick Yan has been extraordinary, given the early life of young Zhen Ronghui. As a child, Zhen's family moved from the manufacturing hub of Guangdong to Hong Kong. They lived in poor circumstances in a small 80-square-meter apartment that could often be "home" to as many as 8 families and 20 people. Zhen was a bright and busy child with many interests and considerable enthusiasm. With his parents busy trying to make ends meet, they paid little attention to their son's studies or how he spent his time, and young Zhen became a lazy student. It was no surprise when he fared poorly in the official examinations for acceptance into high school. Without an adequate high school preparation, it was unlikely that he would find a place in university; and without a university education, future job opportunities would be limited to low-level and unrewarding work. As he later reflected, human beings sometimes must face difficulties in order to change and grow.

Although faced with the added hardship of traveling a considerable distance to the only high school that would accept him, he redoubled his efforts. Two long years later, after achieving top scores that properly reflected his potential, Zhen was admitted to the highly respected University of Hong Kong. While Zhen's engineering studies progressed uneventfully, he began to question whether a stable career as an engineer would satisfy his aspirations. When the general manager of Hewlett Packard (HP) Hong Kong visited on a campus recruitment drive, Zhen eagerly sought an interview. Impressing with his candor and enthusiasm, he persuaded the GM to give him an opportunity in HP's sales team. After graduating with a bachelor degree in engineering and a master in philosophy, Zhen took up the HP offer and set about proving himself as an exemplary employee.

It was a role that he seemed to be born to. Through sheer hard work, persistence, and a gift for selling, he was soon HP's top salesperson in Hong Kong by a considerable margin. Zhen was both admired and envied by his colleagues, however as his reputation grew, the challenge diminished. Having developed a solid base of large and loyal clients, he was able to maintain his unsurpassed sales record with limited effort. As he would demonstrate throughout his career, comfort, stability, and a high salary were not his primary motivators. Zhen began to realize that, in order to propel himself into the ranks of senior management, he must earn an MBA. To everyone's amazement, HP's Marketing Executive of the Year resigned to continue his studies.

In spite of having no background in the French language, Zhen set his sights on studying at the prestigious French university, INSEAD. In lieu of a formal entrance examination, candidates were to engage in a vigorous, 20-minute, face-to-face interview with one of the program's professors, an impossible task for someone with just three months of language preparation. Zhen prepared and memorized a 20-minute presentation and, when the professor asked the first question, he spoke deliberately and without pause for the entire allocated interview time. It was a characteristically bold move, and it succeeded.

Zhen focused his studies on Western business operations and structures, believing that this would prove to be invaluable to his career progress. In 1989, after earning his MBA from INSEAD with distinction, the bold and optimistic young man was offered a position in the London office of Bain & Company, one of the world's foremost strategy consulting firms. Zhen quickly gained a reputation for his detailed analyses and deep insights into financial structures and operations. His managers relied heavily on his skills and other divisions openly courted him. Within two years, he was promoted to a management track, and in 1991, Bain appointed him China manager in its HK office. He reveled in the new responsibility and was subsequently appointed to open the firm's Beijing office.

By 1994, Zhen, now known in business circles as Rick Yan, had transformed himself from a management rookie to one of the youngest VPs in the company's history. However, he still had itchy feet. China's rapid development was creating many incredible success stories. If he were to take advantage of these once-in-a-lifetime opportunities, he knew that he must build an organization of his own. As early as 1991, he had been investing in outside projects, and while his results were mixed, he was honing his entrepreneurial skills.

Zhen's attention began to focus on two areas: recruitment and the Internet. For decades, the idea of searching for a job was unthinkable in China. On leaving school, most people were assigned to a job, and usually that was where they remained for their entire working life. By the turn of the century however, millions of university graduates were scanning job ads and vigorously competing for the best opportunities. In the late 1990s, the Internet was presenting a whole new economy and unique opportunities in almost every field. Recruitment was shaping up as a prime industry for an Internet-led paradigm shift. Zhen's own experience in searching for employees at Bain convinced him that there was a large and profitable gap in the market as well as significant deficiencies in existing product offerings. Here was the opportunity for which he had been searching. In October 1998, together with some colleagues from Bain & Company, he established *Career Post*, a weekly circular containing classified job listings in Beijing.

Although the print product quickly grew to a weekly circulation of 300,000, Zhen was always mindful of the emerging online medium. He soon launched career-post.com, which operated in tandem with the traditional print product. By today's standards, it was a simple site that was little more than a static newspaper presentation on a series of web pages. However, as new software applications were developed and introduced, the website's user base soared. Zhen and his partners had exploited a highly profitable gap in the market: specialized services catering to the urgent needs of rapidly growing white-collar segment. At the same time, they had created a unique "clicks and mortar" model, a website operating in parallel with a trade newspaper. The response from the market convinced them to replicate the model to other cities throughout China.

By this time, venture capital was racing into new Internet ventures and Zhen was keen to fund his ambitious plan to develop a leading brand. With US$14 million in venture capital, he relaunched the site under the name of 51job.com, a clever Chinese play on words with the implied meanings of "I want" and "no need to worry."

Zhen had reached another point in his life where he would exchange stability, comfort, and a high salary for the uncertainty and challenge of an entrepreneurial venture. After an 11-year career at Bain & Company, he resigned to dedicate himself full time as the CEO of 51job. Under his leadership, between 1999 and 2004, revenue grew from less than US$1 million to US$43 million. 51job's hybrid model was a proven success and the website was developing into a sophisticated offering of human resource services for both employers and job seekers. Nevertheless, for Zhen, reaching one goal is merely the first step toward the next: a NASDAQ listing.

The IPO was completed on September 29, 2004, and with the interest and excitement surrounding the listing, the stock price closed the day with a 51% gain. Throughout 2004, fueled by media hype rather than performance or fundamentals, the stock price continued to climb from the US$14 issue price to US$55. Then, a sudden slowdown in the recruitment market led to disappointing results in the fourth quarter of 2004. The company missed its first earnings guidance as a publicly listed company and the stock plunged as many shareholders sold their positions. As CEO Zhen put it, the company experienced a "perfect storm."

Although the HR services industry in China has undergone several ups and downs, including the severe impact of the global financial crisis, 51job has maintained its leadership position. In recent years, several foreign investors have taken strategic stakes in Chinese online recruiters. With the high-scale economies available to the industry, Zhen always anticipated consolidation so his confidence is unshakeable. Looking forward, he expects 51job to hold its market position during the economic slowdown and to take advantage of the market turnaround from a position of competitive and financial strength.

Zhen has become a business icon in China and has built 51job into the largest recruitment company in the nation. Along the way, he has made a valuable contribution to driving industry innovation. Yet, for all of his success, Zhen remains an enigmatic figure with leadership values that are rare, if not unique. He is a CEO without the trappings of an elaborate corner office. He is constantly on the move between departments and locations and is legendary for the time he spends in the air. While this might imply a hands-on micromanager, nothing could be further from the truth. Zhen sees himself as the coach, motivating and guiding his team but rarely becoming involved in the details of their work. His leadership style is the antithesis of the traditional Chinese power-distance dichotomy as he continually seeks to minimize the physical, psychological, and organizational distance between himself and his employees.

Zhen Ronghui, the "Golden Tiger," is a born leader, fearless, a daring fighter, and always in a hurry.

TERENCE R. EGAN

Sources

Forbes (2010), "Business profiles: Rick Yan", available at: http://people.forbes.com/profile/rick-yan/237 (accessed 28 January 2010).
Robertson, B. (2007), "Help wanted", *Forbes* (Asia), 26 March, available at: http://members.forbes.com/global/2007/0326/020.html?partner=yahoomag (accessed 15 April 2010).
51job (2010), "2009 Annual Report", available at: http://ir.51job.com/ir/AnnualReport.php (accessed 15 April 2010).
互动百科 (2010), "甄荣辉", ["Zhen Ronghui", *Hudong.com*], available at: http://www.hudong.com/wiki/%E7%94%84%E8%8D%A3%E8%BE%89 (accessed 28 January 2010).
全球品牌网 (2010), "前程无忧甄荣辉: 从寒门虎子到亿万富翁", ["Zhen Ronghui: From my impoverished family to billionaire", *Globrand*], 13 March, available at: http://www.globrand.com/2010/365148.shtml (accessed 28 January 2010).

Zhou, Yunfan (周云帆 b. 1974)

Deputy director of Zhongguancun Science Park in Beijing, Zhou Yunfan is the cofounder, former chairman, and chief executive officer of KongZhong Corporation, a leading mobile Internet company in China that delivers wireless value-added services to consumers through multiple technology platforms including wireless application protocol (WAP), multimedia messaging service (MMS) and JAVA, short messaging service (SMS), interactive voice response (IVR), and color ring-back tone (CRBT). The company operates three wireless Internet sites that enable users to access media, entertainment, and community content directly from their mobile phones, and designs and operates mobile games, including mobile online games, downloadable offline games, and WAP games.

Born in Beijing in 1974, Zhou graduated from Tsinghua University with a bachelor's degree in electronic engineering in 1997. He then went on to Stanford University to pursue postgraduate study, acquiring a master's degree in electrical engineering two years later. At that time, with the Internet industry booming, Zhou made the decision to go back to China with two classmates: Yang Ning and Chen Yizhou. Together, they successfully created a major Chinese Internet portal, ChinaRen.com, which focused on the new generation of educated Chinese by providing an alumni service that enabled people to connect online. Like all other websites of the time, they began by advertising: Zhou once spent RMB 40 million one night for outdoor advertising signs. With huge advertisement input, this portal was soon well known among the public and became one of the top 10 websites across the country.

When reflecting on his decision-making process for returning to China and launching ChinaRen, Zhou noted: "We do have some advantages at that time. Firstly, we are familiar with the culture in China and abroad, American VC would be more rest assured to us returnee entrepreneurs; secondly, we have a team with strong professionalism, then there are not too many returnees from universities like Harvard and Stanford in China after all; what's more, not too much development space was left in America, while it is totally different in China, which is a promising market" (Zhou, 2008). He also remarked on the irrational exuberance during the early stage of Internet development: "At that time, people doing Internet works all thought about attracting users and expand popularity only, but not making money. When the investor give you one million dollars, he want you to spend it so quickly to draw more attention that more investors will give you 10 million, 20 million and more money. They all think the faster you spend the capital, the more capable you are" (Baidu, 2010).

However, when the dot-com bubble finally burst in 2000, the partners were no longer able to run the portal. The Internet era provided many valuable learning experiences for Zhou and his team. According to him: "I learned plenty of things from that while other people may take 10 or 20 years to get. Just like the roller coaster, extremely fast, I was dropped to the valley from the peak" (Zhou, 2008). With the pressure from venture capital, the partners made the decision to sell the company to Sohu.com for US$30 million.

Following this semi-successful venture, Zhou began to think about what was the profitable segment of the Internet market. Two years later, he sent a resignation letter to Sohu and initiated his second attempt at Internet communications, establishing an innovative website named KongZhong.com along with Yang Ning. To start again, they eagerly sought for capital, but most VCs were reluctant to invest again. Therefore, Zhou and Yang had to sell all their stocks in Sohu – 440,000 shares each and gave up all their options in order to raise the initial fund. Years later when reflecting on the experience, he realized he should have been more patient at that time, as he sold all his shares of Sohu when the price was at its lowest, hence losing tens of million dollars in transaction.

After raising necessary capital for company registration and initial launch, the partners were once again broke. In 2002, Zhou and Yang went to Hong Kong for the second time to raise money. Each of them took a laptop and went through building-by-building, visiting more than 20 investment banks and venture capital firms. Finally, they were able to secure US$3 million. This time, Zhou and his partner found their niche. While the major competing portals believed SMS to be a profit sector, Zhou did not want to be a follower in technology development. Instead, he believed that mobile bandwidth should not be a limitation, so handset devices needed more applications and that KongZhong.com could take the leading position in this market. Therefore, on 18 March 2002, KongZhong Corporation was founded. This mobile portal focused on 2.5G and 3G services such as MMS, WAP, and JAVA. Zhou and his colleague aimed at the demands and preferences of the target customer segments, and combined with its advanced technology and product expertise, they have developed and provided services to meet users' changing requirements.

In the 3G era, cell phone users reach a higher penetration rate than personal computers. As most things can be done with cell phone in the future, the advantage of cell phone compared with computer is that one can take it everywhere, and get on Internet to watch news, movies, listen to music, and play games. Different platforms, different operators, and different cell phones can offer different services, but to the general users, they may not remember the particular service, but the brand. Therefore, Zhou believed that they first had to improve the content, perfect the service, and make the brand known by more people. Zhou envisioned his role in this undertaking: "I will give myself an A when the users can think about KONGZHONG as long as they get online with cell phones" (Baidu, 2010).

On 9 July 2004, KongZhong Corporation was successfully listed on the NASDAQ (KONG). Consequently, not only KongZhong was one of the youngest Chinese companies ever to be listed, but also the two cofounders, Zhou Yunfan and Yang Ning, are the youngest founders among the listed companies in the world. Since then, KongZhong has played a significant role in the telecom value-added service fields in the world. By the end of 2006, KongZhong had grown into a company with more than 800 employees throughout its different operations, such as wireless Internet, KongZhong Mammoth, etc.

To be a technology pioneer and entrepreneur twice, Zhou defined the word "fast." He commented: "If you cannot run fast enough, cannot expand your company to a large scale in a short time, then maybe your business model should wait. Once a good business model is coming out, others will follow you, so you have to be fast enough" (Wu, 2007). According to him, in an era of knowledge economy, how fast one moves will decide his or her success or failure. "There is no other industries can grow up so fast in a short period like the Internet. The Internet make the world informationized and changes people's life. To make a website or a company so widely known in such a short time is unimaginable in a traditional industry, so FAST must you start a company in such environment" (Wu, 2007).

In 2008, Zhou announced his resignation from KongZhong and went on to become a government official of the Zhongguancun Science Park. In charge of human resources, international exchange, and collaborative affairs, he became the wealthiest and youngest deputy director in the brief history of the Zhongguancun Science Park. Despite his modest background, Zhou has displayed impressive talents in the field of business administration. From a CEO to a government official, he has a great deal of experience. Above all, what really matters for Zhou is that he now has the power and ability to pursue his dream, whether that is to be an accomplished entrepreneur, a happy CEO, or an effective government official.

William X. Wei

Sources

百度百科 (2010), "周云帆", ["Zhou Yunfan", *Baidu Encyclopedia*], available at: http://baike.baidu.com/view/251912.htm (accessed 4 September 2010).

互动百科 (2010), "周云帆", ["Zhou Yunfan", *Hudong Encyclopedia*], available at: http://www.hudong.com/wiki/%E5%91%A8%E4%BA%91%E5%B8%86 (accessed 4 September 2010).
吴晓婧, 任绍敏 (2007), "空中网周云帆: 无线互联爆炸性发展周期将临", *第一财经日报* [Wu, X.J. and Ren, S.M., *"Zhou Yunfan: Wireless Internet facing the booming* era", *China Business News], 12 October, available at:* http://media.people.com.cn/GB/40606/6369853.html (accessed 12 September 2010).
周云帆 (2008), "无线互联网将改变世界" [Zhou Yunfan: Wireless Internet will change the world], 15 January, available at: http://blog.it863.com.cn/html/37/837-2057.html (accessed 12 September 2010).

Zhu, Demiao (Dennis D. Zhu 朱德淼 b. 1964)

Zhu Demiao, the managing director of Oaktree Capital (Hong Kong) Limited once said, "Prior to 40, I worked for my own financial well being; after 40, I am working for the societal well being" (Wang, 2007). This, in essence, captures the crux of a successful yet enigmatic Chinese entrepreneur, who flourishes in the elusive private equity sector. At the age of 46, Zhu seems to have the world under his feet.

While many revered investment banks and hedge funds collapsed as a result of the latest global financial crisis, the more credible private equities continue to thrive, especially in the emerging markets such as China. In 2005, Zhu was lured by the founder of Oaktree Capital, a private equity (PE) firm based in Los Angeles, to lead its Chinese operation. His first and foremost task was to establish relationships with the Chinese Government and expand Oaktree's Chinese investment portfolio. A veteran in the Chinese financial market and armed with long established relationship with the Chinese Central Bank, Zhu took the order to heart and launched three offices in Hong Kong, Beijing, and Shanghai within a few years. Currently, Oaktree Capital has more than US$60 billion in managed assets across multiple specialized investment strategies. A growing percentage of these assets are residing in China.

How does this southern provincial Chinese boy end up leading and facilitating immeasurable growth for one of the most credible private equity firms in the world? With much humility, Zhu attributes his success to luck. Or is it? As the youngest high school student, among more than 10 million students, to pass with flying colors at China's statewide exam, luck had little to do with it. Being interviewed and handpicked by a renowned accounting researcher, Professor Yang, during his entrance exam for the master's degree in economics at China's Ministry of Finance Research Institute, was by no means a fluke either. In 1982, at a tender age of 18, Zhu was the youngest graduate to be admitted to China's Ministry of Finance Research Institute. He continues to be the record holder till this day.

Of course, intelligence will only leapfrog a person's career so far. Zhu's curiosity, open mindedness and relentless pursue toward the "perceived impossibilities" led him to the land of opportunities – the United States of America. His extensive travel to Chicago and Hong Kong during his tenure with the Ministry of Finance gave him his first taste of "the world". Despite intensive training within the Ministry, he yearned for an adventure and a fresh start in the United States; in particular, he was attracted by the teaching style and the Nobel Prize clad faculty at University of Chicago. At the time, his life savings of US$20,000 would only cover one year's tuition. Undeterred, he ventured to Chicago in July 1990 nonetheless.

University of Chicago is known for giving free reign to its faculty on research topics and providing total flexibility to students in choosing subjects that are of interest to them. This freedom allowed Zhu to choose second-year subjects during his first-year of MBA program. Little did he know this upside-down decision eventually earned him an internship at FMC (Food Machine Corporation). His Zhu's knowledge on Monte Carlo simulation impressed the FMC personnel during the interview given the Monte Carlo modeling was generally a second-year subject. After a mere two month internship, FMC decided to hire him full time, pay for his second-year tuition in full, assign a dedicated secretary and an office with a vast view of Lake Michigan. A full-time investment analyst by day and a student by night, Dennis continued to excel within FMC. At the end of the second year with the corporation, the ambitious Zhu started weighing his options.

Throughout the 1990s, the financial market was going through an overhaul with the introduction of new "innovative and financially engineered" products and a surge in global mergers and acquisitions (M&A) in the banking industry. The largest cross-border M&A in the financial services industry occurred in 1988 when Credit Suisse merged with First Boston. In 1992, through incessant suggestions from an ex-colleague, Zhu interviewed with Credit Suisse First Boston. Impressed by his talent and attitude, the company offered him a position and a choice of working at any of the company's global offices. Given Chicago is the largest bond and secondary market by trade volume, naturally what better city to learn about capital market but the Wind City?

A predictable return is expected on an efficient market with informed investors. However, many people believe that success in the current inefficient capital market is generally 50% talent and 50% luck, as above-average returns commensurate with higher risks. Zhu admitted during an interview that high IQ, great communication and analytical skills definitely helped in this exhilarating business. As the Head of China Businesses, Zhu was responsible for corporate finance, fixed income, equities and risk management businesses within the divisions of Equity Capital Markets and Investment Banking. He was hailed as the first native Chinese holding such a prestigious position at a large global investment firm. In 1997, Zhu shined in the financial sector again, when he convinced China's Ministry of Finance to offer a 10-year bond that attracted US$1 billion worth of investment. The investment far exceeded the original estimate of US$300 million.

Attracted by JP Morgan's long established standing in China and the opportunity for greater improvement on its operations, Zhu took another leap of faith in 1999. Throughout his seven years at JP Morgan, he advised senior leaders of major clients in Asia including large corporations, banks and Chinese governments on financing, mergers and acquisitions, risk management, business strategies, as well as monetary and fiscal policies. Faced with internal and external challenges he relentlessly focused on formulating and executing strategies to build JP Morgan's investment banking practice and capital markets business in the region, developing and maintaining important business and government relationships, and providing strategic advice on new businesses and transactions to the senior management of JP Morgan Chase. His most recent role was as managing director, member of Asia Pacific Executive Committee and chairman of Greater China Operating Committee at JP Morgan Chase.

Through his relationship and network he had built as a young graduate, Zhu has established himself as an invaluable bridge between his firm and the Chinese government.

After joining the Oaktree Capital Management in 2005, Zhu decided to contribute one-third of his time to career, one-third to his family and the rest to charitable work. Shy from media about his role at Oaktree and directorship roles at other companies, he continues to try to live up to his societal obligations.

KIRSTY S. F. TAN

Sources

Wang, H. (2010), "Chinese returnees: Impact on China's modernization & globalization", Brookings Institute, 6 April.

王红茹 (2007), "朱德淼: 流转自如于资本市场", *资本推手: 10位海归投资银行家* (王辉耀主编), 中国发展出版社, 北京 [Wang, H., "Zhu Demiao: At Ease at the Capital Market", in Wang, H. (ed.), *Capital Movers and Shakers: Ten Overseas Returnees in Investment Banking*, China Development Press, Beijing], pp. 18–37.

Zhu, Min (朱敏 b. 1948)

A successful Chinese entrepreneur, philanthropist, and computer engineer, Zhu Min is mostly known for his innovative accomplishments as a legendary businessman and the founder of WebEx Communications.

Zhu was born in 1948 in Ningbo, Zhejiang Province. During his formative years, he lived through the so-called Great Proletarian Cultural Revolution, a violent mass movement that resulted in social, political, and economic turmoil in the People's Republic of China that began in 1966 and concluded with Mao's death in 1976. For 10 years, he was sent to the countryside doing all kinds of field labor. Finally, Zhu was able to change his fate by passing the new resumed national college entrance examination in 1977, and was admitted into the Zhejiang Agricultural University. After earning his BS degree in 1981, Zhu worked briefly and then enrolled himself in the graduate management science program at Zhejiang University, a top-ranked public university that was founded in 1897 and has around 39,000 students. It was here that Zhu was able to demonstrate his academic capabilities. In 1984, with the top grade in his class, he won a scholarship for study at the elite Stanford University in the United States, where he later received his MS degree in engineering.

Zhu then moved to Silicon Valley and worked in the high-tech industry for over 20 years. The IBM Scientific Center at Palo Alto is where he first gained his in-depth technology knowledge. Afterward, he served as the deputy to the chief technical officer at Price Waterhouse and then at a software company, Expert Edge, where he served as the vice president. In 1991, motivated by his inner entrepreneurial spirit, Zhu founded Futurelabs. Specialized in customized IT solutions for each organization it served, this high-tech company was designed to provide IT outsourcing services, technology consulting, software development, project management, technical support and maintenance to small- and medium-sized business, government, universities, and some *Fortune* 500 global enterprises. In 1996, Futurelabs was purchased by Quarterdeck for US$13 million.

In 1995, Zhu founded ActiveTouch with Subrah Lyar. The company changed its name to WebEx Communications a year later, out of Zhu's commitment to the advancement of real-time, interactive Internet communication. With a clearly defined mission, WebEx quickly grew to be the largest resource for interactive Internet and Internet conferences worldwide. WebEx products include Meeting Center, Training Center, Event Center, Support Center, Sales Center, MeetMeNow, PCNow, WebEx AIM Pro Business Edition, WebEx WebeOffice, WebEx Connect, and others. An example of one of these applications, the Meeting Center, recreates face-to-face meetings with real-time information, treatment, and voice and video distribution capabilities. In July 2000, WebEx was successfully listed on the NASDAQ. Due to Zhu's visionary leadership, *Forbes* named WebEx one of the 25 fastest-growing technology companies for five consecutive years; *BusinessWeek* also named Zhu among its e.biz 25 list for the part he played in creating web conferencing with WebEx and turning it into such a lucrative company.

In recent years, one large organization Zhu has connected with is the New Enterprise Associates (NEA). Based in Baltimore, Maryland, NEA is one of the world's main venture capital firms, which has a focus on IT and health-care investments. NEA's most well-known investments include Apple, TiVo, Neutral Tandem, and Jupiter Networks. Among over 500 corporations invested by NEA, approximately 200 have gone public while 195 have been acquired. Since Scott Sandell, an NEA general partner, knew Zhu had set up several software development teams for WebEx in China, and NEA was looking to expand to China and invest directly in startup companies there, he and a WebEx board member invited Zhu to become a venture partner. Zhu has since worked directly with NEA's technology and health-care sectors in sourcing and probing for new investment possibilities with a deliberation on opportunities in the growing Chinese market.

On May 13, 2005, Zhu resigned from WebEx and left the United States in order to become a full-time venture capitalist in China. Shortly after, Cisco took over the company on March 15, 2007, and absorbed WebEx into its own operation on both sales and technology levels. After leaving WebEx, Zhu founded Cybernaut, a venture investment fund that operates an incubator in Hangzhou, Zhejiang Province. Built on Zhu's professional experience, this firm is designed to help entrepreneurs grow their business by providing them with business strategy, founder mentoring, execution guidance and support, IT technology platforms, fundraising and exit strategy, and global resources. Zhu's ultimate goal is to help entrepreneurs build global enterprises. Under his leadership, Cybernaut has put much emphasis on establishing a global vision and true partnership, with a key focus on team and experience. The value Cybernaut adds to clients includes global business and infoware.

In 2005, NEA announced its backing of Northern Light, a venture capital fund cofounded by Zhu and others. Zhu was critical in helping NEA to develop into the principal investor in Speadtrum Communications in Shanghai. More recently, NEA also functions as a sponsor, or strategic investor for Cybernaut. This means that it ultimately invests in Cybernaut and supports the daily business operations. Besides his venture capital work, Zhu currently serves as a science and technology consultant to the San Jose municipal government, associate of the University of California President's Board on Science and Innovation, member of the Board of Directors of the Hua Yuan Science and Technology Association (HYSTA), and colleague at NEA. Zhu had previously served as the president of HYSTA, a nonprofit organization that promotes the technological, professional, and scientific advancement within the global Chinese business community. Founded in Silicon Valley in 1999, HYSTA has since grown from a group of foreign students to major Silicon Valley business leaders. Aimed to cultivate US–China business affairs, HYSTA members share their experiences and knowledge with new Chinese professionals entering the business world.

Zhu's most recent endeavor was the launch of the Zhejiang Innovation Institute (ZII). The purpose of ZII is to enhance global innovation and industrial exchange. This institute fosters entrepreneurship by providing a global stage for entrepreneurial organizations, partners, and thought leaders to come together and search for ideas and practice. In its short history, ZII has already had a positive influence on the future policy development and the process of enterprise outreach. As one of the most recognized alumni, Zhu recently donated US$10 million to Zhejiang University. In 2007, he was named the most Active Angel Investor in China and was listed as one of the top 10 Zhejiang businessmen during the same year. In addition, Zhejiang Public Relations Association made Zhu the honorary president, and in 2008, *Forbes* named him the one of the best investors. As a shining example of a Chinese businessman who rose up from humble beginnings to accomplish great feats, Zhu's life has inspired many young Chinese students who dare to dream big and never give up in their undertakings.

MICHAEL A. MOODIAN, YIFANG ZHANG AND MARGARET MINNIS

Sources

Cybernaut (2008), "Min Zhu", available at: http://www.cybernaut.com.cn/en_about_us1.html (accessed 5 June 2010).

Fu, S. (2008), "An interview with Min Zhu, Webex founder and active venture investor in China", *Journal of Asia Business Studies*, Fall, available at: http://findarticles.com/p/articles/mi_6777/is_1_3/ai_n32095025/ (accessed 28 June 2010).
Zhejiang University Innovation Institute (2007), "Min Zhu, founder and president", available at: http://www.zii-china.org/zii/web/detailed/member?id = 19 (accessed 28 June 2010).

Zhu, Yunlai (朱云来 b. 1957)

Known to the West as Levin Zhu, the eldest son of China's previous premier Zhu Rongji, Zhu Yunlai is the last person who would willingly admit in public to the powerful connections and influences of his father. Zhu is widely known as the CEO of China International Capital Corporation Limited (CICC), the country's first and largest China-based international investment bank. A well-respected business executive, Zhu is also highly recognized. In 2004, he was listed by *Fortune* magazine as one of the Top 25 Most Powerful Business Leaders in Asia; and in 2005, he was honored with the Asian Banker Achievement Award for Investment Banking.

The company that Zhu heads is very significant to China's business growth and development. Headquartered in Beijing, with offices strategically situated in Hong Kong, Shanghai, Shenzhen, and Singapore, CICC has built a comprehensive knowledge base on China's legal, regulatory, economic, cultural, business, and market environment. The firm is well poised to offer sound solutions and services to epoch-making business transactions in telecommunications, power, transportation, oil and gas, petrochemicals, metals, mining, and finance. Globally oriented, CICC has served as an indispensable and influential bridge between China and the rest of the world. In addition to offering domestic clients with insights on strategic, managerial, and financial trends from abroad, the company also helps international corporations craft and executes strategies suited to the Chinese economic, cultural, and business environment.

Zhu's early childhood interests and studies were in the sciences. Born in 1957 to Zhu Rongji and Lao An in Changsha, Hunan Province, Zhu showed a strong interest in atmospheric physics at a young age. In 1981, Zhu obtained his BS in atmospheric physics from the Nanjing Meteorology Institute. He then started his career at the China Meteorology Bureau before going abroad to pursue graduate studies. In 1994, Zhu successfully completed his dissertation titled "The Large-Scale Hydrologic Cycle and Its Role in Asian Summer Monsoon Variations Induced by Indian Ocean Sea Surface Temperature Anomalies" and graduated with a doctoral degree in atmospheric physics from the University of Wisconsin at Madison.

In the later stages of his life, Zhu developed an interest in business and finance. From 1995 to 1998, he accumulated knowledge in Western investment and finance that paved the way for his future success. Zhu started his studies in accounting at DePaul University in Chicago and graduated with a master's degree. In 1995, Zhu became an accountant at Anderson Bank at Chicago. In 1996, he left Chicago for

Boston, where he worked as an investment consultant for Credit Suisse First Boston, an investment bank based in Switzerland. During the two years there, Zhu was widely recognized as an able and hardworking businessman.

Zhu's return to China was prompted by a chance in the Chinese government policy. In 1998, as a result of a new policy implementation from the Chinese central government, which prohibited the employment of the children of high-level communist cadres with foreign companies, Zhu became a returnee. His return opened up a new career gateway. He moved to the newly returned Hong Kong and joined the CICC. Established in 1995 by Wang Qishan in a partnership between the China Construction Bank and Morgan Stanley, CICC is China's first joint investment bank. While there, Zhu presented a 500-page report that provided financial services to a gigantic state-owned company with 72 branches in China. Although few people knew him as the first son of former Premier Zhu, many people were impressed by the scope and depth of his research proposals and reports.

In his developmental years, Zhu had been involved in several successful endeavors. After he joined CICC in 1998, Zhu participated in the overseas IPO of Petro China and took the lead in many projects such as the mobile assets acquisition of China Telecom (now China Mobile) and the overseas IPOs of Sinopec, Chalco, China Telecom, China Netcom, China Life, PICC, Air China, China Shenhua, and China Construction Bank. With many of these accomplishments, Zhu was promoted to the management committee of the company in 2000 and was named CEO in 2004. Under Zhu's involvement and leadership, CICC has expanded immensely. It not only opened branches in Shanghai, Shenzhen but also increased its international presence, including a new branch in Singapore in 2008. The business diversity has also increased. CICC became the central China trader that issues overseas stock. The transactions with China Life and PICC in 2003 alone earned CICC a 14th ranking among all international IPO underwriters.

Zhu plays an important role in bridging Asia business leaders and facilitating business understanding between the East and the West. He attended the Asia Business Council (ABC) in the fall of 2009 at Taipei, Taiwan, where he met with President Ma Ying-jeou along with other ABC members. He was invited to China–US Business Leaders Roundtable at New York City on April 15, 2010. This roundtable is sponsored by China Entrepreneurs Forum and New York Stock Exchange Euronext, both of which share the common interest in promoting exchange, understanding, and dialogue between influential business leaders in China and the United States.

Zhu's achievements and influence have been widely acknowledged in China and abroad. In 2004, Zhu was invited to speak at the Beijing International Finance Forum, where top finance and business leaders held dialogues on the future of global finance. In 2005, while naming Zhu as the 15th Most Powerful Business Leader in Asia, *Fortune* magazine described him as the only person with the capacity to integrate the global financial system with the local Chinese economic system that is closely monitored by Chinese government. Despite his fame, success, and influential contributions, Zhu prefers the life of a low-key business executive. He wears casual and simple clothes and attempts to work as an ordinary employee in a simple office. He does not like to use his father's influence to help with his business and avoids media appearance and interviews.

PEILING ZHAO AND MARK MUNOZ

Sources

Emerging Market Forum (2006), "International capital flows, domestic capital markets, growth and development in emerging market countries", available at: http://www.emergingmarketsforum.org/meetings/global/2006/2006%20Global%20Meeting%20Participants%20Brochure.pdf (accessed 20 May 2010).

Lee, H. S. (2008), "Levin Zhu Yunlai and Morgan Stanley", *Asia! Through Asian Eyes*, 12 December, available at: http://www.theasiamag.com/cheat-sheet/levin-zhu-yunlai-and-morgan-stanley (accessed 20 May 2010).

家庭周末报 (2005), "朱云来: 亚洲最具影响力的商界领袖之一" ["Zhu Yunlai: One of the most influential business leaders in Asia", *Family Weekend*], 17 March, available at: http://www.gmw.cn/01wzb/2005-03/24/content_202949.htm (accessed 20 May 2010).

人民网 (2009), "朱镕基长子朱云来二度访台, 马英九将接见" ["Zhu Yunlai, the oldest son of Zhu Rongji, will visit Taiwan again and meet with Ma Ying-jeou", People.com], 18 September, available at: http://cq.people.com.cn/news/2009918/200991810557.htm (accessed 25 May 2010).

Zou, Qifang (Robert Zou 邹其芳 b. 1950)

Attending college at 25; traveling to the United States for his MBA at 37; establishing Arrail Dental at 42 – this is Zou Qifang, for whom every time he started something new, it looked like he was always later than anybody else. However, when his contemporaries were content with the status quo, Zou always bravely initiated the challenge, and his core dispositions of "prestige" and "tenacity" made him a winner every time.

Zou is the founder, CEO, and president of Arrail Dental Group, one of the leading dental service companies in China. Established in 1999, Arrail Dental has grown stronger by utilizing its accumulated dental experience, and then adapting it to meet individual customer needs. The company is currently headquartered in Beijing and continues to build on its strong links in China. As a small but dynamic company, Arrail Dental has more than 200 employees in China with 10 clinics in Beijing and Shanghai, and with 92 treatment suites in Shenzhen. Under Zou's leadership, the company has clearly defined its mission: to provide its customers with high-quality dental services at a reasonable price; to establish the largest dental service network in China; and to offer an opportunity for its associates to fully develop their potential.

The success of Arrail Dental was a reflection of Zou's life, who grew to become a successful entrepreneur through adventure and persistence. Zou was only 16 years old when the Cultural Revolution suddenly began. The political turmoil also torn his large family apart, as he had to leave school for a construction work along with 300 other high school students. There he spent several years as a manual worker mixing cement. Zou, however, was not satisfied with being a laborer forever. In order to change his fate, he started to read anything he could find. One day Zou discovered an English teaching channel on the central broadcasting radio station. He was enthralled, and ever since he listened to the program at every opportunity and developed into a remarkable English speaker. Finally, at age 25, Zou realized his dream and became a college student. When he told his English-learning story in Tianjin Foreign Language College, his younger classmates were astonished. Four years later Zou left college to face the challenge of choosing a profession. At that time, the most desirable job was working in the area of foreign trade, yet Zou chose the pharmaceutical industry based on his own sharp intuition.

After working briefly as a translator in the state-owned Tianjin Pharmaceutical Bureau, he joined GlaxoSmithKline (GSK) China, which at that time was not well known in China. Within six years, through hard work and with his remarkable capabilities, all his supervisors became his subordinates. In 1988, under Zou's leadership, GlaxoSmithKline China became the most famous brand through its gigantic advertisement campaign in television across the country. This was a pioneer event in Chinese television marketing. However, the more Zou became interested in business management, the less satisfied he was with his fragmented experiences gained through many years in the workplace. When he discovered that an MBA education could bring him a higher level of understanding, he gave up his executive position in GlaxoSmithKline in 1992, and applied without hesitation to the MBA program of the Wharton Business School in the United States.

At Wharton, Zou was enlightened with new knowledge in management and finance, and was informed and inspired by the lectures of such notable people as Peter Drucker, Bill Gates, and Michael Dell. The American way of thinking – independent, self-confident, and innovative – deeply moved Zou. Two years later, Zou graduated from the Wharton Business School along with a loan of US$80,000. Turning down the employment offers from three American companies, Zou accepted a job with a bank in Hong Kong and paid off his debt within a year. However, Zou still felt discontented with his career choice, as he believed that his strengths were not being applied. His heart lay with marketing and the pharmaceutical industry. As a result, one year later he transferred to an American consulting company engaged in management strategy consulting in the China Market for multi-international corporations. Although it was a brand new challenge, with his understanding of the Chinese market, especially when medicine-related projects were involved, Zou accomplished the task with ease. Meanwhile, he was seeking the opportunity to establish his own business. "Being a professional manager, no matter how capable I am, I will never be able to change the roles for a large company." Zou locked his attention firmly onto the pharmaceutical industry, from which his confidence and wealth were first gained, and where lay his accumulated professional work experience along with his personal contacts.

At the end of 1996, during a conference in Hong Kong, Zou came across his old friend, Henry Winter, the former president of GSK China, who has since established an international pharmaceutical investment fund and had just purchased an American company producing dental implants. Winter wanted to explore the China market with dental implants and asked for Zou's opinion. Zou became excited and immediately launched an investigation. He went to China and researched more than 10 cities. However, the results of the research revealed that for China in the dental market the most needed service was not providing dental implants but providing superb dental care. Zou's intuition led him to believe that a market gap existed and a great business opportunity was waiting.

In 1998, Zou resigned from the consulting company and busied himself with the birth of his own business – Arrail Dental. In April 1999, financed by several investors, Zou opened his very first dental care facility in Beijing, which was positioned as the first high-end dental clinic in China. Twelve years later, Arrail Dental has become the leading dental care provider among all competitors in the growing Chinese market. Arrail is also pursuing other high potential service areas such as dental implants. Perhaps the force of Zou's success derives from his own lips, "Maintain a peaceful mind, and keep an upward inner force."

XIAOWEI SUN

Sources

胡冰 (2007), "邹其芳: 牙缝里做出大生意", *创业英雄: 10位海归创业先锋* (王辉耀主编), 中国发展出版社, 北京 [Hu, B., "Zou Qifang: Big business out of gaps between teeth", in Wang, H. (ed.), *Entrepreneurial Heroes: Ten Overseas Returnees in Entrepreneurship*, China Development Press, Beijing], pp. 115–137.

商务周刊 (2007), "瑞尔齿科集团总裁邹其芳: "诚信"助飞成功", ["Arrail Dental Group CEO Zou Qifang: 'Good Faith' boosts success", *Business Weekly*], 6 July, available at: http://ceo.icxo.com/htmlnews/2007/07/06/1155856_0.htm (accessed 20 July 2010).

Zou, Shenglong (邹胜龙 b. 1972)

A computer engineer by training, Zou Shenglong is the founder and president of Thunder Networking Technologies in Shenzhen, China. Its main product, Xunlei, which means swift thunder in China, is the most popular download manager program developed by Zou and his company, which is based on the core technology of P2SP (peer-to-server-and-to-peer) data transfer engine.

Arrived in the United States in 1996, Zou Shenglong's fate as the future founder of Sandai, the original parent of Xunlei, began shaping when he switched his major from economics to computer science at University of Wisconsin–Madison without consulting his parents. Though this should not have been too surprising to his father Zou Dejun, himself a prolific technologist and inventor. Zou Dejun was initially an aspiring researcher and was invited to join the prestigious University of Science and

Technology of China in 1982, participating in a national key research project involving the development of electron accelerators, but left the institution due to some social strains and the ensuing disappointment in his ostensibly inadequate treatment as a scientific autodidact by the academic establishment there. Subsequently, however, Zou Dejun had the privilege of becoming the general manager of technology for the Shenzhen Science and Technology Parks Corporation, a subsidiary directly initiated and promoted by special status courtesy of the Chinese State Council. It is this career in Shenzhen that afforded the senior Zou the opportunity to continue to groom his 16-year-old son, who entered the Sir Ellis Kadoorie Secondary School in 1988. By 1992, Zou Dejun was determined to have his son study abroad and thus raised the first-year tuition of US$15,000 on his own.

Following his undergraduate degree, Zou Shenglong went on to study for a master's degree in computer science at Duke University, where he met his future business partner in Sandai, Cheng Hao, by three years his junior. Upon a visit in the summer of 1999 to Silicon Valley, Zou was impressed by the bustling digital industry and e-commerce atmosphere and decided to stay. For the next three years, he first worked as the manager of core products in Nuasis Corporation, where he not only familiarized himself with the development of the US IT industry, but also gained valuable exposure to the processes of financing Internet startups by witnessing a two-round US$45-million deal come into fruition. In quick succession, Zou then started up three companies of his own: IPNet, Chinaflow, and MuseTech. Within Silicon Valley's own community of Chinese businesses – albeit small, though somewhat tightly knit and formally represented via the Hua Yuan Science and Technology Association – Zou Shenglong met Xu Yong, a Biology-PhD turned sales executive. Working for the Baidu founder Li Yanhong (Robin), it was not long that Xu Yong introduced Zou Shenglong to Robin Li. Later on, even Cheng Hao ended up working for Robin Li.

The Silicon Valley episode spurned Zou's ideas about the emerging domestic Chinese market. He analyzed various aspects and concluded to its deficiencies in several respects, such as insufficient storage space for e-mail systems, inadequate content distribution systems, but particularly, a shortage of organic and domestic financing. Upon his return to Shenzhen in 2002, it is the confluences of these several factors that allowed Zou to initiate a strategy in his own right for this particular market. A peer-to-peer technology, funded predominantly by foreign investment: Xunlei, synonym for the product and the corporation marketing it (renamed from Sandai to a more literal Thunder, a.k.a. Xunlei) Network Technology Company Ltd. of Shenzhen in May 2005. From then on, Zou's life itself became intimately and intricately linked with the evolution and destiny of this pet project.

While classified as a download manager rather than simply a BitTorrent client, Xunlei is developed on the principle that the technology is not entirely peer-based, rather a derivate of it in the form of peer-to-server-to-peer. It involves a central server that coordinates, collects, and controls the fragments of files existing in a distributed environment on end-user machines, and thus can optimize the provision of such disbursed content, unlike previous technology that focused on simply locating it. Additionally, it achieves that without compulsory file sharing but with proprietary speed technology that leverages the peers yet only for public files.

In its early stage the venture was small and unscalable, consequently the focus of all involved was on developing the technology, including Zou Shenglong and Cheng Hao, who had put in long hours at that time writing computer codes themselves. A first funding breakthrough occurred when the angel investor Zhou Hong dedicated RMB 100 million. Soon after, Sandai secured its first million-dollar funding for the development of Xunlei from the IDG Technology Venture Investment Fund, upon being impressed by Zou's product demonstration at the China International Hi-Tech Fair in May 2003. However, initially the 2004 version of Xunlei's Thunder 2 was technologically problematic, mainly because it lacked speed, an important disadvantage for online gaming. The fortunes started turning, when Cheng Hao promoted the ever-improving tool and a video download accelerator, to be realized later as Xunlei Kankan in the gaming industry by connecting to Kingsofts Lei Jun in Beijing in mid-2004.

Meanwhile, in terms of financing the business model, the tide turned quickly and decisively with the advent of Morningside Ventures, the 1986-founded US arm of Hong Kong's Chan family Hang Lung Group, originally started in 1960. By October 2005, outside investors had contributed in excess of US$10 million, which allowed Xunlei to rapidly expand from 40 to 200 employees in 2006 and to finally launch a fully branded file sharing website Xunlei.com. By the end of the year, it was reported that the Xunlei software had been used by more than 120 million users, and the site had been visited by 40 million users monthly. In the following year, the newly developed download accelerator had reportedly been downloaded over 80 million times. Eventually the Xunlei family of products has spanned a variety of applications far beyond the original simple P2SP client that include Xunlei Kankan, a video-on-demand service, and Gougou, a search engine specialized in multimedia searches, and the company website has ultimately become China's top video and movie search engine.

Xunlei's success eventually resulted in a third round of financing in early 2007, increasing IDG VC partner's amount to US$45 million and involving groups such as Ceyuan Ventures, and Fidelity Asia Ventures. However, the more spectacular moment on record occurred on January 4, 2007, when Google foresighted the market potential and made a highly strategic acquisition of a 36.4% stake in the company for US$5 million.

Some challenges to Zou Shenglong's prominent venture surfaced in 2008, when several media companies such as 20th Century Fox, Columbia Pictures, Paramount, Universal, Warner Brothers, and Disney enjoined the US Motion Picture Association in a RMB 7-million copyright infringement litigation against Xunlei. While this lawsuit was quickly dropped in the Shanghai Pudong People's Court for technical reasons, Zou was put on alert. He quickly substantiated his defense by pointing to the fact that his company did not condone nor allow to download pirated software through Xunlei. Indeed Xunlei Kankan's strength is not only it is a high-definition, DVD-quality video service on demand technology, but also its possession of the associated copyrights and its collaboration with the concerned content and service providers. However, it is particularly Xunlei's Gougou product that continues to represent some exposure. In fact, not only from an intellectual property perspective but also from a privacy and security point of view: its advertising pop-ups are of continued concern about computer viruses, especially of the Trojan kind.

Notwithstanding the latter issues, by 2008 Xunlei had finally established itself with a 70% share of the download market, and generated 65% of revenue via advertising and 20–25% via distribution of online games and movies. Zou Shenglong attributed this success to his original idea of not actually generating content but simply facilitating its distribution. The technical lead now falls to Cheng Hao, who was preparing Xunlei for an expansion into the video distribution market segment. A Thunder Video version of the product would attract a new category of users and would allow the industry to further overcome some bandwidth problems.

By late 2009, the fortunes and impact of Zou's initiative continued to reverberate through the IT industry unhalted, fueled by yet another high-profile investment, this time on the part of SNK Media Asia, and hence ostensibly completing his father's aspirations for a highly successful, foreign-educated Chinese returnee entrepreneur-son.

JONATAN JELEN

Sources

Associated Press (2007), "Google teams up with China's Xunlei", 6 January, available at: http://www.gmanews.tv/story/25822/google-teams-up-with-chinas-xunlei (accessed 9 August 2010).

Richards, J. (2007), "Google gains edge in Baidu fight", *Times*, 7 January, available at: http://business.timesonline.co.uk/tol/business/industry_sectors/technology/article1289796.ece (accessed 9 August 2010).

Wikipedia (n.d.), "Xunlei", available at: http://en.wikipedia.org/wiki/Xunlei (accessed 9 August 2010).

郦晓 (2008), "360度邹胜龙: 后下载时代的迅雷进程", *腾讯科技* [Li, X., "Zou Shenglong in 360 degrees: The swift development of post-downloading era", *Tencent Technology*], 7 October, available at: http://tech.qq.com/a/20081007/000052.htm (accessed 9 August 2010).

Zuo, Xiaolei (左晓蕾 b. undisclosed)

An exceptional female economist, Dr. Zuo Xiaolei has extensive working and studying experiences in Europe, the United States, and Southeast Asian countries. An active columnist on world economic events, she has analyzed domestic and global monetary and fiscal policies, the reform of exchange rate and interest rate mechanisms, and Chinese housing policy. Although largely optimistic, Zuo occasionally sounds alarms on the security of Chinese foreign currency reserves due to the United States and European sovereign debt crises. Zuo and her economist husband, Tang Min, have played a key role in China's transformation from elite to mass higher education.

Born in Guangdong Province, Zuo has had multinational learning and teaching experiences. Upon receiving a BS in mathematics from Wuhan University in 1982, she studied European economy and statistics in two French universities from 1983 to 1986. Zuo subsequently earned an MS in 1988 and a PhD in international finance and econometrics from the University of Illinois at Urbana-Champaign in 1992. She then taught at the National University of Singapore (1992–1997) and the Manila-based Asian Institute of Management (1997–2001). Thereafter she returned to serve as chief economist in Galaxy Securities Company Ltd., one of the largest investment firms in China.

Before her investment bank position, Zuo worked on several research projects, ranging from Malaysia's auto industry to rural China's microfinance. One of the projects she completed was the Guizhou-Hunan Mountainous Region Rural Financial Service Report, sponsored by a German firm. More significantly, Zuo has impacted Chinese society with her co-sponsorship of higher education enrollment expansion.

During the 1990s Asian financial crisis, Zuo and her husband Tang Min, a former economist of the Asian Development Bank, witnessed the slowing of the Chinese economy amidst shutdowns of state-owned enterprises and lay-offs of millions of workers. To delay entry into the problematic job market by millions of high school graduates, the couple advocated using education as a tool to stimulate the economy by boosting domestic consumption. They jointly issued a public letter in November 1998 proposing a radical expansion in higher education enrollment (Tang and Zuo, 1999). Published in the *Xinhua Internal Reference*, the letter came to the attention of the State Council. Then-Premier Zhu Rongji and other top leaders perceived merit in the proposal and implemented it within just a few months. As a result, Chinese universities currently churn out record numbers of graduates each year, on a scale that surpassed the United States by 2005 as the world's largest producer of college graduates (Lin, 2008). However, the quality of education has suffered in China, and unemployment upon graduation emerged another social problem as an outcome of the expansion.

In spite of broad scrutiny of their policy's wisdom, Zuo and her husband defend their original proposal of endorsing enrollment expansion. In 2006, Zuo wrote in her blog an article entitled "The Expansion Enhanced Educational Justice," in which she attempted to clarify college education as an incomplete "public goods," one that the central government should not finance entirely. Instead, private citizens who consume college education should pay for part of the cost. Regarding the disadvantaged students who are unable to pay for the service, she suggested that they be given free access. Her husband also appeared on television in programming such as "Why College Graduates Have a Hard Time Finding a Job," thus further addressing the issue. Whether it will ultimately be viewed a success or failure, the economist couple has been intimately associated with China's university expansion policy.

Before her investment bank position, Zuo's academic papers appeared in the *Journal of Statistical Computation and Simulation*, *Journal of Advance in International Banking and Finance*, and the *Journal of Statistic Planning and Inference*, among others. Since she joined the Galaxy Securities Company, Zuo has been vigorous in writing op-eds and newspaper columns, analyzing economic policies and major world events. A Sina columnist, she has also been interviewed by *China Daily*, *Shanghai Securities News*, *Guangzhou Daily*, *China Business Journal*, etc.

Since 2007, the world has entered a deep recession triggered by the housing bubble in the United States. As an economist based in Beijing, Zuo wrote extensively discussing the danger to China's large foreign exchange reserve as a result of the American recession, the Dubai fallout and European debt crises. Her public advice to the Chinese government is to diversity via purchasing more resources in Africa and elsewhere, instead of investing exclusively on securities, including sovereign bonds. Although agreeing with other economists that purchasing the US national debt is not an ideal choice for China, she cautions the limitation of investing in material resources.

As a world economic watcher, Zuo has focused on the European debt crisis. In an article published in *Shanghai Securities News*, she analyzed the three stages of European debt crisis management: formulation of the €750 billion European bailout plan, bank stress tests, and the financial austerity plans to trim European welfare scales. When asked if these measures will avert future crises, Zuo concludes that a third depression is unlikely to occur. Although Europe is not bottoming out, it is not likely to trigger the third depression. Despite her prediction, Zuo is against global bailouts, claiming they resemble "creating a credit bubble to fight against the asset bubble."

When the $2.4 billion Coca-Cola's bid to acquire Huiyuan Juice Group was blocked in March 2009, Zuo defended the government decision. Though the Ministry of Commerce overruled the market, Zuo said that Huiyuan's business would not suffer because of the failed bid and that the Ministry's rejection conformed to international practices, thus protecting China's domestic industry. When the consumer price index (CPI) rises in China and worries of serious inflation might occur in July 2010, Zuo reminds her readers that "each economy has its own tolerable level of inflation," and that due to the rises of both rural and urban income growth rate, China is unlikely to experience serious inflation in two to three years (*China Daily*, 2010).

CHUNJUAN NANCY WEI

Sources

China Business Focus (n.d.), "RMB appreciation can't stop foreign exchange reserve hike", available at: http://en.cbf.net.au/Item/601.aspx (accessed 16August 2010).

China Daily (2010), "Slowdown ahead, but no hard landing", 7 July, available at: http://www.chinadaily.com.cn/business/2010-07/07/content_10075045.htm (accessed 16August 2010).

Lin, J. (2008), "China's higher education expands", *The Faculty Voice* (University of Maryland), Vol. 21, No. 4, p. 8, available at: http://www.facultyvoice.umd.edu/All%20past%20issues/2007-2008/May_2008_Vol21_No4.pdf (accessed 16 August 2010).

Women of China (2008), "Zuo Xiaolei: Keeping a distance from the stock market", 9 January, available at: http://www.womenofchina.cn/Profiles/Businesswomen/201069.jsp (accessed 16 August 2010).

CCTV (2009), "左晓蕾: 银河证券首席经济学家" ["Zuo Xiaolei, Chief economist of Galaxy Securities"], 17 February, available at: http://finance.cctv.com/special/dawosi1/20090217/107837.shtml (accessed 20 August 2010).

汤敏, 左晓蕾 (1999),"关于启动中国经济有效途径的思考: 扩大高校招生一倍的建议", *经济学消息报* [Tang, M. and Zuo, X., "Pondering on effective means of promoting Chinese economy: Suggestion on doubling higher education enrollment", *News on Economics*], available at: http://finance.sina.com.cn/review/20041023/15201102716.shtml (accessed 16 August 2010).

左晓蕾 (2006),"大学扩招提升了教育的公平性", *新浪财经* [Zuo, X., "The college expansion enhanced educational equity", *Sina Finance*], 10 March, available at: http://finance.sina.com.cn/economist/jingjixueren/20060310/09412406769.shtml (accessed 20 August 2010).

左晓蕾 (2009), "若美国国债降级, 或将爆发更大全球危机", *上海证券报* [Zuo, X., "If U.S. national debt rating is downgraded, a bigger global crisis might occur", *Shanghai Securities News*], 14 December, available at: http://finance.oeeee.com/a/20091214/282181.html (accessed 20 August 2010).

左晓蕾 (2010), "第三次大萧条渐行渐远: 从银行压力测试看欧洲危机三部曲", *上海证券报* [Zuo, X., "The third depression may be behind us: Trilogy of European crisis from the bank stress test", *Shanghai Securities News*], 30 July, p.6, available at: http://paper.cnstock.com/html/2010-07/30/content_37097.htm (accessed 20 August 2010).

About the Editors

A graduate of Peking University and Southern Connecticut State University, **Wenxian Zhang** is a recipient of the Cornell Distinguished Faculty Award, Arthur Vining Davis Fellow and Professor of Rollins College in Winter Park, Florida, where he joined the rank of Arts and Sciences faculty since 1995. He is a Research Associate of Rollins China Center, and has team-taught courses on Chinese history and cultures and frequently taken students on field study trips to China. Zhang is also a recipient of the Patrick D. Smith Award for his academic work with Dr. Maurice O'Sullivan on *A Trip to Florida for Health and Sport* (Florida Historical Society, 2010). In addition to *The Biographical Dictionary of New Chinese Entrepreneurs and Business Leaders* (Edward Elgar, 2009, with Alon) and *A Guide to the Top 100 Companies in China* (World Scientific, 2010, with Alon), he has published many scholarly articles on information studies, international librarianship, historical research, and Chinese business management.

Dr Huiyao Wang is the Director General of the Center for China and Globalization, Vice Chairman of the China Western Returned Scholars Association, Vice Chairman of the China Talent Research Society of the Ministry of Human Resources, and Vice Chairman of the China International Economic Cooperation Society of the Ministry of Commerce. He has also served as the Task Force Leader for the Global Talents Strategy Study Group of the Chinese Government Coordination Office for Talents and also as an Experts Team Leader for the Economic Committee of the Overseas Expert Advisory Group of Overseas Chinese Affairs Office of the State Council, as well as an advisory member of the CPPCC Beijing Committee. Dr Wang is also an Asia Fellow at Harvard Kennedy School, a Senior Fellow of the Asia Pacific Foundation of Canada and was a Visiting Fellow of the Brookings Institution in the United States. He has taught as adjunct professor at the Richard Ivey Business School of the University of Western Ontario and the Guanghua Management School of Peking University. A leading Chinese authority on Chinese returnee research, Dr Wang has published a series of books in recent years on the study of contemporary overseas returnees, which include: *中国留学人才发展报告* (2009), *当代中国海归* (2007), *缤纷海归* (2007), *创业英雄* (2007), *魅力学者* (2007), *资本推手* (2007), *叱咤华尔街* (2007),*财富裂变* (2007), *巅峰职业* (2007), *海旧时代* (2005), *创业中国* (2005).

Dr Ilan Alon is the George D. and Harriet W. Cornell Chair of International Business at Rollins College, Executive Director of the Rollins China Center, and Visiting Scholar and Asia Fellow of the Kennedy School of Government at Harvard University. He has published numerous books, peer-reviewed articles, and chapters on China, and is a regular featured keynoter in many professional organizations. Alon has cooperated with Zhang (co-editor) on many publications, including ones mentioned in Zhang's biography above. Some other recent books on *China include China Rules: Globalization and Political Transformation* (Palgrave McMillan, 2009), *The Globalization of Chinese Enterprises* (Palgrave McMillan, 2008), *Business and Management Education in China: Transition, Pedagogy and Training* (World Scientific, 2005), *Chinese Culture, Organizational Behavior and International Business Management* (Greenwood, 2003), and *Chinese Economic Transition and International Marketing Strategy* (Greenwood, 2003). Alon is also a recipient of the Chinese Marketing Award and the prestigious Huge McKean Award for his work on education in China. He has taught courses in top Chinese MBA programs including Shanghai Jiaotong University, Fudan University, and China Europe International Business School. He is also an international business consultant, with experience in China as well as other countries.